# A CULTURAL HISTORY OF MEMORY

VOLUME 1

**A Cultural History of Memory**
*General Editors: Stefan Berger and Jeffrey Olick*

**Volume 1**
A Cultural History of Memory in Antiquity
*Edited by Beate Dignas*

**Volume 2**
A Cultural History of Memory in the Middle Ages
*Edited by Gerald Schwedler*

**Volume 3**
A Cultural History of Memory in the Early Modern Age
*Edited by Marek Tamm and Alessandro Ancangeli*

**Volume 4**
A Cultural History of Memory in the Eighteenth Century
*Edited by Patrick Hutton*

**Volume 5**
A Cultural History of Memory in the Nineteenth Century
*Edited by Susan A. Crane*

**Volume 6**
A Cultural History of Memory in the Long Twentieth Century
*Edited by Stefan Berger and William Niven*

# A CULTURAL HISTORY
# OF MEMORY
# IN ANTIQUITY

*Edited by Beate Dignas*

BLOOMSBURY ACADEMIC
LONDON • NEW YORK • OXFORD • NEW DELHI • SYDNEY

BLOOMSBURY ACADEMIC
Bloomsbury Publishing Plc
50 Bedford Square, London, WC1B 3DP, UK
1385 Broadway, New York, NY 10018, USA
29 Earlsfort Terrace, Dublin 2, Ireland

BLOOMSBURY, BLOOMSBURY ACADEMIC and the Diana logo are trademarks of
Bloomsbury Publishing Plc

First published in Great Britain 2022
Paperback edition first published 2024

Copyright © Bloomsbury Publishing, 2022

Beate Dignas has asserted her right under the Copyright, Designs and
Patents Act, 1988, to be identified as Editor of this work.

Series design: Raven Design

Cover image: © An allegorical representation of The Apotheosis of Homer, signed by a sculptor
from Priene, a Greek town in Asia Minor © Werner Forman/Getty Images

All rights reserved. No part of this publication may be reproduced or transmitted
in any form or by any means, electronic or mechanical, including photocopying,
recording, or any information storage or retrieval system, without prior permission
in writing from the publishers.

Bloomsbury Publishing Plc does not have any control over, or responsibility for, any
third-party websites referred to or in this book. All internet addresses given in this
book were correct at the time of going to press. The author and publisher regret
any inconvenience caused if addresses have changed or sites have ceased to
exist, but can accept no responsibility for any such changes.

A catalogue record for this book is available from the British Library.

A catalog record for this book is available from the Library of Congress.

ISBN: HB: 978-1-4742-7337-4
PB: 978-1-3504-0857-9
Set: 978-1-4742-7384-8

Series: The Cultural Histories Series

Typeset by RefineCatch Limited, Bungay, Suffolk
Printed and bound in Great Britain

To find out more about our authors and books visit www.bloomsbury.com
and sign up for our newsletters.

# CONTENTS

| | |
|---|---|
| LIST OF ILLUSTRATIONS | vi |
| GENERAL EDITORS' PREFACE<br>*Stefan Berger and Jeffrey Olick* | viii |
| Introduction<br>*Beate Dignas* | 1 |
| 1  Power and Politics<br>*Boris Chrubasik* | 17 |
| 2  Time and Space<br>*Stéphane Benoist and Ilaria Bultrighini* | 37 |
| 3  Media and Technology: Mediatic Frameworks of Memories in Ancient Times<br>*Elena Franchi* | 51 |
| 4  Knowledge: Science and Education—Writing as "External Memory" and its Role in Ancient Science<br>*Han Baltussen* | 65 |
| 5  Ideas: Philosophy, Religion, and History<br>*Luca Castagnoli* | 83 |
| 6  High Culture and Popular Culture<br>*Anne Gangloff* | 101 |
| 7  The Social: Rituals, Faith, Practices, and the Everyday<br>*Beate Dignas* | 117 |
| 8  Remembering and Forgetting<br>*Elizabeth Minchin* | 133 |
| NOTES | 147 |
| BIBLIOGRAPHY | 169 |
| NOTES ON CONTRIBUTORS | 201 |
| INDEX | 203 |

# ILLUSTRATIONS

## INTRODUCTION

| | | |
|---|---|---|
| 0.1 | Apotheosis of Homer relief. | 1 |
| 0.2 | Limestone block from a funerary monument. | 6 |
| 0.3 | Tabula Iliaca Capitolina. | 9 |
| 0.4 | Assyrian scribes taking records. | 12 |
| 0.5 | Terracotta *loutrophoros* depicting funeral rites. | 13 |

## CHAPTER 1

| | | |
|---|---|---|
| 1.1 | Harmodius and Aristogeiton. | 18 |
| 1.2 | Tetradrachm of Antiochus II. | 22 |
| 1.3 | Didyma, Sanctuary of Apollo. | 23 |
| 1.4 | Plan of the Forum of Augustus. | 25 |
| 1.5 | Silver coin of Tryphon. | 31 |

## CHAPTER 2

| | | |
|---|---|---|
| 2.1 | Section of the *Fasti Praenestini*. | 38 |
| 2.2 | Remaining structure of the Olympieion in Athens. | 39 |
| 2.3 | Coin of the Emperor Commodus. | 42 |
| 2.4 | View of the processional frieze on the Ara Pacis. | 43 |
| 2.5 | View of the processional frieze on the Ara Pacis. | 44 |
| 2.6 | Bust of Caligula-Claudius. | 48 |
| 2.7 | Inscription with erasure after *damnatio memoriae*. | 49 |

## CHAPTER 3

| | | |
|---|---|---|
| 3.1 | Delphi, Temple of Apollo. | 57 |
| 3.2 | Reconstruction of the Temple of Concordia. | 58 |
| 3.3 | Map of "Graecia." | 60 |
| 3.4 | Ajax the Lesser drags Cassandra from the Palladium. | 61 |
| 3.5 | Bust of Caius Marius. | 62 |
| 3.6 | Coin of Philippus. | 64 |

## CHAPTER 4

| | | |
|---|---|---|
| 4.1 | Expansion of knowledge. | 67 |
| 4.2 | Cabalistic analysis of the mind and senses, 1617 | 69 |
| 4.3 | The Law Code of Gortyn. | 70 |
| 4.4 | Laehn and Themes of Books. | 78 |
| 4.5 | Laehn and the "Annular Structure." | 79 |

## CHAPTER 5

| | | |
|---|---|---|
| 5.1 | Mosaic depicting Mnemosyne. | 83 |
| 5.2 | Socrates and his Muse. | 85 |
| 5.3 | Donatello, Bust of a Youth, detail. | 88 |
| 5.4 | Orphic *lamella*. | 90 |
| 5.5 | Writing with a wax tablet. | 95 |
| 5.6 | Portrait of St. Augustine of Hippo. | 99 |

## CHAPTER 6

| | | |
|---|---|---|
| 6.1 | Homer and the nine Muses. | 102 |
| 6.2 | Solon. | 108 |
| 6.3 | Thales. | 109 |
| 6.4 | *Togatus* Barberini. | 113 |
| 6.5 | Relief from the tomb of the Haterii family. | 115 |

## CHAPTER 7

| | | |
|---|---|---|
| 7.1 | Engraving of the Acropolis of Athens. | 120 |
| 7.2 | Painted wooden tablet from Pitsa. | 121 |
| 7.3 | Coptic pilgrim flask. | 122 |
| 7.4 | The Menelaion. | 124 |
| 7.5 | Syro-Hittite Kuttamuwa stele with Aramaic inscription. | 126 |
| 7.6 | Fresco depicting the arrival of Io in Canopus. | 130 |

## CHAPTER 8

| | | |
|---|---|---|
| 8.1 | View of the Tomb of Achilles. | 134 |
| 8.2 | Engraving showing Kalliope, the Muse of epic poetry. | 136 |
| 8.3 | Ionic column built to commemorate the Battle of Marathon. | 140 |
| 8.4 | Engraving showing Klio, the Muse of history. | 141 |
| 8.5 | Fragment C of the honorary inscription for the heroes at Phyle. | 143 |

# GENERAL EDITORS' PREFACE

### STEFAN BERGER AND JEFFREY K. OLICK

Any project titled *A Cultural History of Memory* begs a number of questions from the very beginning. For instance: What does it mean that this project is a *cultural* history, rather than some other kind of history? (What other kind of history might it have been?) In turn, what makes memory a feasible and interesting topic for such a history? (It certainly isn't immediately obvious that it would be.) Finally, why a cultural history rather than *the* cultural history? (After all, with forty-eight chapters spread over six volumes, how many more cultural histories of memory could one imagine?)

## CULTURAL HISTORY

*A Cultural History of Memory* is but one entry in a series of cultural histories already and soon to be published by Bloomsbury, including cultural histories of Animals, the Human Body, Food, Gardens, Women, the Senses, Dress and Fashion, the Theatre, Work, Law, Money, and Hair, among many others. The publisher has taken a light hand in prescribing the orientation of these projects, leaving the definition of cultural history to each project's senior editors. And this is very well, as there are many different ways to inflect the idea of cultural history, and different approaches are likely appropriate to the different subject matters. In turn, we have not imposed any particular definition on the editors of the six volumes in this current project, nor have they on the authors of the forty-eight chapters that comprise the total product. That being said, we have relied on a broadly shared understanding of the purposes and tools of cultural history in framing this particular entry in the series, and it is clear that its many authors have as well, though perhaps with occasional divergences.

Namely, contemporary cultural history, at least as it has been practiced in and on the West (and this is one of the important limitations on the project we will discuss below), has defined itself in contrast to at least three other approaches (on the historiographical developments sketched in the following pages see in greater detail Berger, Feldner, and Passmore (2020)). First, there is a broadly defined "traditional" political historiography, dominant in the nineteenth century, that wrote the story of states, their leaders, and their wars. These "high politics" approaches, of course, fully advanced the claim to "objectivity," particularly since the matters they studied—states, their leaders, and their wars—have been quite well documented. These approaches, nevertheless, not only studied the world of nation-states and their high politics but were often part of defining the claims of those states and glorifying the achievements of their leaders, so their claims to be value-free and scientific were obviously dubious ones.

Following this, though at different times in different parts of the world, and only partly under the influence of Marxist perspectives, there developed a vibrant interest in "economic" and "social" history alongside, and sometimes in contrast to, the traditional political histories: the stories not of the "great men" and the great achievements, but of economic processes and social structures. Like political history, this was often presented in national containers and sometimes served the purpose of highlighting the particular "achievements" of nations in the economic and social spheres. Only later did a nascent Marxist historiography, often relatively weak in the universities before the 1970s, come to understand this study of history to be part of a struggle not merely to interpret or understand history, but to change it, as Marx famously put it in his eleventh thesis on Feuerbach.

A stronger concern for ordinary people in social history, however, only occurred with the turn to "history from below," sometimes also referred to as history of everyday life, micro-history, or historical anthropology. This was largely a development that gathered momentum from the 1970s onwards. "History workshop" movements that often became supporters of this new, more human-agency centered understanding of social history, critiqued older forms of social history for being too focused on structures and processes and thereby for ignoring human agency. Furthermore, these approaches criticized the adherence of much of social and economic history to modernization theories and teleologies of progress that appeared to many practitioners of historical anthropology as outdated. The interest of these historians in the everyday had made them turn to anthropology and, inspired by anthropological methods and theories, they set out to change understandings of the social and cultural. As Robert Darnton has put it, "The anthropological mode of history [. . .] begins from the premise that individual expression takes place within a general idiom" (quoted in Hunt 1989: 12). In other words: history had to start from individual human agency and then locate it within a wider collective field.

More difficult to understand is the next form of "traditional" historical interest that was always a lesser strand when compared to political and economic/social history: namely, intellectual history or the history of ideas. Like "traditional" forms of history that focused on states, wars, and high politics, intellectual history has often focused on a narrow slice of life as well: the thoughts and ideas of other great men than politicians (though sometimes them too), mainly artists, scientists, philosophers, and others whose writings are seen to have captured, defined, and led the "spirit" of an age. To be sure, intellectual historians are quite interested in the contexts and structures that enabled the great thinkers to produce their great works, as well as in how those great works affected the less great thoughts of the cultures and societies that produced them. The recent influence of the so-called "Cambridge school" around Quentin Skinner and J.G.A. Pocock is a good example of such contextualization of great thinkers. Internationally even more influential has been the "history of concepts"—shaped seminally by the German historical theorist Reinhart Koselleck. Conceptual history is now a truly global undertaking and one that takes seriously the belief that we need to thoroughly historicize our key concepts in order to understand how people made sense of the world and how they consequently acted in the world.

Next to political history, economic and social history, historical anthropology, and intellectual history, cultural history now forms one of the great traditions of historical writing, reaching back to the very beginnings of professional historiography. Jacob Burckhardt and Johan Huizinga are just two examples of classical representatives of cultural history that can still be read with great pleasure and benefit by contemporary cohorts of students. However, older cultural history often had a strong emphasis on studying "high culture" and thereby distinguishing what was "true" and "worthwhile" culture from "popular culture" or simply "trash." When a "new cultural history" began to conquer history departments in the 1980s, it democratized older forms of cultural history by redefining culture in broader and more inclusive terms. Furthermore, many of its practitioners were much influenced by the "linguistic turn" and theories associated with poststructuralist approaches (Toews 1987: 879–907). Like historical anthropology the new cultural history was dissatisfied not only with an older political history interested mainly in "high politics" but an older social and economic history reducing the past to structures and processes. Unlike an older intellectual history, it was also not so much interested in "great ideas" but instead in ordinary thoughts and practices. Whilst the initial interest in language led cultural historians to study discourses, many soon realized that discourses had to be related back to practices. Furthermore, practices had much to do with things and objects, in other words, materials that needed to be considered to have an agency of their own in history. The history of material culture could thus build on the linguistic turn and practice theory, but it carved out a niche of its own in a field of cultural history that became increasingly compartmentalized as we enter the new millennium after 2000.

Marxist social historians like E.P. Thompson and Geoff Eley spearheaded new understandings of the history of society that took on board many of the insights of the new cultural history without ever abandoning an appreciation of the Marxist understanding of social developments. Thompson, for example, focused not only on the economic condition that made the English working class, but on "the way [. . .] material experiences are handled . . . in cultural ways" (Merrill 1972: 20 f). This happened, according to Thompson, through "cultural and moral mediations." In turn, however, Gareth Stedman Jones moved the discussion even farther afield from economic reduction when he declared that "We [. . .] cannot decode political language to reach a primal and material expression of interest since it is the discursive structure of political language which conceives and defines interest in the first place" (Stedman Jones 1983: 21-22). For the "new cultural historians" in this tradition, then, what they, in part following Emile Durkheim among others, called "representations" became of primary interest. And, as Roger Chartier put it, "The Representations of the social world themselves are the constituents of social reality" (Chartier 1982: 30). This is because, as Lynn Hunt writes, "All practices, whether economic or cultural, depend on the representations individuals use to make sense of their world" (Hunt 1989: 19). The goal of cultural history is thus, as again Chartier defines it, to show "how, in different times and places, a specific social reality was constructed, how people conceived of it and how they interpreted it to others" (Chartier 1998: 4). In this, Chartier followed Lucien Goldmann, who had defined worldviews—the true subject for intellectual historians who were interested in culture more broadly—as "the whole complex of ideas, aspirations and feelings which links together the members of a social group [. . .] and which opposed them to members of other social groups" (Goldmann 1967: 17). And this is indeed the approach that most of the authors in these six volumes have taken, though in an obviously wide variety of ways in and for a wide variety of contexts.

# MEMORY

The turn toward memory, especially understood as a collective or cultural phenomenon, can in fact be seen as—though not only as—another inflection of the new cultural history (Berger and Niven 2014). Its interest in representations and discourses encouraged an interest in memories as constituting those representations and discourses. Whether it was written in pursuit of a nostalgic longing for a great national past, as is evident in some of the contributions to Pierre Nora's seminal seven-volume study on the realms of memory of France (Nora 1981–7), or whether it was conducted in the search for understanding and possibly overcoming the consequences of traumatic events in the past, like genocides or wars, memory history has linked contemporary memories to processes of sense-production in the present that gave rise to very different and always contested understandings of the past.

It should already be obvious, then, that the cultural history of memory undertaken in the forty-eight chapters that follow is not just about recall or other basic cognitive processes. Though the concept of memory employed across these six volumes is sometimes the lay understanding of memory as what and how people can recall in different times and places, the majority of the chapters take memory to be something broader. Memory may seem to take place within individual minds, yet for most of the last century numerous scholars both within and beyond cultural history have understood memory more broadly (Olick, Vinitzky-Seroussi, and Levy 2011). Individual memory always takes place within social contexts, with social materials, from social positions, and in response to social cues. So whatever neurological or mental processes it involves, these are obviously deeply embedded in structures and contexts that extend far beyond the individuals whose minds engage in remembering, traditionally understood. Individuals, moreover, employ many technologies of memory—for instance, chanting or writing—which exist outside of themselves and are not part of their brains, and which vary across social settings and in their impacts on individual mnemonic processes. In this way, it becomes perhaps clearer why memory is such a rich terrain for cultural (and other!) forms of history.

However, many of the chapters that constitute this cultural history of memory take yet another step beyond the mind—that is, beyond what Maurice Halbwachs, one of the key figures in contemporary thinking about memory, called the social frameworks of memory, to see memory as an inherently social activity (Halbwachs 1950). We often—even most often—remember together. Social psychologists understand that there are significant differences between remembering alone and remembering in a group, whether this is a matter of simple recall (e.g. when a group of individuals can reconstruct memorized lists more completely than the sum of individuals alone via cuing and other social processes) or in narrative process (e.g. when a family retells a story of an experience they have shared, and the complete narrative emerges from the many voices involved, which bring different pieces than everyone necessarily would have recalled). However, some scholars argue that groups themselves remember; for instance, they build libraries and fill them with materials, they curate representations of the past in museums and elsewhere in ways that transcend the resources of individuals, and they preserve knowledge that very few individuals recall (Assmann 1992). As such, scholars often refer to social, collective, or cultural memory—the forms and traces of the past that transcend the capacities or even interests of individuals—and many do not believe these forms of memories are merely metaphors (see Erll 2008). The field of memory is thus a vast one, and it is clear that understanding all the different forms of memory—from the neurological to the museological—requires, and is an appropriate subject for, all the resources of cultural history.

Having said that, the development of memory studies since the 1980s has been characterized by the gradual constitution of a new discipline that was self-consciously transdisciplinary. Of all the disciplines that constituted this new field, historians were arguably in a minority. Literary scholars and sociologists were far more numerous, and, as all six volumes in this series demonstrate, a cultural history of memory cannot do without referencing a range of literary, sociological and other disciplinary approaches to memory.

Apart from its characteristic transdisciplinarity, which had a major impact on memory history, however, the latter also remained, for quite some time, tied to the national container that, as we have already discussed, had been so strongly established in the historical sciences in the century roughly between 1850 and 1950. The move of memory history to *transnational* forms of memory has only been a relatively recent development, following a general trend in historical studies to criticize "methodological nationalism" and move to more transnational forms of historical writing, emphasizing interlinkages, adaptations, and transfers. However, as a perusal of any of the hugely successful conferences of the Memory Studies Association will show, most scholars today still focus on national memory.[1] Transnational, let alone global memory is not practiced very widely,[2] which also reflects a major difficulty for a cultural history of memory; there are simply not enough scholars who can truly synthesize vast amounts of work on a particular theme in a global perspective. Here we can only trust that our failure will be an inspiration to future generations of scholars to move to more global perspectives on memory history.

Where our six volumes have hopefully been more successful has been in moving histories of memory away from their fixation with trauma, especially national trauma. The huge body of work on the memory of genocides, in particular the Holocaust, and the equally massive amount of work on the memory of wars, especially the two world wars, but also the Vietnam war and a range of civil wars, is an indicator of to what extent memory scholars have homed in on traumatic events in the past. Undoubtedly, much of this work has been incredibly valuable and inspirational, but the six volumes that we introduce here, whilst not ignoring genocides and war, also intend to highlight a range of other areas in which memory history can be usefully applied.

If *A Cultural History of Memory* tries to escape memory history's bias toward "methodological nationalism" and toward traumatic events in the past, it also deliberately—and structurally—seeks to introduce a longer-term perspective and to show how memory history is a relevant and intriguing exercise for older periods of time. Once again, looking from a bird's eye perspective over the field of memory history, we see a massive concentration of work in the modern period, basically from the late eighteenth century to the present day. But the first four of our six volumes underline to what an extent the history of memory benefits from considering older time periods. As general editors, we particularly hope that modernists (of whom we are culpable examples) may delve into the writings on pre-modern times, as it will reveal not only substantial differences, but also, and certainly more striking to us, amazing similarities when considering the role of memory for cultural sense-production.

## A CULTURAL HISTORY

Finally, what of the definite article "A" Cultural History of Memory. In the first place, across a work as extensive as this one (or these ones), it is obvious that there are many different approaches to the subject matters. Though all contributing to this cultural history, the authors come from numerous different disciplines and specialties, have different foci, bring to bear different interests and expertise even within this "one" work. We do so, moreover, from numerous different countries, languages of origin, and periods of study, though the list, however extensive, is still limited in significant ways. In the second place, however, much as the publishers did not lay a heavy hand on the forms of cultural history to be employed, they did determine that all the volumes should have the same structure. Hence, we came up with eight themes that had to be the same across all six volumes. In choosing broad themes—power and politics, media and technology, knowledge: science and education, time and space, ideas: philosophy, religion, and history, high and popular culture, the social: rituals, practices, and the everyday, and remembering and forgetting—we sought to give the volume editors the space to adapt those themes to the particular foci appropriate to different times and geographies. As any reader of the six volumes will realize, the editors made good use of that leeway, but this also leads to the phenomenon that different authors have put the emphasis of their respective chapters differently and usually in line with their own specialisms.

The publisher also dictated the epochal labels we employed, and they determined that the eight topics addressed in each chronologically constituted volume should be nominally the same as the topics in the other volumes. Much as we appreciated the reasons for this—for instance, so that a particular theme could be followed across the epochs, or that someone interested in a particular epoch could recombine the history of memory we have produced for that epoch with the history of something else addressed in other entries in the series—this constraint did raise concerns for us and our colleagues. For instance, no single chronology labeling applies uniformly for different areas of the world (e.g. not every society or culture identifies the same antiquity, or an antiquity at all). And the present chronology is a very Western one indeed. Moreover, the application of these labels can be anachronistic. After all, the people whose forms of memory we are studying in a particular age did not understand themselves as having that particular place in history (e.g. the people in the antiquity we have studied did not think of themselves as inhabiting an ancient world). Finally, had we not understood the imperative of recombination of themes and periods, the editors of each epochally-defined volume might have wanted to label the eight chapters differently from the editors of the other volumes, since the same relevances did not necessarily obtain in the same ways in different periods.

Nevertheless, much as the ground we have collectively covered here is vast indeed, we might still hope—if not for other, at least for additional work in this vibrant field on this fascinating subject. We hope that, despite the additional works that might be possible—and that we hope will be produced—what we have to offer here will be of use to as many as possible. The field of memory studies is a relatively new one. But the sophistication of the chapters (and volume introductions) we have the pleasure of presenting here shows that much as the field has a long way to go, it is well on its way.

# Introduction

BEATE DIGNAS

At some point in the third or second century BCE, a poet who had won a musical contest had this marble votive relief[1] set up in a sanctuary in Alexandria.[2] Its sculptor, Archelaos of Priene, had signed his work and guided viewers through the complex visual composition with the help of inscribed labels that name many of the figures. The relief is arranged in several horizontal zones. At the top, a reclining Zeus engages with the goddess *Mnemosyne* (Memory), depicted slightly lower to his right.[3] Below, we see the nine Muses and Apollo, who plays the lyre in a cave. On the same level, on the far right, an unnamed figure, who probably represents the commissioning poet, clutches a scroll and stands on a pedestal, with a tripod in the background. In the lowest register, Homer is seated on a throne

FIGURE 0.1: "Apotheosis of Homer Relief," signed by Archelaos of Priene. Hellenistic, 300–100 BCE, Alexandria (?). Found in the seventeenth century in the Via Appia, Rome. Credit: Werner Forman/Universal Images Group/Getty Images.

holding a scepter and a scroll. *Chronos* (Time) and *Oikumene* (the Inhabited World) are placing a crown on his head, and he is flanked by the kneeling personifications of the *Iliad* and the *Odyssey*; to the right, personifications of various genres of literature and moral qualities (among them *mneme*—"memory") guide a sacrificial bull to an altar placed before the enthroned poet.

There has been much scholarly discussion on the Archelaos relief or, as it is also entitled, "Apotheosis of Homer relief"—on its potential original contexts, on its allegory of poetic inspiration and bookish environment, on its depiction of epiphanic encounters, and above all on its characterization of Homer as a quasi-divinity of universal status (e.g. Zeitlin 2001: 195–200; Newby 2006: 156–78; Clay 2004: 55–8). Does the relief also capture or perhaps form an ideal entry point, visually, into a "Cultural History of Memory in Antiquity"? Admittedly, the relief stems from a specific context and environment, and the narrative and message it sent to its contemporary viewers may only be interpreted correctly if one considers this background.[4] However, there is no doubt as to the representative character of many of its features. It attests to the immense cultural authority that the figure of Homer possessed throughout classical antiquity, in space and time. It certainly alludes to the role of myth as both "timeless" and "past," simultaneously reservoir and receptacle of the poet's work. It is a gift to the gods, a lasting monument, a memorial of personal success and a vision of individual and cultural inspiration. Not least, it features the personified goddess Memory as consort of the father of the gods, as a patron of Homeric and any poet's art in past and present.[5] The relief certainly addresses many of the themes and "agents" that this volume seeks to examine and may even contribute to their interpretation.

The tapestry of ancient cultures and memories in a period spanning 1,300 years is as varied as in any other equally wide-ranging geographical and temporal framework. The scholars who are contributing to this volume are fully aware that their thinking from and with examples, and their comparisons, will always represent a specific selection and that they may find challenging otherness if they looked at areas outside their own expertise or simply added differentiation to the interpretation. Regardless of how sharp the focus on "memory" is kept and, within this subject, on the defined themes of each chapter, shortcomings will be apparent. As my own entry to the subject, the Archelaos relief, bluntly illustrates, "antiquity" is often short for "classical antiquity," and this is often the equivalent of "Greco-Roman antiquity." Classical scholars have increasingly become aware of the mind-sets and perspectives relating to such a limited focus, but while this awareness has produced fruitful interdisciplinary work and a much more refined understanding of cultural interactions, pursuing historical memory research that respects "memory" as powerful and specific *and* dynamic and diffuse in multi-cultural societies needs more than a widened perspective. This Bloomsbury series aspires to historical comparison and expects the current volume to make strong statements of correlation (or idiosyncrasy). Whether distorted by Helleno- as well as Romano-centric templates, or by a lack of range, the fine line between inappropriate simplification and unhelpful over-differentiation is hard to find.[6] Likewise, looking "inwards" from a narrow "classical" perspective, it would be a mistake to assume anything like a homogeneous cultural identity with respective homogeneous types and markers of memories. With an eye towards diachronic interpretation, it is equally problematic to assume that concepts and uses of memory remained static over centuries, and tackling that problem creates another fine line between discerning ancient perspectives and patterns and surveying ongoing change.[7]

To attempt a systematic characterization of the meanings and contexts of ancient memories is therefore extremely challenging, if not impossible. This is already clear when one tries, as the editors of this series have, to break down the subject into meaningful thematic chapters that apply to all volumes. Inevitably, the themes addressed in this "ancient volume" respond to chapter headings in a "period-appropriate" way while trying to keep an eye on the later volumes. Between chapters, recurring themes, specific moments in time as well as developments stand out and reflect the fact that the study and application of memory have many facets. Memory is a multiform creature that, while constantly undergoing metamorphosis, at times experiences rites of passage, and it has significance in all areas of society—political, social, and religious—that cannot always be discussed in neat categories without overlap. Here, the ancient world is no exception but paradigmatic, e.g. in its embedded religion and, for long periods, its emphasis on the autonomous city-state. On the one hand, it is not surprising that such idiosyncratic features emerge across the volume, and as they bear enormously on the roles and functions of memory they require discussion. On the other hand, the series offers the wonderful opportunity to adopt an open and inquisitive mind. We need to ask whether certain memory themes have not been addressed in ancient scholarship because they cannot be explored, or because they would impose anachronistic categories on the ancient world, or because scholars of antiquity have simply not attempted to transfer to their own research the insights of memory studies on later periods as well as new theoretical approaches.

These considerations and caveats apply equally or even more so to an introduction that wants to bring observations together and talk about shared and qualifying characteristics of memory categories "in antiquity," and perhaps even tries to "fill the gaps." However, I am hoping to draw attention to some of the parameters that apply to memories in the ancient world and in scholarship on this world. In preparation for the eight chapters of this volume, I shall try to highlight some of the thematic focal points that have generated ancient memory studies and the analysis of which helps us grasp antiquity better than we would without them. Finally, there is the question whether the role of and approach to memory experienced fundamental change within the period, and what was its trajectory.

## PARAMETERS

The intense research output of the last decades has yielded a virtually unlimited range of expressions when it comes to categories and functions of memories. Scholars of antiquity have not only been at the receiving end but also contributed creatively to this situation. One begins to wonder how fruitful it is to engage in the debate and how necessary to adopt a stance on "cultural," "collective," "communicative" memories, and their relationship with "tradition," "intentional history," and other memory-related terms.[8] In contrast, the broad use of the term as one that relates to anything to do with the past shows that memory studies need a conceptual framework and careful thought about the terms used.[9] In the face of this dilemma, an introduction may err on the inclusive side and leave it to the thematically more focused chapters to exemplify, test, and illustrate ideas.

Quite naturally, in this as in the later volumes in the series, Jan Assmann's idea and definition of "cultural memory" are chosen as the starting point of many chapters (Assmann 1992; Assmann and Hölscher 1988). Assmann's background as a scholar of Egyptology and Classical Archaeology is not co-incidental, and an interest not only in autobiographical and social or communicative memories, but also in memories relating to and stemming from a remote past, is not surprising when we study the ancient world and its characteristic modes, such as religious rituals and poetic traditions. In their difficult quest to reconstruct a political narrative of the periods they are studying, scholars of antiquity have always consulted what we label "cultural memory," in all its expressions and versions, eagerly and desperately. The snowball that started rolling with Halbwachs' and Assmann's seminal studies was sorely needed in the context of this task. Without an awareness that "collective memories" are not only different from individual memories (or even the sum thereof) but also highly constructed, ancient research will be fundamentally flawed. An enormous number of case studies illustrating the extent to which self-representation and official versions of a collective past distort or even fabricate a community's historical past has been published since the 1990s.[10] The frustrating aspect of this necessary research trend has been outweighed by the many insights we have gained, relating to both the concepts and expressions of memory, memorization, commemoration, and to their historical impact and utilization by groups and individuals at specific times and for specific reasons. Given this combined need and output, "getting tired" of memory studies, or "returning to hard core historical reality"[11] are no options for scholars of antiquity—which makes it almost superfluous to point out why this volume, still, after a plethora of studies on the subject, is useful and important. Moreover, and this is crucial, a lot of work needs to be done, not least because we have begun to investigate the relation between memory and history in more subtle ways. The way ancient cultures remember their past does not have to be *either* constructed according to a contemporary political agenda *or* based on an actual historical past, and personal memories do not have to be formed in entirely different ways from collective memories (e.g. Dignas 2012: 119–43).

Hardly any reflection on "Memory" can escape the question of its relationship with "History."[12] Answering this question can be an endless and fruitless task, filled with many varied assertions of how the two do *not* relate, and with finding more and more complexity (e.g. Cubitt 2007). Here, I resort to Simon Price's "optimistic" approach that emphasizes a "productive" relationship and sees the study of different memory contexts at the heart of the historian's task because these contexts are imbued with the self-understanding of the people and peoples we are trying to study (above all Price 2012; in more general terms Poole 2008; Ricoeur 2004). Arguably, it is because of this that one could see the ancient world as a paradigm and "ideal playground" for the memory scholar. Firstly, many "memory layers," as well as "networks of memories" are beautifully represented in the written and material remains of antiquity, and it is precisely the ways in which they are fashioned, distorted, preserved or erased through which we can learn about the historical process as such. It appears that our evidence is deeply characterized by the fact that ancient "identity" and "memory" appear exceptionally strong. Responsible for this is a continuing desire to link the present to the remote past, which creates many contexts in which memories were constructed. The ancient historian therefore has the right tools with which to work: places and objects from the past, monuments and iconography, and textual narratives with a primary purpose to memorize and commemorate. This is paired, secondly, with our desire to understand the ancient world through its own self-perception.[13] Let alone the opportunity of tapping into this world by way of "oral history," personal testimonies are a desideratum in all respects. Memory of the past, however, is profoundly about "self-understanding." Thirdly, ancient historians have always been aware that the processes of creating memories and of forgetting are ongoing. Within the centuries that comprise the ancient world, new semantics were constantly imposed on or adopted by monuments and rituals of the past. Continuing this process, "classical reception" in all periods of history in its own ways has fashioned the memory of the ancient world according to the needs of ever changing contemporary worlds, and this continues, of course, in present scholarship that draws on selected evidence and a variety of contrasting representations.

This approach does not confront the relationship between "History" and "Memory" head on but rather deals with it in a creative way. It is a fruitful way forward for our own research on memory, but we may still have to ask to what extent it matters that ancient societies themselves do not seem to be as concerned with the differences between the two, whether stark or nuanced, and how ancient historiography specifically engaged with this question. Although we find explicit ancient references that assume a homology between the two categories,[14] it would be wrong to claim that there was a lack of awareness that both History and Memory were ambivalent and linked in complex ways.[15]

Research has primarily focused on "attitudes towards the past"—here, as a genre, historical works differ from poetry and oratory. Importantly, scholars increasingly argue that this difference does not lie in the contrast between "popular memory" and a critical reaction against it, on the part of a new emerging genre of historiography. Jonas Grethlein has suggested that it was the different ways in which narratives negotiated the tension between past experiences and human expectations in order to help their audiences cope with the uncertainties of the future. Within the genre, there was also the challenge of representing the past in light of the hindsight of the present, with which individual authors dealt differently, oscillating between an emphasis on experience or teleology (Grethlein 2010 and 2013). Catherine Darbo-Peschanski observes an unstable conceptualization and limited appreciation of memory in all historians. She assigns very clear-cut "temporal frameworks" to each historian: Herodotus' *Histories* are based on a "time of justice," the works of Thucydides and Xenophon on a "time of human nature," and that of Polybius on a "time of fate/fortune" (Darbo-Peschanski 2019: 162). As a consequence, Herodotus becomes a historian who saw his role as that of a "judge of *logoi*," compared to the *mnemones*, magistrates of memory who we know from epigraphical sources. Thucydides, in turn, recognized an emotional *mneme* as an important psychological faculty but not as a reliable cognitive power (ibid. 172–4). These interpretations illustrate the challenges of relating memory to the genre and its representatives. The aim of contrasting individual historians from the memory-perspective tends to reduce their work to one dimension, and this dimension again has an impact on our understanding of nuanced memory-layers and functions in the texts. We also have to acknowledge that, while we want to approach the complexity of memory in an analytical, theoretical way, ancient narrators may approach the subject rather instinctually, yet not bluntly. Much work remains to be done here, also from a cross-cultural perspective.

## MEMORY IN VISUAL AND EPIGRAPHIC CULTURE

"Viewing" and "reading" the Archelaosas relief is a fascinating experience—this is not least because it encourages us to combine art and text to create a narrative and grasp the expressed memory roles.[16] Many ancient testimonies, however, are void of text. Where does this leave the memory scholar? Partly but not exclusively, the materiality of ancient sources is responsible for the great emphasis ancient scholarship places on both *lieux de mémoire* and the quality of memory media as objects (e.g. Bommas 2011). Pre-historians, archaeologists and classicists working on early Greek epic and its oral tradition have shown successfully that material objects can illustrate a historical consciousness, an awareness of the past (e.g. Alcock 2002; Antonaccio 1994: 389–410; Grethlein 2008: 27–51; Morgan 2014).[17] An "archaeology of the past" has therefore become an important tool for modern scholars to discern attitudes towards the past in pre- or non-literate contexts. When it comes to using this tool, interpretation is crucial, fruitful, and challenging. To give but two examples: Jan Assmann describes ancient Egypt as "bicultural," contrasting an everyday culture and an eternal monumental culture. While the former leaves unintentional imprints of past life, the latter leaves messages, as self-conscious expressions of an ongoing transmission. This duality is visible in two exclusive building traditions, clay and stone, and two writing traditions, namely cursive and hieroglyphic (J. Assmann 1991: 16–26). Clearly, the consequences of Assmann's dichotomy on the conceptions and functions of memory are immense.[18] However, the context of such memory media is crucial for their correct and specific interpretation: Svend Hansen uses the example of grave goods, which are not simply objects of everyday life and thereby its "mirror" but a symbolic selection from a spectrum of available material goods, and this gives them a new function when they are placed in the grave (Hansen 1996: 261).

As a medium that naturally focuses on display, epigraphy plays a major role in creating "intentional history," similar to numismatic testimonies. Fulfilling both a textual as well as a monumental function, inscribed text stands out even more as a specific (and predominantly ancient) memory medium.[19] Here, the "monumental potential, its capacity to convey a strong message qua monument" (Lambert in Foxhall, Gehrke, and Luraghi

**FIGURE 0.2:** Front of a limestone block from the stepped base of a funerary monument, mid-sixth century BCE, Attic. Credit: Artokoloro/Alamy Stock Photo.

2010: 236; Chaniotis 2013: 132–69) was often the factor that decided whether a "text" was publicized or not.[20] It is not coincidental that the contexts in which we find inscriptions are themselves memory contexts: funerary, dedicatory, honorary etc.

Summarizing his observations on the "poetics of memory: the epigraphic construction of memory," Angelos Chaniotis presents a decree from Olbia, in which the city decides to honor a local politician and military leader with a public funeral and a statue. The decree cites the text of the inscription that will praise the deceased for his benefactions, which matched those of his ancestors. The Olbians also give instruction to crown his statue on several occasions every year, and during this process "the Herold will read the text of the inscription to the statue" (Chaniotis 2013; *IOSPE* I² 34, early first century BCE). This is an unusual testimony in that it *tells us* how the inscription was integrated into local ritual and related to the monument of which it formed a part; undoubtedly, though, the same role applied to many inscriptions. While emphasizing the spoken word, the link between the honorary statue and its engraved text also reminds us that we are not looking at material culture in a search for memory media because of a lack of or limited literacy.[21] Finally, the example of the Olbian benefactor also points to the significance of statues as an exceptional monumental memory medium. In cultures that operated in a fundamental way on concepts of "honor" and "shame" as well as "honor" and "benefaction" this medium as the primary tool to confer honor cannot be overestimated (Ma 2007 and 2013).

## LITERACY, THE HOMERIC EPICS, MYTHOLOGY

Yet, antiquity *is* the period that makes us, more than any other, look at the threshold between oral and written culture, which is why ancient memory studies address "writing" and "literacy" from a plethora of angles, and why writing and literacy also loom large in this volume. Whether talking about the acquisition and retention of knowledge, the consolidation of political or religious authority, the availability of and interconnection between media of memory, the introduction and processes of writing hold a central key to our insights. Modern ideas on how literacy, orality and memory relate form an important theoretical framework to these themes. Close analysis of our evidence often illustrates this theoretical framework, but it also cautions us not to seek neat paradigm shifts (above all Small 1997). It looks as if specific as well as broader studies addressing the impact of writing on memory come not only to the same conclusion but also to a conclusion that corresponds to what research on orality has established. While the introduction of writing had an impact on how memory was conceptualized and its functions described, ancient societies did not give up using memory and memories in traditional ways, and the new medium did not replace old memory media that had successfully served to link past and present.

These observations are not easily mapped onto Jan Assmann's influential theories of the impact of writing on cultural memory and the transformative consequences of processes of canonization (especially J. Assmann 2015). Assmann sets out several stages: "sectorial literacy," where writing is restricted to certain domains of culture such as the economy, administration or cult, is followed by "cultural literacy," where writing is applied to cultural texts. This then leads to a split between "the old" and "the new," with the old assuming normativity and timeless validity. In a following phase of "first canonization" evolving "classics" still exist in multiple versions and undergo changes, comparable to oral cultural texts. Only the third step, which Assmann calls "secondary canonization" and which is characterized by "the combination of strict fixation of surface structure . . . and complete semantic transparency," brings fundamental changes, expressed in and linked to the rise of exegesis and commentary (122). The author acknowledges that only when this last stage goes hand in hand with a shift from ritual continuity to textual continuity is cultural memory formed in a totally different way from before, and there come about new ways of relating to a formative past (130). It is not clear, however, how the two are linked, and why this shift is inevitable.[22]

When we look at these transformations it is perhaps fruitful to consider not only media (or single out one medium) but also content. One of the strongest reasons why traditional memory media, above all oral transmission, co-existed vigorously in(to) an age of—to speak in Assmann's terms—cultural literacy or even canonization must be the crucial and unifying role that the Homeric epics and their subject matter played (Price and Thonemann 2010: 105).[23] As is nicely illustrated by the Archelaos relief, the *Iliad* and the *Odyssey* form part of a range of interwoven themes that are closely linked to memory and memories. The oral transmission of the many stories relating to the Trojan War and the fate of its heroes did not end with written versions but with these the figure of Homer enters the stage of "cultural memory creation," and this with an almost magnetic force. While it is not surprising that this moment is often seen as the beginning of every type of cultural memory in the Greco-Roman world, it is itself an example of a response to the Troy story. Homer's relationship with myth is complex, and the poet's role was certainly not simply that of a creator of myth (e.g. Létoublon 2011).

As a site, Troy may be seen as the prototypical ancient *lieu de mémoire*. It experienced the "pilgrimage" of famous visitors from Xerxes to Alexander the Great, L. Cornelius Scipio to Caesar and Augustus, followed by other Roman emperors, who each added to the cultural memories that would be experienced by future visitors and by audiences of literary works that described and suggested such visits.[24] As an event of the distant past, with an array of protagonists of wide provenance in the Greek world, the Troy story offered enormous scope for individual communities as well as Greek culture as a whole to link the past with the present.[25] It created a narrative of an early Greek "history," and it reflected the world of Greek mythology, which was in itself an attractive memory medium, lending itself to tradition, commemoration and memorization.[26]

From an ancient perspective mythical periods and historical periods formed part of a continuum and the former were used to express local identity even more than the latter.[27] Interestingly, the sense of shared history bound up in myth appears to have flared up in certain periods.[28] In the Hellenistic period, interstate relationships were fostered in this way, to do with the new inter-connectedness of this period, the cultural aspirations and policies of its rulers, the attempt of many communities, old and new, to partake in Greek culture and identity.[29] In the Roman empire, in particular during the so-called Second Sophistic, the potential to conceptualize myth entirely within a concurrent political and historical landscape was particularly striking, and it comes across as both natural and a practical skill.[30] This functional use chimes with the conventional interpretation that in this period of Roman domination the Greeks felt the need to assert their cultural identity. While these themes were not necessarily tied to the telling and retelling of the Homeric stories, there is no doubt that "mythology" was a receptacle for cultural memory and that this font was adaptable and open to challenge. The formation of a canon of classical texts was not an obstacle to this phenomenon. In fact, if the Archelaos relief indeed stems from a Ptolemaic context, the depicted cultic worship of Homer would refer to the shrine that Ptolemy IV established, in which the cult image of the poet was surrounded by

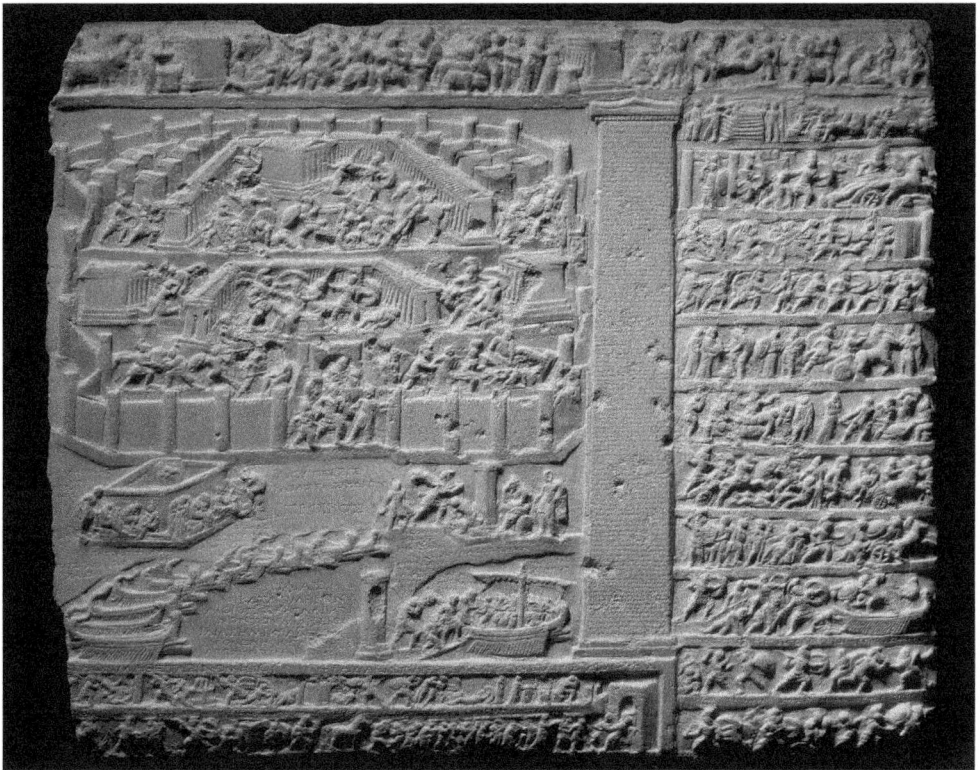

**FIGURE 0.3:** Tabula Iliaca Capitolina with scenes of the Trojan War, first century CE. Via Appia, Rome. Credit: DEA/G. DAGLI ORTI/De Agostini/Getty Images.

representations of the cities that claimed to be Homer's birthplace (Aelian, *Varia Historia* 13.22). For Roman identity and understanding of the past, the Trojan War became equally important during the principate of Augustus.[31] Many components contributed to the creation of this powerful cultural memory, which was driven by the desire of a new imperial dynasty to explain and legitimize itself: the event, the protagonists, the impact on religious infrastructure and the canonization of a poetic work that commemorated all of this. Virgil's *Aeneid*, moreover, allowed the Romans to link Greek and Roman memories of the past and to explain why there was so much overlap between Greek and Roman cultural memory. Interestingly, using Troy as part of a self-image was not an Augustan or Roman invention but followed the example of Greeks who had settled in Sicily and southern Italy.[32]

Foundation myths are arguably the clearest illustration of the ancient blur between history and mythology. They also emphasize the great extent to which looking towards the past was intertwined with understanding the present because these narratives spelled out the *aitia* for contemporary phenomena and identities—they explained why social practices and institutions existed in the present, and they gave these institutions tradition and status. Foundation myths inevitably also contributed to or even created the religious identities of communities.[33] Myths recalled the power of the gods that had led to the foundation of cults, they expressed the existing relationship between gods and human worshippers, and they offered the opportunity for individuals, social groups and entire communities alike to express their identities in religious terms. Local myths referred to specific places and recipients of religious worship, the specific religious infrastructure that was so characteristic for Greek religion. The story and fall of Troy and the *nostoi* of its paramount individual heroes offered many opportunities in this respect, and stories and protagonists "wandered" within and between ancient cultures (Lane Fox 2018: XLVIII–LI). The latter became not only recipients of cult in a wider sense but also, in their characteristics, strengths and weaknesses, "exempla" for individuals in all areas and periods of the ancient world. The Archelaos relief, once more, illustrates not only the existence of hero-cult but shows that this phenomenon extended to the cult of poets, above all but not limited to, Homer (Clay 2004).

## AGENCY AND AUTHORITY

Poets created, transmitted, and guarded cultural memory throughout classical antiquity. Their works were recited, sung, performed, and written down. As recipients of divine inspiration and heroic honors, their versions of the past held authority. How different was this authority from that of other agents that were involved in processes of memory and commemoration? From their respective perspectives, all chapters in this volume address the question of "who controls memory" in the ancient world. It becomes clear that the answer to this question is much more complicated than a list of individual agents or socio-political roles, however narrow the cultural and thematic focus.

Naturally, historiography and its agents play an important role. Thucydides' skepticism of poetry is well known, and Herodotus was cautious in his use of poets as sources (Thuc. 1.9.3; 1.10.3; 1.21.1; Hdt. 2.120). With regard to the formation and transmission of cultural memory, however, many similarities between historiography and other literary genres exist.[34] Moreover, "historiography" is a diffuse genre.[35] I have already pointed to the difficulties of pinpointing idiosyncratic uses of memory in well-known historians, with an interest in Greek and Roman history at large, and beyond. Arguably, reconstructions of local pasts in local settings were the most important tools for creating collective memories within the ancient city-state. Recent scholarship on the individuals and processes behind the creation of local histories, and the ways they related to collective memory, has been prolific (recently Thomas 2019). The Lindian Chronicle, e.g., which set out the history of the cult of Athena Lindia on Rhodes via a list of its votive offerings and epiphanies of the goddess, explicitly spells out which sources were to be used in the process of reconstructing the history of the cult: letters, public records and other testimonies (Higbie 2003). We see the religious officials in the sanctuary, in particular priests, as actively involved in the execution and publication of the record, and various letters of named local priests carry the authority to confirm dedications, alongside the testimonies of Homer and Herodotus, whose master-narratives are complemented by local myth where they present gaps (Higbie 2003: 222–7). While the focus on religious identity and agency may not surprise us in this context, it is important to note that local histories frequently centered on extraordinary detail in cult observance and aetiologies.[36]

The second part of the Lindians' historical record of their sanctuary recalls the epiphanies of the goddess. These were in essence *aitia* for contemporary practices, often in the context of crisis-management, combined with the demonstration of the deity's power and local identity. In their interpretation, we can compare them to other unprovoked divine signs that occurred in sanctuaries: physical signs such as fire, lightning or earthquakes, pragmatic signs such as accidents or irregular behavior, or miraculous signs such as the sweating of a cult statue or the automatic opening of temple doors. These must have been disseminated by oral local interpretations but could also be recorded or physically marked in the very place where they occurred, forming part of the evolving sacred landscape.

As Kai Trampedach has observed, by contrast with the Ancient Near East, where signs had mantic potential per se, in the Greek world such signs were constructed in the aftermath of events, linked closely to the historical contexts in which they took place (Trampedach 2011: 29–44). This means that both epiphanies and other divine signs were closely intertwined with local political history. Similarly, the political context must often have triggered the redaction and publication of sacred histories (Chiai 2013: 84). Religious officials were therefore not directly responsible for the reconstruction of local (religious) history because what they were doing was the consequence of political decisions. As was also the case in Lindos, civic decrees gave instructions for the compilation of records, perhaps initiated by priests but not as agents in a regular and formalized process. In Rome, there were authoritative forms of priestly documentations of history, such as *annals* and *commentarii*. The members of the priestly *collegia* who produced and administered such records were perceived as religious specialists who were to some extent guardians of religious memory. As many rituals formed part of historical commemoration, this memory was also cultural memory in the widest sense, a link that is reflected in religious calendars, *fasti* (Rüpke 2012: 139–152).[37] These emphasized the fact that cults had history, and that their foundations were linked to memories of historical events. Yet again, a political elite that overlapped with the membership in the priestly colleges shaped the religious calendar and decided when to consult the religious specialists.[38]

In Egypt and Babylonia priestly authority was configured very differently, and with consequences for the creation and preservation of cultural memories. In mostly inherited roles, priests and scribes had exclusive access and therefore control over intellectual culture and sacred texts.[39]

However, in particular in Egypt, as sacred texts could not be altered but had to be memorized and recited verbatim, this control was limited by the authority of the text, which was characterized by immanent divine power. In a world of changing uses of scripts, from hieroglyphic or demotic to Greek, the authority of the old, sacred language was particularly significant. As Richard Gordon has shown clearly with regard to the magical papyri, when users emphasized the authority of the old language they did so to increase their personal authority, but this was not necessarily an example of the manipulation of the past (Gordon 2012).

A priestly caste in Egypt, a Roman senatorial elite that held membership in the religious *collegia*, Greek poleis in which elites proposed civic decrees and instructed their own priests to produce local (sacred) histories—should we assume that controlling memory and memory media was a matter of social status in the ancient world? And was this world qualitatively different with regard to social stratification, in other words, did the class and class-conscious societies as we undoubtedly perceive them create patterns of memory creation and reception that have nothing to do with differences between "high" or "popular culture" in other periods? In Chapter 6, Anne Gangloff shows that there are no simple answers to these questions, that in many ways the basic and necessary concept of "shared memories" forbids a dichotomy and that group identities cut across such categories, however one defines them. At this point, one may also ask whether memory in ancient societies was "gendered." In general, one can say that it was to the extent to

**FIGURE 0.4:** Two Assyrian scribes taking records, from the Palace in Nimrud, 730 BCE. Credit: Zev Radovan/BibleLandPictures/Alamy Stock Images.

which agency itself was gendered. Not surprisingly, studies on female agency in Greco-Roman religion provide insights into memory and memory media that relate to female as well as male contexts. In contrast, when scholars observe strongly gendered roles, e.g., in the acquisition of *kleos* or, specifically, in funeral rites, these roles translate into different roles when it comes to memory, remembrance, and commemoration (e.g. Castagnoli and Ceccarelli 2019: 33–4).[40]

Apart from the human agents and the media through which they operated, we may immediately ask about the uses and abuses of memory control. The creation and manipulation of collective memories by entities of state authority, be it autocratic rulers or, at the other end of the spectrum, the "people" in the radical democracy of classical Athens, are central to the discussion, and the case studies explored in Chapter 1 could be juxtaposed with many further examples. In an ancient world where looking towards tradition was a given and where following tradition was a marker of excellence per se those capable of steering collective memory forged their own power. Inevitably, the examination of "time and space," the focus of Chapter 2 in this volume, also tends to look towards political impact and control. However, ancient memory studies are beginning to

**FIGURE 0.5:** Terracotta *loutrophoros* depicting funeral rites, late sixth century BCE, Attic black-figure. Credit: Artokoloro/Alamy Stock Images.

emphasize that "manipulation" and "abuse" can be exaggerated, and scholars do not feel compelled to perceive danger in either remembering or forgetting but show more ease when assessing the complex interrelations and perspectives involved in these processes.[41]

In a similar vein, it is time to acknowledge that not every form of memory is ultimately part of or used as a vehicle to convey "collective memory." The temptation to exaggerate here is again great, in particular with regard to an ancient world for which we question concepts of "private" and "public" or at least see them as differently and less clearly applied. "Public" and "private" can be misleading categorizations if we are steered by the observation that to a large extent the creation of cultural memory depends on public display of memory media—underneath that framework, however, we need to point to individual and more private memory (functions), especially in iconographic contexts.[42] Admittedly, the dichotomy between "private" and "public" does not correspond straightforwardly to qualifiers such as "individual" and "social," let alone "collective." However, as the demarcation of a "private sphere" is often seen as the central prerequisite for individual identity, the relationship and interaction between memory created and stored on a private basis and that circulating in the public realm are important. Moreover, current research in memory studies is continually refining the classification of different types of memory, and while some categories are widely accepted we look at the blurry edges of each type and, beyond this, point to aspects where thinking in distinct terms is unhelpful and prevents us from exploring the social connections that initiate memory processes.

## METAMORPHOSIS—CONTINUITY AND CHANGE

My discussion of parameters as well as selective themes has shown that "big conclusions" evoke "big caveats," that generalizations evoke counter-examples. This means that we should be cautious and not argue from analogy or transfer interpretation from one context to another. However, the memory studies in this volume will draw on and compare their case-studies with insights relating to other periods of ancient or modern history. To some extent we need to fill gaps in order to draw significant conclusions, and at times patterns of thought and behavior familiar to the modern reader can very fruitfully and correctly bring ancient sources to life.[43] Such juxtapositions sharpen a "period focus" that examines how the distinctive qualities of the ancient world bear on memory concepts and practices within this world. In its selection of topics, this introduction has made an attempt towards this, albeit brief and with a strong emphasis on Greco-(Roman) antiquity. Beyond the question of how the ancient world forms a contrast to other periods in its uses of memory, we need to address the question of continuity and change within the period. Was there an evolution of the uses of memory, or can we single out particular moments when such uses became exceptionally important? This task of describing a general development of memory functions, or even, *pars pro toto*, the changing attitudes to the past, is probably the most difficult. What can and should we compare? How narrow do memory contexts have to be to actually trace change? As many studies tracing "memory" over a long period have shown, a very sharp focus, often on place, can be highly instructive and open our eyes to approaches to and an understanding of other contexts (e.g. Minchin 2017; Chaniotis 2016). However, memory is linked to places, to political events, to culture, to societal groups, to individual experiences, and many more constantly evolving and interacting factors. We may observe continuity rather than change, or vice versa, by changing our lens and perspective only marginally.

It is somewhat easier to ask about the impact of political changes on the creation of memories, and this has indeed been an important focus of ancient memory studies. It would appear that, also for the ancient world, the existence of *lieux de mémoire* is largely dependent on decisive historical shifts (A. Assmann 1999: 309–22; Hartmann 2012, 292–3; Galinsky 2016b: 30). Interestingly, our familiarity with the world of antiquity as "a museum world" makes it easier for us to understand this phenomenon. Viewing "a past otherness" provokes and intensifies memories, which can at this point still be used and re-fashioned in certain ways.[44] Far from clear, but fascinating, is the interpretation of this process, in both political and psychological terms. Rosalind Thomas, e.g., describes the local histories that emerged in the Greek world in particular from the fourth century onwards as a reflection of the "shifting military and political situation of the Greek city-states" and "the need to comply or negotiate with dynasts and kings of the Hellenistic period, and the larger and more cosmopolitan world after Alexander" (Thomas 2019: 28). She goes as far as to propose a de-politicization of the *polis*. This interpretation sees the approaches to and uses of the past completely in synchronization with political history, or at least as a direct reflection of this. Memory creation is at the heart of this relationship, but the causal link is not simply "compensation" or "rebellion" etc. In turn and despite its challenges, paying attention to memory creation leads us to understand political processes and changes. One only has to look at how memory studies have enhanced the scholarly debates on the cultural policies of Hellenistic kings and communities, on the so-called Second Sophistic, or the rise of Christianity and the genesis of a late antique world (Alcock 1993, 2001 and 2002; Alcock, Cherry and Elsner 2001; Cordovana and Galli 2007).

Given the extent to which religion and written culture as individual entities surface as guardians and catalysts of memory production, it is not surprising that the rise of Christianity is one of the phenomena that has seen much interest also in the field of memory studies. There are a number of reasons to argue that memory in early Christianity and a Christian late antiquity was transformed fundamentally in both conscious and subconscious ways (Galinsky 2016a; see also Thonemann 2012 and Busine 2012). The sacred canon of the Bible promoted a version of the past to the status of timeless present. The reconstruction of the memories of Jesus' life and his sayings was central to the forming of a Christian identity and tapped into many memory media and *lieux de mémoire*. From creating Christian semantics to coming to terms with a pagan past, cultural memory had to be created and reinterpreted, and the phenomenon of "forgetting" looms larger in this context than any other. Christian iconography and visual programs used pagan artistic *spolia*, sometimes to ridicule the past, always to celebrate the Christian triumph (Eusebius, *Life of Constantine* 3.54).[45]

Moreover, memory in St. Augustine's *Confessions* holds a key place in theoretical approaches to memory in late antiquity and in the seismic changes in its conceptualization. While the author's models were rooted in Platonic philosophy, his transposition of memory to the individual, to the "core of one's self," enabled psychological and pedagogical pathways that were fundamentally new (Castagnoli and Ceccarelli 2019: 29–30; see also Chapters 4 and 5 in this volume). Yet, traditional memory rituals and practices were continued and imitated because they were powerful, accessible and adaptable tools in the creation of new collective memories (Busine 2012; see also Chapter 7 in this volume).

Archelaos of Priene has been a guide to this introduction after all: the visual language of his monument has helpfully highlighted the "hubs" where ancient memory studies and memory scholars meet and pause, before they take off in many different directions, with as many different itineraries. The relief links the present with the past and the future. Its own interpretation by scholars oscillates between contextualization and de-contextualization, processes crucial to the work of the historian as well as to that of memory. While the lowest register sees Homer as the recipient of cultic honors, immortal, forever and everywhere, there are many more elements to the composition, not least the anonymous poet in the present, who sees himself as much an "off-spring" of Zeus, *Mnemosyne*, the Muses and Apollo as Homer was. The plethora of figures that participate in the ritual depicted here refer to themes that are central to the framework and uses of memory: *Mythos* and *Historia*, *Physis*, *Arete*, *Mneme*, *Pistis* and *Sophia*.

# CHAPTER ONE

# Power and Politics

BORIS CHRUBASIK

## POWER, POLITICS AND MEMORY

In perhaps 426/425 BC—give or take a few years—"the council and the people" of Athens, decided to enact a public decree (*IG* 1³ 131, ll. 1–6. For the dating, Tracy 2016: 113–16), by which they granted dining rights in the *prytaneion* to the closest descendants of Harmodios and Aristogeiton, quite likely for all time. This decree was inscribed in stone and publicly displayed. Receiving dining rights, *sitesis* in Greek, in the *prytaneion* was a great honor, an even greater one if they were granted for life (Osborne 1981, but note MacDowell 2007).[1] There is no information about these descendants, but Harmodios and Aristogeiton were very well known in fifth-century Athens. The details about their deeds, and most importantly their motivations, varies in Greek historiography, but what all sources agree on was that during the celebrations of a city festival in 514 BCE the two men murdered Hipparchos, the brother of Hippias, the tyrant of Athens.[2] The fourth-century *Athenaion Politeia* narrates that Harmodios was struck dead on the spot, while Aristogeiton died during the interrogations that followed (Aristotle, *Ath. Pol.* 18.4. See also Thuc. 6. 57. 4, with Hornblower 2008: 450). It was the events of 514 BCE that were on the minds of the Athenians when they granted *sitesis* to the descendants of Harmodios and Aristogeiton.

The inscription that displays the decree is only one of many examples of how the *demos* of Athens remembered the deeds of Harmodios and Aristogeiton, and I shall argue that the deeds of these two individuals were appropriated by and formed a part of the cultural memory of the Athenian democracy. This chapter surveys three entities of state power within the ancient world: the city of Athens, as an example of a Greek city state; a Hellenistic kingdom; and the early Roman empire, and it shall discuss how exemplary each was in remembering a distinct past in order to stabilize its respective political position. It shall be seen that "cultural memories" can be created to underline a specific political entity's right to rule that it might otherwise not possess. And while the political agents of the ancient world could not benefit from the neurological insight of the twenty-first century, they seem to have been acutely aware of a remarkable aspect of the human mind: that outright falsehoods—if repeatedly affirmed by authorities to be the opposite (that is, true)—can indeed become truths in one's personal and societal memory (e.g. Stock, Gajsar, and Güntürkün 2016: 386–8, with further literature). It is tempting to interpret kings' and emperors' actions as direct attempts to use references to the past in order to strengthen and stabilize their positions (e.g. Orlin 2016). That said, this model of cultural memories as a means of power is ultimately one-directional. Cultural memories do not sit in a vacuum, they react to other memories, and—most critically—people and

**FIGURE 1.1:** Harmodius and Aristogeiton, Roman marble copies; Naples, Archaeological Museum. Credit: Paul Williams/Alamy Stock Photo.

memories of different categories react to them. As I shall outline below, the Athenian democracy's claim of how tyranny ended and democracy began was not uncontested: already in the fifth-century there were other stories of these events that were actively remembered, and this has an impact on the persuasiveness of cultural memories as a tool for political power. I shall discuss examples of contesting memories concerning the three groups under discussion and argue that while cultural memories of power were instrumental for those who created them, the process was highly interactive. The following questions and their answers are essential: why did certain memories matter? What were the audiences they tried to address, what were groups' reactions to these memories, and, finally, what does all of this tell us about cultural memories of power and the power of cultural memories? The evidence does not allow me to come to firm conclusions on all of these points raised in every example, but these questions will lead to a nuanced treatment of the relationship between politics, power, and cultural memories. The first part of this chapter will give three stories of ancient cultural memories of power, which will be contrasted by contesting memories in the second part.

I mentioned already that there is further evidence from Athens that underlines the exceptional commemoration of Harmodios and Aristogeiton. At some point after the events—dates vary between c. 509 and the early 480s BCE (discussion in Azoulay 2014: 39–50)—both men were honored by the Athenians with two bronze statues in the Athenian *agora*, the city's busiest market-place. These were the very first statues in Athens to depict mortals, and after the initial statues were taken as war booty to Persia after the Persian sack of Athens, apparently in 477/6 the Athenians commissioned a new pair of statues, and Roman copies of this second monument survive (for the date: *FGrHist* 239: A54) (see Figure 1.1). In addition to the valuable sets of statues to commemorate these two individuals, Attic drinking songs—*skolia*, performed at drinking parties—emerged during the fifth century, famous enough that in one version or another they survived the time period to be collected and written down in four sets by the late second-century CE author Athenaios of Naukratis. One of these versions (*PMG* Page 893) praises their exemplary behavior and underlines that it was they who made Athens a place of "equality under the law," a place of *isonomia* (note that Bleicken 1995: 66 emphasizes the notion of political equality as the main concern). Frequent citations in Athenian comedies suggest the songs' popularity, for example in the *Acharnians*, performed in 425 BCE. Moreover, citations of specific lines could further suggest that the wording of these songs may not have changed significantly from the fifth century to when they were written down by Athenaios.[3] Also, Herodotus, composing his *Histories* in Athens in perhaps the 430s, has the Athenian general Miltiades exclaim in a speech encouraging a positive decision on whether or not to engage the Persians at Marathon: "It is now in your hands, Kallimachos, either to enslave Athens, or to make her free and to leave behind you for all future generations a memorial more glorious than even Harmodios and Aristogeiton left" (Hdt. 6. 109. 3, tr. De Sélincourt, slightly modified).

What we see in these episodes is that by some point in the first half of the fifth century BCE Harmodios and Aristogeiton had become the saviors of Athens in the Athenian public conscience. They had saved Athens from tyranny and paid for this with their own lives: they were heroes. The examples from Aristophanes also demonstrate the public knowledge of this image of the "tyrant slayers." Yet, as outlined in the previous paragraph, the drinking songs further underline that they were not only the slayers of tyrants, they were also the bringers of *isonomia*, and became champions of the Athenian democracy.

The extraordinary honor of large bronze statues was paid for by the Athenian state, and—after the second set of statues was set up in the 470s—they also may have served to remind the young Athenian democracy of the threats to this form of political constitution, perhaps even, as Tonio Hölscher put it, "to encourage the *demos* to embrace the ideology of the tyrannicides" (Hölscher 1998: 158–60).[4] The enactment of a public decree to feast the heroes' descendants in the *prytaneion* was a further conscious act to underline the memory of the heroes.[5] We do not know how worried "the Athenians" (or groups of Athenians) were in the months leading up to the moment when this decree was set up, but it is not too hypothetical to assume that a perceived threat to the established order was there. The *topos* of Harmodios and Aristogeiton's deeds is strikingly present in Aristophanes' comedies of the 420s (when the decree was enacted), and the placement of Thucydides' account of the tyrant slayers within the chronological context of the Sicilian campaign, directly after the recall of Alkibiades and before the profanation of the mysteries, underlines a concern of an overthrow of government in the early 410s (Thuc. 6. 53–8, see Teegarden 2014a).[6] After the overthrow in late 411, and after democracy was re-established in 410, apparently this public notion of standing up for one's form of government and keeping in mind the memory of Harmodios and Aristogeiton was put in a public oath to be sworn by all Athenian citizens (Andoc., *On the Mysteries* 96–8).[7]

There are many more examples of how Harmodios and Aristogeition were invoked, but the ones cited will suffice for the purpose of my argument (Raaflaub 2003. For the long history: Azoulay 2014). For the Athenian democracy of the fifth and early fourth centuries, these two sixth-century elite members of society were slayers of tyrants and defenders of democracy: their deeds could serve as exempla for good civic behavior, also underlining the dangers other forms of government—and that of tyranny in particular—entailed. Over the period of the fifth century, the deeds of the two tyrant slayers were actively remembered through statues, lore, and songs, recast and shaped throughout the development of time if necessary. While modern scholars have attempted to draw the distinction between memory and history (e.g. Galinsky 2016b: 2–3), for the Athenians in late fifth-century Athens, their memory *was* history. It is thus not surprising that the author of the *Marmor Parium*, a chronological list dated to the Hellenistic period, equates the murder of Hipparchos by Harmodios and Aristogeiton with the end of tyranny (*FGrHist* 239. A45).[8] All of these actions of the Athenians, generating a historical aetiology of the Athenian democracy with a clear direction towards the future,[9] can be described as the construction of cultural memory. As has been argued by Jan Assmann in his seminal work on *das kulturelle Gedächtnis*, one of the prime incentives to create cultural memories and to engage in acts of remembering was the desire to uphold power, the desire to rule (J. Assmann 1992: 70–1).[10] The fifth-century Athenian *demos* created cultural memories of tyrant slayers to safeguard their democracy, and to strengthen the position of their state in a time of possible internal and external threats, most explicitly mentioned in the oath all Athenian citizens had to take to act against the overthrow of democracy. The Athenian democracy re-imagined a story of its origin, particularly at a time when individual memory of the tyrant slayers would have died out in the middle of the fifth century.[11] The monuments, the drinking songs, and the overall familiarity with the *topos* of the tyrant slayers were the corner stones on which these cultural memories were founded. They were the Athenian democracy's "places of memory," the now very familiar and generally applied term coined by Pierre Nora for the *lieux de mémoire* of France (e.g. Nora 1989),[12] including both places that were real and those that were abstract. All of these were constructed by human society and they served the Athenians to suit their political life.

The Hellenistic East was a world that emerged tumultuously after the death of Alexander the Great in Babylon in 323 BCE. The new kings of this world had a particular need to persuade both their subjects and their opponents that it was indeed they who had the right to be kings.[13] The creation of cultural memories that aided the stability of these ruling families is one (perhaps even central) aspect of their attempts to maintain their kingships. The largest of these kingdoms—reaching at its largest extent far east into modern-day Afghanistan and west into modern-day Turkey—was ruled by Seleukos, one of the former commanders of Alexander's army. He was a powerful individual, who fought actively in battles to extend his domains until he was assassinated by one of his courtiers when he attempted to return to Macedonia (e.g. Mehl 1986 and Kosmin 2014: chs. 1 and 2). His son Antiochos I already had been made co-ruler during his father's reign, and it was primarily this fact that supported Antiochos' claim to his father's empire. Yet, given that aside from personal loyalties this was a world where rights to rule due to blood did not exist per se, the continuity of the empire with Antiochos I as its king was not a guarantee (Chrubasik forthcoming),[14] and it is surely not accidental that Antiochos I can be credited with the active attempts of creating a "Seleukid" identity for this large land mass he had inherited, and that he intended to pass on to his descendants.

The three central elements of this identity-creating process are quintessentially to do with the creation of cultural memories, both bluntly and ingeniously drawing on the commemoration of Antiochos I's father and his family. One measure regarded the appropriation of space in a monarchical sense. Antiochos I re-organized large parts of the empire and continued his father's policy to found cities in the names of his relatives. In other words: the Seleukid kings inscribed themselves into the landscape of the empire and attempted to make it a Seleukid space (Kosmin 2014: 103–19; 186–92). A further measure concerned time. Instead of using regnal years as an annual reckoning—which was typical in the Ancient Near East and Macedonia—Antiochos I continued the annual count from his father's first regnal year, reminding the empire of its origins (Kosmin 2014: 100–2; Kosmin 2018). This reckoning was continued by his successors, who also placed specific emphases on their ancestors, systematically referring in communications to royal directives as "just as was done under our grandfather" (e.g. *SEG* 37: 1010. 40–1, dating to 209 BCE). This continuity was also expressed in the royal silver coinage of the Seleukid kings (see Figure 1.2). While each king from Antiochos I onwards was portrayed with his own individual portrait on the obverse of these coins, for a century the reverses of these coins—depicting the god Apollo, usually sitting on an omphalos—continued very similar types that had been initially issued in the reign of Antiochos I. Even when alternative reverse designs were introduced, this original, and by that point "Seleukid," type was used until the end of the empire. This ensured that any new design entered circulation as a marker of Seleucid authority and itself became over time a "traditional" marker of the authority of individual Seleukid monarchs (Fleischer 1996; Chrubasik 2016: 19–20). In addition to emphasizing continuity, Antiochos I also forged a relationship between the House of Seleukos and the sanctuary of Apollo at Didyma in Western Asia Minor (Antiochos I's gifts to Didyma: *I.Didyma* 479).[15] While the dynasty's founder had been a benefactor to the sanctuary (*I.Didyma* 424), it was quite possibly the historiographers of Antiochos I who *remembered* that it was this god who had prophesized kingship for Seleukos when Alexander the Great and his army visited the sanctuary in his conquest of

Asia Minor in the late 330s BCE (for the legend: Diod. Sic. 19. 90. 4; App., *Syr.* 56. 283; Lib., *Or.* 2. 99).[16] Seleukos I's descendants gave lavishly to the sanctuary and most likely also paid for the rebuilt colossal temple (see Figure 1.3). It was from the reign of Antiochos I onwards that Apollo became the continued dominant feature of the Seleukid silver coinage. By the time of Antiochos I's grandson Apollo had become a "relative" (*syngenēs*) of the Seleukid kings (*I.Didyma* 493. 6–7).

It becomes clear that the Seleukid kings, who during the period between 312 and 165 BCE used only two male royal names, in many ways did everything they could to evoke their direct line to the dynasty's founder.[17] The city foundations in the names of members of the royal families, the re-foundations of ancient cities such as Jerusalem and Babylon under their new name of Antiocheia, the large presence of other everyday markers such as seals and coinage, and the tapping into religious authority must have been an effective way of reminding the culturally highly diverse population of the empire of their royal dynasty. While some people in the empire surely continued to identify themselves as Babylonians, Jerusalemites, or Prieneans—as a consequence of the new city foundations—many people became Antiochenes, Seleukeians, and Apameians. As such they not only integrated this Seleukid marker to become an ethnic marker of their individual origin, but it also commemorated both these individuals' identity and the cultural memory of the empire.

While the Greek cities of the coast of western Asia Minor maintained their own calendars, royal letters and also public documents written by communities in other parts of the empire or on royal land were dated to years of the Seleukid era, "when Antiochos and Seleukos, were kings in the 45th year" (*I.Laodikeia* 1. 1–3, dated to 267 BCE). Even among those communities that continued to use their own calendars, some nonetheless celebrated local games such as the "Antiocheia," festivals named after a king of the dynasty (e.g. *SEG* 50: 1195. 28) or had one or more of their tribes named after members of the Seleukid household (*SEG* 59: 1406A. 24–25 at Aigai). In the Ionian city of Teos, e.g., the honors for Antiochos III and Laodike III were celebrated on the most important days of the civic community, and two examples will be offered: first, on the day on which the new magistrates enter office, they were asked to perform sacrifice on the common hearth not only to the Charites and to Memory but also to the king whose cult image was set up in the *bouleuterion* (*SEG* 41. 1003 II: 29–38); secondly, a new foundation in the *agora* was

**FIGURE 1.2:** Tetradrachm of Antiochus II; Smyrna, 261–246 BCE. Credit: with courtesy of the American Numismatic Society.

**FIGURE 1.3:** Didyma, Sanctuary of Apollo. Credit: PHAS/Getty Images.

dedicated to the queen and this fountain was to be central to all communal sacrificial offerings. Also, the ritual baths for new brides were to be drawn from this fountain (*SEG* 41. 1003 II: 70–86). Through constant evocation the Seleukid royal couple was clearly deeply inscribed into the web of the Tean community, and this became an integral part of civic memory (*SEG* 41: 1003. For the ritual: see Chaniotis 2007). The fact that we find private cult observances for the kings beyond the civic level illustrates to what extent communal identity affected and translated into individual identity (*OGIS* 246). The relationship between the Seleukid kings and their subjects thus created relied entirely on the kings' promotion of an arguably fabricated memory that they were kings of a dynasty, and that they (and only they) had the right to rule their empire. Admittedly, they added to this web of active remembering of the past an almost permanent display of present military success and conquests, but this too was embedded in the commemoration of previous kings' military achievements and conquests: Antiochos III frequently evoked (and at times imagined) the conquests of his ancestors, and the kings of the second century actively remembered the earlier *anabasis* of Antiochos III into the upper satrapies. By emulating it through similar campaigns, they invoked the memory of this all-powerful king.[18] The domino effect of this constant evocation of dynastic legitimacy—through the coins in people's coin pouches, the dating of their public documents, etc.—meant that the inhabitants of the vast empire participated in these acts of remembering and contributed—consciously and unconsciously—to the shaping of a Seleukid space.

Looking at the kings of the Hellenistic world clearly illustrates that the rulers of newly created political entities had a strong interest in shaping and promoting a memory of their origin and that they did so in order to stabilize their positions as legitimate monarchs. The Roman world of the late first century CE bore witness to processes that were remarkably similar. The death of Marcus Antonius in August 30 BCE marked an end to the long civil war that had plagued Roman society for a large part of the first century CE.[19] The political power of the one remaining warlord, Imperator Caesar *divi filius*, soon to be named Augustus, could not be questioned, yet it was the translation of this de facto political scenario into a stable system that would provide a challenge for the coming generations.

Ancient Rome is often described as a memory culture par excellence (Galinsky 2016b: 17), an environment where monuments (and their inscriptions) in the city of Rome invited the viewer to remember the illustrious deeds of Roman nobles, and where civic life saw a large number of publicly performed gestures—such as the taking of public office, and the celebration of deceased family members—that invited and required the nobles of Rome to participate in active acts of remembrance (on the *pompa funebris*: Flower 1996: 97–127. On the *contio*: Morstein-Marx 2004). With long-standing traditions of nobles who inscribed themselves into the physical and visual fabric of the city, and in particular late republican strongmen such as Marius, Sulla, Pompeius, and Caesar, there were clear patterns that Augustus could follow to cement his special position. Yet this new strongman of Rome must have also been very aware of the precarious position of his predecessors as well as his own, and that many "stabilizing acts" proved unsuccessful for the generals of the past because they went against the grain of a deeply non-monarchical Roman past (on Marius and Sulla: Stein-Hölkeskamp 2016). The content, range, and success of the Augustan activities in this respect have been treated *in extenso* by scholarship and need not be re-iterated here (e.g. Zanker 2003; Strothmann 2000; Eder 2005; Gowing 2005; Havener 2016). But since the reign of Augustus is often treated as the ideal example of the connection between cultural memory and political power, let me single out a few of Augustus' measures that are particularly insightful.

Two examples of Augustus' building policies had an exceptional impact on Roman cultural memory. Augustus deeply changed the physical structure of the southerly part of the Campus Martius and also the area north of the Forum Romanum through the construction of the Forum Augustum (see Figure 1.4). The monumental building complex of the Temple of Mars the Avenger, and the surrounding Forum of Augustus which framed it, was inaugurated in 2 BCE, and has often been described as a key symbol of the political program of Augustus' reign (e.g. Zanker 2003: 198). As Wolfgang Havener has recently underlined, it was the combination of two vows of revenge that were centrally marked by the temple, that of the young Augustus against the murderers of his father (this is why the temple was vowed to be built) and that of the Roman state against the lost standards of the Parthian campaign (those standards were displayed in the temple once they were returned). This united theme of revenge in addition to the statuary underline the rightful role of Augustus for the Roman empire (Havener 2016: 171–3). The Forum of Augustus was also a history lesson, displaying statues and honorific inscriptions for more than 100 of illustrious Roman men from Aeneas to Drusus, the stepson of Augustus (Zanker 2003: 213–17; La Rocca 1995: 82–3; Luce 1990). Here, everyday Romans who walked across the forum could learn about the achievements of Roman men that linked the past with the present, and the growth of the empire, from its beginnings until the reign of Augustus. Here, as in other areas, Augustus attempted to codify Roman history and create an orthodox narrative of past events: it has been pointed out that in this version of Roman

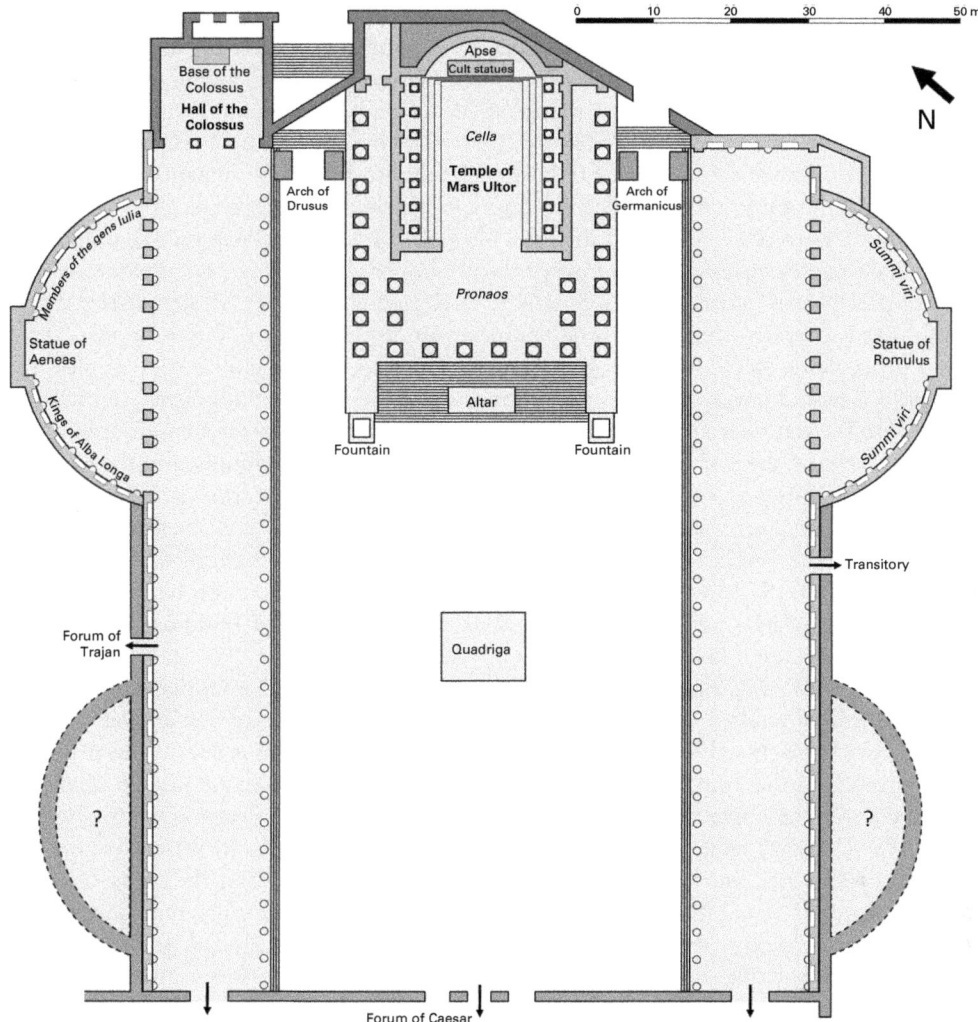

**FIGURE 1.4:** Plan of the Forum of Augustus, with Temple of Mars Ultor, Rome. Credit: Wikimedia Commons (Public Domain).

events, some individuals, such as Cicero, Cato, and Marcus Antonius, are strikingly absent (e.g. Gowing 2005: 145). It is no coincidence that both the focus on the long history of Rome, culminating in Augustus' reign, as well as Augustus as the pinnacle of Roman statesmanship were also key topics in the literary cultures of the Augustan era (for Livy and the Forum: Luce 1990; Farrell and Nelis 2013).

The re-shaping of the southern Campus Martius is another example where Augustan building activities had a similar impact on the symbolic landscape of a particular area. In addition to the physical changes to the area, the new buildings clearly changed how this space was used by visitors and how they viewed it. During the reign of Augustus, the theater of Marcellus—begun under Caesar—was built and inaugurated, the temples of Bellona and Apollo Sosianus were re-built and built respectively, and the Porticus Metelli was revamped as the Porticus Octaviae (Haselberger 2007: 133–7; Orlin 2016: 125–6). Both the theater and the Porticus were named in honor of members of Augustus' family. References to republican noble families and their dedications for the republic, such as the Temple of Pietas and the temples of Jupiter Stator and Juno Regina, were masked (as argued by Orlin 2016: 135–9). Physically, these new building complexes must have not only crowded the southern edge of the campus, but also must have changed the route of the Roman triumph to reflect the new topography of the area due to the close proximity of the buildings to one another (Orlin 2016: 135–6).[20] It is generally argued that both the renovated temples of Jupiter Stator inside the newly designated Porticus Octaviae, as well the temples of Bellona and Apollo Sosianus, were re-dedicated on 23 September. If this hypothesis is correct—and even if the temples were re-dedicated in different years—the ritual processions to the temples and the annual festivals to celebrate the temples' re-dedications would have no longer been connected to their original founding, but instead be held on the day that also coincided with the birthday of Augustus himself (e.g. Orlin 2016: 137–9). By the end of Augustus' reign, he had inscribed his family into the physical structure of key sites of the city of Rome, such as on the Campus Martius and the Palatine. With the re-dedications of the temples and the shifting of their *natales templorum* he not only changed the Roman ritual calendar, and of course he also changed the calendar in general (Samuel 1972: 156–8), he also further placed himself at the heart of central Roman festivals, thus replacing memories of republican votive buildings with those connected to his reign (as argued by Orlin 2016: 135–9).[21]

Augustus—not unlike the Hellenistic kings—inscribed himself and his achievements into the physical landscape of the city of Rome and beyond. The two examples of large building works discussed here offer an insight into Augustan attempts not only to promote the centrality of the emperor, but also to influence the landscapes of Roman memory: with the Forum of Augustus and the *summi viri* Augustus offered visitors a history lesson of the Roman past, lecturing them on who were important men in the history of the Roman republic that were worth remembering and becoming part of the active memory of the emperor's visual history of the Roman republic. These acts of remembering thus also included conscious acts of forgetting (Flower 2006: esp. 1–13), and we can not only see this in the striking absence of obvious republican *summi viri*, but also even more clearly in the rebuilding of the southern edge of the Campus Martius. Here, Augustus' building policies officially re-cast the role of traditional Roman religion, illustrating through acts of renovation and re-dedication his care for the city of Rome and its past, and simultaneously re-writing their context to be closely linked with his persona and political leadership (as also explicitly mentioned in *Res Gestae* 19. 1–21.1).

The three settings that I have sketched above show readily how, in the Greco-Roman worlds, three very different institutions of state authority expressed and corroborated their claims to power by evoking and manipulating memory, and by creating repetitive acts of remembering accordingly. The first, the *demos* of the city of Athens, actively remembered its origin and linked this closely to the deeds of pre-democratic heroes of the past that could be presented as, and become signifiers of, the democratic present of the city. The second setting described the attempts of the Seleukid kings to inscribe themselves into the landscape they controlled. Through acts of conscious remembering of the founder of the Seleukid house and the first Seleukid king they created a dynastic Seleukid identity of themselves and the inhabitants of their kingdom. The monumentalized connection between past histories and the present with a clear trajectory towards the future which—

in the language of Barry Schwartz—underlines its constituting factors (Olick and Robbins 1998: 124), is also visible in the building policies of the Roman emperors and—as briefly discussed—with the example of Rome's first emperor.

Needless to say, the acts of remembering in Athens, the Seleukid empire, and Augustan Rome were not monolithic acts, they clearly were not static but rather dynamic, changing over periods of time: the cultural memory of the Athenian democracy between, say, the middle of the fifth and the middle of the fourth centuries BCE was hardly the same. Rosalind Thomas successfully demonstrates how elements of fifth-century Athenian stories were either forgotten or reported differently in fourth-century contexts, also underlining the mutability of stories, as well as memories (Thomas 1989: 242–57), even if it is not always possible to obtain the fine grain detail that would be needed to carefully plot the development of Athenian cultural memory. Similarly, it is not always possible to determine when which cultural memories of the Seleukid empire were activated and remembered. While it is quite likely—to give just one example—that the Seleukid royal cult was initiated under Antiochos I, it was sixty years later, in the reign of Antiochos III, that we have significantly more evidence for it, perhaps also suggesting that it was more widely propagated at that time.[22] The cultural memories that proponents of state authority put forward were clearly employed with varying intensity and/or were modified throughout their lifecycle, always fluctuating and evolving. Many of these layers of different emphases are no longer accessible to the modern viewer, and some of the finer modifications and alterations must be accepted as untraceable. That said, there are moments when these memories are questioned, and these moments can give us some insight into these layers. While this section has argued that cultural memories were utilized for political purposes and that acts of remembering were employed to stabilize the political position of the ruling authorities, the following section shall investigate these moments of questioning. We must ask what the power of dissenting and contesting voices in those circumstances in which we can hear them is. What do contesting voices tell us about power and cultural memories, and the local manipulation of power and politics?

## CONTESTED POWER, CONTESTED MEMORIES

Pour to Kedon also, attendant and do not forget him
If wine is to be poured to good men

—PMG Page 906[23]

If the cultural memory of the Athenian *demos* of *c.* 380 BCE was something approximating to the story laid out in the first pages of this chapter—honoring the heroes who killed the tyrants—it is critical to emphasize that this was not the *only* memory of the Athenian past (see chiefly Thomas 1989: 238–64). Herodotos and Thucydides are quite adamant to point out that tyranny did not end with the murder of Hipparchos. For Herodotos, the Spartan king, Kleomenes, was the main subject of his narrative at this point. Together with the Athenians who wished to be freed from the tyranny he besieged (expressed in the singular form of the verb) Hippias and his supporters on the Acropolis and eventually expelled them from the city (Hdt. 5. 64. 2). Thucydides disagrees with the Athenian communal memory (Thuc. 6. 54. 1) and writes that the tyrant was deposed "by the Lakedaimonians and the Alkmaionidai in exile" (Thuc. 6. 59. 4).[24] Rosalind Thomas demonstrates persuasively that the Lakedaimonian involvement was still widely remembered in the Athenian public memory in the fifth century, as Aristophanes makes reference to the Spartan aid in his *Lysistrata*, performed in 411 BCE (Thomas 1989: 245–6, on Aristophanes, *Lys.* 1150–4).[25] Some Athenians, therefore, knew that the tyranny had not ended with the death of Hipparchos. Perhaps more importantly, however, for Herodotos, Athenian democracy also had not begun with the death of the tyrants. According to his narrative, it was the Alkmaionid Kleisthenes, who "when the *demos* sided with him, gained the upper hand against his opponents," and it was Kleisthenes again who, in a different passage, "set up democracy in Athens" (Hdt. 5. 69 and 6. 131. 1). This connection is made even more clearly in the *Athenaion Politeia*, composed probably in the early 320s BCE. While the author takes Herodotos' account as a guidance, he explicitly states that not only "the Alkmaionidai bore the greatest responsibility for the expulsion of the tyrants, and resisted them for most of the time," but also adds a drinking song for Kedon—quoted as an epigraph above—who apparently was remembered as an Alkmaionid and had attacked the tyrants unsuccessfully on a previous occasion (Aristotle, *Ath. Pol.* 20. 4–5, all translations of this text are those of P.J. Rhodes' Penguin translation).[26] The *Athenaion Politeia* goes further, claiming that it was "for this reason (*dia tautas tas aitias*) that the *demos* placed its trust in Kleisthenes" (Aristotle, *Ath. Pol.* 21. 1). If the often repeated argument that *isonomia*—while initially part of an invective against the tyrants—was quickly associated with the reforms of Kleisthenes is correct (e.g. Bleicken 1995: 66–7; Rhodes 1998: 1143 with further literature; Pleket 1972: 69–77),[27] it is striking that this Kleisthenic catchphrase (if it ever was that) also became associated with the tyrant slayers at some point: while we have evidence of the first lines of the songs in the comedies of Aristophanes, the earliest written evidence of the last stanzas of *skolia* 893 and 896—those that mention *isonomia*—dates from Athenaios (see above, n. 3).

Thucydides is outspoken about the events of the late sixth century and emphasizes that "both the Greeks generally and the Athenians themselves are quite wrong in what they say about their tyrants and about this episode" (Thuc. 6. 54. 1, tr. S. Hornblower). He relishes in the explanation that Harmodios and Aristogeiton were not tyrant slayers (since, he argues, they murdered the tyrant's brother), nor was the Athenians *demos*, but that, in contrast, the tyranny had been ended by the Spartans and the Alkmaionidai.[28] While Thucydides chose to describe the differing historical narratives as right (his reconstruction of the events) and wrong (the Athenian version), he himself was aware that it was not how *all* Athenians remembered this moment in their city's past. According to his narrative, it was after all the Athenians who were in "constant fear and suspicious" because the Lakedaimonians had overthrown the tyranny (Thuc. 6. 53. 3). As outlined in the first pages of this chapter, as a collective group the Athenian *demos* of the fifth and fourth centuries chose to remember the origin of its democracy in a specific way. Other groups, who also were part of the *demos* of the Athenians, however, remembered the past differently: they remembered the Lakedaimonian involvement in the ousting of the tyrants and the achievements of Kleisthenes in setting up the democracy. Even other groups—as argued by Greg Anderson—supplanted the foundation of the democracy to the period before the tyrants so that the democracy after the tyrants was only restored (Anderson 2007).

It is beneficial to differentiate here between different categories of memory. In addition to the cultural memories of the Athenian *demos*, some of these memories could—at least in the fifth century—be what Jan Assmann describes as communicative memories, memories that are activated through communal remembering or family hearsay (note Thucydides' use in 6. 53. 3) which could extend for four generations, perhaps up to eighty years (J. Assmann 1992: 51–2).[29] The narrative of Aristophanes' *Lysistrata* follows the lines that the Athenian old men "remember" because they had been there, much like Michel Foucault's French who did not find the memories of their past represented in de Gaulle's historical characterization of 1940s France (Foucault 1975: 25–6).[30] Perhaps it is in this context that one ought to place Thucydides' characterization of Athenian knowledge: since he acknowledges Athenian awareness of differing memories, which is also indicated in Aristophanes' comedies, one could argue that—unless he is merely inconsistent—what Thucydides is trying to achieve in his discussion is not to question the Athenian understanding of their past. Rather, he contests and questions the predominance of the Athenian official memory of the origin of their democracy. If indeed this hypothesis is accepted, this could perhaps offer one of the few emic contemporary reactions to cultural memories that are so often invisible.[31]

For Rosalind Thomas, the role of Kleisthenes and the Alkmaionidai is also part of the popular Athenian knowledge. Thomas is surely correct that Jacoby's distinction between an "official" and an "Alkmaionid" version of events is too simple (Thomas 1989: 241–2).[32] The Alkmaionid references in the narratives of Herodotos and Thucydides, and even more accentuated in that of the *Athenaion Politeia*, seem to be too broad and long-lasting to be only part of a family tradition, particularly so if one were to accept Assmann's time frame of *c.* 80 years for communicative memories. Why where the Alkmaionid memories so important to the fifth-century historians and to the author of the *Athenaion Politeia*? Thomas persuasively argues that Herodotos' references to the curse of the Alkmaionidai and the bribing of the priestess of Delphi are hardly oral family tradition material, and that they must stem from different traditional strands (as argued by Thomas 1989: 250 and not fully explained in Jacoby 1949: 162), underlining that really the memory of the Alkmaionid involvement in the origin of the democracy went beyond that of the family alone. This is further suggested in their presence in fifth-and fourth-century historiography, and while the Alkmaionid story may not have been a contesting cultural memory, it was certainly very present in the Athenian public conscience. The reasons why the Athenian cultural memory ultimately focussed on the tyrannicides and lacks references to the Alkmaionidai in particular are hard to establish, ultimately due to the nature of the sources regarding the early fifth century. That the Alkmaionidai—whose position within Athens during the time of Kleisthenes must have been remarkable—had completely ruined their political capital in Athens after the Battle of Marathon because they had not shown decidedly anti-Persian leanings before this event is a plausible suggestion (as argued by e.g. Davies 1971: 381 [9688 XI] and Ostwald 1988: 340–2; also implied by Jacoby 1949: 160).[33] This cannot be substantiated by explicit testimonies but the ostracism of the head of the Alkmaionid family in 487/6 points in this direction. Thomas' emphasis on the Alkmaionid curse may also be spot on, suggesting that a de-emphasizing of the Alkmaionid past would have suited Kleisthenes and his family (Thomas 1989: 259–61).[34] It does seem to be the case that after 470 the Alkmaionidai no longer feature visibly in the Athenian political narrative (Davies 1971: 381 [9688 XI]).[35] What we see in the evidence from the late fifth century is a wide spread cultural memory of the Athenian *demos*—one that was articulated in song, actions, and, if Andokides can be relied on, in oaths—that actively remembered how the Athenian democracy came to be (or was "restored" as Greg Anderson 2007: 119–24 has argued). At the same time, this memory was not exclusive; other stories, family traditions, and forms of memories continued to be actively tapped into.

Interpreting the shown plurality of memories on the origin of the Athenian democracy, it is critical to underline that, in this instance, it was not primarily the genesis of the Athenian democracy in itself that was contested. All mentioned stories (the deed of the tyrannicides, the Lakedaimonian military intervention, and the Alkmaionid reforms) underline the importance of the expulsion of the tyrants. The Spartan associations with Isagoras, their taking of the Acropolis, and their expulsion by the Athenian *demos*, dramaturgically deconstruct the position of the Spartans in Herodotos' narrative: while the Spartans may have been fundamental in the expulsion of the tyrants (Hdt. 5. 64–5), they also hindered Kleisthenes' creation of the Athenian democracy and led to his brief exile (Hdt. 5. 72. 1), devaluing the role of Sparta in the memory of Athenian democracy. Even if, in this instance, Athens—according to Herodotus—was rescued by the Athenian *demos* that besieged Kleomenes on the Athenian Acropolis (Hdt. 5. 72. 2), it was ultimately Kleisthenes who returned and set up the democracy, and his relationship with the end of tyranny is made explicitly in the *Athenaion Politeia* as previously argued. These alternative memories are not what memory scholarship generally characterizes as "contested voices" (e.g. Olick and Robbins 1998: 126–8; Kidron 2016). This is not an alternative voice from political outsiders, from below, from those excluded by national agendas offering a subaltern perspective on Athenian memory, such as Aristophanes' chorus in the *Knights*, who compares Athens to a man with a tyrant's power (Aristophanes, *Hipp.* 1111–14; see Kallet 2003), or, to give just one modern example, the American soldiers who, by inverting their official moral code, used their autobiographical memories to testify against American War Crimes in Vietnam during the so-called "Winter Soldier Investigation" in Detroit in January 1971 (DeGloma 2015: 170–5). In contrast to this investigation, where the "nature" of the Vietnam War was at stake (DeGloma 2015: 172), the Athenian picture needs to be explained as follows: given that the late fifth-century authors Herodotos and Thucydides, as well as Aristophanes, are explicitly making use of some elements of many Athenian memories, it is also critical to underline that at that moment in time, in the mid-420s BCE, they are situated in parallel; they are not necessarily seeking to replace one another. Therefore, unless we ought to argue that—perhaps attractively but also too binarily—Athenian counter memories should be seen as evidence within Athens of a subversive political struggle of elite members who—possibly during the generalship of Perikles or that of Alkibiades—wanted to underline the primary role of the Alkmaionidai in establishing Athenian democracy,[36] the multiple Athenian cultural memories are not necessarily a signifier for political change, that is, a Hobsbawmian change in tradition "when institutional carriers become no longer viable" (Hobsbawm 1983: 4–5; A. Assmann and Shortt 2012: 7). Instead, they co-existed.

It is the idea of a system change that seems particularly applicable to the setting of the Hellenistic world. The Seleukid kings relied not only on military strength, but also on their accepted position at the helm of the empire. While I have outlined some of the Seleukid rulers' attempts to create and manipulate shared cultural memories of the dynasty's origin to create an identity for the Seleukid empire, it is worth emphasizing that the political realities of the day often questioned the overall impact of these attempts. The Seleukid kings were politically challenged not only from the outside, but—from *c.* 240 BCE to *c.* 130 BCE and thus for a significant part of the two hundred-odd year existence of the empire—particularly so from the inside. Usurpers, that is, counter kings, emerged and questioned the authority of the Seleukid king (see the discussion in Chrubasik 2016). While some of these usurpers reigned for short periods of not more than two years, others controlled their empires for up to eight years and even longer. Ancient historiography describes these usurpers' attempts often as fledgling and forced onto soldiers by cruel warlords (Chrubasik 2016: 220–5). Yet the historical scenarios in the Seleukid empire suggest a certain level of success in the usurpers' political undertakings that is not only

FIGURE 1.5: Silver coin of Tryphon; Antioch, 142–138 BCE. Credit: with courtesy of the American Numismatic Society.

reflected in their existence for more than a couple of years but, interestingly, in their use of precisely the methods of memory creation that I outlined earlier.

Usurpers struck coinage—a medium that is traditionally conservative to underline the sustained value of the coin—at times in large amounts, and, in these coins, the usurpers in the Seleukid kingdom strikingly chose to depict themselves quite differently from the visual repertoire of the Seleukid empire: usurpers evoked different divinities on the reverses of their coins and placed different emphases in the creation of their royal portraits, some even broke the Seleukid era and counted their own regnal years (see Figure 1.5).[37] The Seleukid kings reacted strongly to these revolts, punishing perpetrators and their supporters, yet also showed forgiveness and kindness to the areas that arguably had been part of the usurpers' power bases (Chrubasik 2016: 214–20). What is most striking about these episodes is not necessarily that the usurpers in the Seleukid empire chose *personae* for their enterprises that were markedly different to those of the Seleukid kings, but rather that they thought this to be a persuasive tool to control the empire: apparently the citizens and soldiers of cities such as Seleukeia on the Tigris, or Apameia on the Orontes—both named after Seleukid ancestors and thus part of the Seleukid cultural memory—chose not to openly revolt against these usurpers, and, arguably, at times they even supported them.[38] I have argued elsewhere that these episodes, and the success of usurpers, are indicative of the success of Seleukid identity politics (Chrubasik 2016: 227–34). If even the jewels of the crown—the Seleukid capital cities—supported usurpers against the Seleukid kings, the Seleukid empire was not perceived as a "Seleukid" place.

In this context, it is no longer possible to discuss the process of memory creation as a one-way-process. So far, I have emphasized initiators: the Athenian *demos* created cultural memories of its origin, sang songs, swore oaths. This is even more evident in the discussion of kings and emperors, whose agency is paramount: both the Seleukid kings and the Roman emperor, Augustus, created cultural memories by building policies that emphasized a right to rule, thereby constituting themselves and stabilizing their positions. But who were the audiences of these constituting creations and what were their roles? It is unquestionable that the Seleukid kings thought it was advantageous to remember the deeds of their ancestors and to attempt to link their empire to their family. Similarly, the Forum of Augustus underlines, perhaps most visibly, the attempts of the first Roman emperor to combine the remembering of republican achievements with his own person, establishing a unifying cultural memory of the Roman (and now Augustan) empire. Yet it is clearly evident that these creations do not occur on an empty canvas. This is most startlingly demonstrated in the fact that kings and emperors modified their claims to memory over time. While Augustus' successor Tiberius also modified some of his *persona* to distinguish himself from his overly successful predecessor (Gotter 2015), just as the emperor Hadrian had to find innovative ways of being a successful emperor after succeeding the *optimus princeps* Trajan Seebacher forthcoming), it is critical to underline that these changes were not simply reactions to previous rulers: Tiberius' name change to re-introduce the Iulian gentile name that had been abandoned by Augustus in 40 BCE (Havener 2016: 17 n. 41 and 371–5), and thus to re-align himself with part of the cultural memory of the republican noble families—perhaps because the role of the princeps was so much clearer after 14 CE—cannot be ignored, and should be seen as a strong reaction to some forms of Roman (elite?) expectations and direct responses to previous rulers' memories. The Seleukid kings also reacted to usurpers' attempts: Seleukid kings incorporated iconographic elements, such as lavish flowing hair from usurpers, and Antiochos III's emphasis (if not invention) of the Seleukid royal cult should be seen as a reaction and modification of the cultural memory of the Seleukid empire.[39] All these examples strongly suggest that we should interpret power relationships in the ancient Mediterranean world as part of a communicative world, and identity, formed through the creation of cultural memories, was clearly an important aspect of it. Therefore, memory, too, must play a significant role in this communicative framework. For the Hellenistic kingdoms and for Augustus' Roman empire—established through success in wars alone—this was particularly critical, since established forms of legitimacy did not apply to them. Kings and emperors had to be accepted to remain at the helm of their empires (on Rome: Flaig 1992, and building on this: Wienand 2012; Havener 2016; Seebacher forthcoming. On the Hellenistic East: Chrubasik 2016). This can also be transferred to the Athenian democracy: While the *demos* of Athens undertook concerted efforts to delegitimize any other form of government with the exception of its own, this by itself was not deemed sufficient. "Democratic heroes" added a layer to justify the power and age of the *demos*: a *demos* that saw itself as vulnerable to attacks from within at all times.

Considering the apparent need of Hellenistic kings, Roman emperors and the Athenian *demos* to gain acceptance, and the presence of either contested memories or conscious reactive memory modifications, it is tempting to follow a Hobsbawmian road that points to the revolutionizing aspect of altered memory. Here, the Seleukid usurpers' actions may again be a key example. Based on an analysis of the imagery used on usurpers' coinage it seems that indeed they proposed different images of kingship and perhaps—although evidence is too scant to draw conclusions on this—this also included different cultural memories of the past: did Timarchos—a second-century Seleukid usurper who controlled part of the upper satrapies after the death of Antiochos V—rely on the old title of King of Media to generate a "Median" cultural memory for his claim, and thus to gain opposition to the Seleukid kings?[40] Roman emperors were clearly eager to underline both continuity with, but also their distinctiveness from, imperial rule. Certainly, cultural memory, and altered cultural memories are to some extent signifiers of political changes: Whether we can really interpret the late stages of the Roman civil war between Augustus and Marcus Antonius as a war of memories between Augustan Apollo and Antonian Dionysos, as Paul Zanker's analysis suggests (a monumental book in its time: Zanker 2003), or whether we should see the Athenian examples as remnants of political quarrels between those who favored the Alkmaionidai and those who did not, cannot be proven without further evidence. While these are valid historical considerations into questions that are ultimately more complex, it is important not to content oneself with these binary reconstructions. Rather than using these episodes of contestation to focus on the question of the replacement of cultural memories with new ones, it is essential to re-address the question of what the plurality of cultural memories can tell us about the political benefit of cultural memory in the first place. If the Seleukid empire was a Seleukid space—and we have seen that the cultural memory of the Seleukid ancestry was an important element of this equation—but if politically it made no difference, what does this mean? One could of course argue, as ultimately the Seleukid kings prevailed, that their "identity-creating undertakings" were superior, but perhaps this is too convenient an explanation. Two interrelated questions regarding the relationship between cultural and individual (or autobiographical) memories may illustrate the difficulties in assessing the political value of cultural memories.

In general, modern historians content themselves with the long-accepted insight that individual memories may disagree with grand narratives of large-scale cultural memories. The old men of Aristophanes' *Lysistrata* still remember the Spartan help of ousting the tyrants, a communicative memory, openly in opposition to the Athenian cultural memory of the tyrannicides.[41] Studies of contemporary societies have further underlined that individual memories may not necessarily openly disagree with the cultural memories of one's community but still remember the past differently, not caring about macro memories, creating small group memories that work for one's group (e.g. Bodnar 1992 about different forms of American identity in the 1920s). Secondly, individual memories have been shown to be quite creative when family memories form a complete opposite to the cultural memory of the community: one of the distinct outcomes of the seminal study "*Opa war kein Nazi*" was that the human mind adapts family memories in order to fit into the cultural memory of the community. Grandchildren, in particular, who remember kind and loving grandfathers, find heroic explanations to reconcile these memories with their ancestors' Nazi past (Welzer, Moller, and Tschuggnall 2002: e.g. 207–10).[42] It is easy to transfer these patterns to Roman families, whose members fought in the campaigns of Marcus Antonius, and their uneasiness in the Augustan state. The example of C. Sosius may serve as one example for many: quaestor in 39 BCE and governor for Antony of Syria and Cilicia in the following year, he triumphed in 34 BCE against the Parthian backed Judaean leader Antigonos and was in charge of Antonius' fleet at the battle of Actium. He was pardoned by Augustus, became a *XV vir sacris faciundis* in 17 BCE, and the newly re-founded Temple of Apollo near the Circus Flaminius was named after him.[43] The survival of individuals from different systems in a new world order was rather common in the ancient world: Tlepolemos, son of Artapates, from the Lykian city of Xanthos, became regent of the Ptolemaic king in Egypt and in general had a distinguished record of Ptolemaic service. Initially, however, he came from a family with an Iranian name—a family that adapted to life after the Persian empire, he was a *pro poleōs* priest in Xanthos, and he may have resided in Xanthos at the time when the Xanthian assembly passed a decree to inaugurate a royal cult for the Seleukid king Antiochos III: did he try to prevent these movements or did he resign himself to this new phase of the city (Ma 2002: 236–7; Robert and Robert 1983: 168–71)? It is individuals such as C. Sosius and Tlepolemos, son of Artapates, and their position in their new regimes that shall be investigated in the following.

If these individuals are representative of the many people in the ancient world (and their individual and communicative memories) who witnessed dramatic political, and, at times traumatic, changes, and, critically, who remembered the past differently from the successful new political authorities, is there not a danger for historians to overemphasize the persuasiveness of cultural memories as a constituting factor of power? Jan Assmann proposes that cultural memories create and support power per se. The Athenian cultural memory of the tyrannicides, but also the fundamentals of Roman society as a culture of remembering, fit this model quite well: the evocation of Roman noble life during the *contio* and the *pompa funebris*, and the singing of tyrant slayer songs have been interpreted as cores of Athenian and Roman life. Augustus' celebration of the *dies natales* for the temples in the Campus Martius on 23 September was a clear political choice and must have been politically impressive. However, as Pliny the Elder demonstrates two generations later, even with newly dedicated temples, the previous dedicatees are still remembered (Pliny, *HN* 34. 31, as admitted by Orlin 2016: 126).[44] Evidently, the sheer use and presence of cultural memories alone is not a sufficient explanation for their use as a political tool in the ancient world, particularly so since they were rarely monolithic but stood in relation to other—contesting—memories. How, then, did cultural memories and "power" relate?

And here the fates of C. Sosius and Tlepolemos son of Artapates and their relationships with the new regimes in which they lived can give further insight into the relationship between official cultural memories and power. While we only have limited evidence regarding individuals' feelings towards the new regimes, the family of Tlepolemos son of Artapates gives us at least some insight into family memories: the family made a career in Ptolemaic service in the third century, yet the family actively commemorated its Iranian descent through the name Artapates, which is attested until the second century BCE before the family disappears from the epigraphic record. As far as we can tell, neither individual revolted against the political realities of their day or the cultural memories of their new environments. C. Sosius acted as a pardoned, and—as it seems—faithful, agent of the Augustan principate. Aloys Winterling argues that the Augustan principate, in particular, was a place of ambiguity of communication, "doublespeak" (*doppelbödige Kommunikation*), where emperor and senators publicly acted in specific manners that stood in contrast with political realities or senatorial wishes (e.g. Winterling 2011: 26 read with Winterling 2003: 26–9 for the communicative model). While Winterling is mainly interested in the political practice of the early principate (see also Winterling 2005), his model rests on the phenomenon of claiming one thing when meaning something quite different, and this must initially have applied to Sosius and Tlepolemos: it did not matter whether these individuals questioned their new systems at home, but by acquiescing to the cultural memories placed in front of them they also openly declared not to challenge the acceptance of their new masters. While cultural memories were created for the community, in this argument it would be mainly a way of harnessing elite members of communities who, by subscribing (or at least not publicly decrying them) to dominant cultural memories, declared their allegiance to the system in question. This line of argument is attractive, particularly so with regard to the cultural memories of the Seleukid empire and the Roman principate, and perhaps for totalitarian states in general: what people do, think, and discuss at home, can be radically different from public behavior.[45] And, perhaps, one has to accept that cultural memories within democratic city-states and authoritarian states functioned differently. Then again, they might not: the Athenian example of the "official" cultural memory of the tyrannicides and its parallel memories is remarkably similar to the double discourses of memories that have been attested for the two politically very differently organized Germanys: grand stories, official memories, can coexist with family memories that diverge quite radically from the official ones (Welzer,

Moller, and Tschuggnall 2002: 162–4). Elite acquiescence, as described above, is therefore an important constituent that facilitates the consolidation of new public memories, but apparently it did not lessen a ruler's need to actively create, elaborate, and sustain these memories.

The question of autobiographical memories and the relationship with communal memories can be further explained by investigating local responses and local identities. How much did cultural memories *matter* to any local population in its immediate spatial context? Josephine Shaya's emphasis on the "spread" of elements of the Forum of Augustus throughout Italy and even to provincial cities, such as Emerita Augusta in Lusitania, is surely indicative of the persuasiveness of the creation of cultural memories, here conveyed through monuments (Shaya 2013: esp. 95–105). This was particularly so in the long-term: construction on the forum in Emerita Augusta began after the reign of Augustus and may have only been completed under the Flavians.[46] Similarly, an inscribed list of dedications from western Asia Minor demonstrates private devotion to the Seleukid kings, at least fifty years after western Asia Minor was no longer part of the Seleukid empire (*OGIS* 246). To some extent this responds to official Seleukid memories regarding the dynasty's divine ancestors. Yet since, alongside Seleukid kings, kings from other dynasties are also listed, this document also demonstrates the limits of the political power of cultural memories.[47] If the Seleukid kings used the royal family cult to underline their own right to rule, then this document questions the success of these attempts, and rather shows aptly how memories developed over time and may have no longer been part of the memorial worlds they were constructed for. Ultimately, these stories illustrate that the creation of cultural memories worked on different levels in different places, especially in a world where the acceptance of outside rule as such (regardless of the specific dynasty or individual ruler) needed to be achieved. Both the Seleukid kings and the early Roman emperors were successful in creating cultural memories for their regimes. As the previous examples demonstrate, the Seleukid kings received private cult. Also, Augustus' history lessons in the Forum of Augustus were adapted by local communities. That said, the Seleukid example in particular also underlines how these memories were locally adapted and reworked in order to suit local needs.

This chapter has above all addressed the moments when cultural memories were created and considered how communities and, importantly, individuals within them, would have reacted to this process. People could (and did) rely on communicative and other forms of memories and may have been witnesses to the construction of new cultural memories in front of their own eyes. They may have subscribed to these forms of public memory, but, as discussed throughout this chapter, they may have had access to other forms of memory of the past that altered official discourses or offered different—and to them more meaningful—versions. Ultimately, historians of the ancient world cannot get into the minds of the people of the ancient world without written attestations of these individual concerns. Nevertheless, the evidence from other time periods, for example the creative memories of families dealing with their personal Nazi past in light of differing official state narratives (Welzer, Moller, and Tschuggnall 2002: 195–210), should stress the complexity of cultural memories. I have shown that that cultural memories clearly mattered to states, kings, and emperors, and that the recipients of their memory-creating activities formed an important part of the process. I have also expressed a caveat, because there are many elements, in particular with regard to the reception of such memories, that the modern ancient historian cannot retrieve, and we should bear this in mind when postulating the direct political impact of cultural memories in the ancient world.[48] In the light of this, the question of why official creations of the past mattered to entities of state authority requires much further discussion, and we may even question whether such creations should comfortably be identified and labelled as "cultural memories" by modern scholars.[49]

# CHAPTER TWO

# Time and Space

STÉPHANE BENOIST AND ILARIA BULTRIGHINI

## INTRODUCTION: SPATIAL AND TEMPORAL BOUNDARIES

We begin this chapter about the relationships between time and space in the context of ancient cultural memory[1] by discussing how the Romans conceived of boundaries in multiple dimensions. The concept of *terminus* (limit, boundary, as well as the god of the limits himself) illustrates very well how the city of Rome and its people conceptualized their political community, its location, and the sharing of a sacred time. It can hardly be argued that our evidence allows us to trace collective conceptions of time and space back to the origins of a small village in Latium sometime in the eighth century BCE. As is the case with many other aspects of the origins of Rome, most of our written sources date to the first century BCE and to the Imperial period. Archaeological evidence, however, reaches back to a time as early as the fifth or fourth century BCE and provides material traces of the various liminal sanctuaries that existed in Rome between the Fifth and the Sixth Mile—the sanctuaries of Dea Dia, Fortuna Muliebris, Robigo, and Terminus.[2] On this basis, we shall provide an overview of our historical and anthropological enquiry into the various ways in which a collective Roman identity was defined and can be grasped by means of spatial and temporal classifications and perceptions. Literary and epigraphic sources reveal how—*ab origine*—a people (mainly the aristocrats) collectively imagined and understood their territory (the *ager Romanus*), its boundaries, and the rituals that were deemed necessary to maintain the *pax deorum,* (peace of the gods), that is, the gods' continued approval of the collective history of the city of Rome and its citizens (*Populus Romanus, Quirites*).[3]

In his *Fasti*, the Augustan poet Ovid—the only poet we can consider as truly "Augustan" (Millar 1993)—proposes a poetic description of the Roman calendar arranged in six poems for the first six months of the Roman year, from January to June.[4] Ovid's *Fasti* allow us to appreciate the implications of the Julian and Augustan reforms of the Roman calendar for the collective memory in Rome through a comparison of the traditional legends and their new versions. Although many other changes certainly occurred during the Regal and republican periods, their perception can hardly be traced. By contrast, the last century BCE and the first century CE provide abundant epigraphic and literary evidence which has the potential to illustrate the reshaping of time and space in Rome and its empire, *urbi et orbi*. The work of antiquarians like Varro and Pliny offers a fine opportunity for examining such memory manipulations.

When dealing with the month of February, Ovid mentions the god Terminus, as well as the Terminalia festival, which was celebrated on 23 February: "Terminus, you also mark the boundary of the sacred rites'" (2.50; tr. Robinson 2011: 89).[5] This passage

**FIGURE 2.1:** Section of the *Fasti Praenestini*, the calendar of Verrius Flaccus; Praeneste, 9–6 BCE, now in the Palazzo Massimo alle Terme. Credit: Marie-Lan Nguyen/Wikimedia Commons (Public Domain).

suggests that Terminus, the protector of the limits—especially those between different rural properties in the countryside of Rome, whose annual festival could be presented as an idyllic moment for expressing true Roman virtues, was at the same time in charge of temporal boundaries, that is, he provided the time limit by which the last rituals of the month had to be performed.[6] A few decades earlier, Varro had already expressed a similar idea in his *On the Latin Language*: "The Terminalia, 'Festival of Terminus,' because this day is set as the last day of the year; for the twelfth month was February, and when the extra month is inserted the last five days are taken off the twelfth month" (6.13; Loeb tr. Kent).[7] We will not consider in detail the complexities of the pre-Julian, luni-solar calendar of the Romans (Michels 1967; Samuel 1972; Rüpke 1995; Hannah 2005; Rüpke 2011; Stern 2012);[8] for our present purposes it is sufficient to mention the tradition that in the pre-republican calendar the first month of the year could be March;[9] accordingly, by the time of Caesar's reform of the calendar in 46 BCE, which was refined by Augustus in 8 BCE, the Romans may have conceived of their year as having, conceptually, two opening and two closing months: January and March, and December and February, respectively. In the republican calendar, February was the month in which every two years the extra twenty-two or twenty-three days were intercalated to keep the calendar in step with the solar year. In the Julian calendar, leap years were characterized by the insertion of a *bissextilis* day, literally "the second" sixth day before the calends of March, that is, 23 February. The god of the limits, Terminus, was celebrated twice: through traditional rural festivals in the countryside and as a time marker in the epigraphic *fasti*.

With the institution of the Julian calendar and its diffusion in the provinces of the empire, the Roman emperor became the "initiator" of time and space in Rome and throughout the Roman world, as can be exemplified, for instance, by the institution of new eras in the provinces—commencing from the dates of important imperial victories and achievements[10]—and especially by the creation of the calendar of Asia in the Roman East in 8 BCE (Laffi 1967; Buxton and Hannah 2005; Stern 2012: 274–84; Thonemann 2015). At the suggestion of the proconsul of Asia, Paulus Fabius Maximus, the *koinon* of the Greeks of Asia decreed that the New Year in the calendar of the province should fall on 23 September (a. d. IX kal. Oct.), Augustus' birthday; moreover, the same decree established that the first month of the year be renamed *Kaisar* in his honor.[11] In the years following the institution of the Julian calendar, two months were renamed after the two reformers: Quintilis, the month of Caesar's birth, became known as Iulius after Caesar's murder in 44 BCE, and in 8 BCE the month of Sextilis was renamed Augustus, as that was the month on which the emperor had gained his first consulship and most important victories.[12] It is important to appreciate the collective impact of these imperial approaches to time and space, as well as the meaning of Terminus for an *imperium sine fine*.[13] Power without limits: this is how Rome understood its empire. But what were the collective perceptions of the Romans in the provinces, as well as those of non-Roman citizens, the peregrines, some of whom, like the Greeks, had an illustrious history and were full of memories?

A representative case of the role that space and time played in forming and shaping the collective memory of the Greeks in the course of a long span of time, from Archaic times

**FIGURE 2.2:** Remaining structure of the Olympieion in Athens, second century BCE–second century CE. Credit: Wikimedia Commons (Public Domain).

to the period of Roman domination, is that of the Temple of Olympian Zeus in Athens (Santaniello 2011; Whitmarsh 2015). Quite conveniently, this particular example is also relevant to and connects nicely with the subject of our next section, "Foundation(s) and Re-foundation(s)."[14] Also known as the Olympieion, the temple was built over several centuries, beginning in the mid-sixth century BCE under the Peisistratids. The first phase of construction, however, did not progress further than the temple base, and the project was halted by the emerging democratic community when Hippias was overthrown, perhaps as it was symbolic of tyranny in the Athenians' memory (Mikalson 1998: 200; 2010: 208–9, 342; Anderson 2003: 91–92). Work on the Olympieion was resumed hundreds of years later, in 174 BCE, under the Seleucid king Antiochus IV Epiphanes, and was conducted by the Roman architect Decimus Cossutius. However, the death of Antiochus in 164 BCE caused the building works to cease once again. Two further centuries passed before the Roman emperor Hadrian finally completed the structure in 131 CE. The initiative of the *demos*, or perhaps of the Philhellenes, led to the erection of an honorary arch near the temple, which came to represent a spatial and temporal "boundary" between the city of the Greek past and that of the Roman imperial (Hadrianic) present. Two inscriptions are carved on the architrave of the arch, one on each side: the space to the west of the arch, in the direction of the Acropolis, is labelled "the former city of Theseus," while the area on the eastern side of the arch, toward the Olympieion, is described as "the city of Hadrian, not of Theseus"[15] (Willers 1990; Tölle-Kastenbein 1994: 163–165; Camia-Marchiandi 2011). The arch is an honorary monument, and as such, it is not designed as a gate to the city; likewise, the inscriptions on either side of it do not identify two separate parts of Athens. As Tim Whitmarsh phrased it (2015: 53), "the imperial project was to distinguish prior and present time using spatial demarcation, merging temporality and space into a single symbolic expression." In an attempt to create a strong bond with the origins of the city, Hadrian drew on the figure of Theseus, the mythical founder of Athens, and presented himself as its new founder. To further legitimize the Roman authority and his personal claims to the city, during the construction of the Olympieion the emperor embarked on a reorganization of Athens which involved the creation of the *Hadrianis phyle* (tribe), whose thirteenth constituent *deme*, *Antinoeis*, was apparently located in the new south-eastern section of the city developed—or "founded"—by Hadrian (Traill 1975: 31, 103).

The perception of the *princeps* as a new founder, like Hadrian in many provincial cities such as Athens or *municipia* and colonies in northern Africa, stresses the imperial discourse, from Augustus onwards, as an attempt to build a collective memory upon stories of *Res Gestae* made by good emperors as true *conditores*. In that perspective, Roman imperial history provides a way to deal with the past by perpetually re-formulating/re-shaping time (events and legends) and space (shared by gods and humans).

## FOUNDATION(S) AND RE-FOUNDATION(S)

An aspect of collective memory that represents a focal point of vigorous—even fierce—historiographical debates is the question of the origins of cities and civilizations.[16] In this context, part of our evidence is literary and makes a reconstruction of events tempting—even the most ancient ones—which occurred at some point in the past, while part is archaeological and typically difficult to interpret. The mythical story of the foundation of Rome by Romulus remains a vexed question.[17] Should we refuse any reconstruction of the early centuries of Roman history and be "hypercritical," or should we primarily be interested in the perceptions of that remote past in the middle and late republic and during the first decades of the principate? Dealing with the origins of any ancient city requires awareness of the multiple discourses written by ancient historians as well as of modern attempts to reconstruct a scientific account made of *facta et dicta*!

We must be aware that the narratives written by historians such as Livy (*History from the foundation of the city, ab Urbe condita*) and Dionysius of Halicarnassus (*Roman Antiquities*) during the last decades of the Roman republic and the early Augustan period had specific meanings for any Roman citizen in Rome and for any foreigner who was discovering the history of the new masters of the Mediterranean, even though this "national" history could be considered as a Greek history by a Greek audience, in the case of Dionysius of Halicarnassus (Miles 1995; Jaeger 1997; Hurst 1982; Martin 1993; Fromentin 2001; Edwards 1996). Narratives tell a story that is expected to be accepted by the contemporary audience—this is a fundamental aspect that should be kept in mind: a collective memory can never be founded on mere lies, unless these are unanimously accepted.

We will consider Rome as an example in a true imperial perspective: the urban discourse about the origins of the city of Rome is essential if one is to find some positive evidence to interpret the archaeological surveys of Roman colonies and *municipia*, i.e. the self-identification of Roman cities as "little Romes" everywhere in the *Imperium Romanum*, considered as a vast territory under Roman rule characterized by the coexistence of various identities. It is well known that Augustus was almost granted the *cognomen* Romulus by senators during the assemblies in January 27 BCE and finally preferred the far less provocative *Augustus*[18] (Galinsky 1996 and 2005). Augustus paid particular attention to his persona as a new *conditor* (founder) of Rome and the Roman world. In this respect it is useful to quote Livy's introduction to his *ab Urbe condita*, which contains a set of "imperial figures" from the past—Romulus—and the present—Augustus, to emphasize what was not to be considered as "imperialism":

> Such traditions as belong to the time before the city was founded, or rather was presently to be founded, and are rather adorned with poetic legends than based upon trustworthy historical proofs, I purpose neither to affirm nor to refute. It is the privilege of antiquity to mingle divine things with human, and so to add dignity to the beginnings of cities; and if any people ought to be allowed to consecrate their origins and refer them to a divine source, so great is the military glory of the Roman People that when they profess that their Father and the Father of the Founder was none other than Mars, the nations of the earth may well submit to this also with as good as grace as they submit to Rome's dominion.[19]
>
> —Livy, *Praefatio* 6; Loeb tr. Foster

Augustus's successors were equally concerned with the origins of Rome and with the idea of Rome's eternity: Commodus was represented on coins as a city-founder tracing the *sulcus primigenius* (primordial furrow) during the limitation ritual carried out by a carriage with two oxen[20] (Hekster 2002). Maxentius gave his deceived son the *cognomen* Romulus to celebrate the *conditores*, i.e. the founders Romulus and Remus[21] (Cullhed 1994: ch. 3). The festival of the foundation of Rome, the rustic Parilia (or Palilia), a celebration of the herds, which was named after Pales, the goddess of the shepherds, and fell on 21 April (the *Natalis Urbis*), was renamed Romaia during Hadrian's principate in fervent commemoration of the city; similarly, the jubilees—the

FIGURE 2.3: Coin of the Emperor Commodus, *RIC* III 615. Credit: Bibliothèque nationale de France.

*pseudo-ludi saeculares* under Claudius in 47 CE for the 800th birthday of Rome, those under Antoninus Pius in 148 CE for her 900th birthday, and those under Philip the Arab in 248 CE for her 1,000th birthday—were as important as the traditional Secular Games, which were renewed by Augustus in 17 BCE and were subsequently celebrated by Domitian in 88 CE and by Septimius Severus and Caracalla in 204 CE (Benoist 2005: 273–333).

Although it is challenging to fully grasp the specific aspects of the origins of the foundation rituals of Rome from an Etruscan, Greek, and Latin perspective (Briquel 2008), we may assume that a formal legal and ritual procedure of city foundation started to be developed in late republican times. This is the reason why evidence from all over the Mediterranean show that Roman cities—both *municipia* and *coloniae*—tried to trace *ab Urbe condita* (from the moment the city was founded) the various rites which had supposedly been practised by the founder Romulus himself (Liou-Gille 2005). It shall be helpful to look at the reception of those narratives, and especially at the concept of "Roman city" shared by those living under Roman rule in the last century BCE; during this period, the so-called process of municipalization of Italy converted all Italian cities into Roman cities: this was both a spatial and a temporal reorganization, which involved, for example, the establishment of a forum, of a Capitoline temple and of festivals that were part of a civic calendar. Subsequently, during the first three centuries CE, the same process came to gradually change the reality of urban spaces in the provinces (Barchiesi and Scheidel 2010[22]). The epigraphic evidence from Hispania includes legal documents that inform us about the Flavian policy regarding the transformation of foreign cities into *municipia* with Latin rights. The magistrates, along with their families, became Roman citizens, and Roman law started to be increasingly used, until these new *municipia* tried to obtain the privileged status of *colonia*, in order to be perceived and treated like "a little Rome."[23] This circumstance explains why archaeology, and especially aerial photography, tends to paint an oversimplified picture of what may be interpreted as "true" Romanization. It is important to carefully describe the impact of this process on contemporary collective memories. This is reflected, firstly, in the narratives of the origins of Rome in Greek and

Latin historiography; secondly, in the examples all over the Roman world of what defines a city as Roman, i.e. its topographical organization and its monumental setting; and finally, in the societies defined by their political identity and daily rituals, above all the political agenda in Roman practices and a "celebration tool" that we develop in the next section.[24]

Consciously shaping the memory of past foundations offered the opportunity to construct an entirely new sense of Roman identity. As seen earlier, Augustus was fully committed to present himself as a new founder of Rome and the Roman world. Yet he was not simply interested in establishing a link between Romulus's foundation of Rome in the distant past and his own present role as new *conditor* of the Roman *oecumene*. The intense restoration programme implemented by Augustus in Rome, which affected a vast number of temples in every part of the city, had the effect of reshaping the way the Romans remembered their past. The reconstruction of temples was necessarily accompanied by their re-foundation, and in a number of cases the new *dies natalis* for these temples (that is, the date of their re-dedication, which would then become part of Rome's festive calendar) was conveniently moved to 23 September, Augustus' birthday, or to the birthdays of other members of the imperial family. Augustus' re-foundations thus implied a combined intervention on space, through the refurbishment of temples and buildings situated in key spaces of the city of Rome, as well as on time, by moving festival dates in the ritual calendar. By doing so, Augustus deliberately obliterated the early history of these temples from Roman collective memory and replaced it with a new narrative in which the lead role was played by the emperor.[25]

**FIGURE 2.4:** View of the processional frieze on the Ara Pacis, consecrated in 9 BCE. Credit: Wikimedia Commons (Public Domain).

FIGURE 2.5: View of the processional frieze on the Ara Pacis, consecrated in 9 BCE. Credit: Wikimedia Commons (Public Domain).

# CELEBRATION

From foundation rites to ceremonies performed on specific dates of the civic calendar, the idea that ancient Greek and Roman cities were the home to both men and gods is crucial for the present examination. This concept includes, however, the differentiation between sacred and secular space, as well as the notion that time was split into days set aside for the commemoration of the gods and days for human activities (Dumézil 1970; Beard, North, and Price 1998; Scheid 2015). It should however be pointed out that some radical views have recently entered into the debate on the model of "*polis*-religion" and have sought to challenge its long-standing acceptance and validity (Woolf 1997; Krauter 2004).

Livy gives us two excellent examples that reveal the fundamental experience of the divine through the participation in festivals, especially in processions, which celebrated the community of gods and men because both were sharing the same space and time within the city. We immediately sense how Rome conceived of her civic religion and of the communities involved in its celebration. But, interestingly, we wonder whether the author is referring to the Augustan or the old republican city, and which gods and which people are implied as forming those communities. With regard to our focus on "collective memory" these questions illustrate the important function of religious processions nicely. Let us first consider the case of the Volsci, who were expelled from Rome by senatorial decree and whose participation in religious ceremonies was *de facto* forbidden sometime in the early fifth century BCE:

> Games of the greatest possible splendour were decreed by the senate [. . .] A great crowd of Volsci is now in Rome; there are games; the citizens will be intent upon the spectacle [. . .] The senate decreed that the Volsci should leave the City [. . .] But when they had started, their hearts swelled with indignation, that like malefactors and

polluted persons, they should have been driven off from the games at a time of festival, and excluded in a way, from intercourse with men and gods.[26]

—2.37.1; Loeb tr. Foster

We need not dwell on the relationship between Volsci and Romans, nor on the particular context of this decision, which was probably made in 491 BCE (Coarelli 1990); what interests us is the participation of peregrines in Roman *spectacula* (games—*ludi*—held on holidays—*festi dies*) in a civic context—only *ciues Romani* (Roman citizens) were supposed to take part in these festivals—and on the shared sense of interaction with both men and gods associated with the experience of the *spectacula*.

The second example stems from a speech delivered by Camillus about a century later; this passage gives us insight into an Augustan conception of a city full of gods, and of a city perfectly organized by way of time and space—this, in effect, amounts to a definition of *polis*-religion:

We have a City founded with due observance of auspice and augury; no corner of it is not permeated by ideas of religion and the gods; for our annual sacrifices, the days are no more fixed than are the places where they may be performed.[27]

—5.52.2; Loeb tr. Foster

From these two republican examples, given by a historian who lived during the Augustan period, we may infer that we can approach the relationships among communities and practices, festivals, ceremonies, sacred spaces, and a civic calendar (comprising a list of the official *feriae*), in the same way when we look at Rome and at Roman cities in general, and the latter include Greek cities of the Roman East, despite the fact that these had strong traditions of their own, because of their intense encounter with the Roman world.[28] The anthropological and historical implications of the two passages examined above can be summarized as follows: first, the important role of the community—occasionally widened beyond the strictly civic circle of citizens and their families—especially in imperial ceremonies, both in Rome and outside the *Urbs*, in official visits by the emperor and in any festivals relating to the imperial cult.[29] Secondly, the emphasis on the successful organization of the community, in social and political terms, to guarantee and showcase impressive ceremonies that were taking place in various locations, such as theaters, amphitheaters, and circuses (Laurence 1993; Laurence and Smith 1995–6). This can be illustrated by a wide range of evidence from places throughout the empire. Thirdly, we are reminded that a topographical approach to this phenomenon has to be adaptive, matching the dynamic character of what we may define as the "processional tool." Processions "assembled" the different components of cities and transformed spaces through the links they developed between monuments, men and gods. During the *pompae* (processions)—either in the circus, or at funerals, or during the celebration of triumphs—representations of political and social identities were put on stage. These three insights are premises to our understanding of the spatial and temporal dimensions of collective memory (Fless 2004; Benoist 2008; Estienne 2015).

Let us now introduce a further "imperial" image to conclude this section and move on to the next, which deals with identities and mixed memories: what was the impact of the physical presence of the emperor in Rome and in other (Roman and peregrine) cities of the empire—or, in special circumstances, his absence from those cities? We may think about the various processions during which the effigy of the dead or ruling emperors were carried through the urban centers—in the case of Rome, from the Campus Martius outside the pomerial boundary to traditional sites like the Capitoline temple, forum, theater, amphitheater or circus during solemn entries or triumphs, or to the Campus Martius from the Palatine and the Roman Forum during public funerals. The *aduentus* (the solemn arrival of an emperor at Rome or at any other imperial cities) and the triumphal and funeral processions in Rome allow us to reflect on shared images of power and the embodiment of the divine, which shaped the identity of the entire Roman world: the emperor as a conqueror, who bears reference to defeated peoples in his imperial nomenclature (Germanicus, Parthicus, etc.); the emperor as guarantor of security and peace, who, accordingly, is allowed to modify the *pomœrium* (sacred boundary); the emperor being considered as a living Jupiter during the triumphs and, from the early second century CE, eventually becoming a *diuus* (god) as a result of a consecration ceremony (Benoist 2005 and 2008). In other words, the imperial figure was omnipresent in urban spaces throughout the Mediterranean, both through his physical presence and by means of a multiplicity of images. In essence, this imperial figure was produced by a "performed collective memory," fundamentally made of past time—from imperial ceremonies and rituals inscribed on marble calendars and publicly displayed, as well as linear time—through the functions assumed or controlled by the emperor as supreme magistrate—and of space, incarnating the imperial stage *urbi et orbi*: the emperor is Rome and Rome is where the emperor is.

## IDENTITIES

From Polybius to Ammianus Marcellinus, from the mid-second century BCE to the late fourth century CE, Greek renderings of the history of the Romans translate into concrete form the idea of a "Greek Roman Empire," applicable to the first Roman interventions in the debates between Greek cities and the Hellenistic monarchies, to the conquest of the eastern provinces, to Late Antiquity and the creation of an "oriental" empire with Constantinople as its new capital (Veyne 2005; Millar 2006). Polybius wrote a history of the rise of Rome in Greek in order to help his fellow countrymen understand how the Romans had replaced the Greeks in the rule of the Mediterranean world.[30] In the third quarter of the fourth century CE, Ammianus Marcellinus, who was a native of the Greek-speaking eastern half of the empire, chose to write his monumental history of Rome (*Res gestae*) in Latin (Matthews 1989; Kelly 2008). These responses to challenged identities reveal the development of a mixed world that was capable of combining different histories and memories into one "collective civilization."[31] How are we to interpret the range of testimonies that relate to this creation of a global world—the first process of this kind in history, long before the concept was developed at the end of the twentieth century and the beginning of the twenty-first, conceiving of contemporary as connected history? Of course, we do find expressions of local—Greek, Punic, Celtic—cultures throughout the long history of the Roman empire, from the third century BCE to the third century CE: nevertheless, a true "Greek Roman" *ciuitas* came into being as early as the second century CE. This outcome is distinct from a Roman recognition of how Greek culture was becoming part of the empire's very identity, which evolved only partially: while poets such as Horace poignantly expressed this idea (*Epist.* 2.1.156, *Graecia capta ferum uictorem cepit*/"the conquered Greece has conquered her wild conqueror"), traditional senators such as Cato reacted quite differently to the first visit to Rome by an embassy of Greek philosophers representing the three main schools in 155 BCE (Garbarino 1973: 80–6). We find examples of similar opposite reactions from Augustan times to Late

Antiquity (even though the impact of the barbarians engenders new challenges): Antony was presented as a Hellenistic king whereas Octavian was the true defender of Rome vis-à-vis the degenerate *Oriens*; Hadrian was celebrated for his philhellenism and, at the same time, he was considered as a *Graeculus* by senators.

Likewise, Greek authors adapted their descriptions of festivals and ceremonies for Greek audiences. Remarkably, this demonstrates that it was precisely an "insider/outsider" process in the writing of history that came to produce a collective memory, by the use of patterns that emphasized the contrast between "us" and "them" and between "our customs" and "their practices." Our evidence on aristocratic and imperial funerals—the latter corresponding in fact to deification rituals of Roman emperors (*consecrationes*)—comes essentially from Polybius, Cassius Dio, and Herodian. The first meticulously describes the various stages of the funerals of *nobiles*, which would start at the house of the deceased and end in the Campus Martius, where the cremation used to take place, after stopping at the Forum Romanum, where a speech praising the deceased would be delivered. Cassius Dio addresses two momentous imperial rituals: Augustus' funeral in 14 CE and the consecration of Pertinax in 193 CE. Lastly, Herodian analyzes Septimius Severus' consecration in 211 CE. The cultural memory created by such "outsider" testimonies in turn shaped imperial ideology, over time and across space—for example, establishing the template for how emperors had to be celebrated after their death, namely following the model offered by the ceremonies for republican senators[32] (Benoist 2005: chs. 3 and 4). In that vein, the splendid description by Ammianus Marcellinus of the arrival of Constantius II in Rome on 28 April, 357 CE (16.10.1–20), is a programmatic discourse about the persona of the emperor, who lived in the East, in Constantinople, and on that occasion discovered the ancient capital of the Roman empire and her monumental setting (Matthews 1989: 231–5). These narratives are above all attestations of a collective approach to the past and the present, i.e. a collective memory embodied by the emperor(s).

One wonders if this collective approach applied to all "outsiders" alike, regardless of how compatible with Roman religious and cultural practices their backgrounds were. Approached with caution, Jewish and Christian voices in the Roman empire are very helpful here, especially as we have elaborate commentaries on Roman rituals and ceremonies from two authors in particular. Flavius Josephus and Tertullian were witnesses to two crucial moments in Roman imperial history. The former had been an enemy of Rome before becoming a friend of Vespasian and Titus—a circumstance that is traditionally presented as a betrayal. Josephus's description of Vespasian's and Titus's triumph over the Jews (*BJ* 7.63–74 (IV.1)) is considered a goldmine in that it allows us to understand the true meaning of this ceremony and its implications in terms of time—the different moments of the triumph—and space—the procession's route from outside the pomerial boundary to the Capitoline temple (Benoist 2005: 218–21; Edmondson, Mason, and Rives 2005). While Tertullian violently criticized "pagan" spectacles, he nonetheless provides us with very well-informed descriptions of circus games and gladiatorial shows, and, moreover, an analysis of their polytheistic dimensions. As the Christian polemist had previously been a "pagan" and therefore had a first-hand knowledge of traditional festivals his invectives were not based on ignorance and an "outsider" perspective in this sense.[33]

It is problematic to analyze these examples and the respective community identities by setting out theoretical antinomies such as "barbarian and civilized," "Greeks versus Romans," "pagans versus Christians," "Greek Romans versus barbarians," precisely because identities developed and changed over time. Studying the context of late antique cities illustrates this: one may think, for example, of the attitude of Stilicho towards

Honorius in Rome, as well as, subsequently, of the complete lack of awareness on the part of Valentinian III of the traditional function of an emperor as protector of collective memory and, one might say, of his own role as military conqueror! (Roberto 2015).

## CONCLUSIONS

We have tried to position the focus on "time and space" within a discussion of the character and expressions of ancient cultural memory, and this in the context of the collective participation in political actions and religious rituals. In essence, doing so is to consider how populations of ancient city-states (from classical Athens to late antique Rome and Constantinople) conceived of their being part of a world full of men and gods. As a matter of fact, Judaism first and then Christianity—the latter in higher and more decisive proportion—tried to propose a new approach to this crucial entity that could be acceptable in the context of monotheism. Within its framework, however, the fundamental concept remained the sharing of space and time between men and gods,[34] very much expressed as the participation in processions that celebrated the agreement between these two communities (Pietri 1997; Curran 2000). This is a concept closely linked to the meaning of *fides* (a faith resting on relationships based on a contract) and of *religio* (a bond between men and gods and the strict observance of rituals).

**FIGURE 2.6:** Bust of Caligula-Claudius, Sala Rotonda, Vatican inv. 242. Credit: © S. Benoist and A. Daguet-Gagey (eds.), *Un discours en images de la condamnation de mémoire* (Metz 2008), p. 138 fig. 9.

Thanks to the large number of examples from epigraphic and literary texts that collate lists of festivals (calendars) or describe them (e.g. protocols), as well as visual representations of ceremonies, we can reconstruct daily manifestations of collective activities that, crucially, generated sensations and memory. Tracing this process of "making collective memory" sometimes offers us insight into the heart of a community, of its components, and of what was shared by all its members, in many ways its "definition."

Ultimately, however, it is the very same material that reveals the unravelling, or, rather, distortion of this process: passages of texts were erased, monuments were transformed, and marble heads were defaced long before the Christianization of the so-called pagan symbols. This other process, which surfaces throughout antiquity, from archaic Greece to late antique Rome, functioned as a *damnatio memoriae*, the abolition of memory.[35] Yet, with regard to collective memory, and again anchored in space and time, oblivion is part of the process of *creating* such memory, an important strategy in dealing with what we currently call "memory issues."

**FIGURE 2.7:** Inscription with erasure after *damnatio memoriae*, 198–209 CE; Archaeological Museum, Cagliari. Credit: Giovanni dall'Orto/Wikimedia Commons (Public Domain).

CHAPTER THREE

# Media and Technology: Mediatic Frameworks of Memories in Ancient Times

ELENA FRANCHI

## MEDIA MEMORY: MODERN AND ANCIENT

Recent research in memory studies has focused on the effects that different media of memories have on the memories themselves.[1] Of course, interest in the media of memory is as old as memory studies themselves. Developing his theory on collective memory it was already Maurice Halbwachs who pointed to the role of media. However, he conceived of these as neutral transmitters of information and as a mere vehicle to the social dimension of memory—a sort of interface between individual memory and the cadres sociaux (Halbwachs 1925 and 1950; Erll 2011: 154). Ultimately, his focus was on the *cadres sociaux* and not on the *cadres médiaux*. Paul Ricoeur, in turn, implicitly highlighted a difference between literature as a medium of memories and other media, because literature does not simply convey memories but reshapes them in a mimetic context through a process that Ricoeur calls "mimesis II" and that implies a narrative reconfiguration (the emplotment)[2] (Ricoeur 1984: 105–69 and 2000: 15 and 186ff; Giangiulio 2019: 25). Addressing Havelock's contribution to the study of the interplay between oral and written media, Jan Assmann (1992: 139–41 and 162–5) shifts the focus towards cultural frameworks and distinguishes the roles played by different media, e.g. in the processes of "Sinn-Zirkulation" (media that are used to circulate meaning) and "Sinnverfestigung" (the processes of canonization); he argues, however, that "it is not the medium that decides, but the structure and function of the signs."

Recent studies have gone further by looking at aspects that heavily influence memorial processes themselves, that is, the memory-making power of media, and the relevance of the mediatic frameworks beyond the social and cultural ones (Erll and Rigney 2009: 1; Neigers, Meyers, and Zandberg 2011; Dally et al. 2014: 7–9; Franchi 2015a).

From the linguistic turn onwards, a constructivist view of the mediality of reality has increasingly changed our scholarly approach to the mediatic frameworks of memory (Krämer 1998a and 1998b; Seel 1998). Firstly, studies have pinpointed the different ways in which different media convey memory, and they observe that not all remembering practices are media-related at the same level (Kõresaar, Võsu, and Kuutma 2008; Couldry 2012; Kaun and Stiernstedt 2016), or have the same effectiveness and persistence

(Connerton 1989). Secondly, scholars have started to focus on the mechanisms by which different media conveying the same memory content interact and shape one another.[3] As a consequence, the focus has shifted from the individual medium to the mediascape that a medium forms together with other media (Karim 2003; Stahl 2010; Garde-Hansen 2011; Garde-Hansen et al. 2016). This mediascape has been analyzed as a web of intermediality, a continuous interaction between different media, which in turn potentially influences the memory itself (Keightley and Pickering 2016; Adamska forthcoming: 1). Moreover, the roles of intermedia ("media of media") and of processes of remediation,[4] which describe the "formal logic by which new media refashion prior media forms" (Bolter and Grusin 1999: 273) and had been neglected, have received unprecedented attention (Erll and Rigney 2009). Finally, operating on the assumption that all memories are present-oriented, a distinction has been drawn between (mainly) backward looking memories and (mainly) forward looking memories, i.e. past-oriented memories and future-oriented memories (Koselleck 2004; Levy and Sznaider 2006). This distinction in turn has launched an analysis of whether, and possibly how, mediation of memory is influenced by the retrospective or prospective nature of a remembrance (Hajek, Lohmeier, and Pentzold 2016).

As one can expect, not all the issues raised by modern research in media memory apply to ancient media of remembrances; even those that are applicable work in different ways in ancient times (Dally et al. 2014: 6ff). Extreme caution is therefore needed. Moreover, the study of antiquity challenges a media memory approach even more by adding further issues, raised e.g. by the relevance of storytelling, oral traditions, ritual life (Le Goff 1977, passim: XIff, 38–41, 97ff; 120ff; 349ff). A good deal of work has already been done. The papers collected in *Medien der Geschichte—Antikes Griechenland und Rom* (Dally et al. 2014) and in *Memoria Romana. Memory in Rome and Rome in Memory* (Galinsky 2014) provide a general study relating to a number of media and perspectives. Far beyond conceiving of historiography as the only and the very medium of remembrances, classical scholars engaging with memory studies have explored the use of other genres such as poetry, drama, oratory: Marincola, Llewellyn-Jones, and Maciver 2012[5] and the *Companion to Greek and Roman Historiography* (Marincola 2011) are particularly helpful in this respect, especially in their treatment of tragedy and oratory. Literature/tragedy/oratory/historiography have been investigated as media of remembrances in Homer (Strauss Clay 2011), Aeschylus and Sophocles (Scodel 2008; Kyriakou 2011), Demosthenes (Hubbard 2008; Franchi 2016; 2017), Lysias (Piovan 2011), in Athenian public discourse and/or oratory in general (Canevaro 2017a; Steinbock 2013), Cicero (Thornton 2017), Lucan (Gallia 2012), Vergil (Seider 2013), Seneca and Tacitus (Gowing 2005, also with a focus on Velleius Paterculus and Valerius Maximus: Galimberti 2017) and Aulus Gellius (Heusch 2011). Mediascapes of monuments and objects are dealt with in Alcock 2002, with a focus on their potential as media of remembrances and as such their interactions with individuals and social contexts. Calame 2009 addresses poetry and ritual as media of remembrances, and more specifically poetry as a medium of the memory of ritual, above all exemplified in Hesiod and Bacchylides (both as media and as intermedia). The way in which rituals convey specific remembrances of the past is also analyzed in Gould 2001a, Rössler-Köhler and Tawfik 2009, and Beck and Wiemer 2010a. Hans Beck, in particular, has shown how a commemoration festival both conveys memories of past events and founds historical consciousness. Price 2012 emphasizes memory networks in "religious memory": together with textual narratives, other media as objects, representations, places, ritual behavior, and associated myths form a network that defines religious memory and therefore religious identity. Further research brings to the fore ritual and/or more generally religious issues as the object of remembrances, which in turn are conveyed by other media[6] (Dignas and Smith 2012; Cusumano et al. 2013). The complex role played by religious infrastructure and corresponding identity-building memory strategies is another valuable issue. In this context Beate Dignas' analysis of the relation between religious memory created by the Attalids and the pre-Attalid religious infrastructure upon which they built this memory is revealing (Dignas 2012).

Finally, how memories of the past are conveyed via different media in ancient Greece and Rome is studied at the Laboratorio di Scienze dell'Antichità (LabSA) at the University of Trento. A seminal contribution by Maurizio Giangiulio has highlighted how our access to oral stories is always provided by an intermedium and therefore requires more refined methodological tools by modern historians of ancient history (Giangiulio 2005; also 2010c). Further studies have emphasized the role played by mediatic frameworks in conveying and shaping the memory of past events, especially of wars (Franchi and Proietti 2012; 2015; Giangiulio, Franchi, and Proietti 2019, all with further bibliography). Based on Grethlein 2013 and 2014 on future past and teleological perspectives, issues of intermediality of forward-looking remembrances in Athens are dealt with in Franchi and Proietti 2017.

The following case studies serve to further investigate which of the dynamics and issues enhanced by research on modern societies apply to ancient Greece and ancient Rome, and, if so, how they do this.[7] Due to constraints of space it will be impossible to systematically cover all the different media[8] and issues,[9] or to draw comprehensive conclusions; rather, a few trends and starting points for further discussions will be offered.

## A WEB OF INTERMEDIALITY AND REMEDIATION: ORAL TALES, *IMAGINES*, CULTS, AND FESTIVALS

Oral stories are a significant medium of memories in Ancient Greece and there is a rich tradition of studies on this topic (Thomas 1992; Gould 2001b; Luraghi 2001; Mackay 2008; Giangiulio 2010c; Scodel 2014). As one can expect, our access to oral stories is provided via a secondary medium, a sort of intermedium, in the form of historiography (Giangiulio 2010c: 27; Gehrke 2014), poetry or oratory (see below), a circumstance that triggers a process of remediation (Erll and Rigney 2009b: 3; 2011: 165–7).

The most studied intermedium for oral stories in Ancient Greece is historiography, and scholars have focused especially on Herodotus' *Histories*.[10] A typical example of how oral traditions were shaped in Herodotus' web of stories—and, as such, of intermediality and intermedium-dynamics as examples of "genealogies of remediation" (Erll and Rigney 2009b: 6)—is the tale about the Battle of the Champions (Hdt. 1.81–3), which provides a meaningful insight into a specific oral motif connected to Spartan society: the hairstyle.

Herodotus recounts that after the Battle of the Champions, fought around the middle of the sixth century BCE between Spartans and Argives, the defeated Argives decided to regularly trim their hair until they would recover the lost territory of Thyreatis in Cynouria (eastern coast of the Peloponnese), whereas the victorious Spartans let their hair grow (Hdt. 1.82). Herodotus' account of this battle (first-level medium) merges different oral traditions; given that "hairstyle" is of significance in Spartan society it can be assumed that it is part of a Spartan oral tale (second-level medium). Spartan children had to trim their hair when they entered Sparta's famous education system, the *agoge*, and in the Spartan imagery long hair indeed represents the adult male in contrast with adolescents, women and slaves.[11] Imagining their own ancestors with long hair beginning from the victory in the Battle of the Champions, Spartans represented these as males, as adults, apart from victorious, in contrast with the defeated Argives, with their short hair, who were therefore in analogy depicted as non-adults, as adolescents, as women. This opposition and its meaning are familiar to a non-Spartan audience,[12] also to Herodotus, who therefore (creatively) reworks the familiar connotations in his account, further conveying and slightly reshaping the memory of the feature "hairstyle" in the (oral or semi-oral) Spartan tale about this battle. In other words, the meaning of this feature in the medium of Spartan oral tales inevitably changes (even if slightly) once embedded in a written source (Herodotus), that is once the medium, and consequently the audiences, change through remediation. As will appear clear below, the confrontation with writing in parallel with (or/and after) a stage of oral circulation further influences the remembrances which are conveyed.[13]

It is a common assumption that in contrast to Greece, in Rome writing was conceived as one of the most reliable guarantors of memory (Gowing 2005: 25; Walter 2004: 25–6; see, more generally, Assmann et al. 1983; Assmann 2000: 101–23). In consequence, oral stories as media of memory in ancient Rome are understudied and have only recently begun to receive attention, despite the relevance of memory as such in Rome,[14] and although oral remembrances specifically played a significant role throughout Roman history. In archaic and republican times individual oral memories were conveyed from generation to generation: Velleius Paterculus, who wrote during the reign of Tiberius (14–37 CE), proudly declared that his great-grandfather had fought in the Social War between Rome and former Italic allies of 91 BCE (2.16.2).[15] What is at stake here is the so-called "communicative memory."[16] Velleius' statement points to an important difference between oral history in ancient Greece and oral history in ancient Rome: whereas in Greece oral memories were shaped and conveyed in many different milieus, as families, elites, communities or social groups, oral memories in archaic and republican Rome seem to be mostly a matter of families:[17] the *memoria* of the ancestors was celebrated in the "songs sung at banquets" (Cornell 1995; Gabba 2000: 63; Walter 2004: 71ff), in oral narratives (Rüpke 2000: 35), at public games (Wiseman 2014), at funerals, by way of *imagines*, masks and portraits adorning the open central courts of Roman houses (Flower 1996: 32–90 and 185–222), more generally during processions (Latham 2016), or festivals of the dead, as for example the *Parentalia*.[18] Commemorating the dead was a responsibility the Romans took very seriously (Cic., *Sest.* 15; Sal., *Jug.* 4.6), and every family was expected to do this—albeit not in the public arena but among the family (Gowing 2005: 14–15). However, there were also media environments where a slightly wider (and also illiterate) audience was addressed, such as the spectators of the *fabulae praetextae* (Roman tragedies in a Roman setting), of the *pompae funebres* (funeral processions during which *imagines* of the ancestors were carried) and of the first proclamations of the *consules* in a meeting called *contio*.[19] Evidence on these wider audiences is lacking, but it is not difficult to imagine that, as in better documented contexts, these media environments involved a further type of intermediality because while spectators were watching the busts of their ancestors pass by they must have been telling and/or singing their deeds, as well as performing rituals to commemorate them. A variety of media interacted and conveyed accumulative pieces of memory towards building a certain image of the past.

## HISTORIOGRAPHY AND THE CHALLENGE OF MULTI-LAYERED INTERTEXTUALITY AND OF INTERTWINED MEDIA PRESCRIPTIVITY

From a modern perspective, historiography is the most obvious medium of memories; ancient historiography, as an emerging genre, is characterized by important idiosyncrasies. The above cited passage by Herodotus shows how ancient historiography is not completely coherence-oriented—or, rather, it is, but not in a modern sense; moreover, ancient historiography is a very specific medium of oral stories, reported speeches, as well as poetry, and intertextuality, both oral and written, is highly prominent. Here, a special kind of intertextuality is the one involving two (or more) media of the same type, but, in general, intertextuality in all its expressions shows a high degree of intermediality and sometimes even remediation (Erll 2011: 181; Hutton forthcoming: 21). A good example of intertextuality between two different but similar historiographic texts (one of them also conveying oral traditions) is a passage by Thucydides on the Argives' attitude towards their past: here intertextuality is hypoleptic, multi-layered, reiterating remediation because it involves (1) a link between two historiographic media on one level, (2) a link between a historiographic medium and an oral-story medium on a second level, and (3) a link between a historiographic medium and the aural context in which it was performed; in short, a new galaxy of communication is constituted. In addition, the "first-level intertextuality" (intermediality) is conscious and raises questions of intentionality and about a polemical/not polemical attitude. The story runs as follows.

In 420 the Thirty Years' Peace between the Spartans and Argives was about to expire, and the Argives were unwilling to renew it unless the Cynurian land was restored to them. The Spartans agreed that, while a new fifty years truce was to be concluded, both parties were allowed to formally challenge each other over this no man's land, "as on a former occasion, when both sides claimed the victory." In this narrative Thucydides, writing some years after Herodotus, clearly refers to him (1.82), where we learn that during the battle neither side could gain advantage, and that both were convinced to have won: αὐτοὶ ἑκάτεροι ἠξίωσαν νικᾶν (5.41.2) clearly refers to Herodotus' αὐτοὶ ἑκάτεροι ἔφασαν νικᾶν (1.82.6). Here intertextuality between two historiographic media is hypoleptic,[20] and intentional: it allows Thucydides to refer in a few words to core information that is not questionable. Apart from this, intertextuality is fostered by a third medium, which is oral, and this on a double level: the tale reworked by Herodotus is oral, and the context of the *akroaseis* (public lectures) delivered by Herodotus is both oral and aural.[21] Patterns such as this foster in turn an approach to intertextuality that mixes oral, semi-oral and written media and plays with the audiences' knowledge of all of these (Franchi 2011; Foster and Lateiner 2012).

Investigating various historiographic texts as media conveying memories on the same events allows us to highlight how memories are selective. Evidence points to the fact that under the shadow of the principate Livy reshaped the story of the republic in order to show continuity with the past, providing the reader with a sense of wrong and right (Liv. *Praef.* 3; 10–12; Gowing 2005: 21–3; Galinsky and Lapatin 2015). Central characters such as Romulus, Camillus, or Scipio are assimilated with Augustus.[22] This approach was taken further by Velleius Paterculus, for whom there was no sharp dividing line between the republic and the principate because he saw the rise of the *principes* as a form of restoration after the civil wars (Kuntze 1985: 155–68; Sion-Jenkis 2000: 22 and 161–2). A good example is his narrative and appraisal of M. Livius Drusus (tribune of plebs in

91 BCE), who is transformed into a proto-typical defender of the republic (2.14.2–3). In accordance with this attitude, the emperor Tiberius is represented as the *continuator* of his illustrious republican family (2.94.1–2).

Certain media can also limit the shaping of memory if they convey a prescriptive knowledge. Jörg Rüpke has analyzed the extent to which the memory of religion in Valerius Maximus' *Exempla* (written during the reign of Tiberius, 14–37 CE), was influenced by the "knowledge of religion." The knowledge resulting from different pieces of information scattered in the *Exempla* is systematic, itself constituting a medium that differs from other media, such as mythological narratives, which are more fluent and more exposed to continuous change. A twofold process is at work: a specific version of past religion is transformed and systematized to create "knowledge," and vice versa: knowledge of religion proves to be prescriptive for the future (and therefore to limit a shaping of the past). Since Valerius Maximus' brief narratives are centered on individuals, they are able to reduce historical complexity and at the same time to assemble a universe of norms perceived as universal and of prescriptive value: this universe of norms offers both a perspective from which to interpret the past and guidance for the future (Val. Max. 1.1.1; Hickson Hahn 2007: 235; Rüpke 2016: 98–100).

## MONUMENTAL LANDSCAPES AS MEDIA SHAPED BY AND SHAPING THE PAST: COUNTER-MONUMENTALITY, RELIGIOUS MONUMENTS, AND THE MEMORY OF WARS

When it comes to the relevance of objects as media conveying the memory of the past, one is bound to recall Proust's famous recollection that the taste of a madeleine dipped in tea brought back to him the memory of his aunt's madeleine.[23] How objects influence the manner and the matter of what is recalled in antiquity has been studied by prominent scholars (Zanker 1988; Favro 1996; Rehak and Younger 2006; Dally et al. 2013: 190–436). It is not only that the physical objects among which we live shape our memory. Monumental landscapes in which we live have a strong impact on what we remember and what we forget. Since "memory" signifies an active process that is recreated as such each time we engage in the act of remembering, the connection between memory and objects works in both directions (Radley 1990: 49; Orlin 2016: 116 ff.; Adamska forthcoming: 18; Edwards forthcoming: 10 and 13). Changes in the landscape shape the memory of the past, even when they are unintentional, and new objects might attract stories to cluster around them. This implies that not only the construction but also the reconstruction of monuments and their interpretation constantly reconfigures the memory of the past; beyond this, the process can generate a completely new past (Lowenthal 1975: 33; Gabba 2000: 21; Hölscher 2001; Dally 2013 et al.: 21). Similar dynamics are well exemplified by a monument set up in Delphi by the Phocians, of which a rectangular base with the marks of statues' feet featuring a dedication is preserved: "The Phocians dedicated a tithe [?] from the spoils of the Thessalians [?] to Apollo[?]" (*Syll.*³ 202B).

The base now stands on the southwest side of the terrace of the Temple of Apollo in the so-called *halos* (a round open space close to the temple of Apollo)[24], inside or immediately outside of which the fragments were found (Franchi 2016: ch. 6). The monument should be dated to sometime in the middle of the fourth century, most probably to the second half (Franchi 2018). Scholars have tried to link the base with the

**FIGURE 3.1:** Delphi, Temple of Apollo. Credit: Creative Commons (Public Domain).

battles against the neighboring Thessalians of the sixth century BCE and identified the related offerings by the winning Phocians as those recounted by Herodotus (8.27–28), Pausanias (10.1.8–10) and Plutarch (*mul.virt.* 2) (Keramopoullos 1907; Pomtow 1915; Daux 1936: 146 f; Franchi 2018). Some of the statues represent the mythical struggle for the tripod between Apollo and Heracles, and others represent Apollo, some heroes, and the generals of the Phocian-Thessalian battles. However, one cannot ignore the possibility that the monument was erected in the fourth century after the battle of Argolas, won by the Phocians over the Thessalians in 355 (Diod. 16.30). In fact, the one does not exclude the other, and a focus on the media conveying the memories of these battles is helpful towards finding an answer to the question. Firstly, an analysis of the medium of the narratives about the Third Sacred War (356–346 BCE, between the Phocians and the Delphic Amphictyonic League, led by the Thebans and later by the Macedonians) reveals a Phocian propensity to strongly shape the present and the—both archaic and more recent—past (Franchi 2015b). Secondly, an analysis of the media the Phocians used to shape Delphi's monumental landscape reveals their tendency to reconfigure the past according to present needs by using counter-monumentality, i.e. "the installation of a thematically opposed artwork before an existing monument, or simply a range of antimonumental practices such as defacement" (Starzmann 2016; Osborne 2017: 164 ). Near our monument in the *halos* there is one erected by the Boeotians (Jacquemin 1999: no. 99) and another one by the Pieres (Jacquemin 1999: no. 411), who at this point can be considered Macedonians (Diod. 16.31.7; 34.4–5).[25] The Boeotians, Macedonians, and Phocians were the main actors in the Third Sacred War: the three monuments expressed certain spatial politics and engaged in a sort of "war between monuments." The medium of the monuments conveys and shapes specific memories of the past, which in turn are shaped by the position of these monuments and the relationship between them. Thirdly, this counter-monumentality could have triggered a memory of a remote event by its recalling a more recent one (Argolas: 355). By celebrating a recent victory over the Thessalians, the Phocians would also have commemorated an old battle fought against the same enemy and mentioned by Herodotus.

The Romans consciously used monuments as an important medium (Pliny, *NH* 34.14 with Gabba 2000: 143; Cic., *Sest.* 26; Varr., *ling.* 6.49 with Walter 2004: 32–3). The history of the Temple of Concordia shows how reconstructions of monuments continuously reshaped the past and reconfigured present needs, to the extent that they created an entirely new past. The temple was erected by the consul L. Opimius after the death of C. Gracchus in 121 BCE as a sign of concord between plebeians and patricians.[26] Augustus put Tiberius in charge of yet another restoration in 10 BCE. The *dies natalis* of the temple, the day on which the festival in honor of the divinity was held, was moved from 22 July to 16 January: Eric Orlin suggests that this happened because 16 January was the day in 27 BCE on which the *princeps* had received the name Augustus from the Senate, thus eliding the prior history of the building. Its name was changed, too, from Temple of Concordia to Temple of Concordia Augusta: "rather than attempting to create the façade of a peaceful resolution

**FIGURE 3.2:** Temple of Concordia, Rome, reconstruction. Credit: Falkenstein Photo/Alamy Stock Images.

to an internal quarrel, the new Temple of Concordia took for granted the notion of an Augustan peace at home," (Orlin 2016: 23) also looking hopefully to the stabilization of the frontier in the years in which the disaster in the Teutoburg Forest (9 CE, three Roman legions were destroyed) had occurred and the Pannonians were revolting (Galinsky 2007: 75). The visual appearance of the temple was also changed dramatically, with the new façade nearly twice as long as wide and a variety of colored marbles used; interestingly, Tiberius' spoils from Germany were used to fund the project (Kellum 1990).

## MEDIA AND A SHARED SENSE OF BELONGING: INSCRIBED MEMORY MEDIA VS. PERFORMATIVE EMBODIED MEMORY MEDIA

Connerton 1989 and, for antiquity, Price 2012 distinguish two different kinds of memory, which in our perspective represent two different kinds of media of memory: the first is inscribed memory (objects and texts), the second is performative embodied memory (ritual and other formalized behavior). It is noteworthy that both are used to shape the past in order to foster a common sense of belonging within a group, and that both do this by forging genealogies and the image of "national" cults and "national" heroes. They do this in different ways, however. Whereas inscribed media of memory clearly aim to create coherence by reconciling, combining or (alternatively) by erasing contradictory data and thus convey more selective memories, performative embodied media of memory highlight aspects and narrative elements more suitable for performance and ritual enhancement, an emphasis that is not necessarily coherence-oriented.

The way in which the Locrian sense of belonging was fostered through cults, inscriptions and even the creation of genealogies is very enlightening. The Locrian territories comprised two regions, usually known in modern terminology as Ozolian Locris and Opountian Locris, which were separated by mountain ranges and by the *ethnos* of the Phocians.

The Locrians' sense of belonging as a single *ethnos* is attested to by an important inscription of *c.* 500 BCE, found at Chaleion in Western Locris. The stone records a law concerning the foundation of a new colony in Naupactus (*IG* IX, 1$^2$.3.718). Naupactus was resettled by the eastern Locrians, but in lines 46–7 it is clearly stated that the law also applied to Chaleian settlers.[27] The mythical ancestor Locrus received a genealogy that steers our interpretation in the same direction (Dominguez-Monedero 2010: 77ff; Daverio Rocchi 2013: 142). His grandfather was Amphictyon, his father Physcus and his son Opous. The choice of his grandfather's name emphasized his role in the Amphictyony of Delphi, that of his father the leading city of the Ozolian Locrians (Physkeis), and that of his son the main city of the eastern Locrians: i.e. Opous (Daverio Rocchi 2015: 192). The ritual of the Locrian maidens and the cult of Ajax also reflect the intention to construct and consistently foster a pan-Locrian sense of belonging, but in a different way (Daverio Rocchi 2013: 146). Once a year for a thousand years the Locrians were obliged to send to the shrine of Athena at Ilion (Troy) two maidens, in order to atone for their ancestor Ajax the Lesser's rape of Cassandra, the daughter of the king of Troy. Curiously, this tribute was paid by the Locrians of eastern Locris, but explicitly in the name of *all* the Locrians (cf. Polyb. 12.5.7). At the same time, a tradition developed that saw Ajax the Lesser transformed from a violent rapist into a brave warrior, the national hero of *all* the Locrians.[28]

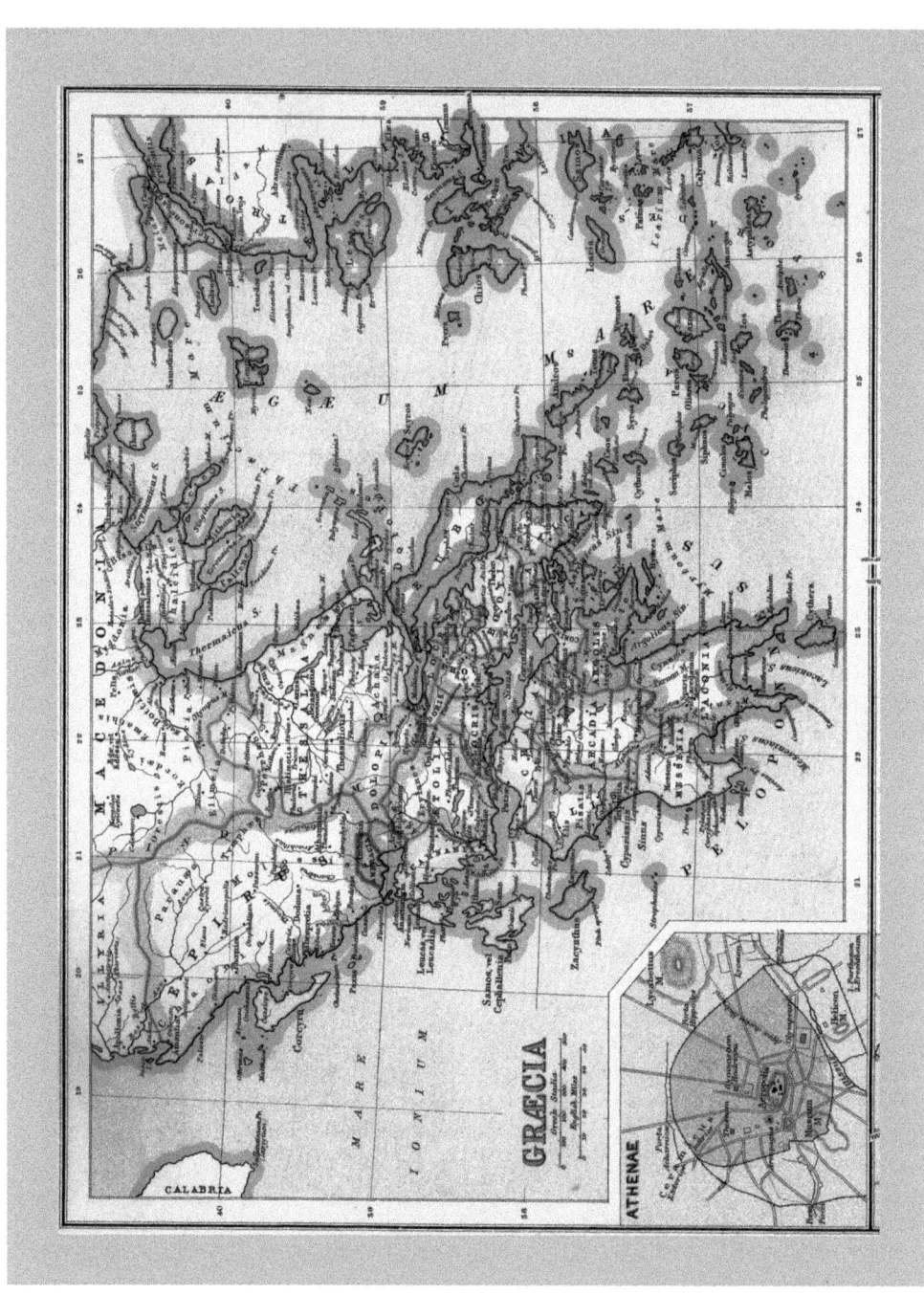

**FIGURE 3.3:** Map of "Graecia" (1902). The provinces of Ancient Greece, with inset of Athens. From the *Century Atlas of the World* John Walker & Co. Ltd., London. Credit: Unknown Artist/Getty Images regions.

**FIGURE 3.4:** Ajax the Lesser drags Cassandra from the Palladium; Tondo of an Attic red-figure cup, *c.* 440–430 BCE, now in the Louvre collection, G 458. Credit: Wikimedia Commons (Public Domain).

The famous Elogium of Marius (*ILS* 59) provides a nice example of how inscribed media of memories can shape the memory of the past in order to construct a coherent and fitting image of a national hero. Usually attributed to the Forum Augustum (*contra* Spannagel 1999: 318–20), the *Elogium* of Marius (157–86 BCE), the famous Roman general and statesman who reorganized the structure of the legions and defeated the invading Germanic tribes, is some kind of official verdict on Marius' career, recorded for posterity among the Augustan *elogia* of illustrious Romans, a deeply rooted tradition in ancient Rome.[29]

As Beard puts it, Marius' *Elogium* is "expertly reticent" with the aim to transform him "from butcher of the civil war to hero of the Republic" (Beard 1998: 88; Gowing 2005: 142–3). Indeed, the *Elogium* lists the following achievements: he was consul seven times, praetor, tribune of the plebs, quaestor, augur, and military tribune; he waged war with and captured Jugurtha, the king of Numidia; in his fourth consulship he destroyed the

**FIGURE 3.5:** Bust of Caius Marius (186–157 BCE); Rome, Museo della civiltà Romana, RVB-11040. Credit: Roger Viollet/Getty Images.

army of the Teutones; in his fifth, he routed the Cimbri; in his sixth, he freed the republic when it was wracked by sedition sown by the tribunes of the plebs and the praetors, who had seized the Capitol; and with the spoils won from his victories over the Cimbri and Teutones he built a temple to Honor and Virtue. At the same time, the *Elogium* omits some low points of Marius' career: e.g., that he secured his fourth consulship in 103 BCE with guile (Plut., *Mar.* 14.7–8 with Gowing 2005: 143); that he had a reputation for faithlessness (Liv., *Per.* 69; Cic., *Rab.Perd.* 10.28); and that he showed exceptional cruelty during the civil war of 87—86 BCE (Liv., *Per.* 79-80 with Gowing 2005: 143). As Gowing puts it, "some viewers [. . .] would have to know their history very well in order to supply from their own memory the low points of Marius' career"[30] (Gowing 2005: 143). Through the genre of the *elogium* memory conveyed by inscriptions becomes selective and can prevent intertextuality in order to convey or manipulate a specific image of the past.[31]

## CREATING COLLECTIVE IMAGINARIES AND PAST MEMORIES THROUGH THE MEDIUM OF COINS

A close link between coins and *memoria* was strongly perceived and expressed, especially by the Romans: Livius Andronicus translated the goddess mother of the Muses Mnemosyne as "Moneta," having "moneta" and "memoria" an etymological connection according to the common Roman interpretation.[32] Even if the spread of ancient coins was limited, coins were mediatic frameworks that functioned as social agents and means of social change, and they legitimized ruling members and their policies and alliances by connecting them with a glorious past (Gell 1998: 16–19; Tsouratsoglou 2002: 11).

Spartan kings made use of these qualities by endorsing fictive genealogies on coins. The main iconographic theme of the coins minted by Spartan Hellenistic kings is Heracles, the mythic ancestor of the Agiadai and the Eurypontidai (Hdt. 6.52) (Palagia 1986: 137; Cartledge and Spawforth 2002: 295; Palagia 2006: 208; Stafford 2012: 140). The use of Heracles on the obverse of the silver coins minted by King Areus (309 to 265 BCE) goes further and points to Sparta's relations with the Ptolemies (the Hellenistic dynasty in Egypt) and his aspirations as Hellenistic king.[33] Indeed, it is not by chance that Areus issued Sparta's first coinage, plausibly to finance the needs of the Chremonidean War (Grunauer-von Hoerschelmann 1978: 1–6; Mørkholm 1991: 149; Hoover 2011: 139). Ptolemy I Soter, first as a satrap between 323 and 305 BCE, had already issued familiar coins of the Alexandrine type, with the head of a beardless Heracles wearing a lion's skin headdress on the obverse and [ΑΛΕΞΑΝΔΡΟΥ] Zeus seated in his throne on the reverse (Grunauer-von Hoerschelmann 1978: 1–6; Mørkholm 1991: 149; Hoover 2011: 139), thus endorsing links to the same Heracleidae ancestry (Hölbl 2001: 92–8). Theocritus (*Idyll.* 17; 24) provides further evidence that the kings, especially Philadelphus, promoted strong ties to Heracles in order to consolidate their dynastic power.[34] By linking himself to Herakles in a similar way, Areus tapped into and strengthened both the core of Spartan identity and the contemporary alliance with Ptolemy Philadelphus (Pagkalos 2015: 146).

Similarly, fictive genealogies play a key role in the coinage of the late Roman republic. Familial, symbolic achievements of the ancestors of a *gens* (a group consisting of individuals claiming descent from a common ancestor) were combined with symbols of achievements of other *gentes*, thereby creating fictional genealogical links, which suited the concerns of Romans at the critical period of transition from republic to principate (Walter 2004: 95; Smith 2019). Moreover, these coins were closely interconnected and created a fabric of intertextuality. Karl-Joachim Hölkeskamp has shown how the Marcii traced themselves back to the legendary king Ancus Marcius, who was considered to have been a grandson of king Numa Pompilius: both kings are represented on a denarius of a C. Marcus Censorinus from the year 88 BCE (*RRC* I, no. 346/1a–i) (Von Ooteghem 1961: 7–11; Crawford 1974: 78; Papini 2004: 157–9; Farney 2007: 264; Hölkeskamp 2016: 189–90);

**FIGURE 3.6:** Coin of (L. Marcius?) Philippus, *RRC* I, no. 425/1; Rome, 56 BCE. Photo: Creative Commons (Public Domain).

Ancus Marcius is also portrayed on the obverse of the coinage of a Philippus, probably L. Marcius Philippus, *consul suffectus* (elected to complete the term of a consul who vacated office before the end of the year) in 38 BCE (*RRC* I, no. 425/1) (Farney 2007: 272; Hölkeskamp 2016: 190).

It is intriguing that the reverse features an aqueduct bearing the inscription AQUA M(A)R(CIA), built in the late 140s by a Marcius of another family: Q. Marcius Rex, *praetor urbanus* in 144 BCE (Crawford 1974: 448–9). The equestrian statue represented on the aqueduct is dressed in a *toga*, a distinctive garment reflecting the citizen's rank, as was typical for the statue of Tremulus, who was consul in 306 and defeated the Hernici (Liv. 9.43; Cic., *Phil*. 6.13), and whose famous monument was in front of the Temple of Castor (Plin., *HN* 34.23).[35] Late republican *gentes* reinforced their status by minting coins that represented glorious wars, and there are further examples. The tradition of the *spolia opima* dedicated by the consul Marcellus in order to remember his victory at Clastidium against the Insubres, a Gaulish population settled in Northern Italy, was evoked through a *fabula* by Naevius (writing in the third century BCE) but also on a denarius of P. Cornelius Lentulus Marcellinus (Crawford no. 439, with Flower 2000: 47). Eventually it became so significant that it was reinvented and helped to shape traditions about earlier dedications, but more importantly, it was used by Augustus to express his connection with the Marcelli and thus to legitimate the new ruling family (Picard 1957; Flower 2000). Fictive genealogies connecting families to glorious military victories of the past were not only displayed on coins but also reinforced through intermediality (coins+monuments/coins+historiography/coins+*fabula*, and so on) and *hypolepsis* (the example of the aqueduct). The very fact that different media conveying interconnected memories and engaging different audiences are displayed makes us wonder whether ancient initiators and recipients were aware of the different mediating effects triggered by different mediatic frameworks. Again, the *cadres médiaux* prove themselves as a new frontier of research in memory studies.

# CHAPTER FOUR

# Knowledge: Science and Education—Writing as "External Memory" and its Role in Ancient Science[1]

HAN BALTUSSEN

## INTRODUCTION

The role of memory in ancient science is closely linked to the problem of knowledge preservation. To acquire and hold on to knowledge is fundamental for human societies (Galinsky 2016b: 4–5). In his fascinating recent book on the history of paper, Mark Kurlansky has recently made an interesting suggestion towards answering the question of which factor sets us humans apart from other animals. He proposes that we should—rather than think of opposable thumbs, building, communicating, even making music—consider our tendency to *preserve information*. He writes:

> There is one truly unique human trait: people *record*. They record their deeds, their emotions, their thoughts, their ideas . . . they have an impulse to record almost everything that enters their minds and preserve it for future generations.
> —Kurlansky 2016: 2[2]

The statement may not be without a certain rhetorical exaggeration, but the author is surely right that it is *one* of the distinctive human features. A study of how ancient science (broadly conceived) undertook to record its insights raises two crucial questions for our purposes, namely how knowledge could be transferred reliably and how it was organized for educational purpose.

Knowledge retention also plays an instrumental role in the identity of individuals and groups. In this context, it is generally acknowledged that a change occurred with the introduction and increased use of writing. In Greek culture, the importance of memory for living beings was, as we will see, taken for granted. That *Mnemosynē* (memory) was crowned the Mother of the Muses also indicates that the Greeks understood its central importance. As a core faculty of human mental activity, memory assists us in navigating the world, provides stability to our identity, and creates a common understanding of our past (Halbwachs 1925 and 1950; Galinsky 2016b: 4ff).

My argument in this chapter revolves around the central idea that writing was not only important for recording precious information, but that the advent of writing played a significant role in the rise of science. In the context of this volume I propose to treat written records as an "external memory," in contrast to our natural or "internal" memory. Such an approach assumes a more active role of an "external" memory on the nature of the study of science than one might expect. Words on paper can stimulate critical assessment and evaluation in a more analytical way. The correlation has not been studied at length for ancient science. But since the 1980s important work has been done by classical scholars, anthropologists and historians to chart the broader "literary turn" (Goody 1978; Harris 1989; Johne 1991). Famously, Walter Ong and Eric Havelock pioneered the study of "orality" and the effects of writing on society (Ong 1982; Havelock 1982 and 1986; Small 1997). The most recent and clearest attempt to capture the role of literacy in ancient Greek science and culture can be found in the collection of essays entitled *Written Texts and the Rise of Literate Culture in Ancient Greece* (Yunis 2003). This volume also helps to frame important aspects of my chapter. A major point made in the volume is that literacy did not *replace* orality but became an important new feature of intellectual pursuits. A nice illustration of this is found in Aristotle, who in discussing lack of self-control (ἀκρασία) inadvertently also informs us that men under the influence are still capable of uttering "scientific proofs and verses of Empedocles, and those who have just begun to learn can string together words, *but do not yet know*" (*EN* 1147a15–18). The point he wants to make is that memorization does not entail understanding, in this particular example due to inebriation (i.e. reproducing the words of Empedocles is a form of mechanical and ineffectual "knowledge"). In other words, he already saw that there is a way to retain information without really knowing what it means.[3]

First, a few comments on method and terminology. I will use "science" and "scientific understanding" very loosely as the kind of (specialized) knowledge that was pursued by rational means and aimed for rational explanations as opposed to mythological narratives. Clearly for this period much of "science" also includes topics that caught the interest of philosophers. Such a traditional description may need a few qualifications, but it is still a convenient one (Buxton 1999). In addition, I shall elucidate how the transmission of this kind of knowledge to subsequent generations was facilitated by the successful use of *well-structured* writings. My title employs notions originating in well-established orality studies, which have emphasized the dynamic interaction between knowledge acquisition and preservation, but also takes inspiration from a recent perspective in philosophy concerning the so-called "extended mind," that is, the idea that our cognitive activity does not merely depend on our brain. As Clark and Chalmers have put it, "some accept the boundaries of skin and skull," but others do not (Clark and Chalmers 1998: 7). My use of extended memory or mind is a derivative and weaker version of the stricter external cognitive influence in the analysis of memory. Our dependence on external technologies (writing being one) to enhance and facilitate our natural memory also facilitates the expansion of knowledge.[4]

On a smaller scale, the new literacy in the sixth and fifth centuries BCE did something very similar, but here for the first time. Kurlansky (2016: 19) noted about Plato: "Tellingly he called writing 'artificial memory'."[5] Where today computing devices have accelerated the expansion of information (so-called "big data"), so too the introduction of written records ultimately led to an accelerated change in how knowledge was acquired and structured. This holds in particular for *specialized* knowledge in ancient Greece. Given that the archaic and classical periods did not yet have a very clear separation between academic disciplines as we understand them, we draw on various related areas of higher learning.[6]

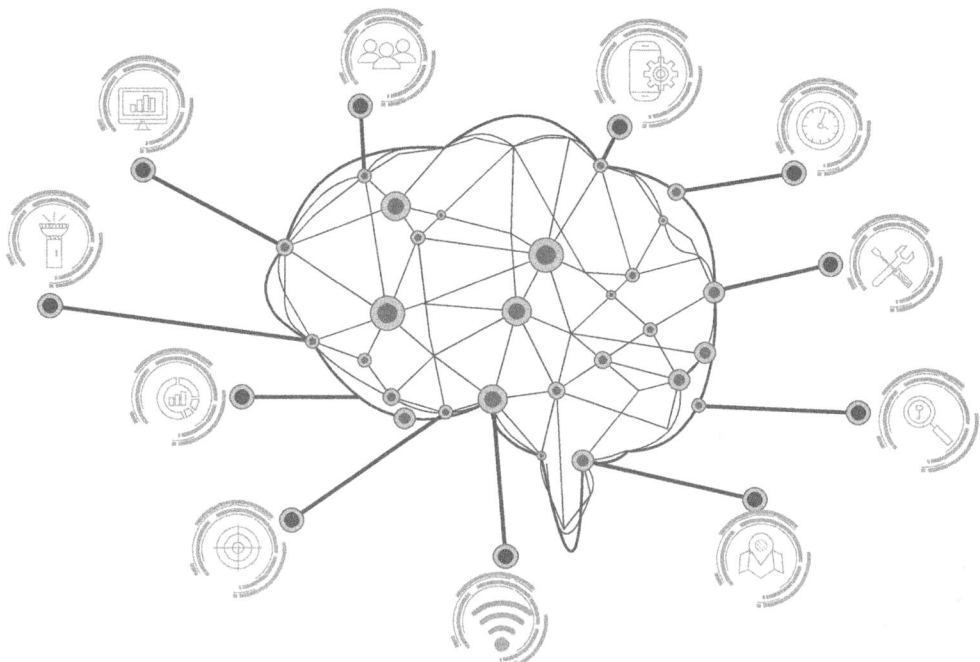

FIGURE 4.1: Expansion of knowledge. Credit: Getty Images.

I will examine four "stages" that feature writing ("external memory") and scientific endeavors in the Greco-Roman literate age. A few opening comments on Homer will characterize the oral tradition. Next, we are able to "sample memory" in medical literature, by examining the first scientific discipline, the Hippocratic works; after this I will move to Aristotle, who pioneered "biology." I will then jump forward to the Roman era (Hellenistic science lacks sufficient evidence), focusing mostly on the prime example of grand-scale data collection, Pliny the Elder's *Inquiry into Nature* (*Naturalis Historia*) in the late first century CE, and another similarly expansive author in the field of medicine, Galen of Pergamum. This approach serves to illustrate how the growing bulk of knowledge in various scientific areas tended to produce large data-collections, which also needed a principle of organization: Aristotle's *Historia Animalium*, Theophrastus' *Historia Plantarum*, Cicero's *Orator*, Pliny's *Historia Naturalis*, all offered new elaborate structures (reflected in the table of contents), based on thematic and causal principles (Kahn 2003). The use of writing facilitated such structuring criteria. The new style of narrative reveals how the change from an internal to an external memory arose when natural memory was enhanced by an artificial one.

## THE IMPACT OF LITERACY ON CRITICAL THINKING: HOMER TO SIMONIDES

In many areas of learning the ancient sources reflect an awareness that a good memory was a major asset for intellectual pursuits. This is of course unsurprising in an oral culture. That the introduction of script and writing initiated an important transition from being an oral culture to becoming a more literate one, also stands to reason. The new skill of reading was probably not available to the many, but, where present, it had a considerable impact on how knowledge became stored and perceived (Harris 1989). Jack Goody already characterized literacy's impact perceptively (1978: 37).

The specific proposition is that writing, and more especially alphabetic literacy, made it possible to scrutinize discourse in a different kind of way by giving oral communication a semi-permanent form; this scrutiny favored the increase in scope of critical activity, and hence rationality, scepticism, and logic to resurrect memories of those questionable dichotomies.

This strongly suggests that at some point written records were no longer merely used in the context of recording household storage (as Linear B suggests) but became responsible for a fundamental change in how humans began to cope with, and went far beyond, the limits of their natural memory. Goody (and others) emphasize(s) the more detached, critical and logical ways of thinking that arose as a consequence (Ong 1982: ch. 3, especially 36–57). Viewed as an artificial memory, writing functions as external memory in ways the internal one is unable to. As Goody (1978: 37) concludes, "No longer did the problem of memory storage dominate man's intellectual life; the human mind was freed to study 'static' text (rather than be limited by participation in the dynamic 'utterance'." Writing had become humanity's ultimate tool of knowledge.

But how exactly did the introduction of writing affect the acquisition and transfer of knowledge? And how did notions of memory and its role influence those who were increasingly better educated? All indicators suggest that the transition from orality to literacy took place sometime in the period between the Homeric age (*c.* 1200–750 BCE) and our first clear example of an *explicit mnemonic technique* linked to the poet Simonides, who died *c.* 465 BCE. The deeply oral culture of the Homeric epics reflects the importance of internal memory as the receptacle of family history, identity and ethnic continuity.[7] Moreover, its fundamental importance as a mental capacity is also, and most clearly, illustrated by the existence of the epics themselves, which were originally transmitted through memorization and performance. The capability to achieve such a feat of extraordinary retention (they comprise a total of *c.* 25,000 hexameter lines) was not just a matter of prodigious memory and talent, but also due to various structuring elements such as training, the use of meter (music) and formulaic phrases: as Milman Parry and Albert Lord showed long ago, even in the twentieth century Slavic bards were able to demonstrate similar performance acts, which were structured by repetition and music while allowing for a degree of improvisation (Parry 1950; Lord 1960).

The powerful memory and oral style of Homeric bards preserved knowledge of all kinds, from shipbuilding to military strategy to religious practices to household economics—but the limits of such a process are also evident. Transmission was mechanical, which does not always encourage independent thought. To commit it to memory, the knowledge embedded in the epics required proper "scaffolding" by way of meter, formulaic phrasing, and long apprenticeship. Even when this is provided, the human mind is not able to master an infinite accumulation of facts and insights, and memorization cannot extend indefinitely. Perhaps the evidence of Linear B on Crete (end of second millennium BCE) gives us a first indication as to how humans found ways to "memorize" a random set of data with the help of writing. The lists were tools to record particular everyday details such as storehouse inventories.[8]

The "new memory" could free up thinking once the burden of memorization was reduced. Literary and performative activities were associated with the daughters of

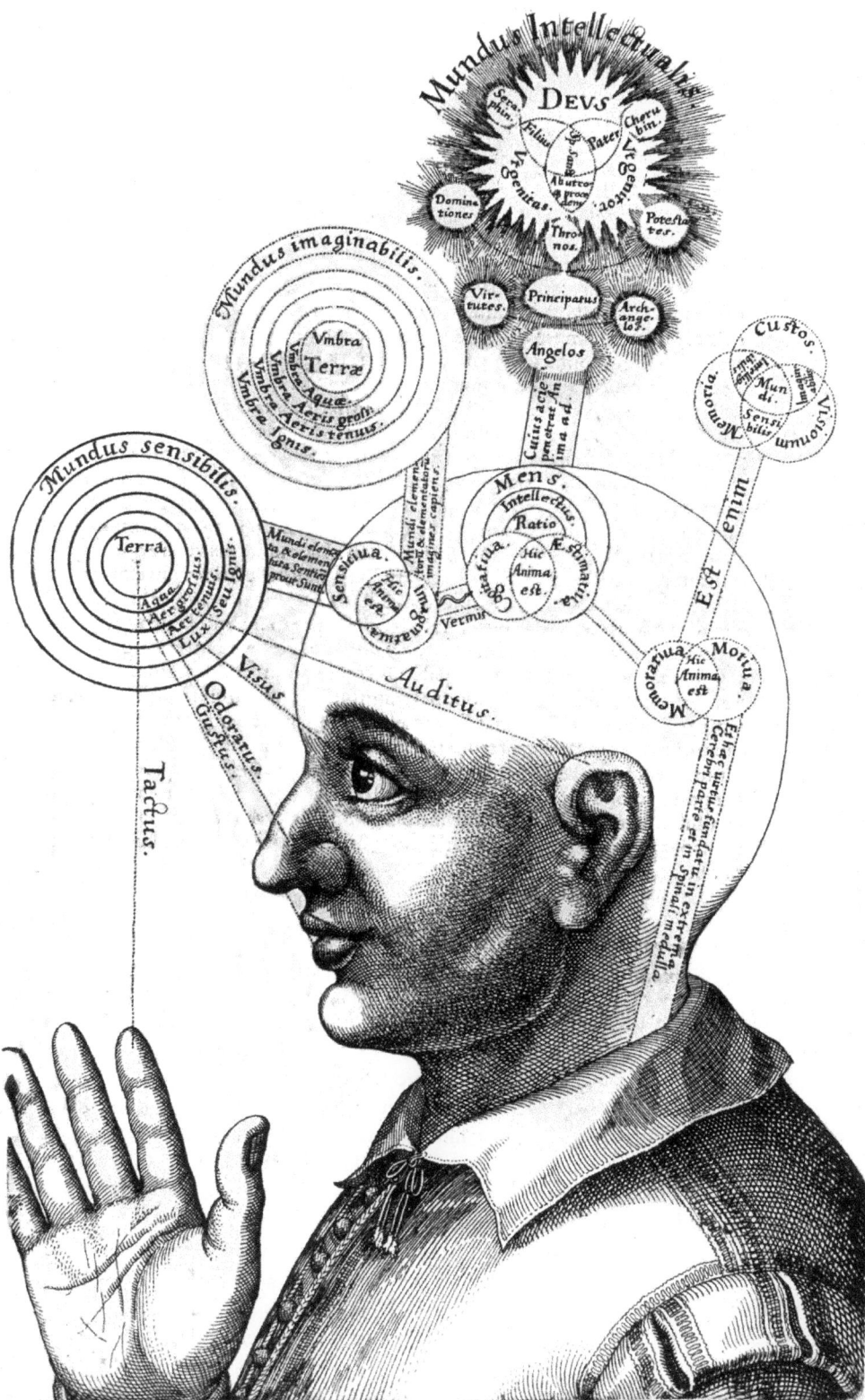

**FIGURE 4.2:** Extended mind. Cabalistic analysis of the mind and senses, 1617, artist unknown. Credit: Oxford Science Archive/Heritage Images/Alamy Stock Photo.

**FIGURE 4.3:** The Law Code of Gortyn, Crete; first half of the fifth century BCE Credit: Corbis Documentary/Getty Images.

Mnemosyne: the Muses gave the Greeks dance (*Terpsikhore*), song (*Kalliope*), religious hymns (*Polyhymnia*), poetry (*Euterpe*), tragedy (*Melpomene*), comedy (Thaleia), mime (*Erato*), history (*Keio*), and astronomy (*Ourania*).[9] The list is weighted towards the performing arts, but it includes astronomy as the major science. This form of aetiology and "reverse engineering" strengthens the idea that a community possesses cultural capital, pointing to both the divine inspiration of these skills and their mysterious origin.

The turn came with one poet, Simonides of Keos (*c.* 552–*c.* 465 BCE), or so the sources tell us (Suda, Cicero, Quintilian). The reports agree on his prodigious memory, but the details are controversial. The late encyclopedic compendium *Suda* informs us that he had a remarkable memory (Lefkowitz 1981: 54). Another source, a Hellenistic papyrus (*POxy* 1800 i.36), suggests that his mnemonic skills arose *from* his poetry (Lefkowitz 1981: 54). Earlier reports claim that he did not just have a capacious memory but also a special mnemonic technique. The most famous story tells of Simonides assisting in the identification of dead bodies from memory in a collapsed dining hall, which he had left just before an earthquake brought it down (Cic., *De Orat.* 2.86.341–5; Quint., *Inst.* 11.2.11–16).[10] He is said to have been able to recall all the names of the victims because he remembered *where* they had been seated. Thus began the special technique of mnemonics in which objects and their place are correlated, a "science of memorization" (Yates 1966).

It is not surprising that the transition is dated in such vague terms (*c.* 500 BCE): an oral culture can hardly be expected to keep a precise record of its own permutations and intellectual progress. Only indirectly can we trace a simultaneous rise of prose texts (continuous script instead of poetic form, hexameter and other metres). The Ephesian

Heraclitus (*c. 535–c.* 475 BCE) is said to have deposited his written prose in the Temple of Artemis, the Artemisium (DL 9. 6). It stands to reason, then, to place a cultural shift in the late sixth and early fifth centuries BCE, as the period that offers the clearest signs of change from oral to written culture. The pioneers who advanced and embraced the new trend were the sophists and legal rhetors (Small 2012). Mnemonic techniques became part of rhetorical training, with further refinements over time as we can see later in Rome (see below).

Before examining the evidence from the Hippocratic Corpus I would like to address Plato, who stands in a way on the threshold of the use of writing as irreversible and illustrates an ambivalent stage in the attitude towards writing and memory.[11] He was in fact fighting a rear-guard battle: while he wrote a considerable amount, he also tried to resist the influence of writing. By his choice of genre, the dialogue, he wanted to reinforce his view that anything written had lost the lifeblood of oral communication, the exchange of ideas, question and answer, in short, the traditional format of Greek aristocratic education. Thus, paradoxically, he protested *in written form* against the deleterious effects of writing. His warning that it would cause human memory to decline is expressed in his story of Theuth, the Egyptian god of writing (*Phaedrus* 274a–277b). What we now consider a benign enhancement of our brain's capacity—paper and electronic devices as parts of our "extended mind"—Plato dismissed as a destructive force for our memory.[12]

## THE RISE OF MEDICAL SCIENCE: THE HIPPOCRATIC CORPUS

As the first discipline approaching what we now consider a science, rational medicine clearly grasped the value of note taking for medical practice, and the Hippocratic writings are a prime example of how scientific knowledge became recorded for the use of future work and training *by and for* physicians. We do not know for certain when Hippocrates became active, but his working life is dated to around 450–420 BCE.[13] The use of written records for describing diagnosis and treatment must have supported the knowledge of presumed medical symptoms and cures, and must have made it possible to teach medicine to a much wider group of students than was the case in traditional form—teacher to trainee transmission of knowledge (often father to son) (Dean-Jones 2003: 98). The influence of writing is abundantly clear by the mid fifth century: the first ethnographer, Herodotus, was another Greek to make good use of writing, recording the customs and stories of a wide range of peoples and documenting the conflict between the Greeks and the Persians.[14]

The habit of taking notes on medical cases and treatments was a revolutionary step in the trajectory to preserve knowledge. It immediately had a clear utilitarian purpose and physicians appear to have been aware of their own significance from the start, proudly displaying this awareness in their writing. We find several statements to this effect, for instance, in *Ancient Medicine* (=VM) 20 we read:

> And I think that <u>one cannot know anything certain</u> regarding nature from any quarter other than from medicine; and that this knowledge is attained when one comprehends the whole subject of medicine properly, but not until then; and I say that <u>this investigative approach</u> (ταύτην τὴν ἱστορίην) shows what man is, by what causes he was made, and other things accurately.
>
> —*VM* 20, slightly modified

This comment on accuracy in a written treatise is further reinforced in the same work,[15] when the author establishes a link between *proper* knowledge and accuracy:

> ... it is a task to learn this [balanced knowledge] <u>accurately</u>, so as not to commit small blunders either on the one side or the other, and in fact I would give great praise to the physician whose mistakes are small, for perfect accuracy is seldom to be seen, since many physicians seem to me to be in the same plight as bad pilots, who, if they commit mistakes while conducting the ship in a calm do not expose themselves, but when a storm and violent hurricane overtake them, they then, from their ignorance and mistakes, are discovered to be what they are, by all men, namely, in losing their ship.
>
> —*VM* 9

The success of rational medical science relied significantly on note taking as a more reliable form of (external) memory. Note how the passage also speaks about "learning" (καταμάθειν) as a major aim of the profession. Moreover, in the so-called "Hippocratic Oath" the didactic attitude is already taken for granted in the stipulation that every new doctor should also teach and preserve the knowledge (*Oath* §2): "To regard him who has taught me this *technê* as equal to my parents and [...] to judge the offspring from him equal to [my] male siblings and to teach them this *technê*, should they desire to learn ..." (tr. von Staden 1996). One might add that, while the medical knowledge referred to (but not articulated) in the oath is meant to stay within the medical "brotherhood," the ethical views encoded in the oath are clearly listed and thus themselves preserved for the future.

How, then, does the Hippocratic Corpus, a body of around sixty-five works (many not considered to have been written by Hippocrates himself), make use of memory in a more technical sense? Two aspects in particular can be highlighted: (1) the role of memory in pathologies and diagnoses, and (2) the role of memory in recording and preserving knowledge. On the first point, several short references to memory in the healing process illustrate that the ability to remember was considered a significant feature of good health. For instance, at *Epidemics* 1. 4. 4 we find a remark that speculates on how a patient had lost their memory: "Eleventh day. Slept; complete recovery of her memory, followed quickly by renewed delirium." The statement seems to emphasize "*complete* recovery" as the notable detail, although a further symptom ("renewed delirium") also indicates that this does not mean return to full health.

As to the second aspect, we find frequent comments relating to the value of writing and transferring knowledge. Some of these represent a genuine reflection on the writing process, others focus on the crucial role memory plays in the medical art. In general, very little explicit reflection on its value is found except in specialist literature. Thus, at *Precepts* 1 we read (my emphasis):

> ... one must attend in medical practice *not primarily to plausible theories, but to experience combined with reason*. For a theory is a composite *memory of things apprehended with sense-perception*. For the sense-perception, coming first in experience and conveying to the intellect the things subjected to it, is clearly imaged, and the intellect, receiving these things many times, noting the occasion, the time and the manner, *stores them up in itself and remembers*.
>
> —*Precepts* 1; tr. Loeb

This general reflection offers a definition of a "theory," which puts a lot of weight on an empirical grasp of things *combined with* memory. It is, one might say, a matter-of-fact approach to knowledge, and perhaps rather obvious to us, but the contrast with "plausible theories" signals a specific choice in a debate (with philosophers) over the best way to proceed in medical practice. The focus on memory here implies awareness of how collecting facts and details via sense perception can have an accumulative effect. This rudimentary epistemology chimes with the practical considerations that physicians tended to follow.

Comments on various degrees of knowledge appear in a work entitled *On Ancient Medicine*, a deeply polemical work:

> Since a physician must at least (I think) *know* this, and be at great pains to know, about natural science, [. . .] what man is *in relation to foods and drinks*, [. . .] It is not sufficient to *learn* simply that cheese is a bad food, as disagreeing with whoever eats of it to satiety, but *what sort of disturbance* it creates, and *wherefore*, and *with what principles* in man it disagrees.
>
> —*VM* 20, tr. Loeb

Here, the emphasis is on not just knowing what "human" is, but also their relation to foods and drinks, and certain reasons and fundamental features. In other words, as objects of study "humans" are not isolated entities, but creatures whose various bodily functions depend on the interaction between body and food. This dynamic relation also requires physicians to have conceptual suppositions about the body and how the relevant factors will respond to the impact of certain foods.

The significance of transmitting knowledge in *written* records is also brought out in clear terms in several works of the Corpus and especially in *Epidemics*. This work attempts a systematic record of symptoms, diseases, and their impact. In one passage we again see a clear link between accurate knowledge and writing, also suggesting that written records contribute to a correct understanding of the medical art (*Epid.* 3. 2. 16, tr. Loeb; my emphasis):

> The power, too, to *study* correctly what has been *written* I consider to be an important part of the art of medicine. The man who has learnt these things and uses them will not, I think, make great mistakes in the art. And *it is necessary to learn accurately* each constitution of the seasons as well as the diseases; what common element in the constitution or in the disease is good, and what common element in the constitution or in the disease is bad; what malady is protracted and fatal, what is protracted and likely to end in recovery; what acute illness is fatal, what acute illness is likely to end in recovery. With this *knowledge* it is easy to examine the order of the critical days, and to prognosticate. <u>One who has knowledge of these matters</u> can know whom he ought to treat, as well as the time and method of treatment.

The skill now incorporated in medical art is one that allows the physician to *study* and *learn accurately* the things that have been *written* (a very similar sentiment in *Epid.* 3. 3. 16). It is evident that medical science takes written records and reflection for granted at this stage. This attitude can also be observed in *VM* 1 and (again) 20, where a dual mode of communicating (speech and writing) are accepted as the norm:

> All who, on attempting <u>to speak or to write</u> on medicine, have assumed for themselves a postulate as a basis for their discussion—heat, cold, moisture, dryness, or anything else that they may fancy—who narrow down the causal principle of diseases and of death among men, and make it the same in all cases, postulating one thing or two . . .
>
> —*VM* 1, tr. Loeb

> Certain physicians and philosophers assert that <u>nobody is able to</u> <u>know</u> medicine who is ignorant as to what man is; he who would treat patients properly must, they say, learn this. But the question they raise is one for philosophy; it is the province of those who, like Empedocles, have <u>written</u> on natural science, what man is from the beginning, how he came into being at the first, and from what elements he was originally constructed. But my view is, first, that all that philosophers or physicians have <u>said or written</u> on natural science no more pertains to medicine than to painting . . .
>
> —*VM* 20, tr. Loeb

The assimilation of writing as the key to retaining knowledge is most clearly on display in a passage from *De articulis* 46–7, in which there can be no doubt that the author uses writing to polemicize against other writers, subsequently clarifying that an audience with access to his argument in the written form may learn from it (my emphasis):

> *Wherefore, then, do I write all this*? Because certain persons fancy that they have cured patients in whom the vertebra had undergone complete dislocation forward. Some, indeed, suppose that this is the easiest of all these dislocations to be recovered from, and that such cases do not stand in need of reduction, but get well spontaneously. Many are ignorant, and profit by their ignorance . . .
>
> —*Art.* 46; tr. Loeb

> I have *written* this *expressly*; for it is a *valuable piece of knowledge to learn* what things have been tried and have proved ineffectual, and wherefore they did not succeed.
>
> —*Art.* 47

A similar didactic motive must be behind the comment in *De fracturis* 25, but this time the written word appears erroneous, when a method of flawed bandaging is discussed and rejected (my emphasis):

> Wherefore I would not have *written* so much on this subject, if I had not well known that this mode of bandaging is unsuitable, and yet that many conduct the treatment in this way, whose *mistake* it is *of vital importance to correct*, while what is here said is a proof, that what was formerly written as to the circumstances under which bandages should be tightly applied to fractures or otherwise has been correctly written.
>
> —*Fract.* 25

This selective set of passages illustrates clearly how both the *adaptation* of writing as such and the *emphasis* on its *value* are so well-developed and common that they must have started earlier than the fifth century BCE. The various works may well have had different authors, so the passages discussed here cannot be regarded as the view of one person. Yet, or rather, in any case, they reveal that at this point in the development of medicine as a science, polemical writing and medical records were considered part and parcel of the emerging discipline and its educational mission. Like laws and storage records, the practical usefulness of writing had been recognized and fully conceptualized.

The implications of the new technology for education were also significant because writing per se more easily spreads the knowledge it contains. The traditional apprenticeship in practical fields such as trade, manual labor, and applied science started to be supplemented with written instructions (handbooks, manuals). Reading and writing supported and reinforced this trend. There was, however, at least one drawback (for a second one, see the following section on Aristotle). In medicine in particular, we find reports of imposters, posing as physicians because they had managed to acquire medical books. It looks as if the problem of quacks and imposters arose *because of* the presence of books. The claim to knowledge became extended beyond a person's internal memory by way of an "external memory," the book. As Lesley Dean-Jones, pointing to the rise of frauds and quacks in the fourth century alongside the rise of medical writings, puts it:

> By the fourth century doctors felt threatened by the unregulated circulation of medical ideas in a way that did not occur before written texts were used. *Decorum* 4 comments that those who think they know medicine from words (*logoisi*) rather than from education (*mathêsios*) "show themselves up like gold proved by the fire to be dross".
> 
> —Dean-Jones 2003: 120–1

Similar complaints about quacks and "non-doctors," *hoi mê iatroi* or *aniatroi*, can be found in *Regimen in Acute Diseases* 6, *Precepts* 7, *On Sacred Disease* 2 (Dean-Jones 2003: 106). In these cases, Dean-Jones (107) argues, the authority of physicians was mostly based on who their teachers were, which suggests that there was already an established appreciation of education linked to the reliability of knowledge.

## THE RISE OF BIOLOGY: ARISTOTLE

Aristotle has been hailed as the first scientist in a more modern sense (Leroi 2014). With regard to his use of writing he continued in the same vein as the medical tradition, perhaps inspired by the fact that his father was a physician. But he also offered a new perspective. While Plato was clearly aware of Hippocrates, and would hardly have objected to his good works,[16] ideological reasons made him critical of the use of writing. Aristotle never had any qualms about recording information. Nicknamed "the Reader," he was also a compulsive writer and even today some think of him as the first scientist with a particular interest in biology. He was a painstaking collector of data and details and a perceptive observer of nature. He was the first to undertake systematic research on large data collections, such as laws, constitutions, dialectical and rhetorical arguments, animals, emotions and virtue. His ability to organize these data is almost unimaginable without the use of writing as a tool.

With regard to memory, Aristotle's studies on animals are undoubtedly the most relevant. Ambitious in scope and rich in detail, the work makes use of a number of organizing principles for his materials, which illustrate how his biology interconnects with more systematic aspects of his doctrines (metaphysics, natural science). The core species is "human," and all other species are measured against this. His pedagogical outlook can be reconstructed from several passages. He declares memory essential for learning (*Eth. Nic.* 6.9; *An. Post.* 1.33) and describes the ideal student in a way that echoes some of Plato's views (e.g., *Resp.* 485–6; *Tht.* 143). An often-overlooked remark made by Aristotle in the last book of the *Nicomachean Ethics* is worth quoting:

> We do not see men becoming expert physicians from a study of medical handbooks [*ek tôn suggrammatôn*]. Yet medical writers attempt to describe not only general courses of treatment, but also methods of cure and modes of treatment for particular sorts of patients, classified according to their various habits of body; and their treatises appear to be *of value for men who have had practical experience* [*tois empeirois*], though they are *useless for the novice* [*tois anepistêmosi*].
> 
> —*Eth. Nic.* 10.9, 1181b21ff. Loeb

It would appear that in Aristotle's view consulting a medical book was not enough to gain a proper understanding, because this required experienced guidance (especially if the notes were written without a well-considered didactic strategy). Taking medicine as a model for method, Aristotle makes a specific point about the limited value of books in relation to applied fields of knowledge.[17] The point is especially relevant because it concerns the art of medicine. All comments imply that learning from books alone is ineffective: the knowledge will have no referent in one's understanding of the actions and things described; that is, a gap will remain between theory and practice, between knowledge and its application. It is worth emphasizing that, nonetheless, Aristotle clearly takes the existence and use of books for granted.[18] The importance of medicine as a model for Aristotle is striking, especially as and when he used it to clarify ethics and its "scientific" basis.[19]

Last but not least, Aristotle is also the only ancient author to have written a work specifically on memory. There is good reason to think that he knew he was making an original contribution. His short work *On Memory* represents a new stage in the emerging interest in the mental process of remembering. The work certainly sets a new standard in the way in which it defines clearly the difference between our memory (location or faculty) and remembering (the activity). The author also closely links memory and the past. As he puts it: "All memory implies a time elapsed; consequently, only animals which perceive time remember, and the organ whereby they perceive time is also that whereby they remember" (*Mem.* 459b; tr. Barnes). In addition, Sorabji's short commentary and exegesis identify the work as a valuable "source for Aristotle's theory of thinking" (Sorabji 1972 and 2006a: 8). In conclusion, we can safely say that Aristotle was the first to theorize the analysis of memory in Greek epistemology.

## ROMAN TRANSFORMATIONS: ADAPTATION AND INTELLECTUAL IMPERIALISM

Culturally the transition from Greece to Rome is famously one of transformation, or, rather, transformation*s*. While some Roman authors were involved in creating larger works on Roman topics (e.g. Varro on language and agriculture, see below), others undertook it to study and adapt a range of Greek intellectual achievements to Latin.

Four figures stand out in Roman culture for their contribution to preserving various kinds of specialized knowledge in their writings: Lucretius' *De rerum natura*, Cicero's rhetorical handbook, Seneca's *Quaestiones naturales*, and Pliny the Elder's *Natural History*. They span a period of about 200 years, from the turbulent late republic in the first century BCE to the equally restless early Roman Imperial period of the first century CE. These four intellectuals represent the Roman intellectual task of converting, transferring, and translating Greek ideas into Roman form. While they differ on account of their chosen genres, they share a sense of imitation and emulation, a notion clearly expressed by the earliest example of "adapters," Lucretius. The process of translating and transforming Greek materials is strongly influenced by both the original text and the drive to adapt it for a Roman audience. Lucretius (105–55 BCE) offers a very clear reason for composing his epic poem on Epicurean philosophy and natural science, fully aware of the difficulty involved (*DRN* 1. 135–9). To him Epicurean philosophy had a salvation message, and Lucretius therefore presented Epicurus as a "savior" of mankind (*DRN* 1. 62–79).

The central ideas are "equanimity" or "calmness of mind" (*ataraxia*) and irrelevance of the gods. These are presented in a broader framework of cosmology, theology, psychology, and human fate. Crucially, the *structure* of the work is partly Epicurus', and partly due to transpositions by Lucretius, as David Sedley (1998: chs. 3, 4, and 7) has shown so vividly in his book *Lucretius and the Transformation of Greek Wisdom*.[20]

The era of encyclopedic endeavors had come into its own in the first century BCE. One might start with Varro's extensive studies of language and grammar: his *De origine linguae Latinae* was dedicated to Pompey and still known to Augustine (*De civitate dei* xxii. 28). His largest work, *Antiquitates rerum humanarum et divinarum*, was in forty-one books (!) and discussed the history of Rome with regard to human institutions and religious practices.[21] Another example is Celsus' *On Medicine* (*De medicina*), a summary of the development and achievements of medical knowledge up to his own time. A prime example of the way in which the progression of written science facilitated large scale works with a more intricate structure is Pliny the Elder's *Natural History*. This real standout among the literature of the early Roman empire shows how, by the first century CE, expansive collections of data had become quite common. Pliny the Elder, as he is known (to distinguish him from his nephew and adoptive son, Pliny the Younger), was a man of some weight, with a career in the army and as a scholar with a broad interest in the natural world. The first large work of this kind, Pliny's monumental *Naturalis Historia* follows a tradition of comprehensive data collection-cum-analysis.[22] It resembles the title of Herodotus' famous historical prose work and a title known for Theophrastus' *Enquiry into Nature* (φυσική ἱστορία) and *Enquiry into Plants*.[23]

The work generated Pliny's fame for centuries to come. Already in the preface ("Dedication to Emperor Vespasian's son Titus," praef. 1; 12–15) the author hints at the value of recording knowledge, despite some self-deprecating remarks so common in dedications. He distinguishes books of "those who merely *publish* their works is very different from that of those who expressly dedicate them to you" (praef.), embedding the dedication in topoi and flattering the emperor's son. In his discussion of anthropology and human physiology Pliny (*NH* 7. 24) later comments explicitly on memory, but his brief chapter limits itself to a few examples of categories of memory in famous men of the past (for his reference to Simonides see above) and injuries entailing the loss of memory. What is more important, however, is to look at the work's emphasis on its own table of contents, and the implementation of a "conscious design," as Laehn (2013: 19) has labeled it. Organization becomes an important aspect of large works, and I would argue that the advanced stage of the use of writing (involving longer and more detailed narratives) required well-developed and clear principles of organization.

In recent decades, Pliny's work has received considerable attention. Moving away from a traditional reading of the work as "encyclopedic," several scholars have proposed a very different approach. Murphy (2004) has suggested that the work was a political statement to alert to the power and expanse of the Roman empire, making the work a (conscious) cultural expression of the imperial period, much like the *Encyclopaedia Britannica* was a reflection and self-representation of the British empire. This analogy works up to a point, in that both share and emerge from a certain optimism that comprehensive knowledge is possible. Laehn (2013) has further supported this political reading and proposed an ingenious hypothesis, on which I shall elaborate in a moment. Concurrently, Doody (2009) has objected to the label "encyclopedia" as too modern, arguing that Pliny's work is nothing like the typical encyclopedic works we now associate with repositories of knowledge forming a tradition that begins with Diderot. While this is a fair point about terminology the work can certainly be called "encyclopedic."

Laehn (2013) proposes an intriguing interpretation by offering a radical rethinking of the work's structure in order to arrive at a far more coherent set of thematic clusters than traditional interpretations can offer. The latter tend to assume a progression from a broad perspective (*kosmos*) to a narrower one of living creatures (via humans, animals, and plants), with additional books on medicines based on plants and animals, and mineralogy. The starting point for Laehn is a small number of the cross-references from later to earlier books. The links are as follows: book 31 refers back to book 8; book 22 to book 10; book 24 to book 15. These references allow Laehn to hypothesize a different organization of the work with a rather unexpected link between the two halves.

| Traditional organization: linear composition | Correspondences leading to a new organization: annular or "ring composition" |
|---|---|
| 1 index | |
| 2–6 kosmos | 1–5 ~ 32–36 inanimate matter |
| 7 man | |
| 8–11 animals | 6–10 ~ 27–31 on animals |
| 12–19 plants | |
| 20–27 medicines from plants | 11–18 ~ 19–26 on plants |
| 28–32 medicine from animals | |
| 33–37 metals and mineralogy | |

In this way Laehn identifies thematic clusters stemming from internal cross-references. The diagram below will illustrate the proposed structure:

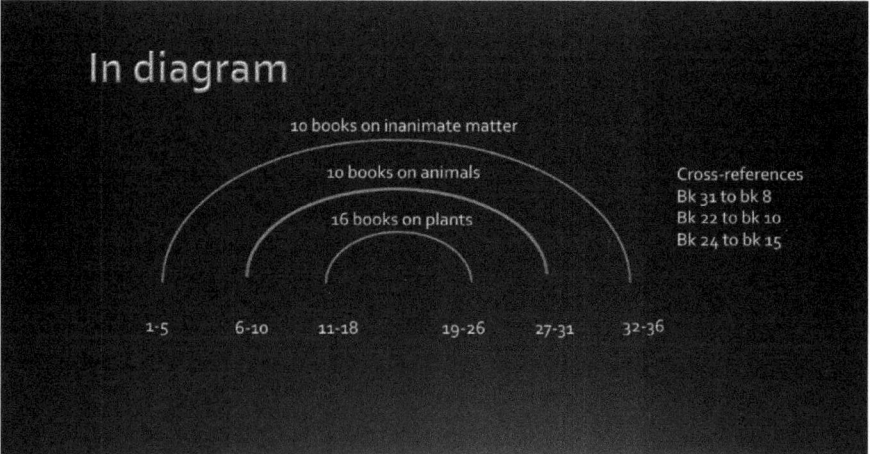

**FIGURE 4.4:** Laehn and Themes of Books. Credit: © H. Baltussen 2019.

The deep interconnection between parts creates a neat plan that links sets of books. The result is an impressive symmetry of the overall structure:

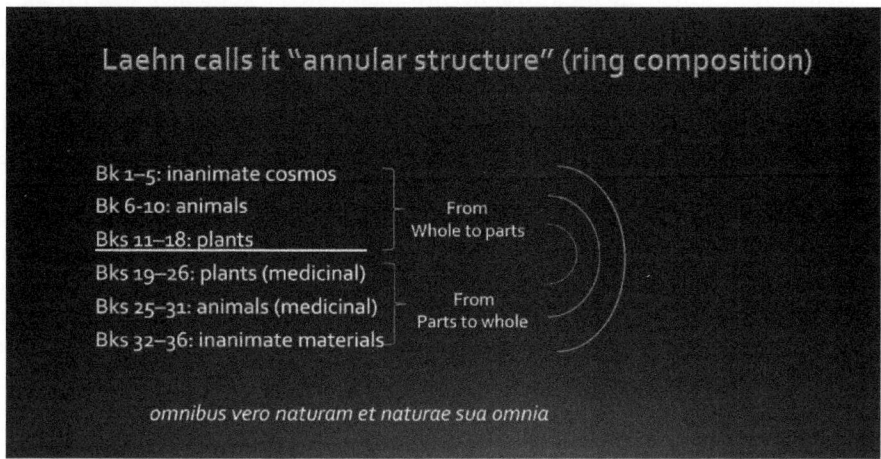

FIGURE 4.5: Laehn and the "Annular Structure." Credit: © H. Baltussen 2019.

The overall structure can thus be explained by a progression that "turns back on itself" halfway through. And the progression is driven by the notions of whole and parts: in the first half we move from inanimate to animate in a way that goes from whole to parts; in the second half we move from animate to inanimate again in a way that goes from parts to whole. Whether we accept this analysis or not, the possibility of an even more complex and sophisticated organization of the material would allow us to attribute to Pliny a well-thought out plan—which identifies a highly analytical, literary writer and presumes an equally sophisticated audience, expected to appreciate the composition.

Accordingly, Laehn concludes (as did Murphy) that Pliny's perfect symmetry encapsulates all areas of knowledge and thus "conquers" the world of knowledge in a way that represents the Romans' view of themselves. Conquests played a major role in the late republic and early empire, and they offered much opportunity for the display of the subdued lands and peoples. This happened above all at triumphal processions and games, which not only honored the military achievements of Rome's generals but also enabled the people of Rome to *see* the distant worlds in all their rich variety. In this view, then, the limits of nature coincided with the Roman order. Pompey actually boasted about his conquests in all (three) continents, also signaled in Agrippa's map of the empire. In other words, expansion of empire inspired something like intellectual imperialism expressed in Pliny's work. If correct, this reading illustrates how sophisticated the data collections had become: while Pliny's work had Aristotelian elements in its DNA, it went beyond this and amounted to a far more comprehensive treatise that captured the Roman empire in written form.[24]

# MEDICAL WRITING ON A GRAND SCALE: GALEN OF PERGAMUM

Roman physicians furthered the transmission and transformation of Greek medicine. In many ways the demands made on the skills of medical practitioners remained very similar.

In the first century CE the physician Soranus, who specialized in gynaecology, offered the following job description of the ideal midwife, who was by now expected to be literate: "A suitable person will be <u>literate</u>, with her wits about her, a <u>good memory</u>, loving work, respectable and generally not unduly handicapped as regards her senses and robust (bearing the 'double burden' of mother and child); and according to some people, endowed with long slim fingers and short nails at the fingertips" (*Gyn.* 1.3, tr. Temkin).

In the second century the philosopher-physician Galen closely echoed the criteria articulated by Plato and Aristotle, namely that students needed a good memory. Galen also tried to live up to Aristotle's famous injunction at the start and end of the *Parva naturalia*, that the philosopher had to have knowledge of medical matters and that the physician should also be a philosopher (*Sens.* 436a19–22; *Resp.* 480b26–30). Galen's contribution to the understanding of memory concerns, as may be expected, mostly cases of malfunctioning memory. His medical approach is grounded in Hippocratic ideas and methods. The humoral theory is the basis for his psychology, i.e. he believed that the soul's activities arose from the elemental balance (*Quod animi mores*). Galen's interest in education and paedagogy is clear from the way in which he endorses certain views of Aristotle and Plato (Baltussen 2017: 588f) He often refers to the qualities of good students: "He [who wants to study medicine and philosophy] has to be quick-witted, have a good memory and be hardworking" (*De ord. libr. prop.* 19.59.2). A work preserved only in Arabic and entitled *On How to Recognize the Best Doctor*) sums up what kind of student will become a good doctor, emphasizing that a student with the right instruction "will be able to describe the doctrines of each of these [i.e., the Ancients]." The perfect student is also able to summarize "those of their successors, outlining the differences and agreements," and add "his own judgment on their differences, justifying correct doctrines and exposing those that are erroneous." Clearly, Galen's educational vision includes a solid knowledge of the history of the discipline and the various positions of each school of thought as found in their writings.

A recent study of crucial texts in the Galenic corpus by Ricardo Julião illustrates this particular medical focus very well and clarifies his clinical view on memory.[25] Galen's theorizing on the matter is quite detailed and sophisticated. Unsurprisingly, the physician concentrates on memory defects. He offers explanations (causes) for the various dysfunctions, suggesting that these are not located in any particular body part but that some are related to psychological states of mind (e.g. stress), and others to physiological states, often depending on the balance of elemental qualities. We find an elaborate account of the formation of memories as well as memory lapses (by describing how some people forget words). In sum, Galen is a great example of memory theory as well as an expert user of the "artificial memory" argued for in this chapter, namely science writing on a grand scale (Julião 2018).

# CONCLUSION

This broad-brush study of the relation between memory and ancient science has attempted to show in an empirical way how "ancient science" was augmented and transmitted with the help of the new technology of writing (viewed as "artificial or external" memory), and how we might characterize the on-going cultural role of memory in this process.[26] As this particular correlation has not been studied at length, my account has drawn on several strands of research, in the fields of classical studies, history of medicine, and anthropology. By using the labels "internal" and "external" in describing different types of memory, I have explained broader features of the trajectory in science: the importance of (natural) memory, the tools in memorization, the role of writing as external memory and proliferation of literacy leading to the rise of "encyclopedic" works.

Early science involved philosophers, mathematicians, as well as physicians. I would argue that these domains of knowledge each represent examples of a broader phenomenon. The earliest harnessing of knowledge in static form by way of recorded facts contributed much to the preservation of human experience and understanding. I have also drawn special attention to the need for memory aids when the bulk of knowledge grew steadily (the word for "notebook," *hypomnêma*, means "reminder"). The early epics suggest that the brain's ability for retention was pushed to its limits, but that initially adding rhythm and repetition could preserve cultural knowledge within oral societies for centuries: I submit that the Homeric epics are the product of an organic system of mnemonics paired with additional training to provide continuity. We can trace the techniques of memory training from the sixth century onwards, via Simonides, the orators and educational commentators such as Plato, Aristotle, and Isocrates. It is equally significant to see how writing aided human memory in urbanized environments, in which recorded versions of common rules became important, such as legal practices being laid down in written form ("laws" or conventions, *nomoi*), and then political thought replicated in government. Once any domain of human interest became studied and written about, literate study would reflect on itself and produce projects in the form of data collections, handbooks, treatises and (proto-)encyclopedic writings, for which Pliny's attempt to collect *all* human knowledge can be seen as a significant highpoint. Admittedly, the development sketched here is a typological outline, but many of its building blocks have been properly described by other scholars (Lloyd 1970; Ong 1982; Havelock 1986; Erll and Nünning 2010; Nutton 2013).

The crucial step for a new scientific approach came with the Hippocratics. Writing was already beginning to establish itself, but the Hippocratic Corpus bears witness to its systematic use and usefulness ("external memory"). Recording medical symptoms and potential cures in great detail allowed for better evaluation of new cases. It assisted in creating a patient history, and a history of particular diseases. Self-conscious comments on the role of writing show that, at least from the fifth century BCE onwards, physicians were very much aware of the importance of recording their findings. This is how "paper" extends human minds and natural memory. Should we be surprised, then, that a close contemporary, the historian Thucydides, who was undoubtedly inspired by Hippocratic writings, described his work as "a possession for all time" (κτῆμα ἐς αἰεί, 1. 22)? Whatever idea of the historian's role this phrase may encapsulate, his claim reflects the view of his time that the human tendency to record is beneficial, and that the written word will outlive the "memes" in our heads. The fact that we can still read (much of) their work is a remarkable achievement. It remains to be seen whether our modern "external memory" in its present vulnerable electronic format will achieve a similar result.

CHAPTER FIVE

# Ideas: Philosophy, Religion, and History*

LUCA CASTAGNOLI

Memory was central to Greek culture from very early on. This centrality is illustrated by the prominent position that Mnemosyne, the Memory goddess, had in the Greek pantheon. In Hesiod's *Theogony* Mnemosyne is represented as one of the earliest, pre-Olympian deities, daughter of Gaia (Earth) and Ouranos (Heaven), sister of Kronos[1] and mother of the Muses. The intuition that memory can give us access to something that is remote from us in space and time is embodied in the genealogy and power of the Muses, daughters of Mnemosyne and Zeus (see Hesiod, *Theogony* 52–63; 915–17). Significantly, when in the Homeric hymn Hermes sings the story of how the gods originally came to be,

FIGURE 5.1: Mosaic depicting Mnemosyne, second century CE. National Archaeological Museum, Tarragona, Spain. Credit: Prisma Archivo/Alamy Stock Photo.

"*first* among the gods he honored Mnemosyne, mother of the Muses" (429–30), before proceeding with the birth of the other deities: it is only thanks to the power of Mnemosyne and her daughters that even a god, Hermes, can sing of a primeval past. It is clearly by virtue of their kinship with memory, then, that already in archaic Greece the Muses represented omniscient sources of super-human knowledge to which human beings can have only indirect access; hence the poet's typical invocation to the Muses, famously exemplified in Homer *Iliad* 2.484–93 and Hesiod *Theogony* 22–33 (Notopoulos 1938; Collins 1999; Yamagata 2005). At the same time, the Greeks thought that this form of knowledge cannot be fully controlled by human beings: to Hesiod's invocation the Muses reply that "we know how to speak many false things as though they were real; but we know, when we will, to utter true things (ἀληθέα)" (*Theog.* 27–8). Although the Muses warn the poet that they can be deceitful, they can, when they want, speak *alēthea*, things that are, literally, "not hidden" or "not forgotten," and thus true.[2]

In Homer's *Iliad*, this privileged access to knowledge is explained by the Muses' presence: "for you are goddesses and are in all places and know all things, while we hear only report and know nothing" (*Il.* 2.485–6); the Muses know directly, by virtue of somehow witnessing (presumably seeing) what they know, while human beings' access to these truths is only second-hand (interestingly Homer suggests that this second-hand access falls short of knowledge). The Muses' memory-knowledge concerns not only the distant past, cosmogonic (e.g. in Hesiod) and heroic (e.g. in Homer), but also the present and the future: the Muses sing "what is, what shall be and what was" (*Theog.* 38).[3] Not surprisingly, human diviners share this omni-temporal knowledge with the Muses: Calchas "knew the things that were, that were to be, and that had been" (*Il.* 1.70).[4]

The same nexus connecting Mnemosyne and the Muses to knowledge and sight is attested in one of Pindar's *Paeans*: "And I pray to Ouranos' well-robed daughter, Mnemosyne, and to her children [i.e. the Muses], to provide facility, for blind are the minds of men, if anyone without the Heliconians seeks the deep path of wisdom" (Pind. *Paea.* 7b, 15-20). Pindar is also explicit as to the source of the Muses' power to inspire the poet, namely memory itself: "the Muse loves to remember" (Μοῖσα μεμνᾶσθαι φιλεῖ, *Nem.* 1.12).

A different tradition made Memory herself (*Mneme*) one of three Muses, together with Practice (*Melete*) and Song (*Aoide*) (Paus. 9.26.2); the triad reflects the connection between memory and the other essential aspects of poetic activity. The existence of such a connection is natural in a culture like that of archaic Greece, in which writing played a very limited role in the transmission of knowledge; but the connection remained alive after the diffusion of writing, as illustrated by the group of Zeus, Mnemosyne and the Muses in the "Apotheosis of Homer" relief of Archelaos of Priene,[5] or by the later reference to the Muses themselves as "Remembrances" (*mneiai*) in Plutarch (*Table Talk* 9.14, 743D).

Given the importance that memory played in early Greek poetry, and in its reflections upon its own authoritative status as the highest source of *paideia* (Simondon 1982), it comes as no surprise that Greek philosophers, who engaged critically with this tradition, showed a sustained interest in the concept of memory. They reflected extensively upon the nature, power, and dangers of memory when proposing alternative models of knowledge, of its sources and objects, of the knowing subject, and of learning and teaching (Vernant 1965, tr. 1983). The two main sections of this chapter will focus on the original and deeply influential ways in which Plato shaped the ancient philosophical discourse on memory. In the conclusion I will offer a very brief and selective overview of some other ways in which different conceptions of memory, recollection, and forgetting characterize philosophical outlooks from the late fourth century BCE (Aristotle) to the fifth century CE (Augustine).

## PLATO ON RECOLLECTION (*ANAMNĒSIS*), KNOWLEDGE, AND EDUCATION

The beginning of a central trend in the ancient philosophical reflection on memory is Plato's choice, in the *Meno*, to tackle the so-called "Meno's paradox," a challenge to the very possibility of enquiry as a route to learning, by introducing the notorious "theory of recollection."[6] According to the theory, learning is indeed possible, and is nothing but *anamnēsis* of what was once known by our souls before their current embodiment (80d–81d). Surprised reactions such as Vlastos', according to whom the "theory of recollection" is "the wildest flight on which Plato's metaphysical imagination ever took off" (1994: 79), fail to appreciate how Plato was consciously engaging with the early cultural and poetic reflections on the power of memory. I suggest that by placing *anamnēsis* at the center of his epistemology Plato creatively transformed the traditional divinely-grounded *mnemonic* wisdom into a human *recollective* process of learning; *anamnēsis* became the label for the (re-)discovery of the truth within ourselves, by means of individual philosophical inquiry and dialectical reasoning, and at the same time for the re-appropriation of our true,

FIGURE 5.2: Socrates and his Muse; Roman sarcophagus, second century CE, now in the Louvre. Credit: Christophel Fine Art/Universal Images Group/Getty Images.

best (divine) natures. At the same time, Plato thought that this process is possible only if we forget the lessons of traditional *paideia*, and the ways of life those lessons lead us to; he thus opposed the rational methods of philosophical enquiry to the passive memorizing practices not only of the poets, but also of the sophists.

Although the idea that *anamnēsis* somehow explains human learning appears in several places in Plato's corpus, the *Meno* is not only the earliest presentation of the idea (Day 1994; Scott 2006), but also the one which best illustrates the critical link between Plato's *anamnēsis* and other, competing ways of understanding the role of memory in human cognition. When at the beginning of the dialogue Meno asks Socrates to tell him how human *aretē* ("virtue" or "excellence") can be acquired (70a), Socrates interprets this request as the symptom of a certain misguided attitude to learning and the acquisition of knowledge: Meno, who has been exposed to the teachings of the sophist Gorgias and enthusiastically accepted them, seems to think that in order to learn something it is sufficient to ask and be told by a knowing authority, and that to know is to remember, and to be able to repeat promptly, the nuggets of knowledge one has been gifted with. This attitude was grounded in a longstanding Greek tradition by which learning by heart the poems of Homer, Hesiod, and other sources of wisdom was considered an essential part of one's education; but the same attitude was also encouraged by the sophists who, while proposing themselves as new, better sources of *paideia*, still encouraged rote memorization as a learning method.[7] Such a method was censured not only by Plato but also by his pupil Aristotle, who at the end of his *Sophistical Refutations* attacked Gorgias and the teachers of eristic for giving their students ready-made speeches and arguments to be memorized, thus failing to teach them the rules of the dialectical art (183b34–184a8).[8]

On the contrary, Socrates, by ironically disavowing personal memory of the teachings of Gorgias (Wygoda 2019) disavows a conception of knowledge as something that can be simply passed on, untested, from the teaching authority to the learner:[9] "I don't have a very good memory, Meno (Οὐ πάνυ εἰμὶ μνήμων, ὦ Μένων), so I can't say at present what I thought about him [Gorgias] back then [i.e. when Gorgias presented his views on *aretē* in Athens]. But perhaps he does know [what *aretē* is], and you know what he said; so remind me what he said. Or, if you like, speak for yourself; for I suppose you think the same as him" (71c–d).[10] Unlike Socrates, Meno does remember well Gorgias' teachings;[11] when what he remembers is submitted to the scrutiny of the Socratic *elenchus* ("cross-examination"), however, Meno reveals himself to be unable to give a full account and defense of what Gorgias (and he) thought about the nature of *aretē*. Since Socrates himself repeatedly disavows knowledge not only of the origin of *aretē*, but also of what *aretē* itself is, Meno once again falls back on his recollection of the words of a different authority, the poet Simonides: "Well, Socrates, I think that excellence is, as the poet says, 'to rejoice in fine things and have power'" (77b). It is when this conception of *aretē* also fails to withstand Socrates' *elenchus* (77c–79d) that Meno finally admits his perplexity (*aporia*) and raises the puzzle that has come to be known as "Meno's paradox." If neither Meno nor Socrates have any knowledge of what *aretē* is, let alone of how it can be acquired, "how are you going to search for this, Socrates, when you don't know at all what it is? Which of the things that you don't know will you set before yourself, when you are searching for it? And even if you do come across it, how are you going to know that this is the thing you didn't know?" (80d). In the absence of a teacher who can transmit the required knowledge, the very possibility of learning anything through the sort of enquiry that Socrates has encouraged Meno to pursue seems to be blocked by the paradox.[12]

Although Socrates claims that the argument is "eristic" or "contentious" (ἐριστικὸν, 80e2), and that it does not seem to him to be "good" (καλῶς, 81a1), he does not undertake to examine the shortcomings of its logic, but contests directly its conclusion, by introducing the notion of *anamnēsis*. He claims to have "heard" from some priests and priestesses and from some divinely inspired poets, like Pindar (whom he recites extensively by heart at 81b–c), that

> the soul of man is immortal, and at one time ends life—what people call dying—and at another is born again, but never perishes [. . .]. So, since the soul is immortal and has been born many times, and has seen both the things here on earth and those in the underworld and all things, there is nothing that it has not learned. So there is nothing surprising in its being possible for it to recollect things concerning both excellence and other matters, seeing that it knew them before also. For since all nature is akin, and the soul has learned all things, nothing prevents it, if it has recollected one thing—what men call "learning"—from discovering all the other things, if one is courageous and does not weary of the search. For the whole of searching and learning is recollection (τὸ γὰρ ζητεῖν ἄρα καὶ τὸ μανθάνειν ἀνάμνησις ὅλον ἐστίν). So one should not be persuaded by that contentious argument.
>
> —81b–e

The way in which Socrates defuses Meno's paradox is interesting not only in its own right, but also when we consider it against the background of Socrates' earlier (implicit) rejection of traditional sources of *paideia*. For his acceptance of the view that all learning is *anamnēsis* of what our soul came to know before birth could appear to rest on uncritical trust of the religious and poetic authorities he mentions, and on his memory of what he heard from them; and this reliance would also contradict the very idea that the acquisition of knowledge is the result of an active process of recollection "from within," prompted by philosophical enquiry. However, while the reference to these authorities may well be Socrates' opening ploy to pander to Meno's intellectual inclinations and pique his interest, it becomes immediately clear that Socrates' own endorsement is rooted in reason,[13] and that he wants Meno's acceptance to be similarly justified. When asked by Meno to "teach" him *how* all learning is recollection, Socrates protests that according to the theory of course he cannot *teach* Meno, and Meno cannot learn *from him*; but Socrates can try to *show* Meno the learning is *anamnēsis* (81e–82a). Socrates does so by showing how Meno's slave is able to solve a geometrical problem whose solution he does not know, and was never taught during his life, simply by being questioned by Socrates in a way which resembles the *elenchus* that he used with Meno. The slave is not told what answers to accept or reject at any given stage of the examination, but progressively Socrates' questions lead the slave to "see by himself" the incorrectness of his initial answer, and finally to understand the correct solution (82a–85b). From this Socrates concludes that true beliefs concerning the geometrical problem must have already been in the slave's soul, and that these beliefs were simply "stirred up" by Socrates' questioning, in a process of *anamnēsis* which in the end could deliver full knowledge (85c–d). It is a difficult question, which I cannot pursue here, whether what is latent in the soul since birth is innate *knowledge*, true opinions, or rather some kind of rational capacity to reason correctly and to discriminate the truth about certain matters, a capacity that is somehow the remnant of our (now lost) pre-natal knowledge of those matters. What is clear is that the kind of *anamnēsis* which constitutes learning differs from the ability to recall what one has been taught in the past, whether in this life or even in the previous one: in the end, the slave does not recall having been told the correct solution in some previous existence; he recollects the solution itself "from within himself" with the aid of Socrates.

When *anamnēsis* is first introduced Socrates claims that we can recollect "all things" (πάντα χρήματα), because our souls have "seen" and learnt "all things" before, in previous lives and in the underworld; clearly, however, what the slave recollects (a geometrical truth, and its demonstration), and what Meno is encouraged to try to recollect (what *arête* itself is), are not historical or empirical events or data, but non-temporal, abstract, universal truths which could not be accessed through ordinary experience (e.g. could not literally be "seen" through our eyes). Although our present capacity for recollection is somehow grounded in some kind of cognition that our souls enjoyed in the pre-natal past, the object of their recollection is not itself the past. There is no indication that Plato would have wanted to claim, absurdly, that we could somehow come to know, by *anamnēsis*, how the gods first came into being, or the names and deeds of the heroes who fought in Troy, or what the weather was like in Athens on this day 100 years ago.

What is only implicitly suggested by the choice of examples in the *Meno* is confirmed by the *Phaedo* and the *Phaedrus*, where we are told that what we can come to know through *anamnēsis* are purely intelligible eternal universal essences, the "Forms" (*eidē* or *ideai*), and not sensible particulars located in space and time.[14] The human capacity to grasp the Equal Itself, the Good Itself or the Just Itself is in fact used as a premise in an argument for the pre-existence of the soul in the *Phaedo* (72e–78b);[15] in this way the

**FIGURE 5.3**: Donatello, Bust of a Youth. Detail medallion with the "Chariot of the Soul"; Florence, Museo Nazionale del Bargello. Credit: B. Dignas ©; courtesy of the Museo Nazionale del Bargello, Florence.

doctrines about the soul from the priests and poets who first introduced *anamnēsis* in the *Meno*[16] find rational support in an argument founded upon central tenets of Platonic metaphysics and epistemology.

Similarly, within the eschatological myth in which the soul is represented as a winged chariot, in the *Phaedrus* (Griswold 1986; Ferrari 1987; Werner 2012; Capra 2014) the capacity for recollecting the Forms is singled out as what distinguishes the human souls from those of non-rational animals:

> a soul that never saw the truth cannot take a human shape, since a human being must understand speech in terms of general forms, proceeding to bring many perceptions together into a reasoned unity (δεῖ γὰρ ἄνθρωπον συνιέναι κατ᾿ εἶδος λεγόμενον, ἐκ πολλῶν ἰὸν αἰσθήσεων εἰς ἓν λογισμῷ συναιρούμενον). And this is recollection (ἀνάμνησις) of the things our soul saw when it was traveling with god, when it disregarded the things we now call real and lifted up its head to what is truly real instead.
>
> —249b–c

The myth also offers an explanation of how our souls came to know, before our birth, what we can now recollect. In the interludes between cycles of ten incarnations, when they are free from their bodily prison, following the gods' lead in a sort of heavenly procession the souls are afforded a chance to "see" the Forms themselves.[17] As long as a soul manages to catch at least partial sight of the Forms, it remains free from reincarnation; if it fails to see, because of the impediment caused by its lower, appetitive part, it is filled with forgetfulness (*lēthē*), loses its wings and falls down to earth (248a–b). Notice how, for a discarnate soul who lives, as it should, in the company of the gods, divine memory-knowledge is afforded by direct contact with and constant attention to the Forms, rather than past experience and retention, in a way that resembles the traditional description of the Muses' memory-knowledge.

Not only is the capacity for *anamnēsis* central to our identity as rational beings, then, and to our potential for (re-)acquiring knowledge during this life; it is a failure of memory, forgetfulness of the Forms, that explains the fall of our souls, our cognitive limitations as human beings, and our incapacity to live virtuously in accordance with the best part of our nature, divine reason. Here Plato's reflection on the role of recollection in human existence intersects with another important strand of the ancient tradition: Orphism.

"Orphism" is the name of a heterogeneous set of theological and anthropological doctrines, mystery cults and purification rites. The Orphics claimed the mythical Orpheus, son of the Muse Calliope (and thus grandson of Mnemosyne), as their prophet. The central Orphic belief is that, as the result of an original sin, the human souls have been condemned to endure bodily existence, as in a prison, through a cycle of reincarnations. The Orphic purification rituals and life-style rules were meant to help the initiates to regain their place with the gods, and instructions were given as to how the soul should behave after death to achieve this goal.

These instructions are recorded in some gold "tablets" or "leaves" (*lamellae*) dating from the sixth century BCE to the third century CE (West 1983; Betegh 2004; Bernabé and Jiménez San Cristóbal 2008; Edmonds 2011). Some of the extant *lamellae* mention a lake of Memory, from whose waters the thirsty soul should drink in the underworld, while carefully avoiding another spring (evidently, of Forgetfulness); one *lamella* invites the underworld gods to accept the *lamella* itself as "a gift of Memory" (Μνημοσύνης τόδε δῶρον), while two *lamellae* claim to be a "work of Memory" (Μνημοσύνης τόδε ἔργον), presumably because

FIGURE 5.4: Orphic *lamella*, mid-fourth century BCE; J. Paul Getty Museum. Credit: The Getty Museum Open Access Images (Public Domain).

they function as memory aids that the initiate needs in order to take the right course after death. Indeed, an Orphic hymn calls on Mnemosyne to "awaken the memory of the pious ritual in the initiates and send forgetfulness far from them" (*Orph. Hy.* 77.9–10). Here the goddess Mnemosyne is not called upon to teach us of great divine or human deeds from the past; she is asked to help an individual soul to remember who she is and find her way back to her original divine status, i.e. she has a soteriological role. A formula that the Orphic initiate had to pronounce, "I am a child of Earth (Gaia) and of Starry Heaven (Ouranos)," shows the Orphic belief in man's affinity with the gods, and in particular the brotherhood of the initiate to Mnemosyne, who was herself the daughter of Gaia and Ouranos.

The role that memory plays as an instrument of redemption in the Orphics is transformed by Plato into a celebration of the philosophical activity as a form of purification of the soul. Undergoing certain rites of initiation, and remembering a series of rituals or formulae, or the map of the treacherous paths of the underworld, will not help our souls to re-gain their original status; it is philosophical enquiry that will prompt our recollection of the eternal, divine truths to which our souls are most akin, and will thus grant us the most divine form of life here and now (*Phaedrus* 249c).[18] In addition, this way of living will be rewarded by just gods in the afterlife, and as a result of this our soul might even hope to manage to escape the cycle of reincarnations altogether (248e–249a).

The description of the underworld geography in the Orphic tablets also finds an echo in several Platonic dialogues: in the myth of Er in the *Republic*, for example, the souls of the dead who are about to return to the world of the living after choosing the pattern of life they will follow in their next reincarnation assemble in the "Plain of Oblivion" (Λήθης πεδίον), and drink the water of the river Ἀμελής ("Carelessness") (621a). Although the souls cannot avoid drinking, because of the terrible heat, and will thus forget their previous lives and their post-death experiences upon re-birth, we are told by Er that some of them will drink more than necessary, if their thirst is not restrained by philosophical understanding (621a). I suggest that with this detail Plato is, once again, appropriating and transforming Orphic ways of thinking about the dangers of forgetfulness: presumably the souls who have drank too much of the water of oblivion will be unable (or, at least, less able), in their next incarnation, to recollect the eternal truths akin to them, the Forms, and to appreciate their own immortal, quasi-divine nature.[19]

Albeit in interestingly different ways, in the *Meno*, the *Phaedo*, and the *Phaedrus* the human potential for acquiring knowledge through rational enquiry is consistently described in terms of *anamnēsis*. Although other Platonic dialogues are silent on the role of recollection, and adopt different models for human learning and education, these models seem to capture some of the same core insights. In the *Theaetetus* (148d–151d) and the *Symposium* (206b–212b) knowledge is not transmitted to us from external sources, but in the right conditions our fertile souls will be able to "give birth" to it from within (perhaps with the help of an expert Socratic "midwife"); in the latter dialogue it is even suggested that we are born "pregnant," and the long process of "intellectual gestation" which is propelled by our innate love for beauty and (ideally) culminates in philosophical enquiry allows us to bring the pregnancy to term (Burnyeat 1977; Sheffield 2001; Rawson 2006; Kahn 2006). The "embryonic" knowledge with which we are all born can be compared with the innate and latent knowledge or true beliefs which, on most interpretations of *anamnēsis*, underlie our learning. In the *Republic*, we encounter the idea that knowledge of the Forms will result from a sort of "intellectual vision" (Scolnicov 1988; Ferejohn 2006; Kahn 2006; Reeve 2012):

> Education (παιδεία) isn't what some people declare it to be, namely, putting knowledge into souls that lack it, like putting sight into blind eyes. [. . .] The power to learn is present in everyone's soul and the instrument with which each learns is like an eye that cannot be turned around from darkness to light without turning the whole body. This instrument cannot be turned around from that which is coming into being without turning the whole soul until it is able to study that which is [i.e. the Forms] and the brightest thing that is, namely, the one we call the [Form of the] Good. [. . .] Then education is the craft concerned with doing this very thing, this turning around, and with how the soul can most easily and effectively be made to do it.
> 
> —518b–d

I take the reference to those who think that *paideia* is "putting knowledge into souls that lack it, like putting sight into blind eyes" to be a reference to poets and sophists; consider, for example, Pindar's *Paean* 7b and the sophistic attitude to teaching which I have briefly introduced above. Just like the theory of *anamnēsis*, the model of intellectual vision rejects that conception of *paideia* (of which rote memorization is a component) in favor of one which places the innate resources of the learner at the center of the learning process (518d–e). There is no suggestion here that our capacity for intellection of the Forms stems from some pre-natal experience (although, as we have seen, later in book X the myth of Er introduces the doctrine of metempsychosis, and alludes to memory and forgetfulness in that context).[20] Nonetheless, when we consider how central the sight vocabulary was to the explanation of *anamnēsis*, we can appreciate that, if my recollection is of what my soul has "seen" before, learning itself could be described as seeing those things anew. Rather than as alternative models, recollection, intellectual pregnancy and intellectual vision should then be seen as different ways of conceptualizing what seems to be a by-and-large coherent set of ideas about human cognition, learning and the nature of education.

## PLATO ON MEMORY (*MNĒMĒ*) AND THE DANGERS OF WRITING

Although his "theory of recollection" focuses on cases in which what is recollected are not past objects or events in our (current) life, Plato's adoption of the vocabulary of *anamnēsis* is consistent with the ordinary Greek usage of the verb *anamimnēskō*. In the *Phaedo* Plato initially introduces *anamnēsis* by means of everyday illustrations. For example, upon seeing Simmias I can be led to recollect his dear friend Cebes, in the sense that seeing Simmias makes me think of Cebes; or upon seeing a portrait of Simmias I am reminded of Simmias himself (73c–d). Being reminded of X by something else, Y, which is somehow connected with X (by similarity or habitual association) is presented as the general structure of *anamnēsis*; however, the *Phaedo* clarifies that we speak of *anamnēsis* especially in those cases in which we had temporarily forgotten what we are now reminded of (73e). A similar distinction is drawn in the *Philebus*, although the emphasis there is on the fact that when it recollects our soul recalls (*analambanein*) or recovers (*anapolein*) *by itself*, as far as possible, some experience or knowledge it had (and possibly had lost/forgotten) (34b–c), without mentioning that our *anamnēsis* needs to be jogged by something or someone else.

Just as he did not disregard ordinary cases of *anamnēsis*, Plato was interested in ordinary forms of memory (*mnēmē*).[21] The *Philebus* offers what looks like the closest thing to a definition of memory in Plato's *corpus*: memory is "preservation of perception (Σωτηρίαν τοίνυν αἰσθήσεως τὴν μνήμην)" (34a). Although the idea that memory is a kind of retention of past experiences might appear hardly controversial, the focus on perception (*aisthēsis*) is surprisingly narrow, especially since *aisthēsis* here seems to be understood as *sense*-perception:[22] are our past sense-experiences all we can have memory of? The emphasis on sense-perception is confirmed by the analysis, later in the *Philebus*, of how memory contributes to our making judgements (*doxai*). Socrates asks his interlocutor Protarchus to imagine a situation in which someone sees something under a tree from a distance and, unsure, asks himself "what is that?" and then answers to himself "he's a man," or "it's a statue" (38c–d). Thinking and saying something silently within oneself is what making a judgment amounts to (38e).[23] Socrates explains that in such a situation our soul can be compared to a book (38e):

> If memory and perceptions concur with other impressions at a particular occasion, then they seem to me to write, as it were, reports in our souls (οἷον γράφειν ἡμῶν ἐν ταῖς ψυχαῖς τότε λόγους). And if what is written is true, then we form a true judgment and a true account of the matter. But if what our scribe writes is false, then the result will be the opposite of the truth. [. . .] [T]here is another craftsman at work in our soul at the same time [. . .]. A painter who follows the scribe and draws illustrations to his words in the soul (Ζωγράφον, ὃς μετὰ τὸν γραμματιστὴν τῶν λεγομένων εἰκόνας ἐν τῇ ψυχῇ τούτων γράφει).
>
> —39a–b

The reconstruction of the details of the psychological mechanism that Plato has in mind here is tantalizingly difficult and debated (King 2019). For our present purposes, it will suffice to say that the passage can be taken to suggest that memory contributes to the process of thinking and judgment-making by providing some kind of image or representation of what a human being, or a statue, look like; by comparing these mental images with his present sense-perception, the person will be able to ask themselves whether they are seeing a man or a statue, and finally to make a judgment about what they are really seeing, which is "written down" in his soul. This judgment in turn will be turned by the soul painter into some kind of mental representation or image, which presumably will not only accompany the current episode of perception (if he judged so, the person now sees the object *as a man*), but might in turn be preserved as a memory for future use.

While Plato adopted *anamnēsis* to account for the possibility of high-powered forms of cognition, *mnēmē* is here involved in mundane processes of perceptual discrimination and judgment. The example strongly suggests that our memories come from our past perceptual experiences in this life, rather than from some pre-natal access to intelligible truths: it is not the innate grasp of the essence of Human Being or Statue that makes the judgment possible, but the memory of what human beings and statues look like. This is confirmed by another enormously influential Platonic description of the workings of memory, in the *Theaetetus* (Bostock 1988; Burnyeat 1990; Sedley 2004). In the context of a discussion of knowledge (*epistēmē*), and its relation to true belief or judgment (*doxa*), Socrates and Theaetetus stumble upon several puzzles that call into question the very possibility of ever making false judgments (187b–191b). Interestingly, one of these puzzles is reminiscent of Meno's paradox: if I know X, I cannot make false judgments about X (for how could I be mistaken about something I know?); while if I do not know X, I cannot even start to think about it or formulate any judgment about it, let alone a false one. To attempt to explain how false judgments come about, Socrates introduces the role of memory:

> Now I want you to suppose, for the sake of the argument, that we have in our souls a block of wax (κήρινον ἐκμαγεῖον), larger in one person, smaller in another, and of purer wax in one case, dirtier in another; in some men rather hard, in others rather soft, while in some it is of the proper consistency. [. . .] We may look upon it, then, as a gift of Mnemosyne, the mother of the Muses. We make impressions upon this of everything we wish to remember among the things we have seen or heard or thought of ourselves; we hold the wax under our perceptions and thoughts and take a stamp from them, in the way in which we take the imprints of signet rings (ἀποτυποῦσθαι, ὥσπερ δακτυλίων σημεῖα ἐνσημαινομένους). Whatever is impressed upon the wax we remember and know (μνημονεύειν τε καὶ ἐπίστασθαι) so long as the image remains in the wax; whatever is obliterated or cannot be impressed, we forget and do not know.
> 
> —191c–e

The way we can make a false judgment about something we know is by "mis-matching" our memory imprints with our present sense-perceptions: for example, although Socrates remembers/knows both Theaetetus and Theodorus, he could misjudge that the man he is seeing from a distance, Theaetetus, is Theodorus, as the result of hastily mis-matching his memory of Theodorus with his fuzzy perception of Theaetetus, while failing to use the relevant piece of memory/knowledge of Theaetetus (192d–194c). The "wax block" model seems to provide an empiricist account of thought, memory, and knowledge in which our experiences determine what we remember, and what we remember is identified with what we know. Unlike in the *Philebus*, we can imprint/remember not only things we have seen or heard, but also things we have "thought of ourselves," but it is not clear what level of abstraction these "thoughts" could reach, and Socrates' example focuses on sensible particulars like Theaetetus and Theodorus. The model also describes a sort of physiology of memory: different kinds of wax will determine different individual learning and memory capacities and failures, and explain different tendencies to mis-seeing, mis-hearing, mis-thinking (194c–195a). When the wax is deep, abundant, smooth, and of the proper consistency, the imprints are clear, distinct, and long-lasting. Men with such souls, learn easily and remember easily, thus making consistently true judgments. In "ignorant" people the wax is shaggy, dirty, or impure, or too soft or too hard: these people are slow to match imprints and perceptions and often end up misjudging. Those with softer than normal wax will be quick to learn but also quick to forget, and their memory imprints will become easily blurred; those whose wax is too hard will be slow learners, who do not forget easily once they learn, but whose imprints have insufficient depth. Having impure or dirty wax, or too small of a block, will also lead to unclear and indistinct imprints which crowd upon one another.

A notable implication of this model of memory, is that memory/knowledge *comes in degrees* of clarity and precision, and the better our memory/knowledge of something is, the more accurate our judgments about it will be. This implication is sufficient to make us doubt Plato's endorsement of the wax block, given Plato's apparent commitment to the absolute reliability of knowledge elsewhere.[24] Moreover, this model seems to be at odds with the type of innatism underlying the "theory of recollection." No mention is made of the possibility that some imprints are already in our memory wax *since birth*; the imprinting process is described as a consequence of experiencing/learning things we did not know *before*. As we have seen, Socrates introduces the wax block as a for-the-sake-of-argument hypothesis to account for the possibility of false judgments, and not as something he is committed to. At the end of the passage, the model is discarded exactly because it is unable to explain some forms of false judgment in which the mis-matching of memory and perception is not involved, like the judgment that 7+5 is 11 (195d–196c).[25] Does this mean, however, that for Plato the model is a complete failure in explaining the workings of memory? One could accept that the model is too narrow, by focusing exclusively on a certain type of experiential memory, and misguided in identifying this type of memory with knowledge, but also allow that it offers a promising account of that particular type of memory and its role in perceptual judgments (Sedley 2004: 139). This would explain why the (presumably later) *Philebus* adopts without qualifications a similar account in which memory is understood as preservation of perception.

However that may be, we should not forget that Plato's enormously influential descriptions of memory in the *Philebus* and the *Theaetetus* are not original inventions, but philosophical appropriations of metaphorical ways of thinking and talking about memory deeply entrenched in the culture of his time.[26] It is well attested and widely recognized that the introduction of writing had a profound impact upon Greek conceptions of memory and memorial practices (Havelock 1963; 1982; Thomas 1992; Small 1997; Derderian 2001). With the transition from an oral culture dominated by memory to one in which writing and literacy became more and more important, early and classical Greek poets and thinkers often conceptualized writing as a sort of externalized memory, on the one hand, and memory itself as a kind of internal writing, on the other (Agócs 2019). To mention only one example here, in the tragedy *Prometheus Bound*, Prometheus exhorts Io to remember what he is about to say: "I shall tell you about the wanderings on which you will be driven: write them on the memorious tablets of your mind (ἥν ἐγγράφου σὺ μνήμοσιν δέλτοις φρενῶν)" (788–9), where the act of fixing something in one's memory is conceived as an internal inscription. The *deltoi* ("tablets") were thin boards with a hollow center filled with wax used for writing. As Agócs notices, when applied to the mind the wax "tablet-metaphor involves a transference: even as the tablets are an image of the remembering mind, they have a memory of their own—the 'memory' of the wax" (2019: 73–4).

But acknowledging the cultural context of Plato's adoption of the metaphors of the wax block and the book of the mind is only the beginning of the story. The adoption is a creative one, through which Plato wanted his audience to reflect on the epistemological shortcomings of these metaphors, or at least of the types of memory they illustrate. I have

FIGURE 5.5: Writing with a wax tablet. Red-figure cup from Cerveteri; Douris, *c*. 480 BCE; Berlin, Staatliche Museen F2285. Credit: Wikimedia Commons (Public Domain).

mentioned above how the rejection of the wax block model in the *Theaetetus* could be interpreted as part of this reflection. Once again, I want to suggest that we will miss something important if we fail to place Plato's descriptions of memory as a kind of internal inscription in the context of his polemics against rival models of learning, teaching and the acquisition of knowledge. In the final part of this section I will outline how, in the *Phaedrus*, Plato's analysis of the dangers of writing for memory (Derrida 1972; Ferrari 1987; Morgan 2000; Werner 2012; Capra 2014) can be interpreted as another subtle defence of the value of philosophical "recollective" inquiry.

After Socrates' "palinode" speech in praise of love (*erōs*), in which the myth of the soul as a winged charioteer and the function of philosophical *anamnēsis* are presented (see p. 89 above), Socrates and Phaedrus discuss what good rhetoric should look like, before turning to the question of how writing can be used either in an acceptable way or improperly (274b). In a way reminiscent of the *Meno*'s introduction of *anamnēsis*, Socrates says that he will report "what I've heard the ancients said, though they alone know the truth. However, if we could discover that ourselves, would we still care about the speculations of other people?" (274c). The story Socrates heard is that when the Egyptian god Theuth invented writing and presented it to the king of the gods, Thamus, they disagreed on the usefulness of the invention. According to Theuth writing "is something that, once learned, will make the Egyptians wiser and will improve their memory; [. . .] a potion for memory and for wisdom (μνήμης τε γὰρ καὶ σοφίας φάρμακον)" (274e). Thamus protested that actually writing

> will introduce forgetfulness (λήθην) into the soul of those who learn it: they will not practise using their memory because they will put their trust in writing, which is external and depends on signs that belong to others (διὰ πίστιν γραφῆς ἔξωθεν ὑπ' ἀλλοτρίων τύπων), instead of trying to recollect from the inside, on their own (οὐκ ἔνδοθεν αὐτοὺς ὑφ' αὑτῶν ἀναμιμνησκομένους). You have not discovered a potion for memory, but for reminding (οὔκουν μνήμης ἀλλὰ ὑπομνήσεως φάρμακον); you provide your students with the appearance of wisdom, not with its reality. Your invention will enable them to hear many things without being properly taught, and they will imagine that they have come to know much while for the most part they will know nothing.
> —275a–b

The first part of the passage could suggest that the danger identified by Thamus is that writing will ultimately damage our ability to memorize, retain, and recall information. We are all familiar with the ways in which having written information constantly at hand makes us less likely to remember that information ourselves, and in time can lead to some atrophy of our own mnemonic capacities; think for example of the meanings of foreign words listed in a dictionary, telephone numbers stored in our phone's memory, or historical or scientific data readily available on the internet. But this is not what Thamus, and Plato with him, is really worried about. The reference to *recollecting things by oneself from the inside* is reminiscent of the discussion of *anamnēsis* earlier in the dialogue; this is also confirmed by the second half of the passage, in which it becomes clear that the main problem with writing is that it encourages students to passively accept what the written text says, exposing them to ideas they don't really understand. Being reminded (*hypomnēsis*) of what other people have said about a certain subject is essentially different from recollecting, i.e. coming to understand and know, something by oneself, through one's own intellectual resources (*anamnēsis*). All a written text can prompt is *hypomnēsis*, but by doing so it will impair the "best" use of memory, *anamnēsis*. Access to written works generates in those who read them only an illusion of knowledge but is an obstacle to the process of actual learning.

The idea that a written text is a poor aid for learning is developed through the analogy with painted portraits, which at first sight could appear to be alive, but if asked something will remain silent. Similarly, the written text cannot engage with the readers' questions, or defend itself, but will keep repeating always the same, with the same voice, to all readers, irrespective of what they know and do not know (275d–e). These charges might appear to miss the point of how good writing can actually inspire independent thinking. But closer examination shows that the opposition here is not between writing and orality *tout court*, but between certain misguided ways of understanding the function and value of a written text, and certain correct ways of using language in the process of teaching and learning. Socrates explains that oral speeches which only aim at creating conviction without questioning or explanation, like the public displays of poets, sophists, and orators, are, after all, no better than their written counterparts (277e–278a). Earlier in the dialogue Phaedrus had offered to declaim by heart what he remembered of Lysias' speech about love; but since Phaedrus had a written copy of the speech with him, Socrates had encouraged him to read directly Lysias aloud (228d–e). Phaedrus' "orality," wholly dependent on his uncritical memorization of Lysias' text, would have been no better than the orality of poets or sophists. The problem with the new technology of writing, then, is that written texts are liable to be misunderstood by their readers as authoritative sources of knowledge, but in this way the introduction of writing only "upgrades" and reinforces the traditional oral, passive "memorizing" model of learning which Plato objects to. On the contrary, the philosopher who has knowledge of the Forms can aid his interlocutor's learning (presumably, his recollection from within) through the "living speech" of philosophical conversation: he does not sow the seed of his knowledge in written words, but "chooses a proper soul and plants and sows in it discourses with knowledge—discourses capable of helping themselves as well as the man who planted them, which are not barren but produce a seed from which more discourses grow in the character of others" (276e–277a). This is how philosophical discourse "is written down (γράφεται), with knowledge, in the soul of the learner " (276a).[27] Provided that we do not misinterpret the writing of philosophical *logoi* in the learner's soul as the transmission of knowledge, this description can be understood as a consistent account of the role that a philosophical teacher plays in prompting and aiding a process of *anamnēsis* in his student.

One final observation, circling back to the accounts of the *Theaetetus* and the *Philebus*: in light of what we have just seen about the unsuitability of writing to transmit knowledge, Plato's adoption of the writing metaphor for our memory of past sense-experiences could bear important, albeit implicit, connotations as to the insufficiency of that form of memory for our pursuit of knowledge (implicit connotations that we, the readers, are prompted to see by ourselves by engaging with Plato's *logoi* in the dialogues).

## CONCLUSION: AFTER PLATO

The British philosopher and mathematician Alfred North Whitehead once wrote that "the safest general characterization of the European philosophical tradition is that it consists of a series of footnotes to Plato" (1929). The question of whether different ancient philosophical traditions construed memory (and forgetfulness) in radically alternative ways is one I cannot pursue here.[28] But whatever we make of Whitehead's grand claim, there is no doubt that most of the later Greco-Roman philosophical reflection on memory is deeply indebted to the rich Platonic insights I have sketched in the previous two sections. We should not forget, however, that those insights were themselves the result of sustained critical engagement with the culture of Plato's time.

One of the questions that was at the center of the Greeks' speculation throughout, starting from its mythical manifestations, both before and after Plato, is whether memory itself should be identified with knowledge, or rather seen as a necessary but not sufficient condition for it. In his poem, which aims to offer a new description of *physis*, including a theology which debunks traditional conceptions of the gods, the philosopher Empedocles still invokes a πολυμνήστη, "much-remembering," Muse (DK 31B3). We have seen how Plato rejected the epistemological value of certain forms of memory, and especially of certain passive uses of memory, and how he identified the highest achievements of philosophical dialectic as a form of *anamnēsis* of eternal, intelligible and divine objects.

Several developments of the later Greek philosophical tradition can be seen as reactions to Plato's nuanced discourse on memory. Many, within the Platonic tradition, endorsed and systematized Plato's insights (Tarrant 2005; Helmig 2012).[29] Many others, from Aristotle onwards rejected the kind of innatism underlying Platonic *anamnēsis*, and re-focused on memory as a fully human experience, which we share with lower forms of life (including most animals), and on its role in the preservation of our past experiences within a broadly empiricist epistemology. But even these critics ended up adopting the same vocabulary and imagery for conceptualizing memory that Plato had explored, but either discarded or considered epistemologically inferior. For example, in the theory of memory he developed in the first chapter of *On Memory and Recollection* (Sorabji 1972 and 2006a; Bloch 2007; King 2009; Castagnoli 2019) Aristotle fused Plato's imagery of imprints on wax (*Theaetetus*) with Plato's language of memory pictures (*Philebus*):

> For it is clear that one must think of what is so generated by means of perception in the soul and in the part of the body which contains it as a sort of picture (οἷον ζωγράφημά τι), the having of which we say is memory; for the change that occurs marks in a sort of imprint (οἷον τύπον), as it were, of the percept, as people do who seal things with signet rings (καθάπερ οἱ σφραγιζόμενοι τοῖς δακτυλίοις).
>
> —*Mem.* 1, 450a27–32

Later on, to express their rejection of Platonic innatism the Stoics adopted the image of the human mind as a *tabula rasa*: "When a man is born, the Stoics say, he has the commanding-part of his soul as a sheet of papyrus ready for writing upon (χάρτην εὔεργον εἰς ἀπογραφήν). [. . .] The first method of inscription is through the senses. For by perceiving something, e.g. white, they have a memory of it when it has departed. And when many memories of a similar kind have occurred, we then say we have experience" (Aetius 4.11.1–4) (Ierodiakonou 2007). Strikingly, the empiricist process which from sense perception, through the accumulation and preservation of memories and the emergence of a unified "experience" (*empeiria*), finally leads to knowledge and scientific understanding,[30] had been sketched and rejected by Socrates in the *Phaedo*, in the same dialogue that placed *anamnēsis* of intelligibles at the center of Plato's epistemology:

> When I was a young man I was wonderfully keen on that wisdom which they call inquiry into nature [. . .] Do we think with our blood, or air, or fire, or none of these, and does the brain provide our sense of hearing and sight and smell, from which come memory and opinion, and from memory and opinion which has become stable, comes knowledge?
>
> —*Phaedo* 96a–b

The investigation into the physiology of memory, envisaged in this passage as an interest of the early natural philosophers, and the study of the phenomenology, pathologies, and therapeutics of memory were of course pursued in ancient Greek medicine, and are attested from the Hippocratic writings to late antiquity (Julião, Lo Presti, Perler and van der Eijk 2016; Baltussen: this volume). But ancient medicine also debated the role of memory in the construction of medical knowledge. A branch of medical empiricism, espoused by the so-called "memorist" (*mnemoneutikoi*) doctors, emphasized the cognitive and performative role of memory in medical theory and practice, in opposition to various forms of medical "rationalism" (Frede 1990). A skilled doctor's extensive and structured memory of past observations of symptoms and therapeutic effects, both personal (*autopsia*) and collected from others (*historia*), was considered by the "memorists" cognitively rich enough to guide his medical practice, and to amount to medical knowledge.

Although Plato was critical of certain uses of memory, "memory skepticism" as understood in modern philosophical discussions was not among his concerns, and was hardly an issue throughout the ancient Greek discussions of memory.[31] The ancient skeptics, however, not only targeted some of the theories of memory proposed by the "dogmatic" philosophers (Ierodiakonou 2007), but also, in the case of the Pyrrhonists, resorted to memory as a practical "standard" or "criterion" (*kritērion*) of action. A Pyrrhonian skeptic will be able to live his life in the absence of any knowledge, or indeed belief, about the world, by relying on his present perceptions and feelings and what they remind him of on the basis of his past experiences, namely by relying on "commemorative signs" (*hypomnēstika semēia*; see Sextus Empiricus *PH* 2.197–202). For example, his present feeling of hunger will remind the skeptic that, in the past, a similar feeling was satisfied by food; to act the skeptic will not need to discover the hidden essences or causes of things (such as the nature of food and its properties, or the physiological mechanism of hunger, or the workings of the processes of digestion and nutrition). For the Pyrrhonists memory has a fundamental survival function, like in animals; but it should not be taken to be a source of knowledge or an instrument for scientific and philosophical discovery.

There is another hot topic in modern discussions of memory that was surprisingly under-theorized in antiquity: the role of memory in securing the *personal* identity of individuals over time,[32] and in constructing their self-knowledge and self-understanding. We have seen how for Plato the capacity for *anamnēsis* was distinctive of our identity *as human beings*; but far from being essential to define who we are as individuals, our excessive attachment to our *personal* memories of our bodily experiences in this life is

**FIGURE 5.6:** Portrait of St. Augustine of Hippo. Cecco del Caravaggio, 1610–20; Veroli, Museo Del'Abbazio. Credit: De Agostini/Getty Images.

actually an obstacle to philosophical enquiry and *anamnēsis* (Capra 2014; on Plotinus Clark 2019). At the end of antiquity, Augustine, a Latin thinker deeply influenced by Greek culture, although mostly via its transformations in the Roman world of the late republic and empire, adopted epistemological and pedagogical models deeply rooted in the Platonic tradition of thinking about the powers of memory, and tailored them to the framework of his Christian theology (Hochschild 2012). In particular, at certain times he seemed to endorse a form of innatism strongly reminiscent of Plato's "theory of recollection," especially in *Confessions* X (Teske 2001; Castagnoli 2006), and the idea that real learning can only come from the "teacher within" (*On the Teacher*), and not from the reception and memorization of teachings from external secular sources (Burnyeat 1987). But he ultimately went well beyond that tradition, when he identified memory as the core of our *individual* selves: "Great is the power of memory. It is a true marvel, O my God, a profound and infinite multiplicity! And this is the mind, and this I myself am" (*Conf.* 10.17.26). He thus recognized memory as an essential source of self-understanding and self-transformation, while using a work of memory, the *Confessions*, to re-construct and make sense of his own spiritual journey, and to inspire his audience to undertake a similar journey. From this point of view, we could say that with his philosophy of memory Augustine was at the same time the last of the Greco-Roman ancients and the first of the moderns.

# CHAPTER SIX

# High Culture and Popular Culture*

ANNE GANGLOFF

## INTRODUCTION: CONCEPTS, SOURCES, AND APPROACHES

In Hesiod's *Theogony* (*Th.* 53–79), the union of Mnemosyne and Zeus gave birth to the nine Muses that preside over the development of human thought in all its forms: eloquence, persuasion, wisdom, history, mathematics, and astronomy (Figure 6.1).

This myth reminds us that memory is at the heart of every culture, because it is both its foundation and its means of transmission. Thus, to understand a culture one must examine the function and place of memory in this given culture. It allows us to address a delicate point: the division, within any hierarchical society, between High Culture(s) and Popular Culture(s). Can one argue that the former refers to a social elite that controls the access to knowledge and memory and thereby imposes its cultural norms? And that the latter either builds on the reception of these norms, more or less clumsily imitated (because of a lack of resources), transformed, or through the will of the dominated group (or groups) to distinguish itself and defend its specificity? This proposed distinction between High Culture and Popular Culture, which dates from the 1960s, was severely criticized in the decade that followed. Pierre Bourdieu, in *La distinction* published in 1979, formalized a theory of cultural legitimacy that relegated popular culture to those unable to access a higher volume of cultural capital because they lacked the necessary means to do so (Bourdieu 2010). He, therefore, denounced the building and the highlighting of a High Culture, which introduced a cultural gap between the social elite and the others. In the 1970s, interest in the topic shifted to cultural exchanges, agency and different modes of appropriation. However, since the 2000s, there has been a renewed interest among historians of different periods in the study of so-called "popular" cultural practices:[1] my chapter on the place and role of memory in elite and non-elite cultures should be viewed in this context. I purposefully use more neutral—although none easier to define—expressions, elite and non-elite cultures, to avoid the terms high culture and popular culture, which nowadays often have a negative connotation.

I wish to raise two main questions: firstly, can we identify in the Greek and Roman worlds types of memory that were the building blocks of elite identity and, in contrast, other forms of memory that pertained to the non-elite, characterizing them and defining them as coherent social groups? Secondly, what were the functions and place of memory in ancient elite and non-elite cultures? Before addressing these points, we need to clarify

**FIGURE 6.1:** Homer and the nine Muses; Mosaic, Vichten, second century CE. The Muses appear in the same order as in Hesiod, *Theogony* 53–79. Credit: The Picture Art Collection/Alamy Stock Photo.

our use of core terms and the parameters of their relationship, namely "culture," "elite," and "memory," and underline the difficulties encountered by the historian in their exploration.

### *Memory and culture*

As we intend to study collective cultures, we must consider a culture as both the product of interactions within a group and between different groups from different cultures, as well as a social legacy, i.e. "everything a society or group transmits, including outside an educational system" (Inglebert 2005: 5). A culture refers to a set of various forms of knowledge, practices, objects that make up a familiar environment of social representations that are used to define a human group (whether it is a particular community or a social layer) as a coherent system. Every culture is thus engendered by a collective memory and confers an identity.

### *Elite and non-elite in antiquity: culture divided?*

Can we actually closely link the differences in the control of knowledge and in the creation of memory with a divide between elite and non-elite ancient culture, and can we, moreover, presuppose that the intellectual and the social elite were to a much greater extent the same entities in antiquity than in current developed societies, because access to education was strictly limited to a social elite? What were the specific premises that defined elite and non-elite culture in the ancient world? Greek and Roman societies were characterized by several overlapping legal subdivisions (men/women/children, free/non-free, citizens/non-citizens, aristocrats/people), which must be taken into account in any definition of the elite and the non-elite, and which changed in different periods and places. The economic factor, which looms so large in the stratification and interpretation of modern societies, should not be overlooked: it is included de facto in some of the legal subdivisions, but it also goes beyond them, because, as we shall see, wealthy non-citizens could evolve in a similar cultural environment to that of citizens who possessed the same level of fortune.

For Rome, one can use a common division found in ancient literature, namely between *plebs* and aristocracy:[2] the elite was made of members of the senatorial and equestrian orders, which constituted the aristocracy, while the non-elite included the *plebs* as well as slaves and non-citizens. This division is especially useful from a heuristic point of view: recent research by Cyril Courrier presented in *La plèbe de Rome et sa culture (fin du IIe s. av. J.-C.-fin du Ier s. ap. J.-C.)* led its author to study the "*plebs* media," an expression that singles out the upper layer of the *plebs*, wealthy and quite literate, likely to imitate, by the end of the republican era, aristocratic cultural norms (Veyne 2005; Courrier 2014: 356–409).

A peculiarity of the Greek world is the existence of terms that identify a cultural elite, but cannot strictly distinguish this from the social elite: in the classical period these are the *kaloi kagathoi* ("Good and upstanding," an expression the meaning of which is still debated), and during the early Roman empire the *pepaideumenoi*, "cultured people," who appear to be linked to the evolution of the so-called Second Sophistic, a period during which the memory of the past was of considerable importance.[3] The *pepaideumenoi* were first and foremost culture specialists (sophists, philosophers, orators, etc.), but also prominent local citizens and aristocrats, both men and women, who played leading roles in their cities and documented their adherence to the values of *paideia* in inscriptions and visual culture (Borg 2004). This phenomenon should be seen in the context of the promotion of Greek culture under the Antonines and the opening of the Senate to eastern elites, which began under the Flavians, especially from Trajan onwards.

It becomes clear that the concepts and terms at stake were for the most part specific, complex, and evolving. The attribution of "memory" to these is even more intricate, not least because there are different forms of memory and memorization.

## *Memory divided?*

Memory is a concept anchored in time, and in this perspective the distinction made by the Egyptologist Jan Assmann between communicative memory and cultural memory is fundamental, because it highlights the variety of functions and operating modes of memory, depending on a given time frame (Assmann 1992). Building on the research by art historian Aby Warburg on social memory, Assmann draws a distinction between two forms of memory:

(a) "communicative memory," which cannot exceed three generations. It encompasses what the Romans meant by *nostra memoria* or *memoria hominum*, referring to everything that could be remembered in human memory. The figure of three generations seems to be invariable; Rosalind Thomas, who has studied aristocratic genealogies in Athens in the classical period, also observes the appearance of major distortions and transformations of facts beyond the third generation;[4]

(b) "cultural memory," based on cultural codifications that imbue objects with meaning, and on institutionalized mnemonics, to overcome the lack of natural memory, e.g. Athenian aristocratic genealogies.

The first form, which is a social relational memory, helps men live well together, while the second cements the group in the long term. Since it requires the use of special mnemonics, it may be more difficult to access by the non-elite, depending on the type of mnemonics. It is arguable that communicative memory was more easily shared between the elite and non-elite in societies that did not rely on closed caste systems: for example, in Rome there were communication memory specialists who were non-citizens, the *nomenclatores*, whose duty it was to provide for their masters the names of the people these encountered. Nomenclators, however, were not admired for their exceptional memory (Baroin 2010: 157–66); although obviously useful, it was not this type of memory that was most valued. In Rome, as in Greece, it was, in line with Assmann's definition, "cultural memory" that took precedence. Even so, lacking communicative memory put you at risk of being out of step with basic social etiquette: Tacitus (*Ann.* 11.15) and Suetonius (*Claud.* 39–42) describe the emperor Claudius as a scholar, a specialist of the Etruscans, but incapable of mastering communicative memory; for example, he would ask for people he had just sentenced to death, for which he was despised by his entourage (Baroin 2010: 147–8).

Regarding memorization there are further variations within the cultural transmission. The anthropologist Paul Connerton has identified a form of bodily memory, based on habit (Connerton 1989). Postulating that social memory is essentially based on commemorative practices, Connerton argues that participants in commemorative ceremonies were necessarily *used* to them: the relevant information was somehow *silted* in their bodies. He advocates the study of these incorporation practices and sees ritual performances as a privileged vehicle for the transmission of the past. Thus, in the field of religious culture, an approach that emphasizes habitual memory allows us to associate elite and non-elite cultures through the study of collective rites. But one must be aware that not all ritual participants shared the same degree of participation: the priests possessed knowledge that made them the guarantors of the validity of the rites, whereas, in contrast, some spectators (who were not part of the elite) participated in the ceremony only emotionally.

The historian of religions Philippe Borgeaud developed an anthropological approach comparable to that proposed by Connerton on memory and tradition in ancient religious cultures, emphasizing the role played by mechanical memorization: "It is by practice and imitation, by the mechanical repetition of gestures and words transmitted within the framework of a tradition maintained by a social group to which he feels he belongs, that an individual memorizes, without even realizing it, most of the required information to behave in a proper social and religious way. Understood in this sense, memorization leads to the acquisition of innumerable models of action, behavior, thought and sensitivity that define a social and cultural identity" (Borgeaud 1988: 10; Rudhardt 1988). In contrast to this notion of mechanical memorization for all, elite and non-elite, Borgeaud proposes a "deliberate memorization" by certain individuals in the specific contexts of initiatory rituals or educational institutions. This was the case, for example, with the Vestals in Rome, who for ten years learned their priesthood from their elders, before practicing for ten years, then teaching in turn the youngest during the last ten years of their service (Prescendi 2010).

We can generalize this opposition between, on the one hand, a habitual memory and, on the other hand, a deliberate memory which played a special role in the transmission of elite culture. I have chosen two examples to illustrate this type of memory. The first is that of the trained memory of Latin orators, who mastered a famous memorization technique based on the association between a place and an argument in a mental scheme. It helped to transmit a very selective culture, which was the highest degree of elite culture at the end of the republic (Yates 1966; Coleman 1992; Baroin 2007: 153–5; Baroin 2010: 202–30). The second example is that of an institutionalized memory, i.e. framed and transmitted by an institution, such as the Athenian *ephebeia*. In the imperial era, it had become an aristocratic institution that bore the memory of the glorious Athenian military past, which it revived especially during the *ephebeia* competitions (Newby 2005: 187–91, 200).

The "exploitation" of the described "deliberate" and "cultural" memories would tend to apply to a greater extent to elite culture, but there are many notable counter-examples: the already mentioned Roman *nomenclatores* who had a trained memory, the pedagogues and Greek logographers, professional actors; what of the cultural traditions related to the secession of the plebs, attached to the cult of Anna Perenna, who supposedly had fed the plebs during the first secession of 494 BCE, or the consensual "place of memory" that the Aventine had become in the Augustan age?[5] One must also distinguish a plethora of memories according to memorization media: there is oral memory, written memory, visual memory (nourished by monuments, statues, paintings, coinage etc.), and auditory memory, which Nicholas Horsfall has discussed in his study of the culture of the Roman plebs (Horsfall 2003: 11–19 on songs, 31–47 on musical culture). The impact of orality and writing is discussed by Han Baltussen in this volume, but it is clear that it plays a very important role in the definition of memory types and cultural legacies. The question of how far non-elites had access to reading and writing is, of course, decisive to understanding the extent of their culture.

The distinction between these various types of memory raises two further questions: that of the nature of the evidence and that of our own access to the memory and culture of the non-elite.

## *Historiographical problems, sources, and approaches*

How do modern scholars access the different forms of memory, especially of the ancient non-elite? This access is partial and limited: it is no coincidence that, for the Roman world, which has given rise to much research on memory in the context of cultural studies, academic work has focussed on societal groups that were certainly not the most disadvantaged and for whom we have more traces, the urban plebs and affluent freedmen, but not the rural plebs or slaves. It seems therefore logical to think that when it comes to the memory and culture of the non-elite we primarily explore what was *seen*, material and visual culture, and more specifically things that did not immediately raise the question of literacy. But the issue is more complex: Roman monuments, for example, were in many respects "a product" of the elite. One might think that they reflected and created a shared culture and memory.[6] However, an architect who designed a monument, as Vitruvius writes at the beginning of his treatise *De architectura* (*On Architecture* 1.1.1–4), published around 24 BCE and dedicated to Augustus, had to have a considerable culture, built on the practice and mastery of vast bodies of knowledge—literature, drawing, geometry, optics, arithmetic, history, philosophy, music, jurisprudence, astronomy—which each called upon written memory. Vitruvius himself, who was a Roman citizen, may have belonged to the literate *plebs media* mentioned earlier: already having served Caesar he built war machines for Augustus and was in charge of the construction of public buildings and water works in Rome (Vitr., *On Architecture*, Praef. 1–3; 8.6.2; Front., *On Aqueducts* 25.1–2; Fleury 2011).

Let us take the example of *history*, developed by Vitruvius (1.1.5–6), in the context of a monument's iconographic programme:

> Architects ought to be familiar with history because in their works they often design many ornaments about which they ought to render an account to inquirers. For example, if anyone in his work sets up, instead of columns, marble statues of long-robed women which are called caryatids, and places mutules and cornices above them, he will thus render an account to inquirers. Carya, a Peloponnesian state, conspired with the Persian enemy against Greece. Afterwards the Greeks, gloriously freed from war by their victory, with common purpose went on to declare war on the inhabitants of Carya. The town was captured; the men were killed; the state was humiliated. Their matrons were led away into slavery and were not allowed to lay aside their draperies and ornaments. In this way, and not at one time alone, were they led in triumph. Their slavery was an eternal warning. Insult crushed them. They seemed to pay a penalty for their fellow-citizens. And so the architects of that time designed for public buildings figures of matrons placed to carry burdens; in order that the punishment of the sin of the Caryan women might be known to posterity and historically recorded. Not less the Spartans under the command of Pausanias, son of Agesilas, having conquered with a small force an infinitely large army of Persians, gloriously celebrated a triumph with spoils and plunder, and, from the booty, built the Persian Colonnade to signify the merit and courage of the citizens and to be a trophy of victory to their descendants. There they placed statues of their captives in barbaric dress—punishing their pride with deserved insults—to support the roof that their enemies might quake, fearing the workings of such bravery, and their fellow-citizens looking upon a pattern of manhood might by such glory be roused and prepared for the defense of freedom. Therefrom many have set up Persian statues to support architraves and their ornaments. This motive has supplied for their works some striking variations. There are also other narratives of the same kind with which architects should possess acquaintance.
> 
> —Loeb tr. F. Granger[7]

Paul Zanker suggests that this text offers an explanation for the use of caryatids in the Roman Forum, to represent the peoples that submitted to Rome (Zanker 1988: 13). Zanker is an excellent connoisseur of Vitruvius, but who among the contemporary Romans frequenting the Forum had read the architect's treatise?[8] Which spectators could identify the references to the Persian wars, and more precisely to the punishment of the inhabitants of Carya and Sparta's Persian portico (known in antiquity, as is evident from a reference in Pausanias 3.11.3)? It is obvious that the monuments on Augustus' Forum were a shared memory and culture for different audiences, via channels of communication that operated at different levels.

In addition to material culture, the other main approach to the memory and culture of the non-elite has been via literary texts that recorded the reactions of the public to performances, popular songs and public entertainment: this theme has mainly been explored by N. Horsfall in the context of Roman culture. One can also examine the allusions made in public speeches to try to define a shared culture in the targeted audience, or, as S. Forsdyke has done for classical Greece and T.P. Wiseman for Rome, look for the clues of a political culture of the people. Wiseman has analyzed references to past performances to glimpse a common memory that preceded the creation of historiography as a literary discipline. Similar to the Vitruvius example and in analogy to the realm of material culture, such promising research requires great caution because it undertakes to reconstruct sections of "popular" culture through the filter of literary culture (Horsfall 2003; Wiseman 1995; 2008; 2009; 2014; Forsdyke 2012).

Another challenge lies in the imbalance of modern works on memory, which do not approach the Roman and Greek worlds in the same way. For the Greek world, useful syntheses focus on orality and literacy or archiving, rather than on non-elite culture, with the exception of S. Forsdyke's research and works on Aesopian literature or Aristophanes' theater. We miss the equivalent of Catherine Baroin's anthropological study *Se souvenir à Rome*. Michèle Simondon's seminal study *La mémoire et l'oubli dans la pensée grecque* is in fact rooted in the history of ideas and ends with the classical period.[9] The symbolic value of memory was different in the Greek and Roman worlds: whilst the former honored it as a goddess, *Mnemosunè*, this does not seem to have been the case in the latter (Barouin 2010: 41–9). The Greek world may have been, in general, closer to its archaic past because it placed myths and heroes on a pedestal, whereas Rome favored the *exempla* of its aristocratic ancestors. This is demonstrated in Greek and Latin oratory, which—given the importance of oral communication—played an important role in cultural transmission, not only to an elite audience but also to a large number of listeners of any social status. Greek oratory was more conservative, more focused on the past than Latin oratory (which was also more recent). The latter honored writers from the imperial period, such as Virgil and Titus Livius, while the former transmitted a corpus and examples which, for the most part, ended in the Hellenistic period (Pernot 2005: 102–3).

With regard to scholarship on Late Antiquity, this is marked by a vast debate launched in 1960 by Santo Mazzarino on the concept of a "democratization of culture." While we assume that, similar to the situation in the early empire, a form of "limited" literacy, sufficient for basic written communication, continued to be widespread, we see dramatic change in the emergence of new cultural actors, such as women, who were active in the transmission of Christianity, and also the will of the Christian elite to address all and educate the masses even on very complex debates, appropriating vectors that were traditionally popular, such as songs. St. Augustine, for example, composed a non-metrical abecedarian psalm against the Donatists, for "the humblest of people, the ignorant and the illiterate" (*ad ipsius humillimi vulgi and omnino imperitorum atque idiotarum notitiam pervenire*) to "engrave" the debate "in their memory" (*inhaerere memoriae*), responding in kind to other songs by his opponent Cresconius (*Retractationes*, I, 29) (Carrié 2001).[10]

It has become clear that the caveats relating to fundamental concepts and sources are manifold when we bring the study of memory to that of elite and non-elite cultures. Bearing these challenges in mind, it is nonetheless fascinating to ask about memories or memory uses specific to as well as shared by elite and non-elite cultures in the Greek and Roman worlds.

# MEMORIES SPECIFIC?

## *Non-elite culture*

There is an ongoing debate between art historians and historians of the Roman world regarding the existence or non-existence of one or more coherent culture(s) specific to certain non-elite groups. Recent research in art history has indeed opened the way to the non-elite. In his 2003 work, *Art in the Lives of Ordinary Romans*, John R. Clarke wonders about the reception of famous monuments by Rome's non-elite and explores how this group used art in public (cults, performances, at work) and private spheres. He observes that those who commissioned artworks desired to either imitate the elite, or, as in the wall-paintings of the Baths of the Seven Sages in Ostia (about 100 CE), where the greatest Greek sages defecate and give advice on this in iambic senaries (Figures 6.2 and 3), to mock intellectual culture, or to represent realistic scenes.

Clarke comes to the conclusion that it is impossible to understand non-elite art as an expression of a particular social group: we cannot speak of a folk, plebeian or freedman art, but only of an art in the service of ordinary people, who could choose or reject standardized images for their homes, shops, or graves, according to what they wanted to show about themselves. A similar approach is followed by Clarke's student Lauren H. Petersen, who has studied the artistic culture of freedmen, trying to keep texts written by the elite at arm's length, especially the *Satyricon*, in order to avoid *a priori* assumptions originating in the all too famous literary representation of the freedman Trimalchio. In conclusion, she prefers the idea of assimilation to that of imitation and advises not to distinguish artistic production commissioned by freedmen from that initiated by free men and citizens of equal wealth (Clarke 2003: 273; Petersen 2006).

**FIGURE 6.2:** Solon; Ostia, Baths of the Seven Sages (III,X,2). Inscription: *ut bene cacaret, uentrem palpauit Solon* ("In order to poop well, Solon massaged his belly"). Credit: © Evelyne Prioux.

**FIGURE 6.3:** Thales; Ostia, Baths of the Seven Sages (III,X,2). Inscription: *durum cacantes monuit ut nitant* [sic] *Thales* ("To the constipated, Thales recommended that they push"). Credit: © Evelyne Prioux.

In contrast to such approaches, Lucy Grig and C. Courrier postulate that the culture of the non-elite is not depoliticized, and that each social group tends to defend its own cultural specificity (Courrier 2014: 547-600; Grig 2017b: 32). The political culture of the non-elite is found, in particular, in ancient descriptions of the reactions of the *plebs* to certain monuments, events or festivals (Courrier 2014: 547–600). Unfortunately, it is yet again (and still too rare) the literary sources that offer the most developed testimonials when it comes to the question of how various social actors received and reacted to events, monuments, performances etc. which they witnessed or in which they participated. The traditions of the non-elite are then reported through the lens of the elite, a circumstance that brings me back to the problematic "biased" access to the memories and cultures of the non-elite, and it looks as if, ultimately, these can only be reconstructed in a hybrid form, in the form of shared memories. As S. Forsdyke has pointed out, many scholars, representing a range of social science disciplines that study the concept of "popular culture," see this hybrid dimension as inherent to the making of a "popular culture," which evolves from interconnections between non-elite traditions and elements derived from the symbolic codification operated by the elite.[11]

The debate about the culture of the non-elite in the Roman world is therefore based on the use of different kinds of sources and on a different understanding of the notion of culture: on the one hand the focus is on political culture and on the other hand on the postulate that culture is the expression of one's individual freedom to choose what one wishes to reveal about oneself. Anyway, these two different forms of culture (and, to a greater extent, this is probably true of every form of the non-elite culture to which we have access) are shared—or hybrid—cultures: they are based on shared "communicative memory," and create shared "cultural memories."

## Elite culture

It is easier to pinpoint the types and uses of memory specific to elite culture, from the perspective of social distinction. I have selected three representative examples, the first of which brings us back to the emblematic character of Trimalchio.

(A) In ancient societies, writing and literary culture was par excellence a form of selective culture. Homer, at least from the sixth century BCE onwards, was the "founder" of this literary culture. At school, children read the *Iliad* and the *Odyssey*, learning long passages by heart, then developed rhetorical and philosophical analyses of these poems. The aristocratic content of the epics also reinforced their use in terms of social distinction. By the end of the fifth century BCE, Niceratus, the son of the famous Athenian *strategos* Nicias, an aristocrat and representative of the *kaloi kagathoi*, boasted he knew by heart the *Iliad* and the *Odyssey* and could draw from them all the knowledge he needed (Xenophon, *Banquet* 4.6–7). The developing canon of Greek literature and cultural philhellenism showed a remarkable continuity during the Hellenistic period and the early empire. It is therefore not surprising that the lack of knowledge of Homeric culture was considered, in the early empire, to be a blatant proof of a lack of culture which was supposedly typical of wealthy freedmen. Two characters were stigmatized in that way and have often been compared: Petronius' Trimalchio and Seneca's Calvisius Sabinus evoked in his correspondence with Lucilius (*Letters to Lucilius* 27.5–6). However, interpretation and identification of both the historical and the fictional individual are far from easy, especially in the context of an early imperial world when categories of social and political standing were changing dramatically—traditional elites finding themselves side-lined and deprived of status in light of an imperial household and its political infrastructure. These caricatured characters raise issues of identification, or rather of categorization: we wonder if Petronius created his protagonist, the freedman Trimalchio, as representing non-elite culture or, rather, as a representative of a new type of elite that partly imitated and partly despised traditional markers of elite culture. And we wonder, interestingly, if the historical Calvisius Sabinus was a freedman (or the son of a freedman), or a "degenerate" member of the aristocratic Calvisii Sabini family, behaving in a way that the traditional elite expected from a freedman? Here is how Seneca describes him:

> He had the bank-account and the brains of a freedman. I never saw a man whose good fortune was a greater offense against propriety (*indecentius*). His memory was so faulty that he would sometimes forget the name of Odysseus, Achilles, or Priam— names which we know as well as we know those of our own attendants. No majordomo in his dotage, who cannot give men their right names, but is compelled to invent names for them—no such man, I say, calls off the names of his master's tribesmen so atrociously as Sabinus used to call off the Trojan and Achaean heroes. But nonetheless did he desire to appear learned (*eruditus*). So, he devised this shortcut to learning; he paid fabulous prices for slaves—one to know Homer by heart and another to know Hesiod; he also delegated a special slave to each of the nine lyric poets. You need not wonder that he paid high prices for these slaves; if he did not find them ready to hand

he had them made to order. After collecting this retinue, he began to make life miserable for his guests; he would keep these fellows at the foot of his couch, and ask them from time to time for verses which he might repeat, and then frequently break down in the middle of a word.

—Loeb tr. R.M. Gummere

Whatever his "real" social background, Calvisius Sabinus is described as a typical freedman who never received schooling and the kind of rhetorical teaching that trained memory and considered it as an integral part of rhetorics (*Rhet. Her* 1.3; Quintilian, 3.3.1–10). He also disregarded the sociocultural codes that went hand in hand with such privileged education: he had no sense of propriety (*decus*), which was perceived as embarrassing by his guests (Baroin 2010: 164).

The similarities with the literary construct Trimalchio are striking but here, also, we wonder about interpretation. During his banquet he entertains his hosts with specialist Homeric actors, called *Homeristai* (*Satyricon* 59). At the end of the show, the actor playing Ajax, armed with his sword, throws himself onto the meat, chops it up and serves it to the guests (Jones 1991). Such Homeric actors can be likened to mimes and pantomimes, very popular in the imperial era, which were vectors of Greek myths and much appreciated by a wide audience, including the elite at least from the second century CE.[12] But, when Trimalchio launches into the explanation of the show after having read the Latin libretto, he also confuses the names, the families, the mythical episodes: beyond overt exaggeration and burlesque, he is presented as incapable of mastering literary culture. The author may well question how much this literary culture still mattered, to a Trimalchio, who is very much in control at his *cena*, or to a Roman emperor, who was seen to advance and link to himself, financially and socially, freedmen left and right. However, the fact that Petronius and Seneca found resonance in their vivid description of the two characters are indicative of the continuing socio-cultural prejudices of a traditional Roman elite at the beginning of the early empire—a world in which literary culture and the memory of this culture were still perceived as a distinction reserved for an elite.

(B) During the Roman republic, the ruling elite acquired authority from personal experience and, in the words of Claudia Moatti, the mastery of "power knowledge": military knowledge, legal knowledge and eloquence. This is an important difference with the Greek world where knowledge did not automatically entail social status and where aristocrats were educated by teachers who often had a servile origin, and they could use the service of logographers who were not part of the civic elite. The most famous example is the well-known orator Lysias, a wealthy Athenian metic who almost lost his life during the oligarchic revolution of 404 BCE because of his social status, despite his commitment to Athenian civic life. In Rome, certain senators who were magistrates, priests, legal specialists, and orators distinguished themselves by an extraordinary memory which conferred on them an exceptional degree of *auctoritas* and *dignitas*. But here, too, comparable to the challenges of interpreting a character such as Trimalchio to which I pointed above, we cannot be sure that power, knowledge and memory continued to be inseparably linked in the early empire. C. Moatti has drawn attention to the cultural transformations that appeared in the late-republican era, from the second century BCE: "power knowledge" turned into independent scientific disciplines, exercised independently from the *cursus honorum* or in the entourage of a powerful patron.

This phenomenon accompanied the described loss of power of the members of the senatorial aristocracy and the emergence of personal power with Caesar and Augustus.

On a number of levels and for a range of reasons we move from the model of an autonomous senator to that of a *princeps* surrounded by experts, and "memory" is at the heart of this complex change.[13] Varro, who came from a family of equestrian rank and who withdrew from political life after the death of Caesar, is a good illustration: he wrote a short guide on how to preside over the Senate for Pompey, consul in 70, and a book on Roman religion and cult administration for Caesar (Aulus Gellius, *Attic Nights* 14.7; Lactantius, *Divine Institutions* 1.67); Caesar also commissioned him to establish the first public libraries in Rome in order to make great authors accessible. We thus see an expert entrusted with the transmission and dissemination of scholarly and technical knowledge. The same author composed, around 36 BCE, three books entitled *On Agriculture* for his wife Fundania, who had just bought land she wished to cultivate (*De agricultura* 1.1). Technical treatises of this kind played an important role in the creation of shared memories and cultures: Jean-Michel Carrié has pointed out that the numerous technical treatises of the late empire, less literary than in previous eras, reveal a need to communicate with a wider audience (Horsfall 2003: 68–9; Carrié 2001: 36–8).

(C) Another distinguishing feature reserved to the Roman aristocracy was the right to display images of their ancestors (*ius imaginum*; Figure 6.4).

This privilege was manifest most vividly at public funerals, granted to few illustrious men only. Such a funeral was described by Polybius at the end of the first half of the second century BCE (Polyb. 6.52.11–54.3): the deceased was carried into the Forum and into the assembled crowd. Then his son or another relative gave a eulogy praising the virtues and achievements of the deceased, also recalling the great deeds of his ancestors, whose images were present. As this ceremony was public, its main interest, according to Polybius, was political. The entire setting evoked a shared Roman civic and patriotic memory, while also disseminating an agonistic spirit among the audience who would be inspired to imitate the courage and sacrifice for public welfare exemplified by the deceased and his ancestors. This, in the eyes of the Greek historian, contributed to and explained Rome's exceptional success.[14]

Each of my three examples illustrates cultural practices and values used by the social elite to distinguish itself. Each, however, also shows that the very same practices have a tendency to be disseminated or are transformed in a way that create more or less shared memories.

## MEMORIES SHARED

Let us finally turn towards the notion of shared culture and memories. In fact, this may be just the right key to studying "non-elite culture." Restricting the definition of "popular culture" as has been suggested, to the idea of an "unauthorized" culture is unwarranted (Canevaro 2017b; *contra* Parker 2011). We lack the evidence that would allow us to pinpoint and contrast elite and non-elite tastes in antiquity, and even their respective cultural norms do not seem so distinct, as N. Horsfall has demonstrated. For instance, in the field of humor, while Cicero considered the humor of mimes and buffoons to be the antithesis of the orator's intellectual humor, Horace and his friends (including Maecenas and Virgil) embraced it openly. Similarly, in the field of music, it is not always possible to distinguish between "popular culture" and Roman culture at large.[15]

In societies as vast and heterogeneous as were the Greek and Roman worlds, non-elite culture could take many forms, such as a "local" culture, or, from the perspective of *Hellenism* and *Romanitas*, an accessible culture that offered the possibility to create a

**FIGURE 6.4:** *Togatus* Barberini, late first century BCE; Roman senator holding the portraits of deceased ancestors(?); Musei Capitolini, Rome. Credit: Leemage/Corbis via Getty Images.

shared identity and social cohesion. One might think of Plato's famous condemnation of the myths told by mothers and nurses to children: according to the philosopher, the traditional stories spread false and immoral ideas about the gods, ideas that were all the more dangerous because they were introduced to an impressionable and uninformed public. It is clear from this example that it applied to both elite and non-elite children. Although Plato condemned this type of pre-school learning, which he wanted to reform, he was aware that his contemporaries had been almost indelibly marked by shared culture from their earliest childhood (Plato, *Rep.* 2.377c–392a; *Laws*, 10.887d). The main elements that nourished these shared memories were songs, hymns, and public rituals, theater and performances, proverbs, fables, myths and tales—which were told, outside the family circle, by professionals such as the *circulators* (Horsfall 2003: 57 and 98; Courrier 2014: 578), traveling artists who sang, read or recited for small circles of listeners—technical treatises, graffiti, simple inscriptions and, to a certain extent, the visual environment as well as the speeches made by orators in front of a crowd (Horsfall 2003; Courrier 2014: 576–600; Grig 2017b: 21–36).

Similar to what I said earlier about Vitruvius and the shared reception of monumental iconography via differing levels of perception, some very successful orators were able to develop forms of multi-level communication to address a culturally heterogeneous audience. This was probably the case with the sophist Dion of Prusa (c. 40–c. 113 CE), who gave his speeches to enthusiastic crowds. Even though his vocabulary was classical and most people used *koine*, they understood classical Greek and saw it as the backbone of Hellenism. While the pronunciation was no impediment, the complex syntax was, but the speaker reinforced his ideas through repetition and by varying his examples. People in the audience who were not *pepaideumenoi* were therefore able to appreciate the speaker's flights of oratory and the theatricality of his eloquence. Two qualities of his style were recognized in antiquity, "clarity" (ἐνάργεια) and "simplicity" (ἀφέλεια), obtained through his frequent use of images and mythical stories. He favored the use of Homeric myths as a medium of communication, thus selecting known references, and in addition often taking care to explain his allusions and references; yet, his works include many allusions that were accessible to the *pepaideumenoi* in a more complex way because they knew the original context, which activated an additional function of the selected example and allowed a *happy few* to further appreciate an image or some irony, inaccessible to the wider public, who did not lose, however, the overall meaning of the speech.[16]

## BY WAY OF CONCLUSION: A COMMON WILL TO "REMEMBER"

Many challenges to any straight-forward interpretation have emerged in my brief discussion of memory in relation to elite and non-elite culture. What has also become clear, I hope, is that the notion of memories, and in particular of "shared memories" helps us to understand why the study of elite and non-elite cultures in antiquity is so difficult. Whichever research perspective is chosen, the notion of memory can provide a key to enter the debate. Here, it is essential to pay careful attention to the various forms of memory and memorization that existed, in order to analyze our evidence adequately and grasp, if this is the case, the genesis of any group culture.

Finally, one ought to mention a common aspect of ancient cultures, for which for once there is a consensus: there was a strong common desire on the part of both the elite and the non-elite to leave behind a memory of their existence and identity (such as name, age, career or profession, social status or family, place of origin or home, images), whether by way of honorific inscriptions or statues, or by way of funerary markers and monuments (such as a monumental tomb, a *stele*, or *titulus*). In this sense, "memory" and "commemoration" had an extremely important place in ancient cultures. The fact that lasting memory was a driving force in a civic life turned towards glory has been well-demonstrated, above all in my discussion of Roman public funerals. But recent research has also emphasized that the search for a lasting memory is also expressed vigorously in the epigraphy, art and architecture of funerary monuments commemorating members of lower social strata. Véronique Dasen has studied the funeral portraits of children, attested

**FIGURE 6.5:** Relief from the tomb of the Haterii family (CIL VI 19151), early second century CE; Rome, Via Labicana, now Vatican Museums. Credit: akg-images/Nimatallah.

from the Julio-Claudian era, among the elite and the non-elite who adopted aristocratic practices. Plaster casts of children reveal a desire to build a family memory among the non-elite. In the absence of prestigious ancestors, they had invested their children with their ambitions and, in doing so, appropriated aristocratic customs. One can also take the known example of freedman Q. Haterius Tychicus, contractor for public works, who depicted on his funeral monument (*CIL* VI 19151) the buildings he had built in Rome, including the famous Colosseum: through this "urban scenography" the deceased appears as a great benefactor and is assimilated to the powerful men he had worked for (Figure 6.5; D'Ambra 2002: 223–46; Corbier 2006: 19 and 22; Dasen 2010: 109–45).

# CHAPTER SEVEN

# The Social: Rituals, Faith, Practices, and the Everyday

BEATE DIGNAS

## INTRODUCTION

Arguably, the abstract idea of "the social" lies at the heart of all memory studies. If we follow Maurice Halbwachs in his argument that memory is an entirely social phenomenon and that even "individual memory" cannot be addressed outside the contexts of socialization,[1] the following study should capture an unlimited range of individual and collective memory sites, memory functions and memory practices. The term "social memory" is to some extent interchangeable with "collective memory," with which it shares its emphasis on feelings of identity and belonging, and its communicative framework. Yet not only are "the shared remembrances of group experience" (Alcock 2002: v) important here, but also the ways in which communication and the perception of social relevance link the experiences of individuals to society as a whole. Moreover, every society comprises many different memory communities in which the individual participates;[2] these are formed in culture-specific ways, they are fluid and they are determined by many criteria. They also contribute in varying degrees to the individual's personal memories and perception of the past, and ultimately to what is remembered and commemorated in a community.[3] A collective or at least widely accepted image of the past is therefore the outcome of complex negotiations between the described agents—an outcome that has to satisfy the need for the cohesion of the community as a whole.

The listed key themes, "rituals, faith, practices," refer to the realm of ancient religion, which is often the fountain of examples, whether we relate memories to "time and space," "high culture and popular culture," or consider "remembering and forgetting." Given the embeddedness of religious practices in ancient societies, this certainly extends to "power and politics," and given the emphasis on "visible religion" (Luckmann 1967; J. Assmann 2000: 33) that we observe in these societies, the chapter on "ideas" aptly delegates much of its discussion on "religion" to the current chapter. In all its facets, religion was the central medium of public communication about identity, and, as Jan Assmann puts it, ". . . religious rituals are without doubt the oldest and most fundamental medium of bonding memory . . ." (J. Assmann 2000: 11). Inevitably, the current chapter cuts across all chapters in this volume in one way or another, and it develops its distinct thematic focus in close cross-reference to their categories. After a brief critical survey of the overall themes, I want to specifically address the following topics: religious memory media, the commemoration of the dead, uses of the past and memory creation in religious festivals, and the roles of memory in interstate and interfaith relations. As memory media gain meaning through content, and as faith and rituals were themselves media through which memory, commemoration and remembrance were constantly activated, these topics overlap and interlink.[4]

It is both tempting and problematic to explore the subject from a perspective that categorizes ancient religions. The fact that most pagan religions in the ancient world were based on ritual rather than dogma bears on the findings of this chapter, and this is because the agents and media that control memories are directly determined by important premises of this type. However, while all religions looked at antiquity and tradition to legitimize themselves and to explain their codes for religious practice, the mechanisms to formulate and control memory could be very different.[5] Whereas, to give but one example, the knowledge of sacred texts that regulated orthodox religious practices was firmly in the hands of priests and scribes in Egypt and Babylonia, this was not the case in Rome or Greece (Bommas, Harrisson, and Roy 2012; Nielsen 2012: 3–32). In other words, pagan religion in the ancient world comprised a wide range of religious systems that may look more alike than they actually were, and, among these, the defining (and changing) characteristics of Greek and Roman religions are themselves the subject of lively scholarly debate to date.[6]

Yet, we want to make use of the fact that, while religious identity did not entirely overlap with "social identity," in Greece and Rome the paramount emphasis on "civic identity" in social and religious contexts constantly drew the two together. This means that the everyday practices of social groups within communities were bound together by shared religious practices that created "big" and "meaningful" memories through collective experiences, or were themselves part of a fundamental cultural memory. However, there was also social differentiation, and each community comprised many sub-groups with idiosyncratic religious practices: regional units smaller than the city-state, groups bound by specific political or military institutions, family units, socio-economic classes, ethnic groups, gendered and age groups, etc. Both "religious communities" and "memory communities" would have been created accordingly, and not necessarily in identical ways. As I pointed out in my consideration of "the social," the experiences of individuals also link with the formation of memories of the society at large in complicated ways, and this touches on the difficult questions of "personal choice" and "piety" in Greco-Roman religion.

Generalization becomes even more problematic when we look outside pagan faith and rituals. The rise of Christianity within the Roman empire shows memory formation, reinterpretation and manipulation as complex interactive processes between the very different religious systems. From a diachronic perspective, "memory" should also be included in the wider discussion of continuity and change between antiquity and Christendom. In this context, Jan Assmann has forcefully proposed a watershed between "cult religions" and "book-based religions," with strong consequences for the role not only of memory media but also for the formation of cultural memory (J. Assmann 2006: 122–38). Not achievable in a short discussion of this kind, this means that the memory registers of rituals and practices in Christianity should receive careful attention in their own right, and that the book-religion with a much longer tradition in the ancient world, Judaism, should also be discussed.

There is no doubt that "rituals, faith and practices" formed a central part of "the everyday" in ancient societies—the proposed topics of the discussion therefore also fall under what we may define as the part of life "that was taken for granted by individuals, social groups and institutions."[7] Can we, however, conceptualize memory in relation to this "everyday" in ancient societies? While it is immediately clear that any explicit and categorical "exclusion" of memory from the study of "the everyday" would be inappropriate, a systematic approach to this theme is extremely difficult. All cultural practices carried out in the present involve memories of the past as the foundation of and medium for social bonding, regardless of whether the content of these memories has any support in everyday life (J. Assmann 2000: 10f). In terms of the creation of memory, one may assume that the everyday should be attributed little impact, at best gradual and subconscious memory changes—however, active memory politics, as they are observed regularly, can emerge from uneventful changes in ideological frameworks, and the embracing nature of ancient polytheism is an important factor in this.[8]

In the face of this maze of potential gaps and mis-interpretation, one may argue that "the social" always oscillates between cohesive and centrifugal forces—as a matter of methodological approach *and* results, and that this could not be better illustrated than in the realm of memory. I am hoping to show this in the following discussion of the selected topics. This discussion will mainly illustrate its themes through the paradigms of Greek religion and practices but alert the reader to contrast as well as cross-cultural and religious comparability where possible.

## RELIGIOUS MEMORY MEDIA

Testimonies that show remembrance, commemoration, and memory at the heart of rituals and practices in the ancient world abound.[9] The media/memory carriers, operating both within the ancient contexts and in the process of transmission to be analyzed by memory scholars, are manifold.[10] Their nature, and the uses and attitudes towards them are culture-specific and lay the foundations for the "formation, negotiation, contestation, and transmission of social memory" (Steinbock 2013: 22). Undoubtedly, the visual and epigraphic records are of highest significance, and often the physical link between the two intensifies their role as memory signifiers.[11] Inscriptions themselves were referred to as *hypomnemata*, a term that was also used to refer to remembrance days, memorials/monuments, dedications, honorary statues and crowns, and tombs, i.e. had a semantic meaning of something like mnemonic tools and media to control memory (Chaniotis 2013). The list makes it immediately clear that we are dealing with the realms of the social, of religion and ritual, and the everyday. This is especially felt from the fourth century BCE onwards, and the fact that the contexts in which we find inscriptions *and* their contents were crucial memory media suggests that talking about an "epigraphic habit" cannot and need not be the one explanation for this.

Likewise, monuments and artifacts, and architectural programs that filled landscapes related to and inspired religious practices. The physical demarcation of sacred space, the monumentality of altars and temples, the placing of votives in sanctuaries created a memory landscape that was of paramount importance for the ancient worshipper and viewer, and society at large.[12] Sanctuaries were undoubtedly *lieux de mémoire* with the plethora of functions ascribed to these by memory scholars (Haake and Jung 2011; Jung 2011: 9–18). The property of the gods was integrated into city planning and thus firmly linked with the origins of a community, whether exact memory of original borders and landholdings existed or not. Often, the monuments and their spatial arrangement created the setting for ritual activities that added emotional intensity and created memories built on memories. In other words, the monumental memory landscape was "alive" and

FIGURE 7.1: Engraving of the Acropolis of Athens, *c.* 1890. Credit: Hulton Archive/ Getty Images.

facilitated new memories through contexts, some of which will be discussed below. To list but a few: temples were built in fulfilment of a vow before battle, or deliberately left in ruins after the sack of a city; spoils were dedicated by victors at local or panhellenic sanctuaries; hero cult was established and performed at Bronze Age tombs; statues were erected that honored the memory of men, both in a private and public context; ancestor masks were displayed in houses or during funeral processions.

From early on, the history and significance of a sanctuary were expressed by its votive offerings. These were memory media with wide-ranging functions.[13] Individually, they reminded the viewer of the status and piety of the dedicants. As private and public gifts to the gods they commemorated successes in war, in business affairs, in athletic or poetic competitions. They therefore also commemorated the power of the gods. Collectively, they embedded local history in a wider panhellenic physical and mythical landscape and allowed citizens and visitors to learn about the past. There are numerous testimonies that reveal the importance of votives as memory carriers and show how they linked to and enabled further media in this process. Again, their close link with "inscribed text" is important. Together with funerary inscriptions, dedications form the largest category of inscribed text transmitted to us, composed exclusively for this purpose and with the intent to reach their addressees permanently and in large numbers (Chaniotis 2013).

Inscriptions on votives and about votives gave a voice to the objects that explained their existence in more or less detail. Often they existed in the format of inventories, which—whether actually read or with symbolic meaning—narrated and commemorated the tradition of the sacred site and attributed importance in the present.[14] This was undoubtedly intentional. In their most elaborate form, the records formed the basis for or even represented local historiographies. While theoretically the visual impression of each votive offering, and perhaps an indication of the dedicant qua inscription, would have

FIGURE 7.2: Painted wooden tablet from Pitsa; votive, 520–500 BCE. Credit: DEA/G. DAGLI ORTI/De Agostini/Getty Images.

sufficed to impress visitors, cities, or those groups and individuals looking after the sanctuaries, we see a strong interest in creating elaborate offering lists and, beyond this, turning these into a full narrative.[15] Local historians,[16] certainly from the fourth century onwards and with many examples during the Hellenistic period, constructed their narratives out of temple records. John Dillery describes the essentials of such "sacred history" as the thank-offering, its causal background (the *aition*), and the divine epiphany through which it was regularly set in motion (Dillery 2005: 516 ).[17]

A famous example is the so-called *Lindian Chronicle* (Higbie 2003; Shaya 2005).[18] A set of documents inscribed in the sanctuary of Athena Lindia on Rhodes in 99 BCE presents the decree that authorizes the recording of the inscription, followed by a catalogue of votive offerings, going all the way back to mythical times, and a catalogue of the goddess' epiphanies on Rhodes. The list of dedicators (re-)creates the history of the city, beginning with its eponymous hero Lindos, who dedicated a *phiale* inscribed "to Athena Polias and Zeus Polieus." He is followed by other mythical figures—the Telchines, Kadmos, Minos, and Herakles, whose entries are seamlessly succeeded by historical figures—Phalaris, the tyrant of Akragas, the Persian general Artaphernes, Alexander the Great, Ptolemy I, Pyrrhos of Epirus, and King Philip III of Macedon. As a result, the history of the sanctuary emerges through the history of its treasures, and ultimately a list of Athena's benefactors narrates the history of Rhodes (Dignas 2002b: 240–1). The catalogue of epiphanies of the goddess that follows has a similar function of narrating local history—the tales about the miraculous power of Athena Lindia also refer back to the inventory because they explain the goddess' exceptional worship.

With regard to the reconstruction of a cult's history the Lindian example is not exceptional. A famous dossier of inscriptions in which the history of a cult site is narrated from its mythical past comes from Magnesia on the Maeander (Rigsby 1996: nos. 179–279). Here, elements of Trojan *nostoi* are intertwined with typical foundation myths in which the Delphic oracle plays a role as much as the geographical origins of its first settlers. Hans-Joachim Gehrke uses this dossier as his prime example to set out the concept of "intentional history" (Gehrke 2001: 286–313; 2010: 15–33). In his *Liber Memorialis* the second or early third century author Lucius Ampelius recalls the votives that had been dedicated in the Temple of Apollo at Sicyon by heroes of the mythical past. Ampelius' work included the votives as an example of "the things that deserved to be seen and admired most in the entire world" (Prologue; Sicyon: 8.5; Scheer 1996). Yet, we are not dealing with a collection of curiosities or precious objects but rather a city's successful attempt to place its main sanctuary at the center of panhellenic mytho-historical events of the past (Scheer 1996: 373). We do not know how the Sicyonians framed and narrated their story of the sanctuary but we have to assume that their contextualization of the votives was also a mix of testimonies, general traditions, rituals of the community, and the efforts of an individual writer.[19] As material and epigraphic record, the Lindian Chronicle and comparable sacred histories were ". . . intended to be part of the written past, as well as (obviously) a public record of popular memory."[20]

In different ways, the examples of Lindos, Magnesia and Sicyon illustrate the appeal of sanctuaries to a wide range of visitors. The question of ancient pilgrimage and its role as memory carrier beckons, both as a concept and with regard to its agents.[21] As much as sacred sites were important for civic communities and crucially shaped their identities, they were open to the outside world, whether as part of interstate relations, performed by social groups or personally motivated. Within a typology of "ancient pilgrimage" the

**FIGURE 7.3:** Coptic pilgrim flask, fourth/fifth century CE, inscribed "St. Thecla"; Louvre. Credit: CM Dixon/Print Collector/Getty Images.

following are immediately relevant to the rituals of commemoration and memory creation: festival *theoria* and *theoria* to tombs of mythical heroes, pilgrimage to sites of battles, and what we may call "sacred tourism."[22]

In particular in the Roman imperial period, the range of those participating in such travel to religious memory sites was wide and included imperial officials and intellectuals, with a strong emphasis on cultural nostalgia. However, as with the composition of "sacred histories," it would be misleading to dismiss the role of "faith and religious practices" by using the lightweight label "tourism" or "antiquarianism." When imperial officials toured their provinces and were shown around prominent religious sites, the proud presentation of relics relating to Homeric heroes did not simply satisfy their literary interests or reflect their hosts' cultural ambitions—the experience of wonder, the religious topography of such visits mattered.[23] This is important with regard to the mental processes and emotions involved when monuments and places were experienced as memory carriers (Galli 2005: 253–90). I would argue that this also applies to the "intellectual tourism" that is associated with the so-called Second Sophistic and writers such as Pausanias or Plutarch.[24] Regardless of the author's intentions, Pausanias' *Periegesis* illustrates vividly how tempting and captivating it was for any traveler to link places with stories, and thereby to evoke and create intense memories (Pirenne-Delforge 2008). Plutarch himself served Pythian Apollo as one of the two permanent priests for many years, he identified with its religious past and present (Plutarch, *Moralia* 792ff; Dignas 2013). While several of his dialogues illustrate the sanctuary's attraction in the context of cultural tourism, they did not aspire to replace sanctity and worship with philosophical discourse but to let the one inspire the other, and vice versa.

Christian pilgrimage to bible sites is comparable in its attempt to find and assert shared identity—shared cultural and religious tradition. While the memory of the life of Jesus formed the focus of these travels, pilgrimage to the living saints celebrated Christian asceticism and virtues of the present, complemented by the cult of relics and icons associated with the saints' lives in the past. More than memory media, these relics were perceived as objects of veneration and thereby perceived very differently from, e.g., items dedicated by mythical heroes in the Lindian sanctuary of Athena.[25]

## HERO CULT AND THE COMMEMORATION OF THE DEAD

The desire to link oneself to a glorious past characterized individuals, families, and communities alike. They achieved this not only through patrilineal genealogies but also through the worship of heroes that were "a fixed milestone in the largely unknowable past" (Foxhall and Luraghi 2010: 12). Although the Greeks had no collective memory of a Dark Age, the 400-year period between the end of the Mycenaean civilization and the emergence of the early Greek city-states, the late eighth century saw a sharp increase in the number of offerings made at Mycenaean chamber and tholos tombs. This observation is often associated with the emergence of hero cult, a predominantly local phenomenon that existed in Greece until late antiquity. Its historical evolution is far from clear but there is no doubt that it linked in many and meaningful ways with communities' visions and reconstructions of their past.[26] As in many other realms of memory creation, the Homeric poems were "co-opted" in the process (Price and Thonemann 2010: 105; Higbie 2014). Already our earliest hero-shrines were connected with epic or mythical heroes such as Helen and Menelaus at Sparta, Odysseus on Ithaca, Agamemnon at Mycenae (Malkin 1998: 94–199; Currie 2005: 47–59).

**FIGURE 7.4:** The Menelaion, Hill of Therapne near Sparta, eighth century BCE. Credit: De Agostini/Getty Images.

But the plethora of attested heroes are not only those found in myth, epic and other narratives but also those only known from cultic contexts (Ekroth 2007: 100–14). Their worship and cult-places were very similar to the worship of the gods, and they were often in a relationship with a divine cult as well as closely connected to the history of a sanctuary. On a community level, looking back to and establishing the cults of legendary founders formed the beginning of intentional history par excellence, and the *oikistes* appears as a particularly early category of hero. This is not surprising given that such legendary founders can be seen as "locating the social and political community within the cosmos" (Foxhall, Gehrke, and Luraghi 2010: 12).

As Greek hero cult centered on tombs, and as Greek contemplations about mortality and funerary practices often appear in the context of the worship of heroes, this is a theme closely linked to the commemoration of the dead as a general social phenomenon. Aleida Assmann opens her chronological survey of the "Secularization of Memory in

Western Civilization" by saying, "The anthropological heart of cultural memory is the *remembrance* of the dead" (A. Assmann 1999: 22). Undoubtedly, antiquity offers much opportunity to explore this theme. An exemplary study is Sally Humphreys' analysis of funerals and burials in her recent comprehensive study of kinship in Athens. Above all, the author corrects the still widely held assumption that human response to death is essentially conservative, referring to old practices for meaning and consolation, to the effect that funeral and mourning customs hardly changed over time. She points to the "reflexive processes of change" that affected Greek funerals and monuments and argues that changes were shaped by "conceptions of honor." These were themselves evolving under the influence of poetry, the interpretation of the remains of earlier burials and the memories of recent funerals (Humphreys 2018: 319; 331; 361–3).

A chronological survey of how Athenians commemorated death and funerals illustrates a strong mutual interaction between what we might call the private and public realms. In the Homeric epics, the latter realm steers honor and therefore commemoration—family and kinship do not feature in this process much. The contrast instead lies between the "memory of a man's great deeds in battle preserved in the songs of poets and oral traditions anchored to the mound that marked his grave" and "endless anonymity in Hades" (Humphreys 2018: 320).[27] Yet, we observe that from Solon onwards and well into the Hellenistic period legislation regulated competitive funerary display, illustrating clearly that families were active agents in creating lasting memories of their kin, and that there was a public interest in controlling this. Boris Chrubasik has discussed the important social institution of the annual funeral ceremony in Athens, and its role in disseminating "official polis tradition."[28] To some extent this replaced the earlier aristocratic family burials during which, undoubtedly, speeches celebrating the courage and virtue of the deceased individual had been held, showing many similarities with the surviving public orations. The new institution, probably established soon after the Persian Wars, allowed for the qualities and deeds of individuals to be transferred to a normative and timeless description of Athenian identity. This included the myths of the past that were linked to Athens and could be remembered in a "marathonized" way (Steinbock 2013: 51–8).[29]

Beyond the emphasis on the public funeral of the model citizen, we find families and corporate religious associations attending to tombs and the performance of rites there. According to a passage in Demosthenes (24.107), Athenians could even be charged with "ill-treatment of parents" if they neglected ancestral tombs.[30] The same emphasis on both realms applied to the placing of grave monuments. On the one hand the "private realm" is confirmed in the layout of cemeteries, where families were buried together, and families maintained the site and offered libations at anniversaries, on the other hand monuments were deliberately placed alongside roads into cities and actively engaged with the "passer-by." Such a dialogue between the private and public remembrance of the dead also existed in Rome, where rites were regulated by the state in that they formed part of the official calendar but were considered as private rites, conducted by families and clubs. Alongside, there was the institution of the *funus publicum*, paid for and organized by the state and culminating in the burial of an emperor. Soldiers fallen in battle, in Greece as well as in Rome, were collectively buried—which, as has been shown for Athens, offered much opportunity for the creation of collective memories. Interestingly, in the Hellenistic period the institution of public funerals for the war dead appears to give way to the commemoration of ambitious members of the elite. Rich citizens were even able to "prolong their careers as benefactors in death" by setting up foundations that included their own annual commemoration (Humphreys 2018: 330; but see Chaniotis 2005: 188–

204). Visual and epigraphic evidence relating to funerary sites and rites is ubiquitous, and so is scholarly discussion. In essence, the material makes us aware that at all times rituals were characterized by social and historical circumstance and change. We also have to accept that the ways in which Greeks and Romans commemorated their dead do not offer a straight-forward interpretation of their understanding of death.[31]

This insight also bears on any cross-cultural perspective beyond a Greco-Roman framework (Davies 1999: 1–26). While there is no doubt that feelings of grief are universal, the interpretation of many aspects of funeral cult, such as its relationship with the cult of the gods or its potential role in linking the dead and the living, poses many challenges—here, "memory" cannot simply be used as a levelling or unifying key.

As with many generalizing statements in memory studies, scholars often take their own focus of interest as a template. A. Assmann points to "the cult that links the living with the dead as the earliest and most widespread form of social memory," exemplified in the Egyptian "Festival of the Desert Valley, the shared meal between them, a ritual way of reintegrating the deceased ancestors into the family" (A. Assmann 1999: 23). While there

FIGURE 7.5: Syro-Hittite Kuttamuwa stele with Aramaic inscription, eighth century BCE; Zincirli Mound, now Gaziantep Museum. Credit: Images&Stories/Alamy Stock Images.

were commemorative rites and festivals of the dead in Greek and Roman funerary practices, these fulfilled very different purposes.

In Greece, some states, such as Athens, held an annual state festival to honor the dead, the *Genesia*, and the second and third day of the *Anthesteria* in honor of Dionysus were to some extent devoted to the dead. As far as we can tell, apart from their function as remembrance or memorial, these days served to appease the dead and avert any evil they might intend toward the living (Felton 2007: 89).[32] In Rome, the *di manes*, the gods of the dead, were worshipped at the festivals *Parentalia*, *Feralia*, and *Lemuria*, and individually on the anniversary of a person's death; these also served to propitiate the ghosts of the dead, not to reintegrate them into the society of the living (Davies 1999: 146–7; Scheid 2007: 263–71). As S. Humphreys puts it, "What the Greeks hoped to achieve for the dead was perpetual remembrance, by strangers as well as kin. Their dead did not become ancestors [. . .] they became monuments" (Humphreys 1981: 270). These fundamental differences caution our interpretation. We can, e.g., suspect but not be sure that the emphasis on permanent memorials, expressed in elaborate tombs and tomb architecture, can be explained by the desire for immortality precisely because there was no belief in the afterlife as we find it in Christian or Jewish eschatological belief (Walker 1985: 13).

## RELIGIOUS FESTIVALS

In Greek communities every festival was a day of historical remembrance, which stemmed from an aetiology, a narrative of a real or fictional event that led to the foundation of the festival. This means that there was no distinction between a religious and a historical festival (Chaniotis 1991: 123; 2005: 194–5). The overlap is intensified by the fact that there was no conceptual difference between narratives that talked about gods or heroes, and those that concerned historical individuals and their deeds. If there was a distinction between a distant and more recent, known past, this was blurred because the gods had an impact on historical individuals and events, and these individuals could be perceived as heroes or gods (Chaniotis 1991: 123–4). With regard to the concurrence of political and religious memories, and their media, these observations are crucial, and indeed, the nomenclature and proceedings of days commemorating battles, civic freedom, kings or citizens are identical to those of festivals of religious significance: the wearing of garlands, the processions, sacrifices, hymns and prayers, the communal meals, athletic and musical competitions, and often the dramatizations of the commemorated event—in all these aspects the emphasis on the visual and the collective, as well as the use of space and time created an ideal setting for memory formation.[33] Angelos Chaniotis goes even further in his interpretation when he explains the parallels with the Greeks' theological interpretation of history, combined with their "idealization of history," by which he understands the isolation of a historical event from its historical context, to the effect that ". . . historical tradition becomes identity" (Chaniotis 1991: 142).

If this was the case even to a limited extent, one could argue that religious festivals were the most powerful creators and transmitters of collective memories and memory politics. In addition, they also illustrate the complex range of "social memories" discussed at the beginning of this chapter, the interaction between the experiences of individuals, societal sub-groups and the community as a whole. While it was obviously important that the entire community participated in the civic festivals, that a shared image of the past was articulated, we see an explicit and intended display of communities' social components, in particular distinctions of age and gender, but also of kinship. To give but a few examples: civic decrees that established new festivals not only set out its ritual proceedings in detail, they also spelled out which groups, and in what order, formed a procession and performed the rites. There were also rites associated with children's legal status early in life and around the age of puberty. In the Hellenistic period proud families even commemorated their children's participation in ritual performances with statues.

From the fourth century BCE onwards, the military training of the young men, which was a prerequisite for their enrolment as full citizens, saw a new and defined set of rituals, sealed by an oath in which these *ephebes* swore, among other things, to honor the cults of their fathers. Women had their own festivals and rites, such as the *Thesmophoria*, which existed not only in the city of Athens but had their local equivalents in the various *demes*. Such gendered experiences included the wedding festival, undoubtedly the most important ritual in many girls' lives. The fact that the religious calendar was tied to patrilineal descent groups means that even institutions such a *genos* priesthood, which was held for life and passed on within families, always created strong collective identity among the male members of a *genos* but for female members only when they married within the *genos* (Humphreys 2018: 393). References in the literary sources, above all oratory, point to a number of shared ritual activities within families, which are mentioned because they attest to close relationships among members (e.g. Isaeus 8. 15–16; 9.30). New comedy presents the "negative" memories of young men bored by family get-togethers that dwelled on the remembrance of ancestors and tombstones (Humphreys 2018: 390 with references).

Likewise, specific memory communities were created by the regional and local divisions within Attica. The local *demes* had their own political institutions, cults, and festivals, and the tribes had their own political identity, eponymous heroes, and corresponding rituals.[34] Thanks to our rich archaeological and epigraphic evidence, we are able to study the idiosyncrasies of these smaller units, as well as their interface with the collective memories of the community as a whole. Robin Osborne has presented a fascinating comparison between the well-documented *demes* Thorikos and Rhamnous, two coastal communities of moderate size and with some homogeneity in their basic administrative structures (Osborne 2011: 25–43). However, an examination of their archaeological features and of the framework of their religious activities shows that the day-to-day experiences of formal and informal memorials of the past in each of the two must have been completely different. While the people of Rhamnous presented themselves as part of the whole history of Athens, the Thorikians who emphasized their own local past and religious identity; they were, as Osborne puts it, "either proudly independent or inward-looking" (Osborne 2011: 35). There is no doubt that speaking about 'Athenians' relations to the past" at best captures some of the picture and that the *demes* shaped these relations as much as the collective memories evoked in funeral orations.

## INTERSTATE AND INTERFAITH RELATIONS

Whether to integrate or to differentiate subgroups, the powerful role of myth as a memory medium closely interwoven with lived experience had a tremendous identity-building effect within communities (Graf 2011). This effect could also be used for diplomatic purposes, as a foundation for interstate relations. The ancient world was a connected world, and, as the above comments on "pilgrimage" have already illustrated, could generate and cement peaceful interaction. This, also in a cross-cultural context, happened with more intensity and much wider geographical scope from the conquests of Alexander the Great onwards. Memory creation and memory shifts occurred continuously and, arguably, should be addressed in their very specific contexts. However, we see patterns of looking back to the past by pointing to foundation stories that reflected kinship, traditional and reciprocal privileges, and long-standing cultural and political relations. These were bonding strategies as much as communities' attempts to raise their profile vis-à-vis the outside world. Pointing to shared mythical traditions not only enabled communities to link themselves to far-away places but it also allowed cultural "newcomers" to assert themselves as traditional, as stakeholders with regard to a Greco-Roman heroic past.

I already mentioned the "anthology" of inscriptions that reflect the communication between Magnesia on the Maeander and a plethora of Hellenistic communities and rulers concerning the new festival of Artemis Leukophryene (Gehrke 2010). The range of actors involved, the monumental display and its location, the content of the texts, from the Magnesians' foundation story and the collated "evidence" of the sanctuary's history, to the civic decrees introducing the new games—all these elements express the careful and intentional use of the past to great effect. While the level of documentation at Magnesia and presumably the level of effort and response were exceptional, many communities adopted similar strategies (Rigsby 1996; Chaniotis 1988). Already long before the Hellenistic period and with regularly revived regularity, the panhellenic sanctuary Delphi served as a flagship for shared religious and cultural identity and was instrumentalized by communities to lend a divine dimension to the elaboration of their past (Giangiulio 2010b: 131).

New collective memories were also created in the interaction with rulers, crucially facilitated by their integration into the religious life of the cities via ritual transfer from the cult of gods. *Lieux de mémoire* and other visual memory media, such as statues, altars and even cult images, referred to kings and queens and their deeds.[35] In many ways, the traditional and the new merged to create a memory landscape that could be manipulated on both sides as need and political tact required. Many aspects discussed above, such as the identity-building effects of festivals, or the commemoration of the dead, map themselves directly onto these relationships—communities remembered the king in a regular and ritualized way as founder, as epiphanic savior, as civic benefactor.

Another complex phenomenon is the export of cults and their specific practices. Here, the malleable nature of memory is particularly visible when we look at how often new memories were based on distorted memories, in conscious and unconscious ways. A good example is the Isaic cults. They helped to create a certain memory of Egypt in Greece and Rome because their sanctuaries were used as "storage facilities of oral, written or visual knowledge" (Bommas, Harrisson, and Roy 2012: 198, on the Iseum Campense in Rome) developed in close association with religious practices. At the same time, a careful selection of the characteristics that were to remain important for their new identity was paired with fluid adaptation to their new locations and worshippers. The difficulties in tracing the origins and "cultural identity" of the cult of Sarapis are perfect testimonies to this process, in which "memory" formed the key ingredient.

Last but not least, the interactions between the Greco-Roman and the monotheistic religions of antiquity are a challenge in tracing a cultural history of memory. As I already pointed out in the introduction, the rise of Christianity urgently poses the big question of change and continuity. The close link between memory and political context that applies to all aspects discussed so far suggests drastic change. The new religion questioned the

**FIGURE 7.6:** Fresco depicting the arrival of Io in Canopus, first century CE; Pompeii, Temple of Isis. Credit: Alamy Stock Photo.

legitimacy of religious tradition and the mechanisms and media through which sacred memory was controlled in the Roman empire. It rejected the anchoring of the past in stories of panhellenic as well as local gods and heroes and placed, against these, the memory of the life of Jesus and the commemoration of martyrs, who displaced rather than created local identity. Martyrological discourses became a powerful expression of Christian collective memories, the legacy of which endures to the present day (Castelli 2004). Moreover, scripture, biblical memory, was endowed with an authority that could not be questioned. Jan Assmann describes the radical break even more sharply and links it to the reversal of the significance of the media that create cultural memory, namely ritual repetition on the one hand, and the interpretation of canonical texts on the other. The text, he argues, becomes the pivotal factor because the historical acts of revelation and creation are based in sacred writings; accordingly, ritual has only a framing function (J. Assmann 2006: 122–3). If we push, as the author does, the consequences of this premise hard, "coherence" in each is achieved very differently: a culture of learning and understanding the sacred text versus the correct performance of ritual to maintain the world.[36] In turn, equally different social types of priest, media and controllers of sacred knowledge and memory, are created. The one who knows and performs actions has a counterpart in an interpreter and preacher who deals with a sacred realm that is separate from this world. The memory media that matter so much in the world of cult religions, namely holy places, images, statues, symbols and buildings, are denigrated in a "discourse that de-sensualizes religion and dismantles the theatricality of ritual" (128). The function of cultic language, sacred letters and the perfect memorization of these by priests in ancient Egypt illustrate that this is not simply a matter of "writing" or "text" vs. monumental culture—the shift of emphasis from sound to meaning was essential to transform a cult religion into a book religion (129–36).

Comparative research into the role of sacred texts as storage of meaningful memory cautions us to see the divide as straight forward. Daniela Bonanno has compared the recovery of the sacred mysteries in Messenia on an inscribed tin sheet with the rediscovery of the Book of Law under the reign of Josiah, as told in the second book of *Kings* (22–3), and she concludes that the uses of memory are indeed very similar (Bonanno 2013: 63–80). Another example that cautions us not to categorize religious practices according to memory media (or vice versa) too quickly relates to the so-called mystery religions. Whereas Assmann contrasts the need for wide dissemination of the sacred text in book-religions with a principle of secrecy in the mysteries of pagan cults,[37] other scholars (albeit in different pursuits) have often juxtaposed the two in order to demonstrate likeness. In particular, the Orphic mysteries have been interpreted as centered on belief and the authority of sacred texts rather than ritual and sensual experience. In a recent study of the Orphic-Bacchic gold leaves Mark McClay suggests that the character of the *lamellae* is that of objects produced, handled and disseminated by ritual performers. This is also relevant because the theme of memory is paramount in the texts, some of which relate the soul's journey to obtain a drink from the chthonic water of *Mnemosyne*, or reference themselves as objects of memory. Rather than seeing the meaning of this "Memory" in the *lamellae* as a specific Orphic-Pythagorean divinity, the author links the vocabulary of memory to connections with Greek poetry and religion. In modern theoretical terms he calls the *lamellae* an expression of "collective memory in the context of mortuary practice" (McClay 2018; but see Castagnoli in this volume).

In line with the conventional interpretation of the Orphic gold leaves, the references to *Mnemosyne* in healing sanctuaries of Asclepius and in connection with the oracle of Trophonios in Lebadeia are normally taken as attestations to a powerful divinity. Pausanias (9.35.9–13) tells us that worshippers descending into the hole of Trophonios were instructed to drink from the waters of *Oblivion* and then from the waters of *Memory*, and after they had returned to the surface were seated on "the chair of *Mnemosyne*" (Graf and Johnston 2007; Graf 2009: 169–82). In their recent volume on *Greek Memories* Castagnoli and Ceccarelli (2019: 11) link the persistent prominence of "the goddess of Memory" to the strong connections with early Greek song-culture, emphasizing that "this connection remained very much alive also after the rise of the written word to prominence."

Undoubtedly, we see the negotiation and appropriation of "memory" as a very complex process between old and new, where pagan approaches to and contents of memories were transferred to and influenced by other religious identities. A forceful example of this is the verse epitaph of St. Aberkios of Hierapolis, perceptively analyzed in Thonemann 2012. Here, Christians adopted the prolific pagan memory practice of creating and sharpening local identity by linking it to the worship of local heroes—using instead the life of a martyr. Other examples, such as the use and re-use of pagan oracles, or even the ways in which the biblical past was presented to suit present needs, illustrate that the rise of Christianity did not break with approaches to social memory as radically as references to the destruction of pagan monuments and symbols may suggest.[38] Equally, the "deritualization and de-theatricalization of religion" as a consequence of "writing" did not occur as vehemently as theoretical considerations postulate. Ultimately, the historian cannot answer the question of continuity and change without looking at interaction.

## CONCLUSIONS

Initially I proposed that "memory" would be a good focus to illustrate the cohesive and centrifugal forces of "the social." Indeed, it would appear that ancient societies continuously painted images of their past in broad and fine brushes next to and on top of one another. Some colors are dominant, some motifs are big, some small, and many relate to others. Not surprisingly, ancient memory studies and theories have attached themselves to virtually all phenomena of social behavior, to the extent that it is becoming necessary to express caveats.[39]

Focusing on the realm of Greek religious practices, this chapter has shown that this realm was a memory theater par excellence, through which social cohesion and differentiation articulated themselves in multiple effective ways. The range and ubiquitous nature of these practices reveal the importance of a religious landscape within which the remembrance and commemoration of a mythical and more recent past took place. Corresponding to the dominant character of Greek religion as "*polis r*eligion," there is strong evidence of local sacred histories, among which many engaged in "intentional history." Funerary monuments and customs were modeled on and served themselves as models for religious memory culture at large. They did so not necessarily because of a culture-specific conceptualization of death but in close relationship with concepts of honor and hero cult. The regular celebration of religious festivals created and activated collective memories, linked religious experience to political events and thereby forged civic ideology; this potential existed also below the level of the *polis* and the citizenship as a whole, expressing social differentiation and micro-identity qua memory. Tapping into such experiences, Christianity addressed memories and memory formation intensively in order to establish itself as the enemy and heir to pagan religious identities. Altogether, it may be the perceived "antiquarianism" in the ideologies of religion and ritual, to the effect that "change (sometimes radical change) may be disguised by a fundamental rhetoric of continuity," which created so much potential for the use and abuse of memory (Elsner and Rutherford 2005: 31).

# CHAPTER EIGHT

# Remembering and Forgetting

ELIZABETH MINCHIN

## INTRODUCTION

How were the primary activities of memory—more precisely, of remembering and forgetting—perceived in the ancient Mediterranean world? In this chapter I consider evidence from ancient Greece that reflects on the functions of memory, and its various failings, in the light of a range of research from today's world on remembering, forgetting, the inability to forget, and memory distortion. In this context, I begin with the work of Jan Assmann, whose particular interest is in the relationship between one's memory and one's "awareness of selfhood" at both the personal and the collective levels (Assmann 2008: 109). Assmann has proposed that memory operates at three occasionally overlapping levels: the inner, the social and the cultural.[1] At the inner level we locate personal or autobiographical memory. At the social level, with a temporal reach of about eighty years, are the memories we share with those around us; this is what Assmann calls social, or communicative, memory. At the third level we find Assmann's cultural memory, which derives from the remote past, and which is at the foundation of traditional stories, traditional dances and rituals.[2] Two of the earliest texts from the Greek world, the *Iliad* and the *Odyssey*, not only offer as subjects for discussion the act of remembering, but they also exhibit an implicit understanding of the distinctions between personal, social, and cultural memory in the same sometimes approximate way that we do today. It is in these texts too that we find the expression of one of the fundamental principles of cognitive studies: that location and memorability are linked; and that spatial information, along with visual information, prompts the recall of associated material.[3] In the first of the three case studies that make up this chapter I explore how this (originally oral) epic tradition understood these aspects of memory, and how it viewed memory's failings.

From our perspective today, in the twenty-first century, Greeks of the ancient world were remarkably optimistic about the reliability of memory, whether of the individual or of a larger group. My second case study is an account of how the past was remembered in classical Athens. Although fifth- and fourth-century Athens was still largely an oral culture, this was a period in which the possibilities of the new technology of writing were gradually being recognized. As Herodotus observed in his preface (Hdt. 1.1), a written record of the past—a record that preserved its memories—would be a gift of value to generations to come. In this case study I shall focus on the reliability of memory and, in parallel, on the fluidity of oral traditions in the light of a second fundamental principle of cognitive studies: that memory is subject to both transience and distortion. I will examine the extent to which Herodotus recognized the ways in which memory so often failed his fellow Greeks, as he tried to reconstruct the past with future generations in mind. I will refer to important work by Daniel Schacter and Michael Schudson on the failures of memory in order to test ancient world understanding—at least, among the elite of Athens—of these phenomena.[4]

This expressed concern for the preservation of memories and for commemoration which we will observe in the first two case studies suggests that the ancient Greek world was no less preoccupied with the phenomenon of forgetting. The individuals whom we meet in the early Homeric texts, for example, were almost all concerned that their achievements should not fade from the memory of generations to come. But, as the poet makes clear, the capacity to remember, even against one's will—the inability to put something out of one's mind—can be a blight. In this regard he brings to our attention Achilles in the *Iliad* and Ajax in the *Odyssey*, for each of whom remembering (and *not* forgetting) is a cause of constant pain.[5] My third case study will address a remarkable, historical, case in which selective forgetfulness, as it applies to a society, is declared: I refer to the "amnesty" of 403 BC proposed by Sparta, and the efforts of Athenian citizens to heal their state after the civil war of 404/3. And I shall ask how successful was the *polis*'s attempt to put behind them the troubles associated with the rule of the Thirty.[6]

## CASE STUDY 1: UNDERSTANDING MEMORY IN THE ARCHAIC WORLD: THE HOMERIC EPICS

Time and again in the Homeric epics we are reminded of an individual hero's ambition that after his death his name should live on, as *kleos*, in the memory of others. Achilles,

**FIGURE 8.1:** View of the tomb of Achilles (Beşiktepe) in Beşika Burnu (ancient Achilleion); Sir William Gell, 1804. Credit: History and Art Collection/Alamy Stock Photo.

at *Il.* 9.412–13, looks ahead to everlasting glory (κλέος ἄφθιτον, 413), should he decide to remain at Troy and return once more to the fighting. In a similar vein, when Hector, at the critical point in his long-awaited contest with Achilles, realizes that he is facing death, he gathers himself for one last effort, saying (*Il.* 22.304–5):

μὴ μὰν ἀσπουδί γε καὶ ἀκλειῶς ἀπολοίμην,
ἀλλὰ μέγα ῥέξας τι καὶ ἐσσομένοισι πυθέσθαι.

May I not die without a struggle, and without glory,
but do some big thing first, for people in the future to learn about.[7]

And, much later in epic time, at *Od.* 8.72–82, the bard Demodocus fulfils this heroic desire, when he sings of the great achievements of heroes of the Trojan War: their great deeds, and their names, are celebrated and now live on in the community's memory.[8]

We find in the poems an awareness too that markers in the landscape are thought to play an important commemorative function, prompting recollections in passers-by of great heroes and great deeds. When Hector, issuing a challenge to the Achaeans, boasts that he will kill his opponent, he looks ahead to the moment when the Achaeans bury their comrade beside the Hellespont under a great mound; in the future, passers-by will see the mound and, remembering the tale, will speak out about the hero and about the great man who killed him (*Il.* 7.89–90; cf. *Od.* 11.75–6):

ἀνδρὸς μὲν τόδε σῆμα πάλαι κατατεθνηῶτος,
ὅν ποτ᾽ ἀριστεύοντα κατέκτανε φαίδιμος Ἕκτωρ.

"This is the mound of a man who died in battle long ago,
one of the bravest, and it was glorious Hector who killed him."

As the epics demonstrate, it is well understood in archaic Greek society, in practical terms, that the form, the visibility and the durability of the mound will prompt stories about each man for generations to come.[9] But, as Hector implies, at *Il.* 7.91, although the mound will cue these memories into the future, it does not itself retain them. What is required is an agent: in this pre-literate world such a man would be a singer of tales, like Homer himself, or an elder or a guide: someone, that is, who would serve as a keeper of memories for his community. Only then will a passer-by be able to reflect on the heroism of both victor and vanquished (Assmann 2008: 114–15):

ὥς ποτέ τις ἐρέει· τὸ δ᾽ ἐμὸν κλέος οὔ ποτ᾽ ὀλεῖται.

So will some passer-by speak some day, and my glory will not be forgotten.

Like spatial and visual markers in the landscape, prized possessions in the personal sphere also prompt memories. These precious objects, each distinctive in its own way, serve as souvenirs—as reminders of absent friends, of important events and special occasions. Whenever the poet calls to mind a prized possession in order to describe it, he responds to the mental image of the object, and this image in turn sparks a memory, which in many cases will take the form of a brief story.[10] Thus we, the poet's audience, learn of the origins of the gowns in Priam's store-chamber (*Il.* 6.289–95), of Andromache's headdress (*Il.* 22.468–472) and of the golden pin in Odysseus' cloak (*Od.* 19.225–31, 255–7); almost inevitably we recall these vivid stories long after we have forgotten the details of the appearance of each item. Following, perhaps, a longer traditional practice, the poet has thus conscientiously recreated in his narrative a phenomenon observable in the

FIGURE 8.2: Engraving showing Kalliope, the Muse of epic poetry; Hendrik Goltzius, 1592. Credit: Artikoloro/Alamy Stock Photo.

everyday world, the cueing of memory by imagery.[11] Although he might not be able to formulate explicitly, as David Rubin has done, the relationship between visual image and memory, he knows instinctively that such a relationship exists.

We observe in the Homeric poems a similarly instinctive understanding of the distinctions between personal, social, and cultural memory, as Assmann has outlined them. The poet offers us clear representations of each of these modes: Eurycleia's silent recollection, at *Od.* 19.392–466, of how the young Odysseus acquired his scar is presented as a personal memory. Nestor's reminiscences about his past achievements, at *Il.* 1.260–73, 4.319, 7.132–56, 11.670–761, 765–89, and 23.629–45, are personal memories for Nestor, but they represent the social memory of the community of younger heroes who hear them, as are the memories Nestor shares with Telemachus, at *Od.* 3.103–200, 254–328, in response to the young man's enquiries about his father. The poet's own account of the history of the sceptre that Agamemnon now wields (*Il.* 2.100–8), which has been passed from generation to generation, from Hephaestus to Zeus to Hermes to Pelops and down through the generations to Agamemnon, is presented as a cultural memory.[12]

The Homeric poet is confident of the accuracy of the memories he shares: as he begins his song he appeals to the Muses, the daughters of Zeus, who are the source of his information and the guarantors of its truth (for example, at *Il.* 1.1–7, 2.484–93; *Od.* 1.1–10). But he is equally aware that information can slip from our minds. In the epic world that the poet creates Nestor rebukes Patroclus for having forgotten his father's advice that his greater age gave him the right to act as counsellor to Achilles (*Il.* 11.786–90); and Athene accuses Zeus of having forgotten Odysseus (*Od.* 1. 59–60) (a charge vigorously denied at *Od.* 1.65).

In this epic world, however, just as heroes are concerned with failure to remember and to be remembered they are equally troubled by the inability to forget. The poet offers us interesting case-studies, in the figures of Achilles in the *Iliad* and, in the *Odyssey*, Ajax, of the unwelcome persistence of memory, classified by Schacter as one of memory's "seven sins"[13] (Schacter 2001: 161–83; Minchin 2006). Schacter observes that persistence is strongly linked to emotion: emotionally charged incidents are better remembered than events without such an emotional charge. He observes too that we tend to remember negative events in greater detail than positive ones (Schacter 2001: 163–4). Memories of this negative kind often follow the death of a loved one; and this negativity can develop into a crippling persistence. Homer offers a classic case in his representation of Achilles, who cannot forget Agamemnon's insult to his honor, when he strips him of his prize, the captive girl Briseis (*Il.* 1.182–7). He is afflicted in the same way after the death of Patroclus. At *Il.* 22.61 the hero announced his inability to forget that it was Hector who brought about Patroclus's death (Ἕκτορ, . . ., ἄλαστε, . . ., Hector, doer of unforgettable deeds, . . .); at *Il.* 22.386–90 he vowed that he would never allow the memory of his beloved companion Patroclus to fade; and at *Il.* 24.3–18 we observe the hero as he continues to endure the torment of loss and remembrance, even twelve days later (*Il.* 24.31), as he gives expression to his grief by repeatedly maltreating the body of Hector. Furthermore, dwelling on the sorrows of the past, as Achilles does, can lead to counterfactual thinking, when the grief-stricken individual generates alternative scenarios of what might have been (Schacter 2008: 165–7):

τὴν ὄφελ᾽ ἐν νήεσσι κατακτάμεν Ἄρτεμις ἰῷ
ἤματι τῷ ὅτ᾽ ἐγὼν ἑλόμην Λυρνησσὸν ὀλέσσας·
τώ κ᾽ οὐ τόσσοι Ἀχαιοὶ ὀδὰξ ἕλον ἄσπετον οὖδας
δυσμενέων ὑπὸ χερσὶν ἐμεῦ ἀπομηνίσαντος.

> I wish that Artemis had killed her at the ships with an arrow
> on that day when I captured Lyrnessus, having destroyed it.
> In that case so very many Achaeans would not have bitten the dust
> at enemy hands, when I had grown angry.
>
> —19.59–62[14]

Disappointments and failures of all kinds may result in self-perpetuating negativity, and a negative sense of self, as a painful incident is relived again and again (Schacter 2008: 168): the Homeric exemplar here is Ajax of the *Odyssey*, now in the Underworld, and angry still that the armor of Achilles went to Odysseus rather than to himself (*Od.* 11.541–67). Unable to engage with Odysseus despite the hero's conciliatory words, the hero allows his body language (νόσφιν ἀφεστήκει, 544), his stiff intransigence, to reveal his continuing pain. Odysseus does not understand Ajax's continuing anger. A more resilient character, Odysseus views Ajax's inability to engage as a willed incapacity to forget (οὐκ ἄρ' ἔμελλες | οὐδὲ θανὼν λήσεσθαι ἐμοὶ χόλου . . .; could you then not forget your anger against me, even in death? 553–4).

These early literary works from the ancient Greek world indicate already a cultural preoccupation with memory, whether this related to the practical applications of memory (reminding and remembering), the appreciation of the different levels of memory as described now by Assmann, or the understanding that just as the failure to remember may be a personal, a social or a cultural problem so is the inability to forget. These perceptions were not formalized; rather, I propose, they were intuitive, based on the observation of the behavior of others. Thus, the Homeric accounts of the epic heroes' relationships with memory would have been readily understood by their ancient audiences, as they are by audiences today.

## CASE STUDY 2: REMEMBERING THE PAST IN CLASSICAL ATHENS: SOCIAL AND CULTURAL MEMORY IN A LIVING COMMUNITY

In this section I move from a poetic tradition and its understanding of remembering and forgetting, as illustrated by the heroes of an imagined world of the past, to a living community, the world of classical Athens. As I observed above, classical Athens was, for the most part, an oral society; even here, two centuries after the introduction of the alphabet into the Greek world, the written word still lacked "authoritative weight" (Steinbock 2013: 39). By contrast, in the Western world today, we rely heavily on the preservation of written records, and we validate information by consulting written records and documentary sources. Ours is an archive culture. But, to return to fifth- and fourth-century Athens, although written sources were important for some educated memory communities within the *polis*, for most others they were not. Their knowledge of the past was acquired through oral transmission exclusively; its accuracy was, for the most part, not doubted. Most people had no means of checking facts—nor did it occur to them that they should.[15]

While information about the city's past was transmitted, undoubtedly, in the home and in the *deme*, I shall first take one example from the wider social context of large-scale religious festivals, such as the *Panathenaea*, and other cult practices, of public commemorations, such as funerals, and of dramatic performances.[16] As activities celebrated within the *polis*, occasions such as these contributed significantly to Athenians' view of themselves and of their past.[17]

Because of Athens' almost unbroken record of military activity, a public funeral ceremony was held almost every year. The funeral orations delivered on these public occasions became an opportunity for remembrance on a collective scale. Speakers typically included reference to a limited number of topics: Athens' defeat of the Amazons, the expulsion of Thracian Eumolpus from Attica, the expulsion of Eurystheus, and Athens' acceptance of the Argives' request to bury their dead after the attack of the Seven against Thebes. The fifth great topic was Athens' contribution to the Persian Wars.[18] Funeral orations set out the city's past in these terms, as a series of narratives in rough chronological order (Steinbock 2013: 51). Presented in a set form, as stories of this kind so often are, and rehearsed in that same form each year when the dead were commemorated, well into the fourth century, they were a significant source of cultural memory for younger Athenians and, for older citizens, they reinforced through repetition and familiarity connections between the present and the remote past (Thomas 1989: 212–13).[19] They represented both what individuals held in memory and what was thought—by statesman and orators—to be worth commemoration.

Whereas the *polis* brought together the people of Athens as a single body, the individual *deme* was small enough to be a "face-to-face society' (Steinbock 2013: 71) with its own history and identity. That is, older members of the *deme* would have passed on to younger members their own particular personal, social and cultural memories. A third important source of knowledge of the past was the family unit, which fostered, sometimes selectively, its own traditions and memories.[20] Within the family unit memories were passed on to the new generation by parents and grandparents, especially one's father or grandfather, who might then be cited in the assembly or in the law courts as an exemplar of, or an incontrovertible source of knowledge about, the past.[21]

Finally, as in the world of Homer, memorials such as funeral monuments and trophies (τρόπαια) formed a special class of carriers of memory through time. At the site of great battles, an enduring monument in honor of those who had perished preserved their memory for time to come. Erected in conspicuous, or highly significant, locations, or in striking landscapes, such monuments were designed to stir remembrance of those whom a society wished to honor.[22] In some cases these monuments were inscribed with explanatory text (an epigram for the fallen in battle, for example);[23] at other times they were invested with meaning simply through regular commemorative activities held at the site.[24]

We know, however, that human memory is fallible; memories can be eclipsed through the passage of time. Just as personal memory is noted for its failings, its instability, so too, as we observe, is cultural memory. Within two or three generations actual situations and events are forgotten; the "real" past slips away, to be replaced by new information.[25] Although a memorial may remain fixed in the landscape, with the passing of years its interpretation may change. By the fifth and fourth centuries, for example, *tholos* tombs that had survived from the Bronze Age palace-culture had come to be identified with the heroes of ancient epic. Their original occupants had been forgotten; these great tombs were assumed instead to be the memorial sites for recently established hero-cults.[26] And, in the realm of myth, Steinbock notes evidence of "continuous reshaping and reworking" (Steinbock 2013: 190–1) in the archaic and classical periods of the tale of the burial of the Seven at Thebes, a process in which certain elements were elaborated, or compressed, or even omitted, depending on the prevailing attitudes and concerns at the time of the

FIGURE 8.3: Ionic column built to commemorate the Battle of Marathon, fifth century BCE; Archaeological Museum of Marathon. Credit: Prisma/UIG/Getty Images.

telling.[27] As Schudson observes, in connection with active memorialization in the public sphere, there is always a degree of simplification, or crystallization: an account of an event will be reduced to its essentials; protagonists and antagonists will be brought to the fore; and contests of ideas will be made concrete and vivid (Schudson 1995: 355–8).

It was in this fifth-century context, in which the principal mode of transmission of knowledge about the past was still oral, that Herodotus and, only a little later, Thucydides began to write.[28] Although Herodotus was not Athenian, he had spent time in Athens and was deeply engaged with this city (Raaflaub 2002: 152). Herodotus proposed to conduct his own enquiry (*historia*) into how the Greeks and the Persians had come into conflict (Hdt. 1.1). He would record in writing the results of his research, as what we today call history (discussion in Bakker 2002: 3–4). This written text, he claimed, would preserve the memory of the past for audiences in the future (Hdt. 1.1[29]). Herodotus' material had

**FIGURE 8.4:** Engraving showing Klio, the Muse of history; Hendrik Goltzius, 1592. Credit: Gibon Art/Alamy Stock Photo.

been gathered in the course of extensive travels, through observation (αὐτόπτης ἐλθών, 2.29.1), through conversations and interviews with relevant informants who drew on their own memories of people and events (ἀκοῇ... ἱστορέων, 2.29.1), from oral traditions (often highly simplified, as I noted above), and from some limited written sources (Hornblower 2002). In adopting this innovative research method, Herodotus implicitly set himself in contrast with the poet of the Homeric epics, who relied on the Muse to recall on his behalf the story of the Trojan War past.[30] It was Herodotus himself who collected memories, compared them, and evaluated them, and drew his own conclusions about what was credible and what was not.[31]

Herodotus frequently pointed out to his readers those occasions when he drew on firsthand experience; at other times he remarked that his information came at second hand, from local informants, who had heard about events from participants or witnesses. What is interesting in the context of this chapter is that there were occasions on which Herodotus felt that he could not verify the facts of an account, often an oral tradition extending back into the domain of myth or, in one case, a family tradition. In those cases he maintained a critical distance; he was aware of the limitations of his sources, and of the multiple reasons and motivations that made memory unstable and unreliable for historians.[32] In connection with more recent events, for which there might be disparate accounts, he took it upon himself to assess which account was more credible and he recorded his findings for his own world and for posterity.[33] Thus Herodotus led the way in acknowledging the instability of human memory, in understanding the capacity of the mind to distort memories, whether through its susceptibility to transience, to misattribution, to suggestibility or to bias. He recognized that family loyalties and prejudice were factors that led to inconsistent accounts and diverse interpretations of events, and that memory at the individual level and ultimately at the cultural level was likewise subject to these same factors.[34] The sustained critical investigation that Herodotus undertook, in the light of these observations, became the model for the work of all historians.[35]

## CASE STUDY 3: THE DESIRE AND THE STRUGGLE TO FORGET

The world of Homer was concerned for the most part with the effort of remembering, or of not forgetting—that is, of not allowing its heroes and their great deeds to slip from the memory of contemporaries or of generations to come. But there are occasions when one's over-readiness to remember, one's incapacity to forget, becomes a burden, as Achilles in the *Iliad* and Ajax in the *Odyssey* demonstrate so clearly.[36]

Although Homer describes the suffering of individuals who are tormented by personal memories that cannot be erased, he does not dwell on the comparable experience of a community. Herodotus, however, offers us an example (6.21) of the way in which communities try to deal with painful memories: soon after 494, after the sack of Miletus by the Persians, the tragic poet Phrynichus produced a "Capture of Miletus" for his Athenian audience. During the performance members of the audience were overcome by grief. As a consequence, Phrynichus was fined for reminding them (ἀναμνήσαντα) of the disaster that had touched them so closely (for Athens had supported Miletus); and a law was passed that banned the play from the stage. Thus, the people of Athens demonstrated their awareness that memories prompted in the public sphere, in this case the sphere of social memory, could be a disruptive force in the life of the city; in response, they tackled the problem head-on. In the same vein, again in Athens, we hear of an altar to Forgetfulness (βωμός ... Λήθης) that was erected on the Acropolis at the Erechtheum, a fifth-century temple replacing an earlier shrine dedicated to Athena; an altar to Poseidon is also located there. Although Poseidon and Athena had once been in competition, each desiring to be the patron god of Athens, that contest was represented in the Athenian mind as an event quarantined in the past; it was "forgotten," as was any associated bitterness on the part of Poseidon, who had lost the contest. To make this point, the Athenian people subtracted from their calendar the anniversary day of the contest;[37] and they constructed the altar to Forgetfulness, which became, in Loraux's words, "the basis of life in the city" (Loraux 2002: 153–4). Once again, we see the *polis*'s desire to block the prompting of painful memory, even amongst the gods, who thus serve as models of appropriate behavior.

It is time now to talk about the Athenian "amnesty" of 403 BCE—a term which was not used by the Athenians themselves to describe this particular ban on memory. First, the background: following the defeat of Athens in the Peloponnesian War, thirty Athenian oligarchs were selected by the Spartans to run the government of the city and to write new laws. Extremists amongst the Thirty, as they were called, gained the upper hand: popular juries were abolished and supporters of the democracy were removed, along with wealthy citizens and non-citizen residents. Hundreds were executed; many others left Athens. Only through a movement from outside Athens was this rule of terror brought to an end. As Xenophon tells us (*Hell.* 2.4), a small band of democrats, led by Thrasybulus, gathered in Thebes and, advancing from there, seized Phyle; subsequently, and with greater numbers, they seized the Piraeus and there defeated the troops of the Thirty.

**FIGURE 8.5:** Fragment C of the honorary inscription for the heroes at Phyle; Raubitschek (1941), 292, photo of no. 78, frag. C (ID I 16). Credit: © American School of Classical Studies.

Thrasybulus was then able to lead his men into Athens (*Hell*. 2.4.38). Subsequently, oaths proposed by the Spartans were sworn that the democrats with Thrasybulus and the people in the city who had supported the Thirty would "not remember past grievances" (μὴ μνησικακήσειν, *Hell*. 2.4.43).[38]

The re-establishment of democracy, a significant event in Athenian history, was thereafter marked by two series of actions: first, by memorialization, in the stone *stelai* honoring the men of Phyle and the men of the Piraeus, and, some time later, a herm beside the rebuilt walls of the Piraeus and the tomb of Thrasybulus in the public cemetery (Steinbock 2013: 237–45; Wolpert 2002: 43–4; 87–90)[39] and, second, by a significant and necessary effort on the part of the people of Athens to deny the persistence of memory, and to put what should be forgotten behind them.[40] This was not a ban on the act of recounting the past; what was put in place was a check, to limit the seeking of revenge (Wolpert 2002: 77).

Certainly, as Wolpert shows so well, the forensic speeches available to us lead us to the conclusion that the efficacy of the reconciliation agreement was misjudged both by Xenophon and, later, Aristotle.[41] "Forgetting" was not so easy. Nevertheless, the courts offered the people of Athens a forum in which they could retell their version of the past (Wolpert 2002: 71). Even so, if the "amnesty" was to hold firm, a commitment beyond the domain of the law courts was required; what was needed was a willingness on the part of the Athenians, not as individuals but as a community, to forgo recrimination and revenge and to remember the past in ways that fostered reconciliation rather than bitterness and division.[42] Thus, at the level of civic ideology, the people of Athens came to exercise selective memory about the recent past: as Wolpert observes, the men of the Piraeus became the Athenian democracy in exile; the men of the city, who had supported the Thirty, now became the victims of the Thirty. Thus, through a willed distortion of memory, what might have been a separate and troublesome faction was now integrated into the restored democracy (Wolpert 2002: 93).

The "amnesty," this ban on remembering, did not call for, nor did it result in, a total erasure of certain events from the recent past: rather, it provided an interlude in which the bitter pursuit of former foes was actively discouraged; and this check on the pursuit of grievances, although imperfect, gave the citizens of Athens sufficient time to let the natural process of forgetting and healing take place, and sufficient latitude in which to reshape their civic memory of the past, reaffirming a continuing commitment to democracy. Herein lay the reasons for its relative success. This was an exercise in the management of social and cultural memory: in remembering *and* forgetting in equal part.[43]

## CONCLUDING REMARKS

The case studies above, from archaic and classical Greece, have allowed us to observe early attempts at harnessing memory, as society tried to understand and respond to the processes of remembering and forgetting at the individual, social, and cultural levels. The challenge of *not forgetting* is highlighted in the *Iliad*, a world of the imagination in which, as this poetic tradition makes clear, it is the responsibility of each generation to preserve for generations to come the deeds and names of their culture's great heroes. This is a world in which "memory" was thought to be aided by inspiration, thanks to the interventions of the Muse, whose authority was divinely assured. By the time of Herodotus, however, we are in a world in which human memory was viewed as a valuable resource, as a point of access to events of the past; but also apparent were its weaknesses, in particular its susceptibility to suggestion and its capacity for distortion. Herodotus saw his task as a sifting through of memories, to make decisions, as best he could, about plausibility, with the aim of safeguarding valid memories of the past by fixing them in writing. Our third example shows a contrary impulse, the desire of a community to put a check on the dangerous persistence of memory. In the late fifth century a successful reintegration of the people of Athens required a certain amount of strategic forgetting and the creation of a new narrative, a reshaping of memory. The so-called amnesty of 403 BCE allows us to see how this society dealt with the problem of not being able to forget, so that it might continue to function.

# NOTES

### *General Editors' Preface*

1. https://www.memorystudiesassociation.org/ (accessed February 3, 2020).
2. Agenda-setting in this respect was Cesari and Rigney (2014). For a review, see Erll 2011: 4–18.

### *Introduction*

1. Archelaos Relief BM 2191.
2. The precise context, date, and commissioner of the relief are debated among scholars. So as to not distract from the focus of this introduction I present a likely but by no means authoritative version here. Given its findspot Italy and the background of the sculptor in Asia Minor, the relief may stem from a different geographical and cultural context; similarly, I accept, without discussion, the common identification of figures that are unlabeled but recognizable by details of their iconography. For a more detailed interpretation and further references see Newby 2006: 156–78 and 156 n. 1.
3. The figure is not labeled but as the mother of the Muses the identification as *Mnemosyne* is compelling.
4. Again, I limit discussion to a brief note. The specifically Hellenistic culture of learning certainly shines through many aspects of the composition; moreover, the often preferred identification of the portrait faces of *Chronos* and *Oikumene* as those of Ptolemy IV and his wife Arsinoe III would steer towards a very specific historical and dynastic reading. This would include identifying the depicted cultic worship of Homer as taking place in the *Homereion* in Alexandria, a shrine dedicated to Homer by this king (cf. Aelian, *Varia Historia* 13.22).
5. Featuring all nine muses as the daughters of *Mnemosyne*, the relief does not follow a tradition that saw Memory as one of the three muses that were the three essential aspects of poetic work—its intended meaning therefore goes beyond the strong link between early Greek song culture and the Goddess of Memory. On this link see Castagnoli and Ceccarelli 2019: 11.
6. The works of Bommas are exemplary in this respect and attempt consistently to see the ancient world in all its parts, also asking about a "Mediterranean past" and "experience." See especially Bommas 2011 and Bommas, Harrisson, and Roy 2012.
7. For a good summary of the specificity of Greek taxonomies of memory, starting from vocabulary and its meaning and function, see the introduction in Castagnoli and Ceccarelli 2019: esp. 3–5.
8. Cf. Thomas 2019: 21–7 for careful comments on the nuances and misleading aspects of such labels; the author is particularly sceptical of Assmann's concept of "cultural memory" as "authoritative" because it "conjures up a somewhat cosy and uncontested community and culture . . ." (23); in her own work Thomas prefers to talk of "tradition," "official tradition," "city tradition" etc.
9. Alroth and Scheffer 2014's *Attitudes towards the Past*, e.g. are identical with "memory," which in turn is the equivalent of "creating identities"; yet, much in the case-studies presented

in the volume is about memory, and the asset of cross-cultural and -temporal comparison achieved via the link "identity" is evident.

10. By now "classics," works such as Zanker's *The Power of Images in the Age of Augustus* 1989 very much instigated ancient scholarship on memory; to single out but a few fascinating studies: Scheer 1993; Alcock 2002; Flower 2006; for an overview see Beck and Wiemer 2010b: 9–17.

11. Increasingly, studies begin with an almost apologetic acknowledgement that "the subject is no longer new" (see e.g. Hartmann 2012; Galinsky 2016b), or indeed with the reminder that constructed identities built on the manipulation of memories hardly matter in "real" negotiations of power (see e.g. Walter 2007, reviewing Jung 2006, on Marathon and Plataiai as *lieux de mémoire*).

12. Erll and Nünning 2010: 5 reject the antithesis or even importance of a debate history vs memory but rather see history as "but yet another mode of cultural memory," and "historiography its specific medium"; in their introduction to *The Birth of Classical Europe. A History from Troy to Augustine* 2010: 6 Simon Price and Peter Thonemann assert, "The first and overarching theme is 'memory'," and call their volume "a historical study of memory."

13. Price and Thonemann 2010: 8 want to take "seriously how people in the past saw themselves in relation to their own past" and offer "a set of rolling pasts."

14. Galinsky 2016a: 4–5, refers to a range of testimonies, above all Cicero, to make the point that the two were largely identified by the Romans. However, Galinsky acknowledges that they can be distinguished in chronological terms, with *historia* occupying a space beyond the reach of *memoria*.

15. Herodotus' account of the foundation of Cyrene illustrates clearly how well the author was aware of the complex ways in which a historian worked with "tradition" and "memory." For a detailed analysis of this awareness see Malkin 2003: 153–70.

16. Depending on the viewer/reader, the process (and outcome) may vary considerably. Is it the labels that steer the narrative? Do they simply complement the visual impression, or correct/counter-act viewing that ignores them? For analysis and a wide range of case-studies illustrating the juxtaposition of images and words in the ancient world see Newby and Leader-Newby 2006. A problematic "subversion" and "mismatch" between art and label was already noted in antiquity. Dio Chrysostom (31.156) commented on the re-inscribed statues of former athletes, which were "re-used to commemorate weaklings." Modern scholars are able to see the potential of such mismatches "allowing statues to represent two different individuals simultaneously" (Newby 2006: 16).

17. Referring to Hor., *Carm.* 1.2.15, Galinsky 2016b: twenty named statues and monuments as the quintessence of anything that attests to memory.

18. For the importance and further examples of archaeological/monumental/visual memory media see Chapters 3 and 7. Serida 2018 shows that the formative character of the Homeric epics extended to the Egyptian Inaros Cycle and thereby, indirectly, formulated even non-Greek memories of the past.

19. Steinbock 2013: 93 speaks of "corroboration" and "symbolic reminders of the lessons of the past."

20. Chaniotis 1988 is probably the earliest and most comprehensive work focusing on the link between inscriptions, historiography, and memory.

21. Han Baltussen's chapter in this volume addresses questions of literacy, which is, of course, relevant and complex.

22. On "canonization" see also Chapter 4; on the tension/interplay between ritual and textual continuity see also Chapter 7.

23. The authors talk about the "co-option of Homer for nationalist purposes" as "an important step in the creation of a communal past for themselves by the developing citizen-states."
24. See Minchin 2012a, who looks carefully at what these famous men did during their visits to experience the collectively remembered past in a direct emotional and physical way, not least to "inscribe" themselves into Troy's memory stratigraphy.
25. Or, in fact, individuals, for whom the values and heroic examples become formative models. If we ask on the impact of writing and canonization here, the difference may not be as sharp as formulated by J. Assmann 2015: 115.
26. Dowden in Bommas, Harrisson, and Roy 2012: 129, views "mythology as a variety of cultural memory" and even attempts to rewrite the mythology as "to advertise the power of that shared memory."
27. Thomas 2019: 245 attributes this to the fact that "the myths were so malleable." With the same emphasis Chiai 2013: 81–121.
28. See Scheer 2018: 71–91, a diachronic case-study that traces the creative uses of myths to establish political and cultural links between Cyprus and Arcadia.
29. Examples are so prolific that this form of constructing identities is often interpreted as a Hellenistic phenomenon. See Scheer 1993.
30. Cf. Hawes 2014: 185–8. The author endorses the parameters of "intentional history" as proposed in Gehrke 2001. See also Pirenne-Delforge 2004: 50–62, who examines Pausanias' unwillingness to separate myth from history.
31. For a detailed study on the origins of Rome's foundation story as based on descent from Aeneas see Erskine 2001.
32. Erskine 2001 has shown this successfully.
33. On these themes see Chapter 7. On the function of Euripedean aetiologies as bridging the gap between mythical times and the contemporary lives of fifth-century Athenians see, e.g. Romano 2012; on tragedy as "debating the past" see Scodel 2012.
34. See Chapters 5, 7, and 8.
35. The strict conceptual distinction by genre may be misleading in itself. Hornblower 2004 has set out the strong affinities between the victory odes of Pindar and Thucydides' work.
36. Thomas 2019: 56 acknowledges that this was not simple erudition or antiquarianism but that local historians were doing this as "an act of piety and patriotism," "an act of preservation and reverence."
37. See Chapter 2.
38. Undoubtedly, there was a stark contrast to the situation in Egypt and Babylonia, where priests or professional interpreters of the past, such as scribes, controlled sacred knowledge. These, however, often had to memorize the sacred texts, the wording of which was not to be changed. For further discussion see Chapter 7.
39. That the significance and authority of writing could extend to the status of scribes also in early Greece is illustrated in the so-called Spensitheos inscription (*SEG* 27.631; *LSAG* 468 no. 146). In this late archaic decree/contract from Crete a community appointed the scribe Spensitheos and his descendants to the monopoly of acting as "scribe and recorder for the city in public matters, either sacred or secular." The role was remunerated by "subsistence and freedom from all taxes."
40. The authors refer to contexts such as epic poetry, lament and tragedy.
41. See Chapter 8.
42. Cf. e.g. Ng 2016, who does so with regard to honorific statues in imperial Asia Minor.
43. See e.g. Chapter 1, where Boris Chrubasik refers to seminal studies on the memories of Nazi Germany to illuminate the behavior of elites/individuals as a reaction to "system change" in

the Hellenistic world and the Roman principate; also Chapter 6, on "High Culture and Popular Culture."
44. For a discussion of this process see esp. Chapter 3.
45. For a discussion on the "*spolia*" of the Arch of Constantine see Elsner 2000.

## Chapter One

1. Socrates commenting that he was deserving of such honor, as transmitted in Pl. *ap*. 36D, is only one example.
2. The main parts of the story are narrated in Hdt. 5, a long and unusual digression in Thuc. 6. 54–7 and Aristotle, *Ath. Pol.* 18. Note the discussion in Rhodes 1993: 190–1; Azoulay 2014: 29–37 offers a recent summary.
3. Reference to the songs that imply familiarity: e.g. Aristophanes, *Acharn.* 980. Direct quotation of lines for comedic effect: e.g. Aristophanes, *Lys.* 631–3 and the first line of *PMG* Page 893, as well as Aristophanes, *Acharn.* 1093 and the first line of *PMG* Page 894. I see little reason to follow the optimism of e.g. Rausch 1999: 51 n. 229, who follows Ostwald 1969: 125–36, building on the vague definitions of Bowra 1961: 395–6 (cited incorrectly by Rausch), that these *skolia* should have been composed—as a solid unit—before 480 BCE. See Thomas 1989: 258–60, who also does not question the unity of the *skolia*, but who uses the *skolion* as one piece of evidence that suggests the Cleisthenic championing of the tyrannicides (as does Pleket 1972: 69–73). Given that all fifth-century citations are never full citations, I would hesitate to narrow the complete *skolia* 893 and 896 closer in date than to the mid-fifth to mid-fourth century. Perceivably, it could be significantly later.
4. The practical aspects of behaving like a tyrannicide are discussed in Teegarden 2014b: 33–4.
5. The postulated relationship in Teegarden 2014a between the date of the decree and the time that had lapsed since 514 BCE is possible, but—also given the lower date of the text given here—could hardly count as a primary reason; we need to look at the immediate political environment of the 420s.
6. Note, however, as pointed out by Hornblower 2008: 433 that Thucydides' placement of the story at this point in time can ultimately only tell us that Thucydides was aware of this concern; a general Athenian concern is possible, but not certain.
7. For the oath of Demophantos: Teegarden 2014b: 30–40. If one can rely on the historicity of the decree, it would certainly have been a "highly memorable event" (Teegarden 2014b: 35).
8. For Jacoby this was all reliant on the *Atthis* of Hellanikos, but note e.g. Hornblower 2008: 439–40; Thomas 2019: 316–57.
9. For the notion of memory as a model, note Barry Schwartz's comment in Olick and Robbins 1998: 124.
10. Note also Gehrke's classification of intentional history, which fits thoroughly this Athenian scenario: Gehrke 2004: 2; see now Thomas 2019: 22–8.
11. J. Assmann 1992: 50–1 describes this individual memory as "communicative memory" relying on carriers and lasting for not more than four generations or about eighty years.
12. On the applicability of *lieux de mémoire* to the ancient city: Ma 2009.
13. On Alexander's empire e.g. Bosworth 1988 and Briant 2010; on the thirty-year period until the establishment of the Hellenistic kingdoms: e.g. Bosworth 2002.
14. Argead Macedonia had a clearer emphasis on a "right to rule": e.g. King 2010.
15. The Seleukid kings also fostered relationships with other sanctuaries: note Ios., *Ant*. 12. 138–46 for honors for the Temple in Jerusalem and the Antiochos Cylinder for a relationship with the temple of Nabu in Borsippa (see Stevens 2014).

16. On Seleukos and Didyma see now Ogden 2017: 56–8. Ogden 2017: 323 also imagines the legends to emanate from the early decades of the empire but emphasizes that evidence for this is slighter than it appears. By the late third century, he contends, a large part of the legend had been developed (idem: 323 and 325). Ogden 2017: 277–8 emphasizes the importance of Apollo already during Seleukos I's lifetime, but admits, however, that this does not necessarily have a bearing on the legend.
17. Note McAuley 2018 on Seleukid female royal names, which he sees as becoming signifiers for royal titles. His analysis of the royal name Laodike is important, however, he seems to underestimate how much royal names could have become a fashion. Yet if families could choose the name Laodike for reasons other than familial relations, this questions the persuasiveness of his analysis that the continuation of the name also can be a testimony of real blood relations.
18. On Antiochos III and his ancestors: Ma 2002: 50–2. On the kings of the second century and the eastern campaigns, see e.g. Fischer 1970: 108 and Ehling 2008: 203, on the *imitatio* of Antiochos III by Antiochos VII; also Mittag 2006: 317–18 for Antiochos IV's eastern campaigns. It should be noted though that Mittag does not speak of an imitation.
19. For the longer, first-century-context: e.g. Meier 2017. For politics in Rome after the Ides of March 44: Gotter 1996.
20. Note, however, the changed semantic of the triumph in the principate: Beard 2007: 68–71.
21. The complexity of the religious Roman landscape as outlined in Bendlin 2013 may, however, offer an important qualification on how visible and how "felt" these reconstituted memories were.
22. Scholarly debate has also turned around the question of when it began: see van Nuffelen 2004 with further bibliography.
23. Tr. David Campbell, Loeb Classical Library, vol. 144, slightly modified.
24. Thucydides identifies "those Athenians who wanted freedom" (Hdt. 5. 64. 2) with the Alkmaionidai. But note Anderson 2007: 116–17 on Thucydides caught in the web of Athenian memory.
25. See also Anderson 2007: 111–15 on views of the past in the *Lysistrata* and other plays.
26. The evidence for this Kedon as an Alkmaionid is circumstantial and based entirely on this passage, but see Rhodes 1993: 248, who persuasively argues that the textual context should provide the interpretation.
27. Despite its title, Rausch 1999: 369–70 does not add anything to the discussion.
28. For his lengthy discussion of the age of Hippias and the death of Hipparchos: Thuc. 6.54.1–59.2, read with Hornblower 2008: 433–40.
29. These memories are equated with "popular knowledge" in Thomas 1989: e.g. 199–200.
30. Note also Wagner-Pacifici and Schwartz 1991 concerning a memorial for which there was no public consensus. For "autobiographical" memory see also DeGloma 2015. Rhodes 1992: 63 supposes that the "Spartan" element could have been re-introduced under the noble Athenian politician Kimon who named his son Lakedaimonios. If this were the case, the Spartan memory could also be a cultural rather than communicative memory.
31. I owe the reminder that so often modern historians' analyses are based on etic categories to Andreas Bendlin (personal communication); cf. Bendlin 2015: 539.
32. This encompasses the "Alkmaionid tradition" championed by Jacoby 1949: esp. 158–66 (read with the powerful—if not always convincing—account of Podlecki 1966).
33. On forgetting, see Minchin in this volume.
34. For the *ostracisé*: Davies 1971: 379 (9688 X).

35. One could raise the question to which degree the removal of tyrants was too much political capital for one family.
36. This follows the model sketched in DeGloma 2015: 180–3 but is ultimately also the vision of Jacoby 1949: 161–2.
37. On the credibility of coinage: e.g. Meadows 2001. Coins as a political choice: Chrubasik 2016: 17–20. Tryphon's own regnal years: e.g. *SC* 2045 dated to "year 1."
38. The questions of support are difficult but is explicit for Apameia under Tryphon (Ios., *Ant*. 13. 224) and seems clear enough in the case of Seleukeia on the Tigris (Polyb. 5. 54. 10–12 with Chrubasik 2016: 215–16).
39. The difficulties in Ogden 2017: e.g. 323 to establish when certain parts of the legend of Seleukos developed may also point towards the fluidity and malleability of Seleukid cultural memories.
40. Pomp. Trog. 34. may possibly indicate this, as suggested by Kosmin 2014: 256; it may also just be a geographic reference.
41. Surely, the "many" family stories of their anti-tyrannic deeds noted by Thomas 1989: 252 are part of the same picture.
42. The independent study of Leonhard 2002 offers important qualifications and agreement. Note also Stock, Gajsar, and Güntürkün 2016: 385–8.
43. The temple was likely begun by Sosius in the 30s BCE, but the name was kept. For his career: Bartels 2001. See also Haselberger 2007: 83 with n. 105.
44. It should be emphasized that J. Assmann 2000: 38–9 is fully aware of the possible antagonism between these types of memories.
45. The people of the GDR's familiarity with west German television programs in contrast to the official denial of watching "Westfernsehen" is just one example: e.g. Welzer, Moller, and Tschuggnall 2002: 167–9.
46. Trillmich 2009: 466 substantially reconsiders his earlier views in light of recent excavations. Note also the careful remarks of Edmondson 2016: 83 with an updated bibliography up to 2010.
47. Ptolemaic names are probably mentioned in ll. 14–15. It should also be noted that individuals from western Asia Minor frequently served in the Seleukid empire's administration and army.
48. As also proposed in the careful discussion of Ng 2016.
49. I am grateful to Beate Dignas for her invitation to write this paper and for her substantive comments on earlier drafts. Discussions with Ben Akrigg, Andreas Bendlin, Elizabeth Ferguson, and Christian Seebacher have improved details and the argument; all shortcomings rest naturally with the author.

## *Chapter Two*

1. For a general introduction to various concepts about collective and cultural memory, from Halbwachs to Ricœur and Assmann, see the essay by Späth 2016, with extensive bibliography.
2. Scheid 1987, for a first examination of these sanctuaries on the basis of the evidence at our disposal; Scheid 2012, with a new overview in response to some hypercritical comments (e.g. by Ziółkowski 2009).
3. For current approaches to the religions of Rome: Beard, North, and Price 1998; Scheid 2003 and 2015; Rüpke 2007a and 2007b.
4. The last six months have probably been lost, or, perhaps, they were never written. A fine study of the links between Ovid, Augustus, and the *Domus Augusta* is provided by Herbert-Brown 1994. Different perspectives can be found in Barchiesi 1997.

5. Tu quoque sacrorum, Termine, finis eras.
6. *Contra*, Hannah 2005: 108, "Terminus [...] guarded physical, geographical boundaries, not, it seems, temporal ones." Except for intercalary years, which is supposed to be the true meaning of some references by our ancient evidence: Michels 1967: appendix 1 "Roman Intercalation," 145–72, esp. 162–3 with note 8.
7. Terminalia, quod is dies anni extremus constitutus: duodecimus enim mensis fuit Februarius et cum intercalatur inferiores quinque dies duodecimo demuntur mense.
8. Rüpke 2011 is an excellent presentation of the Roman calendar, an English translation of his German 1995 dissertation, revised and summarized.
9. The idea that February was the last month of the republican calendar, which rests essentially on the passage by Varro quoted above and on Cic. *De leg.* 2.21.54, has been the subject of much debate: the general consensus among scholars is that the republican calendar always began in January (e.g. Michels 1967: 97–9; Samuel 1972: 164–5; Hannah 2005: 108). See, however, on the supposed Decemviral reform and the conception of an "archaic" calendar, Brind'Amour 1983: 217–27 and Rüpke 1995: 289–330 ("Die Lex Acilia und das Problem der pontifikalen Schaltung").
10. The practice existed already before the Roman Empire (cf. e.g. the Seleucid era and the Pompeian era) but came to represent a radically new appraisal of time in the imperial perspective. The best recent overview is provided by Feeney 2007.
11. The decree has been preserved in a series of copies that were found in various cities of the province of Asia: see Thonemann 2015, with full references at p. 123 n. 1.
12. Dio 44.5.2, 55.6.6; Suet. *Aug.* 31.2; Macr., *Sat.* 1.12.35. Significantly, the renaming of the month Sextilis as Augustus occurred in 8 BCE, which, as we have seen, is also the year of Augustus' revision of the calendar reform that had been carried out by Caesar in 46 BCE; the same year, moreover, saw the institution of the calendar of the province of Asia.
13. The long passage in Ovid's *Fasti* about the Terminalia (639–78) ends with the public state celebration (679–84): est uia quae populum Laurentes ducit in agros, / quondam Dardanio regna petita duci: / illa lanigeri pectoris tibi, Termine, fibris / sacra uidet fieri sextus ab Vrbe lapis. / gentibus est aliis tellus data limite certo: Romanae spatium est Vrbis et orbis idem. "There is a way that leads folk to the Laurentine fields, the kingdom once sought by the Dardanian chief: on that way the sixth milestone from the city witnesses the sacrifice of a woolly sheep's guts to thee, Terminus. The land of other nations has a fixed boundary: the circuit of Rome is the circuit of the world" (Loeb, trans. Frazer). Cf. Robinson 2011 ad loc. and Barchiesi 1997, "Terminus and the sense of limits of the Roman identity."
14. On the Roman perception of and discourse about Athens starting from republican and Augustan times, cf. above all Feeney 2007, especially chapter 3 "Transitions from Myth into History I: The Foundations of the City," passim.
15. αἴδ' εἴσ' Ἀθῆναι Θησέως ἡ πρὶν πόλις. / αἴδ' εἴσ' Ἀδριανοῦ καὶ οὐχὶ Θησέως πόλις (*IG* II² 5185).
16. For some perspectives about the foundation of cities in classical antiquity, see Reddé 2003. On the traditional and literary conception of the foundation of Rome, see Ternes 1992.
17. In Italy, the vigorous debate about the origins of Rome developed into a controversy between Carandini (1997); Carandini and Cappelli (2000); and Gabba (1999). For two different conceptions of the "beginnings" of Rome in British historiography, see Cornell 1995 and Wiseman 1995.
18. DC 53.16.7–8; Suet. *Aug.* 7.4: Romulum appellari... ipsum conditorem urbis.
19. Quae ante conditam condendamue urbem poeticis magis decora fabulis quam incorruptis rerum gestarum monumentis traduntur, ea nec adfirmare nec refellere in animo est. 7. Datur haec uenia antiquitati ut miscendo humana diuinis primordia urbium augustiora faciat; et si

cui populo licere oportet consecrare origines suas et ad deos referre auctores, ea belli gloria est populo Romano ut cum suum conditorisque sui parentem Martem potissimum ferat, tam et hoc gentes humanae patiantur aequo animo quam imperium patiuntur. For the idea of the *princeps* as *conditor*, see Benoist 2001, with full bibliography.

20. *RIC* III, Commodus, 560, Rome, sesterce, in 190 and Ibid. 616, Rome, sesterce, in 192. On Commodus and his policy of "images."
21. Cf. *CIL* 6.33856 (*ILS* 8935), forum Romanum: Marti inuicto patri / et aeternae urbis suae / conditoribus / dominus noster / I[[mp(erator) Maxent[iu]s p(ius) f(elix)]] / inuictus Aug(ustus); "To Mars the undefeated father and to his eternal city, to the founders, our master the Imperator Maxentius, pious, lucky and undefeated Augustus." The inscription was erased after Constantine's victory. On the process of *abolitio memoriae*, see a few conclusive remarks below.
22. The authors offer a compendium that illustrates a wide range of historical and theoretical aspects relating to this huge subject during the Empire. Specifically on the case of Italy during the republic, see David 1996.
23. Cf. Gonzalez 1986, who draws on a major discovery in Spanish epigraphy which illuminates the process of "municipalization" of foreign cities through the granting of Latin Law. On Latin Law, see Le Roux 2015, the most recent survey by a French specialist.
24. The Latin word *ciuitas* can be interpreted on three different levels: as the community of the *ciues* (citizens), as the city as a political unit, and finally as the whole civilization in its various connotations. For a global approach, see Inglebert 2005. Woolf 1998 is an attempt to renew the concept of Romanization through the specific case of Gaul.
25. The implications of Augustus' building programme for the shaping of Roman memory have been examined by Orlin 2016. Previously, Gros 1976 and Sablayrolles 1981 dealt with the Augustan architectural project in political perspectives to reflect on the impact of Augustus' *impensae* on the urban everyday life, from the *Res Gestae diui Augusti* to the reception by contemporaries and further historians of this euergetic programme. For further references and a discussion of these policies in the context of power-building see Chrubasik in the previous chapter.
26. Ludi quam amplissimi ut fierent senatus decreuit; 5: Magna hic nunc Volscorum multitudo est; ludi sunt; spectaculo intenta ciuitas erit; and 8–9: factoque senatus consulto ut urbe excederent Volsci [. . .] proficiscentibus deinde indignatio oberta se ut consceleratos contaminatosque, ab ludis festis diebus, coetu quodam modo hominum deorumque abactos esse.
27. Vrbem auspicato inauguratoque conditam habemus; nullus locus in ea non religionum deorumque est plenus; sacrificiis sollemnibus non dies magis stati quam loca sunt in quibus fiant.
28. Cf. Beard, North and Price 1998, vol. 1, ch. 6, and vol. 2, ch. 5, with several examples; for a complete overview, see Hermary and Jaeger 2011, which includes an example from the Spartan city Gytheion at the beginning of Tiberius's principate (an inscription about the creation of new festivals, on which see Benoist 2011: 271–2, "Les *Kaisereia* de Gythéion").
29. Foreign residents (*incolae*) are regularly mentioned in inscriptions relating to the imperial cult. For example, at Narbo *coloni et incolae* attended imperial festivals at the shrine of the colony: *CIL* 12.4333 [*ILS* 112]. Cf. Benoist 2016.
30. On the so-called language of empire, which does not correspond to our modern concept of imperialism, see Richardson 2008. For a classical essay about Polybius, see Millar 1987.
31. Suffice to think of the development from Fabius Pictor, who wrote his Roman history in Greek at the end of the third century BCE, to Ammianus Marcellinus, a Greek native who chose Latin for his own work.

32. Polybius 6.53.10–54.2 (aristocratic funerals); Dio 56.34 (Augustus); 74.4–5 (Pertinax); Herodian 4.2 (Septimius Severus).
33. Cf. Tert., *De Spectaculis*, and *Apologeticum*; with Barnes 1985, Wilhite 2007, and Fredouille 2012. For an example of further Christianization of space and time in late antique Rome, see Salzman 1999.
34. This applies also to the case of a unique God, as we can interpret some important aspects of the Christianization of time from new festivals and ceremonies, as well as aspects of the Christianization of space from the Christian topography introduced e.g. in Rome and Constantinople.
35. For some perspectives on the so-called *damnatio memoriae*, a modern phrase used to describe the process of *abolitio memoriae*, see Flower 2006; Benoist and Daguet-Gagey 2007; Benoist and Daguet-Gagey 2008; and Benoist, Daguet-Gagey, Höet-van Cauwenberghe, and Lefebvre 2009. Although terms like *damnati* and formulae like *abolitio memoriae* can be found in ancient sources, *damnatio memoriae* is a modern Latin phrase (see Vittinghoff 1936).

## Chapter Three

1. Literature on media memory is very extensive; due to space requirements, only a few exemplary titles are referred to in this contribution. I am grateful to Beate Dignas and Elvira Migliaro for their precious comments. Any remaining error is the author's responsibility.
2. Ricoeur distinguishes three different levels of mimesis: mimesis I (a prefiguration of a narrative on human action consisting of different elements as e.g. agent, means, goals, and so on); mimesis II (the reconfiguration of this experience through an emplotment which makes it intelligible); mimesis III (a refiguration mediating the world of the text and the world of the reader). It is possible to argue that mimesis II unavoidably limits his "historical value," and indeed narrative reconfiguration ends up requiring more refined methodological tools by historians.
3. Winter and Sivan 1999 suggest to substitute the term "memory" with "remembrance" to avoid the reification of the former, but this has not been followed by other scholars; in what follows I shall therefore use "memory" to design the process of remembering and "memories" or "remembrance"/"remembrances" to design what is remembered. On the risks of reification see Giangiulio 2019: 17–20.
4. Not in the sense of multiple media (music, dance, painting, sculpture etc.) converging in performances that finally result in "scores" and "instructions" becoming artworks in themselves (Higgins 1966; Nöth 1997; Osborne 2002; O'Neill 2008), but in the sense of "medium of a medium" involving a process of remediation as described by Bolter and Grusin 1999: 273.
5. See e.g. Ruth Scodel's and Allen Romano's enquiries on differences and similarities in the past attitudes of historians and tragedians, or Jonas Grethlein's analysis of the techniques through which the Homeric past is recalled in historiography and in oratory.
6. On these themes see Chapter 7 in this volume.
7. I have studied some of the case studies in depth myself, while historians specialized in memory studies in classics have done so for others; this is a summary and comment on the results of their research in light of media memory studies.
8. Regrettably, environments promoting memory such as speeches, theater and schools, or other media such as poetry are not addressed, and forgetting devices (e.g. the much studied *damnatio memoriae*) or *lieux de mémoire*, both in Nora's (1984–92) sense and in a literal sense, are not dealt with here; however, there is considerable literature on these: on theater as medium of "familiar memories" and "community memories," and on *gnome* turned into

narratives by collective memory, see Flower 1995 with further lit.; Gould 1999: 108–11; on the relationship between theater and memory see Sommerstein 1993; Pelling 1997; Beltrametti 2011: 16; on schools as an important medium of memory in Ancient Greece see Nicolai 1992, on schools as media of exempla and therefore of the *mos maiorum* in Ancient Rome in the republican period see Walter 2004: 47ff with previous bibliography, who comments on Cic., *Off.* 1.61ff; *Mur.* 75; Quint. *Inst.* 10.1.31–34; 12.2.29-31; Suet., *Tib.* 2; on speeches as mediatic framework see Franchi 2017 (Greece) and Migliario 2015 and 2019 (Rome), both with further bibliography.

9. For the same reason the (in most cases very extensive) bibliography on the following case studies is cited only selectively, by mentioning only a few seminal works as well as the most recent contribution to consult for further bibliography.
10. Literature is summoned and discussed in the papers collected in Giangiulio 2005; bibliographical update in Munson 2013.
11. Xen., *Lac.Pol.* 11.3; Plut., *Lyc.* 16.11–12; *Lys.* 1; *Mor.* 230B. On the relevance of hairstyle in Sparta, also in order to express opposition, see Hdt. 7.208; Aristotle, *Rh.* 1367A27–31; Plut., *Lyc.* 15; and Franchi 2009 with other sources and previous bibliography.
12. As. fr.13; Thuc. 1.6.3; Aristophanes, *Eq.* 1321–1334. Further sources in Franchi 2009: 75–7, and, more recently, Bershadsky 2012.
13. It is also interesting to note that the writing of oral stories that keep on circulating in parallel triggers in turn hypermediacy, which multiplies the signs of mediation without remediating.
14. Cic., *De orat.* 169: "si barbarorum est in diem vivere, nostra consilia sempiternum tempus spectare debent."
15. Commented by Gowing 2005: 8. See also Cic., *Cato* 21–22, commented by Walter 2004: 34–5.
16. "Kommunikatives Gedächtnis", i.e. the past which is still alive in one's own memory or directly reported by parents and grandparents; Assmann 2000: 20.
17. It has long been commonly assumed that in contrast with Greek elites, Roman noble families had more "stability" and therefore were the very "lords" (cf. Cic., *Mur.* 166; Liv. 27.8.9–10) of a memory that for a certain time was private and only later was presented as the memory of the *populus Romanus* as a whole, after the struggles that led to the ascendancy of the early republic (Timpe 2011). More recent views have highlighted the fluidity of Roman "aristocracies" (Bradley 2015; Smith 2019), with exception of the period between 450 and 367 (Raaflaub 2005); for studies on elites in ancient Greece and Rome see Giangiulio 2016. Neither view implies that elites had total control of memory (much more binding was the *tabula pontificum*, which, however, did not cover all events and stories to be remembered); nor can oral memories by other social groups be dismissed a priori, even if it is not possible to investigate them (Gabba 2000: 61): see Rüpke 2000: 47; Walter 2004: 84ff (with further bibliography and a compilation of sources), 254; Migliario 2015. For collective memory conveyed by monuments and triumphs see Favro 2014 and Migliario 2015, who also observes the role played by the generals and by the *principes* as lords of memory, whereas there is no "national memory" (national memories are typical for provinces: a good example is the Bellum Iudaicum), on which see Flower 1995; Migliario 2015 (vs. Wiseman 1994).
18. On the *laudationes funebres* see Polyb. 6.53–4 with comment of Flower 1995, 178ff; Coel. Ant., *FRH* 11 F 36 (=Liv. 27.27.13) with comment of Beck and Walter 2004 ad l.; Kierdorf 1980; Gabba 2000: 63–5; Walter 2004: 89–108 (with further bibliography); Beck 2005: 333; on the role played by women in the *laudationes* (and beyond: e.g. in the *ossilegium* ritual): Rohr Vio 2017 (with a fresh, documents-oriented *gender* perspective on the media of collective memory) and Zecchini 2017; on the (genealogically shaped) *pompa funebris*, see Flaig 1995; Hölkeskamp 1996: 320–32; Blösel 2000: 37–46; Walter 2004: 89ff, Ungern-

Sternberg 2011; on the *imagines* see Cic. 2 *Verr* 5.36 (ius imagines ad memoriam posteritatemque prodendae); Pliny, *NH* 35.2 with comment of Beck 2005: 16; Tac. 3.76; Walbank 1957 on Polyb. 6.53.7–8; Flower 1996; Spannagel 1999: 263–344; Walter 2004: 89–108 (with further bibliography); Shumka 2000: 150–88; Migliario 2015 (who comments on *CIL* I² 6, 7; 8, 9 [sepulchral inscriptions of the Scipiones]); on the festivals of the dead see e.g. Ov., *Fasti* 2.537ff; cf. Lindsay 1998: 74–6; Dunbabin 2004; on the *Parentalia* see Scullard 1981: 74–5.

19. On the *fabulae praetextae*: Wiseman 1994; Flower 1995 (esp. on contemporary praetextae as a controversial genre in a context of aristocratic competition and as a form of direct control of audience reactions); Rüpke 2000: 42; Walter 2004: 75ff, with a comment and further bibliography on Liv. 7.2; Beck 2005: 303ff; on the first discourse of the consuls in the *contio*: Cic., *leg.agr.* 2.1 with Flower 1996: 154–5; Beck 2005: 23; on the *pompa funebris*: Blösel 2000: 41 (spectators were not only aristocrats); Hölkeskamp 2016: 182. See also Beck 2005: 14ff.
20. I.e. the principle of not starting anew from the beginning but rather, by way of reference, joining in what had been going on and thereby entering into a continuous communicative process (Assmann 1992: 281ff).
21. One of the most influential audiences to which both Herodotus and Thucydides appeal are educated Athenian milieus of the 420s, and even if *akroaseis* are specifically Herodotean, Thucydides' work is also influenced by an akroasis-oriented approach. See Franchi 2011 with previous bibliography, and Wecowski 2016 with bibliographical update. More generally, on the permanent interaction between orality, literacy, and aurality in conveying memories (esp. medieval ones), see Adamska forthcoming: 2 and 6.
22. E.g. Liv. 1.6.4 to compare with Suet., *Aug.* 95; Liv. 1.7.15; 5.50 to compare with *Res gestae* 19–10; 6.4.1; 7.1.9; 6.6.7; see Miles 1995: 89–95; Walter 2004: 402ff esp. n. 122 on pp. 402–3 (more cautious); Gowing 2005: 21ff; Mineo 2015: 145ff.
23. Proust, M. (1913–27), *Remembrance of Things Past. Volume 1: Swann's Way: Within a Budding Grove. The Definitive French Pleiade*, transl. by C.K. Scott Moncrieff and T. Kilmartin, New York: Vintage, 49–51.
24. It is difficult to locate the Phocian monument but it would appear likely that the *halos* represented, in the fourth century, an appropriate place for it: see Franchi 2018.
25. Literature and discussion in Franchi 2018. The Pieres were the inhabitants of Pieria, a region between Thessaly and Macedonia conquered by Philip in the fourth century.
26. The Opimian temple is reportedly attested by numerous authors; it is not clear if a previous temple was built by Camillus in 367 BCE with similar purposes (Momigliano [1942] arguing that its construction formed part of the later Camillus legend) cf. Cic., *Sest.* 140; App., *BC* 1.26; Plut., *Cam.* 42; *C.Gracch.* 17.
27. Cf. also lines 10–11. Bibliography is very extensive, see, e.g. Nielsen 2000: 109ff; Dominguez-Monedero 2008 (with lemma); Daverio Rocchi 2015: 198, all with further bibliography.
28. Cf. the so-called Mädcheninschrift: *IG* IX 1².3.706, with Wilhelm 1911.
29. Hor., *Carm.* 4.18.13; Suet., *Aug.* 31; Dio 55.10; Laprid., *vit. Alex.* 28. Only three fragments of the inscription survive, but the entire text is recorded in the codices of Renaissance observers. Modern editions rely on Theodor Mommsen's reconstruction. See e.g. the Scipionum *elogia* or the *elogium* by C. Sempronius Tuditanus (*CIL* 12, 652; *ILLRP* 335).
30. Such tendency is typical for other media, as Augustus' own *Res Gestae* shows: silent about the unsavory aspects of the emperor's rise to power, it conflicts with other interpretations of the emperor's triumviral career, and the very fact that these interpretations were competing memories is proved by Tac., *Ann.* 1.9–10. Cf. Bonamente 2017.

31. Another interesting case-study analyzed in a similar perspective is the Tabula Lugdunensis: Galimberti 2017: 195–7 and passim.
32. Cf. *FPK* F 23 Morel (cf. [Hom.], *Od*.8.480–1) and Varro *LL* 6.49; Miano 2012, with bibliography.
33. The Spartan king issued silver tetradrachms on the Attic standard (*c*. 17.2g), based on the Alexandrine type, and obols on the Aeginetan standard (*c*. 0.95g). Both tetradrachms and obols bore the head of Heracles (Grunauer-von Hoerschelmann 1978: 1–4, groups I and II).
34. See also Satyrus *FHG* III, p. 165; cf. also a cult statuette depicting Philadelphus with a club, traditionally carried by Heracles (London *BM* 38442).
35. Most of the scholars agree on this identification: Münzer 1930: 1582–3; Lahusen 1983: 47 and 57–8; Bergemann 1990: 156 L 10; Sehlmeyer 1999: 57–60; Schmuhl 2008: 78–9; Hölkeskamp 2016: 190.

## *Chapter Four*

1. I am grateful to the editor, Beate Dignas, for inviting me to contribute a chapter on this challenging theme. I am also grateful to colleagues and graduate students who attended a presentation on some of the material, esp. Margaret O'Hea, George Couvalis, and Emily Chambers for helpful comments during the discussion.
2. The author goes as far as to claim, "It is this urge that led to the invention of paper."
3. A further important point is that of authority and how written versions of scientific knowing could lead to new modes of evaluating this kind of expertise. This question has been given a new significance in the recent volume *Authority and Expertise in Ancient Scientific Culture* (König and Woolf 2017), which contains many insightful essays but was available too late for me to include here. See now also Taub 2017.
4. The technical notion is of an extended mind is far more elaborate, and also quite recent (the phenomenon itself is of course as old as writing itself). A philosophical defence of an extreme version (cognitive processes can take place outside our head) was introduced by Clark and Chalmers (1998). The debate is ongoing; see Rupert 2004; Pritchard 2010.
5. Referring to the *Phaedrus*, Kurlansky must mean 274c–5b, the conversation between Thamus and Theuth.
6. For philosophy "proper" see Chapter 5 in this volume.
7. For a useful list of recent literature on social and cultural memory, see Elsner and Squire 2016: 181 notes 4–5.
8. One may compare lists in archaic poetry, e.g. Hesiod, *Catalogue of Women*; Homer's catalogue of ships in *Iliad* B. See Goody 1978 on lists as an important step towards cultural sophistication. Cf. Wright 2004: 124, who points to lists at Pylos in Linear B.
9. Some of the important sources for this list of ten muses are Hes., *Theog.* 75, Apollod. 1.13, Diod. Sic. 4.7.1, *Orphic Hymn* 76. But there are variants: lists of 3 or 4 Muses exist.
10. According to Cicero, Themistocles dismissed his skill, preferring forgetting to remembering: "I would rather have a technique of forgetting, for I remember what I would rather not remember and cannot forget what I would rather forget" (*Fin.* 2. 104).
11. See also Chapter 5 in this volume.
12. For his famous image of the "clean slate" ("erased writing tablet," *tabula rasa*—not his phrase) see also Chapter 5. By this metaphor he brought brain and paper closer together as part of his so-called "theory of recollection" which has remembering at its heart. In addition, his position on science was well informed but ultimately not one which could commit to its overall function, given the inferior status he gave it as part of this derivative sensible world we live in.

13. Jouanna 1999: 10 places his birth in 460.
14. Cf. Johne 1991, who speaks of a "book culture" ("Buchkultur") in the second half of the fifth century BCE.
15. It is referred to as a *historia*, an "investigation," or the account resulting from it (hence my translation "investigative approach" which I hope captures both senses). The word is also used by Herodotus for his own ethnographic researches (*Histories*, Book 1).
16. Plato's knowledge of the medical science of his day are included at *Timaeus* 72c–76e, 77c–92c.
17. Much like the Hippocratics did, and as Galen would do later; see the following section.
18. Admittedly Aristotle's point is more limited in its original context: he emphasizes the aspect of the *general* versus the *particular* in a discussion of legislation (arguing that a mere collection of laws written down still does not amount to knowledge of justice or a just society).
19. Jaeger 1957 already pointed this out. See also Jaeger 1978, where the author dedicates a whole chapter to the theme "Greek Medicine as Paideia" (III. 3–45).
20. Sedley's choice of "Transformation" in the title is a telling one and reinforced by the fact that it is also the last word in the book (p. 204).
21. Quotations in later authors such as Pliny, Gellius, Censorinus, Servius, Nonius, Macrobius, and Augustine allow us to reconstruct parts of the work. For the edition of fragments see Goetz and Schöll 1910: 199–242.
22. I am grateful to Ms. Emily Chambers for pointing out that the actual composition of the work has the additional complicating factor of slaves assisting Pliny in reading and writing materials. I lack the space here to explore this aspect of the writing process in antiquity, but see Skydsgaard 1968; Dorandi 1991.
23. The source for the first title is late: φυσική ἱστορία is mentioned by Simplicius in his *Commentary on Aristotle's Physics* p. 154.17 (Diels), but it fits the style of the Peripatos (see above text to note 13). The second is in the list of his works in DL 5.
24. Of course, a fundamental difference remains between Aristotle as a philosopher developing his own doctrine, and Pliny who is mostly a collector within a framework of his own making. I am grateful for my colleague Dr. Margaret O'Hea for pointing this out.
25. I am most grateful to Dr. Ricardo Julião (HU, Berlin) for generously allowing me early access to his paper in August 2017, which I summarize on the most relevant points here. The paper is now published in Thumiger and Singer 2018.
26. I have tacitly taken as valid several long-standing theories about social and cultural memory. Some of these have been revised and criticized in recent decades.

## Chapter Five

* Over the last fifteen years, my work on ancient philosophical conceptions of memory has greatly benefited from the feedback of more friends and colleagues than I could mention here. I would like to thank them all here collectively, but in particular Paola Ceccarelli; my understanding of the cultural and literary context in which ancient philosophical conceptions took shape is hugely indebted to what I learnt from Paola as we worked together on Castagnoli and Ceccarelli 2019.
1. For the association between the gods Kronos and Chronos (Time) see Plutarch (*Is. Os.* 32). For earlier evidence of this association see Castagnoli and Ceccarelli 2019: 5–6.
2. For the etymology of ἀλήθεια see Chantraine 1969: 618–9, s.v. λανθάνω; Beekes 2010, s.v. ἀληθής: composed of privative α and λήθη, "forgetfulness," or perhaps, more generally, privative α and the root λαθ- "to be hidden, unknown"; Cole 1983.

3. Cf. also *Theog.* 31–2.
4. For the role of Mnemosyne at the oracle of Trophonius in Lebadeia cf. Pausanias 9.39.3.
5. On the relief see the Introduction to this volume.
6. Throughout the chapter, I put "theory of recollection" in scare quotes: we should not think of Platonic *anamnēsis* as a single, fully worked-out theory to which Plato was committed, but as a set of ideas and arguments that Plato explored non-dogmatically in a number of different dialogues and contexts. The literature on Plato's theory of recollection is vast: see e.g. Vlastos 1994; Scott 1995; Dancy 2004; Kahn 2006.
7. The sophist Hippias of Elis was renowned for his astonishing memory (Pl. *Hipp. ma.* 285d–286a). Yet it is likely that he also used some sort of "mnemonic technique" (*Hipp. min.* 368d). The sophistic treatise *Dissoi Logoi* celebrates the power of memory: "The greatest and finest discovery to be found for life is memory; it is useful for all purposes, for inquiry and wisdom" (9.1), and makes reference to some mnemonic techniques (9.4–5). On ancient "mnemotechniques," including the influential technique of "memory places," cf. e.g. Yates 1966 and 2001; Sorabji 1972 and 2006a; Coleman 1992; Small 1997.
8. For some qualifications on this picture see Sassi 2019.
9. Cf. also *Symposium* 175d: "How wonderful it would be, dear Agathon, if the foolish were filled with wisdom simply by touching the wise. If only wisdom were like water, which always flows from a full cup into an empty one when we connect them with a piece of yarn . . ." In the *Symposium* the poet Agathon is also presented as someone influenced by Gorgias.
10. Cf. also *Meno* 73c: "try and tell me and recollect what Gorgias, and you with him, say [*aretē*] is."
11. Notice the word-play between Meno's name (Μένων) and the participle "remembering" (μνήμων) in Socrates' disavowal of memory quoted above.
12. For detailed analysis of the paradox in the *Meno* and its extensive influence in ancient philosophy see Fine 2014.
13. For some qualifications on this endorsement see *Meno* 86b ("I do not insist that my argument is right in all other respects").
14. On the interpretation of *anamnēsis* according to which it accounts for basic concept formation since early childhood, human beings all recollect (at least some of) the Forms, however partially and dimly. On a different interpretation which has been especially promoted by Scott 1987 and 1995, in the *Phaedo* (but also in the *Meno* and the *Phaedrus*) recollection is an arduous process of philosophical enquiry and understanding that only few undertake.
15. A different argument for the immortality of the soul based on recollection was introduced in the *Meno* (85d–86b). For introductions to the *Phaedo* as a whole cf. e.g. Hackforth 1955; Gallop 1976; Bostock 1986. On recollection in the *Phaedo* cf. e.g. Ackrill 1973; Bedu-Addo 1991; Scott 1995; Dimas 2003; Dancy 2004; Fine forthcoming.
16. For another reference to the "ancient doctrine" of metempsychosis see *Phaedo* 70c–d.
17. For a post-death discarnate vision of the Forms, which presumably will also ground our capacity for recollection in future lives, see *Phaedo* 66d–e.
18. In the *Phaedo*, Socrates claims that those who established rites of purification for a good afterlife (presumably the Orphics) were setting a riddle, since "wisdom itself is the kind of rite to purify us" (69d).
19. Presumably this inability is the result of their deeper forgetfulness of the "sights" and experiences of their after-death journey. For analysis of the myth of Er and other Platonic eschatological myths see e.g. Annas 1982; Halliwell 2007.
20. For an earlier reference to metempsychosis (and possible allusion to recollection) see 498c–d.
21. Although he draws a clear distinction between *mnēmē* and *anamnēsis* in the *Philebus*, at times Plato uses the two terms interchangeably in the *corpus*.

22. In the context of 34b–c *aisthēsis* is associated with what the soul "experienced with the body" and contrasted with "pieces of knowledge" (*mathēmata*).
23. Cf. *Tht.* 189e–190a; *Soph.* 263e–264b.
24. In the *Meno* the stability of knowledge is directly connected to idea of *anamnēsis* at 97d–98a.
25. Socrates then compares the soul to an "aviary," in which we keep the birds/pieces of knowledge we capture/acquire (197a–199c); although the birds are not presented as memories, the claim that when we are children our aviary is empty (197e) is an explicit denial of innate knowledge.
26. Cf. *Timaeus* 26c: "the story has stayed with me like the indelible markings of a picture with the colors burnt in (οἷον ἐγκαύματα ἀνεκπλύτου γραφῆς ἔμμονά μοι γέγονεν)."
27. The philosopher will also write for "amusement" (*paidia*), producing "reminders" (*hypomnēmata*) of what he already knows, for himself and for those who follow in the same footsteps (276d).
28. For some studies of memory in the ancient near-eastern, Indian, and Chinese traditions, included, but not limited to, philosophical approaches, see e.g. Sharma 1983; Assman 1992; Perret 1999; Thompson 2013; Chen 2015; Nadali 2016; Baines, van der Bloom, Chen, and Rood 2019.
29. On Plotinus' conception of memory (including his rejection of the wax block model) cf. e.g. King 2009; Chiaradonna 2019.
30. For Aristotle's own influential description of this process cf. *Metaph.* 1.1.980a27–981a7; *APo.* 2.19. Memory plays a similar role as a central faculty in the Epicurean empiricist epistemology and was an object of study in its own right for Epicurean physics and psychology (memory was understood as a sort of "imprint" or material change in the atomic structure of the mind). Moreover, memorization of the key tenets of the school was fundamental to the Epicurean therapy and way of life (Spinelli 2019).
31. For two interesting but elusively short ancient texts cf. Pl. *Tht.* 166b1–4 (Protagoras) and Eus. *PE* 14.7.9 (the Academic Skeptic Lacydes).
32. Two interesting exceptions are the ancient anecdote about Pythagoras' extraordinary ability to remember his past lives, which he had chosen as a proxy for immortality (D. L. 8.4–5), and Lucretius *DRN* 3.843–64, which suggests that the continuity of our memories is a necessary condition for our persistence as individuals through time (cf. Warren 2001; Sorabji 2006b: ch. 5).

## Chapter Six

\* I wish to thank several colleagues for our discussions on the subject: Julien Alerini, Gilles Gorre, Jean-Manuel Roubineau, Catherine Saint-Pierre, and Christophe Vendries who kindly accepted to review this contribution; for his remarks and for the translation, Alexandre Mitchell (www.expressum.eu); and for her thorough and precious review, Beate Dignas.
1. E.g. Kalifa 2010, who ends his article regretting the lack of research on contemporary popular practices. For antiquity: Toner 2009; Parker 2011; Kurke 2011; de Angelis et al. 2012; Forsdyke 2012; Grig 2017a.
2. A first division between *plebs* and patriciate was replaced in the middle of the fourth century BCE by the division between *plebs* and *nobilitas*; then, at an unspecified date, it gave way to a tripartition between the *plebs*, the equestrian order and the senatorial order, the first order constituting the pool for the second.
3. On the *kaloi kagathoi*, see Bourriot 1995, criticized by Davies 2013; see also Martínková 2010. On Second Sophistic references to the past: Bowie 1970; Gangloff 2013.

4. *Nostra memoria* or *memoria hominum*: Baroin 2010: 29. Thomas 1989: 105, 124–31.
5. Anna Perenna: Ov., *Fast.* 3.523–696; Courrier 2014: 585–6. The Aventine as a "place of memory": Prim 2016; Rutledge 2015: 229–37; Horsfall 2003: 14 notes that the Christianization of society generated a growing need to memorize, but with a certain tolerance towards this memorization: "The Creed, the Our Father, a handful of psalms and a few biblical texts were the indispensable minimum. Oddly enough, though, in comparison with the Jew's urgent intensity in memorising the Torah, and with the ancient Romans' insistence upon following the very letter of every sacred text, the new religion was curiously lax (or merely realistic) when it came to memorisation."
6. Regarding the possibility of a shared memory, different from Maurice Halbwachs' idea of a collective socially framed memory, see Candau 2005.
7. The example of the architect is mentioned by Galinsky 2015: 7.
8. It is obviously impossible to answer such a question, but Vitruvius' fame (for us) goes back to the third century, after his treatise was abridged by Cetius Faventinus.
9. On orality and literacy, one can add to the standard works by Thomas 1989 and 1992 that of Pébarthe 2006. The book edited by L. Grig (2017a) is typical of this imbalance: only two studies focus on the ancient Greek world, one of which being on Aristophanes (Robson 2017). On memory in Classical Greece see Simondon 1982.
10. Brown 1981 rejects the dichotomy between Popular Culture and High Culture and the notion of "popular religion." On literacy in Rome see Corbier 2006: 47 and 74-5.
11. Forsdyke 2012: 6–11, on the mixed nature of "popular culture," and 11–16 on its political dimension. On the back-and-forth movement between "popular culture" and "high culture," see Kurke 2011.
12. See Lucian, *De Saltatione,* on the popularity of pantomimes.
13. See the praise of Q. Fabius Maximus Cunctator by Cato the Elder, *On Old Age* 12–13, *consul* four times, victorious at Tarentum and against Hannibal; Baroin 2010: 127–52. See Moatti 2003; Landrea 2014.
14. Polyb. 6.54: "By this means, by this constant renewal of the good report of brave men, the celebrity of those who performed noble deeds is rendered immortal, while at the same time the fame of those who did good service to their country becomes known to the people and a heritage for future generations. But the most important result is that young men are thus inspired to endure every suffering for the public welfare in the hope of winning the glory that attends brave men" (Loeb tr. W.R. Paton).
15. Cic., *De Or.* 2.59.239 and 242, 60.244, 245 and 247, 62. 251–252, etc.; Hor., *Sat.* 1.5.50–69. Horsfall 2003: 64–74, 75–82; Suet., *Aug.* 74, on popular artists who performed at the *princeps'* banquets. Vincent 2017: 149–64.
16. I would like to express my gratitude to Sophie Minon for discussing this topic with me. On the language and style of Dion of Prusa: Philostr., VS 1.488; Phot., *Bibl.* 209; Schmid 1887: 72–191; Minon 2012: LI–LXVI. On the idea of a multi-level communication: Gangloff 2006: 193–9; 2012: 119–29.

## Chapter Seven

1. While Halbwachs' concept of the "collective memory" (see Halbwachs 1952) is controversial, the idea that it is difficult to distinguish between "individual" and "social" memory (Halbwachs 1925) is followed by many scholars; see e.g. J. Assmann 2000: 3; Erll and Nünning 2010: 5. Powerful in its criticism of the extreme view that remembering always takes place within a group is Ricoeur 2004.

2. See the important work of Steinbock 2013, which investigates social memory in Athenian public discourse of the fourth century BCE. Steinbock sets out to find "constructive ways to integrate the complex, dialectical role of personal memory into a concept of collective memory" (9); see also Misztal 2003: 54.
3. Cusumano et al. 2013: 8 emphasize the recent shift to the individual in research on both Greco-Roman religion and memory as an opportunity. In his own paper Cusumano investigates the efficacy and limitations of oaths to guarantee memory.
4. The phenomenon of local histories told through sacred history is prolific and will be discussed below. See Dillery 2005 and Thomas 2019. For the role of memory in the foundation, articulation and redefinition of Messenian ethnicity via religious media see Luraghi 2008. For an analysis and interpretation of the Andanian mysteries in particular see Deshours 2006 and Gawlinski 2011; with emphasis on hereditary priesthoods see Guettel-Cole 2008.
5. The notorious observation that "tradition legitimizes religion" is one of the most important reasons why religious rites have a historical dimension to begin with. Cf. Rüpke 2012 on the relationship between religion and forms of historiography.
6. With regard to Greek religion see, e.g., Eidinow, Kindt, and Osborne 2016, with ample bibliography on recent debates.
7. See the very useful remarks by Hansen 1996: 257–61, who tries to grasp the term "Lebenswelt" (not quite "the everyday," as he says, but including its "glowing potential") before he applies his observations to the character and functions of votive offerings in archaic Greece.
8. On memory politics and the relationship between memory and ideology see Steinbock 2013: 15. For the introduction of new gods and its impact on the creation of memory see Garland 1992.
9. I am going to avoid a sharp distinction (as postulated by Halbwachs) between "tradition" and "memory" and agree with Assmann (2000: 8) that this distinction cannot be sustained, especially in the context of religious practices.
10. Elena Franchi discusses the media of memories in detail in Chapter 3, the following therefore relates specifically to the themes of the current chapter.
11. See Chaniotis 2016: 90–3. The author sketches the role of inscriptions and images in the creation of memory and identity in Aphrodisias through the city's history. His "broad brush" gives an insight into the processes that transformed collective memory into cultural memory at Aphrodisias.
12. On the physical infrastructure and daily activities in Greek sanctuaries see Dignas 2007: 163–77; on the importance of objects and places as memory contexts in which networks of memory were constructed see Price 2012: 17–22.
13. Hansen (1996: 261–2) distinguishes categorically between bloody sacrifice and material votives, with the former determined by ritual along the lines of anthropological interpretations of sacrifice (Meuli; Burkert).
14. There are many specific and general studies on temple inventories. For an overview and further bibliography see Dignas 2002a: 16–20; Dignas 2002b.
15. Cf. Dillery 2005: 505, categorizing these texts as "a distinct branch of Greek local historiography that focused on the past viewed through regional cult." With reference to Dion. Hal., *De Thuc.* 5.1, Chiai (2013: 82–3) follows the distinction in his analysis of the epigraphical records of the historical memories of a city, people or religious institution. The author further distinguishes between "sacred chronicle" and "sacred history," describing the latter as written by "professional authors" and in "an elaborate style."
16. See now Thomas 2019, a detailed survey and interpretation of polis histories and their stake in creating and reflecting collective memories.

17. But see Thomas 2019: 55, who questions the idea of a separate sub-genre of "religious history," arguing that "the material was simply part of polis histories, including epiphanies." The author concedes, however, that the wide array of material "could be framed by cult, place, *aition*" (56).
18. For the inscription as the best example of how objects represented a context in which networks of memories were created see Price 2012: 17–20.
19. It is important to note this wide-ranging background to what may ultimately come across as an authorized version of the past, "intentional history" of an entire community. Cf. Thomas 2019: 27, on the Lindian Chronicle.
20. Dillery 2005: 516. Thomas (2019: 27) comments on the effect of the epigraphic record as "creating an even more authoritative tradition with the approved stamp of the sanctuary, thus forming an official sanctified version."
21. Elsner and Rutherford (2005: 30) describe pilgrimage "as a mechanism by which the pilgrim comes into intimate contact with a shared cultural or religious tradition."
22. Elsner and Rutherford (2005: 1–11) offer such a typology and think carefully about the advantages and problems of a concept of ancient pilgrimage. The aspects that are relevant here are strikingly similar to the concept of memory, namely "locality and space, movement and identity, individual and collective investments in religious ideals as embodied in material culture within the landscape" (9). Minchin 2012a offers the fascinating example of Troy as a landscape characterized by the "accretion of memories" over time, with famous visitors, from Xerxes to Alexander and Roman emperors not only commemorating the site/the past but adding to the stratigraphy of cultural memory themselves.
23. See Williamson 2005: 219–52, who examines the travels of Licinius Mucianus, governor of Lycia and prominent politician in the early Flavian period. Mucianus was shown a letter from Sarpedon, prince of the Lycians in the *Iliad* and recipient of cult on the acropolis of Xanthus; he also showed special interest in a linen corselet that the Egyptian pharaoh Amasis had dedicated to Athena Lindia. Cf. Pliny, *NH* 13.88.
24. See Jacquemin 2011: 19–27, who argues for a sharp contrast between the memories of privileged travelers and those of "simple Greeks" attached to their local *lieux de mémoire*. She goes as far as to talk about two different memories that ignored each other.
25. Elsner and Rutherford (2005: 31) differentiate Christian pilgrimage by "the material embodiment that offers a sacred goal for the pilgrim." For a detailed comparative study of object-related memory practices in antiquity see Hartmann 2010. Overall, the author's emphasis is on mutual influence and conceptual similarities.
26. Recent research on hero-cult has been prolific and fruitful, contributing much to our understanding of the multi-facetted phenomenon. To name but a small selection, see Pirenne-Delforge and Suárez de la Torre 2000; Hägg 1999 and the useful summary of proposed theories about its genesis in R.C.T. Parker 2011: 287–92.
27. On the increasing significance of the grave monument as memory marker in the archaic period see Sourvinou-Inwood 1995: 117–22.
28. See Chapter 1 in this volume.
29. Steinbock describes the lasting effect of this "social memory carrier" well—in many contexts, such as diplomatic missions, assembly meetings and law court speeches the past was evoked as familiar to audiences from the funeral orations (58).
30. Humphreys (2018: 327) acknowledges that no cases are recorded.
31. Humphreys (2018: 331) refers to an increasing scholarly consensus that archaeological data do not provide evidence for "belief." Notorious legislation regulating funerary display also reveals that funerary monuments and funerary rites were crucial media of social stratification.

They do show us an entire population because their publicity and visibility depended on the social status of the deceased, or other social criteria such as age and gender.
32. The festival at this point was about avoiding and driving away the roaming ghosts of the dead; referring to Isaeus 2.46, Humphreys (2018: 327) considers that any family's obligation to honor deceased members annually was fulfilled at the festival of the *Genesia*.
33. Apart from the modeling on traditional cult, there was also the association with thematically related religious festivals, and the actual integration into coincidental festivals. Cf. Chaniotis 1991: 134.
34. For a detailed analysis of the micro-identities within *polis* religion see above all Sourvinou-Inwood 2000; on religious agency in the Attic *demes* Humphreys 2004: 130–96.
35. On the example of Antiochus III and his wife Laodike in Teos see Chaniotis 2005: 188–204. In this case, the commemoration rituals that were established to create collective memory were abolished later in order to erase this memory when Antiochus lost the war against Rome in 189 BCE.
36. There is also a historical dimension to this argument, in that Assmann (126) sees the principle of ritual coherence fading to the benefit of textual coherence—and he compares this with the Platonic theory of the world-soul and the Aristotelian idea of the unmoved mover, albeit acknowledging, ". . . this did not indeed have any further implications in the practices of the Greek cults."
37. Cf. Assmann 2006: 125; the author refers to Josephus, *Contra Apionem* (2.23) as an illustration of this. Josephus contrasts the perpetual accessibility of the sacred in Jewish religion with the few days of revelation in mysteries in pagan cult.
38. See Goodman 2012; Busine 2012; Smith 2012, who discusses the "adjustments" made to the marble reliefs from the Sebasteion at Aphrodisias, describes a very varied Christian response to pagan memorials, again reflecting how much pagan memory in the cultural context of the Roman empire was either underlying or creatively appropriated by Christian needs.
39. E.g. Ng 2016. Looking at public honorific statues in Roman Asia Minor the author argues (244) that the recycling of statues was lamented by authors such as Dio Chrysostom because it was a deprivation of honor, not of memory. Ng also observes that portraits of elite citizens set up alongside legendary city founders in public sculptural programmes were not necessarily placed with an intention to tap into collective memory.

## *Chapter Eight*

1. On the temporal reach of social, or communicative, memory, see Assmann 2008: 111. See also the important work by Vansina 1985: 23–4, 167–9.
2. Assmann avoids the term "collective memory," first used by Maurice Halbwachs in his ground-breaking work on the way in which a culture retains its memories (Halbwachs 1952). In Assmann's view, Halbwachs failed to make the important distinction between social and cultural memory. "Collective memory," however, continues to be used by many scholars: see, for example, Steinbock 2013: 8–13.
3. For discussion see below.
4. On the failures of personal memory (through its suggestibility, its transience, or its propensity for misattribution), see Schacter 2001: 12–40; 88–111; 112–37; on the dynamics of memory distortion at the broader level, see Schudson 1995 on the related processes of distanciation, conventionalization, narrativization, and instrumentalization.
5. For further discussion, see below.

6. With the coherence of this chapter in mind, I do not discuss remembering and forgetting in the Roman world. Readers will, however, find in the footnotes some references to relevant scholarship.
7. For other instances of this thought, see *Il.* 6.460–1; *Od.* 3.204. Translations from Greek are my own.
8. Cf. *Il.* 9.189: Achilles sings of the great deeds of heroes in the past: their *klea*.
9. On spatial memory, see Neisser 1989: 79–80; Winograd and Church 1988: 5–7; on imagery as an aid to memory: Rubin 1995: 39–64. For discussion of mnemotechnic practice in the ancient world, using *loci* and *imagines*, see Yates 1966: 1–3; on memory and the built environment in Rome, see Orlin 2016.
10. As Paivio 1983 and 1986 has shown, visual imagery is particularly successful in leading us to verbal material.
11. For discussion of the composition of Homer's descriptive segments, see Minchin 2001: 100–31. It is proposed there that the poet holds in memory a "description format" that he has perhaps inherited from earlier poets in this tradition; this prompts him to include information about certain features of each object he describes, as well as a brief history. It is this narrative element that stays in our mind.
12. For further discussion see Minchin 2012b. The poet's awareness of the qualitative differences between each mode is vividly revealed in those bravura moments when he plays these modes off each other. For commentary on the meeting of Hector and Andromache in *Iliad* 6, see Minchin 2012b: 91–4: the initial contrast of and, subsequently, the interweaving of the three modes of memory—personal, social and cultural—contribute to the poignancy of this memorable scene.
13. Penelope too suffers from this affliction (see, e.g., *Od.* 1. 362–4, 16.449–51); in her case, however, her pain is aggravated by the presence of the suitors in the palace.
14. For further examples of Achilles' counterfactual thinking, see *Il.* 18.86–7, 107–10.
15. On sources of knowledge in the oral context: Steinbock 2013: 22–3; and see Thomas (1989: 200–1) for an excellent brief summary. Thomas notes, however, that throughout the fourth century the Athenians became more document-attentive (1989: 83–93).
16. The Panathenaic festival reminded participants and viewers of the contest between Athena and Poseidon, the outcome of which was that Athena became the patron of Athens. On the ways in which cult practices, such as processions, communal meals, and competitions can support other carriers of social or cultural memory, see Price 2012: 22–5 and Steinbock 2013: 65–6, bearing in mind the reservations of John Gould about embodied memory (Gould 2001b).
17. For discussion of the comparable situation in the Roman world, see Wiseman 2014: 57: "[t]he great majority of Romans did not read books; they learned what they needed to know at the *ludi scaenici* and the other festivals of their gods, where epic bards, hymnodists, dramatists, and dance librettists created that composite narrative of the past that we may define as popular memory."
18. On this last theme, see Thomas 1989: 221–36. Indeed, the custom itself of the oration may have been introduced after the victory against the Persians: on the *epitaphios* in general, see Thomas 1989: 207–13.
19. On the "long-standing Greek desire to link the present to the remote past", see Price 2012: 19. On the inherent desire to create a story out of events, see Schudson 1995: 355–8, at 355, who speaks of conventionalization and narrativization: the encapsulation of a version of the past into a recognizable cultural form, that is, the kind of story that meets one's community's expectations. Steinbock (2013: 116–17) argues, too, that a personal memory of an event will

often be shaped in such a way as to make it consistent with the memories of others (or of a "master-narrative").

20. For discussion, see Thomas 1989: 95–154, noting especially her comments on selectivity and distortion (97); and on the telescoping and transformation of family traditions, which can be explained by the "processes of remembering and forgetting in the incredibly unstable and shifting world of oral tradition" (154). For a neat example, see Plato, *Laches* (179b–c): oral transmission through the family, in casual conversation, is taken for granted (Thomas 1989: 101).
21. For examples of the fluidity of family traditions in Athens, see Thomas 1989: 139–44 (Andocides) and 144–53 (Alcmaeonids). These traditions are characterized by conscious and unconscious distortion.
22. The original trophies (usually captured armor) that marked the victories of the Greeks over the Persians at Marathon or Salamis were replaced in subsequent years by more durable stone monuments (Paus. 1.32.5, 36.1).
23. For discussion, see Steinbock 2013: 84–94; but note Thomas's caution: epigrams may be reticent; written commemoration may be only a reminder of what everyone knew at the time. As memory faded even a written memorial became less and less useful: Thomas 1989: 216.
24. For regular offerings, for example, to the fallen at Plataea: Thuc. 3.58.4.
25. On transience in individual memory, which fades unless there is repeated retrieval of the information, see Schacter 2001: 12–40; on transience in collective memory, see Schudson 1995: 346–64.
26. Cf. the *heroön* in Eleusis of the Seven who had fought against Thebes (Paus. 1.39.2); and see also Price 2012: 22, on the later reception of Bronze Age sites in Crete.
27. These compressions and elaborations come about almost unnoticed: human memory is highly susceptible to suggestibility; distortion is the outcome. See too Schudson 1995: 351–5, on instrumentalization: the way in which memory is called up and carefully shaped to address present concerns ("the past is put to work").
28. We know that Herodotus' text was being read in Athens in 425 BCE, when Aristophanes provided a parody of its early chapters (*Ach.* 496–556). Thucydides began to write as soon as the war started (1.1.1): 431 BCE.
29. ὡς μήτε τὰ γενόμενα ἐξ ἀνθρώπων τῷ χρόνῳ ἐξίτηλα γένηται, so that the memory of the past might not be erased among men by the passing of time. Rösler (2002: 79) claims that this is a "modern" ambition. In my view it is not unrelated to the ambitions of Iliadic heroes, that great events and great performances should be preserved for subsequent generations.
30. On Herodotus' alignment with contemporary intellectuals rather than traditional poets, cf. van Wees 2002: 322.
31. As Herodotus says of the Egyptian priests' claim that Helen had been in Egypt not Troy at the time of the Trojan War: ἐγὼ δὲ τῷ λόγῳ τῷ περὶ Ἑλένης λεχθέντι καὶ αὐτὸς προστίθεμαι, τάδε ἐπιλεγόμενος, εἰ ἦν Ἑλένη ἐν Ἰλίῳ, ἀποδοθῆναι ἂν αὐτὴν τοῖσι Ἕλλησι . . . (As for me, I believe their story about Helen, for I reason like this: if Helen had been in Ilion she would have been given back to the Greeks . . .).
32. Cf. his words at 1.5: ἐγὼ δὲ περὶ μὲν τούτων οὐκ ἔρχομαι ἐρέων ὡς οὕτω ἢ ἄλλως κως ταῦτα ἐγένετο, "I am not going to say whether these things happened in this way or in some other manner"; and cf. van Wees 2002: 322. In connection with the Gephyraean family tradition about their Eretrian origins, Herodotus denies it flatly: ὡς δὲ ἐγὼ ἀναπυνθανόμενος εὑρίσκω, ἦσαν Φοίνικες τῶν σὺν Κάδμῳ ἀπικομένων Φοινίκων . . . but, as I learn from my enquiries, they were some of the Phoenicians who came with Cadmus . . .

33. Herodotus regarded it as appropriate to record *all* his data: as he notes at 3.9: οὗτος μὲν ὁ πιθανώτερος τῶν λόγων εἴρηται, δεῖ δὲ καὶ τὸν ἧσσον πιθανόν, ἐπεί γε δὴ λέγεται, ῥηθῆναι. "The most credible version is recounted here; but the less credible must also be given, since it is being told."
34. As Thomas (1989: 250) observes, oral tradition can accommodate different accounts of the same event, even accounts that contradict each other; and cf. her discussion of Alcmaeonid accounts of their family's genealogy (1989: 144–54).
35. Thucydides, perhaps in acknowledgment of Herodotus's method, claims at 1.21.1, with reference to history of earlier times, that he has attempted to be accurate, "on the basis of the clearest indications."
36. See above.
37. On the location of the contest: Hdt. 8.55; on the Athenians' subtraction of the day: Plut., *Moralia* 489b; on the shared temple and the altar to Forgetfulness: *Table Talk* 9.741.
38. Although the term ἀμνηστία was certainly available it was not used in this particular context. The amnesty of 403 BCE was not the only amnesty known in this period: Megara (424 BCE); 422 BCE (Athenians and Bottiaeans); 411 BCE (Samos); 405 BCE (Athens): see Wolpert 2002: 76–7.
39. On the significance of the herm and the tomb (erected after Thrasybulus' death in 338 BC), see Paus. 1.29.3; Wolpert 2002: 89.
40. As Wolpert (2002: 48–9) observes, however, because the Spartans allowed those who had collaborated with the Thirty to participate in the restored democracy, there continued to be dissension and division.
41. Xen. *Hell*. 2.4.43: "even to this day they live together as fellow-citizens . . ."; Aristotle, *Ath. Pol*. 40.2 (on the execution of Archinus; thereafter "no one ever again violated the amnesty"); Wolpert 2002: 48–71, at 52.
42. These same thought processes are already on view in the *Iliad* (Case Study 1, above), in Ajax's appeal to Achilles, at *Il*. 9.624–42. Ajax argues, using the model of the payment of a blood price in the case of murder, that Achilles should accept the generous gifts that have been offered him by Agamemnon, and that in exchange he should curb both his pride and his anger: for the welfare of the community as a whole (in this case the Achaeans), Achilles should give up his desire for revenge on Agamemnon.
43. For discussion of "memory sanctions" in the Roman world, see Flower (2006), who prefers this term to the more commonly used *damnatio memoriae*, which would not have been used by the Romans themselves to identify their sanctions (2006: xix); see also Levene (2012); Kousser (2015). For a discussion of the management of memory in a Christian community in Late Antiquity, see Smith (2012) on Christian efforts in the Sebasteion at Aphrodisias to "deactivate the noxious powers of old gods" (2012: 320) by a careful program of defacing and erasure while still maintaining as much as possible of the monument: the existing monuments were "remastered" to accommodate them to new circumstances.

# BIBLIOGRAPHY

Ackrill, J.L. (1973), "*Anamnesis* in the *Phaedo*: Remarks on 73c–75c," in E.N. Lee, A.P.D. Mourelatos and R. Rorty (eds.), *Exegesis and Argument: Essays in Greek Philosophy Presented to Gregory Vlastos*, 177–95, Amsterdam: Van Gorcum.

Adamska, A. (2020), "Verba volant, scripta manent? The Multimediality in Medieval Memory," in *A Cultural History of Memory*, vol. 2, London: Bloomsbury.

Agócs, P. (2019), "Speaking in the Wax Tablets of Memory," in L. Castagnoli and P. Ceccarelli (eds.), *Greek Memories: Theories and Practices*, 69–90, Cambridge: Cambridge University Press.

Alcock S.E. (1993), *Graecia Capta: The Landscapes of Roman Greece*, Cambridge: Cambridge University Press.

Alcock, S.E. (2001), "The Reconfiguration of Memory in the Greek East," in Alcock, S., D. 'Altroy, C. Sinopoli, and K. Morrison (eds.), *Empires: Perspectives from Archaeology and History*, 323–50, Cambridge: Cambridge University Press.

Alcock, S.E. (2002), *Archaeologies of the Greek Past. Landscape, Monuments, and Memories*, Cambridge: Cambridge University Press.

Alcock, S.E., J. Cherry, and J. Elsner (eds.) (2001), *Pausanias. Travel and Memory in Roman Greece*, Oxford: Oxford University Press.

Alroth, B. and Ch. Scheffer (eds.) (2014), *Attitudes towards the Past in Antiquity. Creating Identities, Proceedings of an International Conference Held at Stockholm University, 15–17 May 2009* [Stockholm Studies in Classical Archaeology 14], Stockholm: Stockholm University.

Ambos, C. et al. (eds.) (2005), *Die Welt der Rituale. Von der Antike bis heute*, Darmstadt: Wissenschaftliche Buchgesellschaft.

d'Ambra, E. (2002), "Acquiring an Ancestor: the Importance of Funerary Statuary among the Non-elite Orders of Rome," in J. M. Højte (ed.), *Images of Ancestors*, 223–46, Aarhus: Aarhus University Press.

Anderson, G. (2003), *The Athenian Experiment: Building an Imagined Political Community in Ancient Attica, 508–490 B.C.*, Ann Arbor: University of Michigan Press.

Anderson, G. (2007), "Why the Athenians Forgot Cleisthenes: Literacy and the Politics of Remembrance in Ancient Athens," in C. Cooper (ed.), *Politics of Orality*, 103–128, Leiden and Boston: Brill.

Annas, J. (1982), "Plato's Myths of Judgement," *Phronesis* 27, 119–43.

Antonaccio, C. (1994), "Contesting the Past: Hero Cult, Tomb Cult, and Epic in Early Greece," *AJA* 98, 389–410.

Assmann, A. (1999), *Cultural Memory and Western Civilization. Functions, Media, Archives*, Cambridge: Cambridge University Press.

Assmann, A. and L. Shortt (2012), "Memory and Political Change: Introduction," in A. Assmann and L. Shortt (eds.), *Memory and Political Change*, 1–14, Basingstoke: Palgrave Macmillan.

Assmann, A., J. Assmann, and C. Hardmeier (eds.) (1983), *Schrift und Gedächtnis: Beiträge zur Archäologie der literarischen Kommunikation*, Munich: Wilhelm Fink Verlag.

Assmann, J. (1991), *Stein und Zeit. Mensch und Gesellschaft im alten Ägypten*, Munich: Wilhelm Fink.
Assmann, J. (1992), *Das kulturelle Gedächtnis: Schrift, Erinnerung und politische Identität in frühen Hochkulturen*, Munich: Beck.
Assmann, J. (1992), *Das kulturelle Gedächtnis. Schrift, Erinnerung und politische Identität in frühen Hochkulturen*. Munich: C.H. Beck. [Engl. Tr. (2011), *Cultural Memory and Early Civilization. Writing, Remembrance, and Political Imagination*. Cambridge: Cambridge University Press].
Assmann, J. (2000), *Religion und kulturelles Gedächtnis: Zehn Studien*, Munich: C.H. Beck [Engl. Tr. (2006), *Religion and Cultural Memory: Ten Studies*, Stanford: Stanford University Press].
Assmann, J. (2008), "Communicative and Cultural Memory," in A. Erll and A. Nünning (eds.), *Cultural Memory Studies: An International and Interdisciplinary Handbook*, 109–18, Berlin and New York: De Gruyter.
Assmann, J. (2015), "Tradition, Writing and Canonisation. Structural Changes of Cultural Memory," in T. Stordalen and S.-A. Naguib (eds.), *The Formative Past and the Formation of the Future. Collective Remembering and Identity Formation*, 115–32, Oslo: Novus.
Assmann, J. and T. Hölscher (eds.) (1988), *Kultur und Gedächtnis*, Frankfurt: Suhrkamp.
Azoulay, V. (2014), *Les tyrannicides d'Athènes: vie et mort de deux statues*, L'univers historique, Paris: Éditions du Seuil.
Baines, J., H. van der Bloom, Y.S. Chen, and T. Rood, eds. (2019), *Historical Consciousness and the Use of the Past in the Ancient World*, Sheffield: Equinox.
Bakker, E.J. (2002), "The Making of History: Herodotus' *Historiēs Apodexis*," in E.J. Bakker, I.J.F. de Jong, and H. van Wees (eds.), *Brill's Companion to Herodotus*, 3–32, Leiden: Brill.
Baltussen, H. (2017), "The Aristotelian Tradition and the Second Sophistic," in D. Richter and W. Johnson (eds.), *The Oxford Handbook to the Second Sophistic*, 581–94, Oxford: Oxford University Press.
Barchiesi, A. (1997), *The Poet and the Prince. Ovid and Augustan Discourse*, Berkeley: University of California Press.
Barchiesi, A. and W. Scheidel (2010), *The Oxford Handbook of Roman Studies*, Oxford: Oxford University Press.
Barnes, T.D. (1985), *Tertullian. A Historical and Literary Study*, Oxford: Clarendon Press (1971, 1st ed).
Baroin, C. (2007), ":Techniques, arts et pratiques de la mémoire en Grèce et à Rome," *Métis*, N.S. 5: 135–60.
Baroin, C. (2010), *Se souvenir à Rome. Formes, représentations et pratiques de la mémoire*, Paris: Belin.
Bartels, J. (2001), "Sosius (I.2)," *DNP*, 11: 745–46.
Beard, M. (1998), "Vita inscripta," in S.M. Maul et al. (eds.) *La biographie antique, Entretiens sur l'antiquité classique*, 44, 83–118, Geneva: Fondation Hardt.
Beard, M. (2007), *The Roman Triumph*, Cambridge, Mass.: Belknap Press of Harvard University Press.
Beard, M., J. North, and S. Price (1998), *Religions of Rome. Vol. 1: A History, and Vol. 2: A Sourcebook*, Cambridge: Cambridge University Press.
Beck, H. (2005), *Karriere und Hierarchie: Die römische Aristokratie und die Anfänge des cursus honorum in der mittleren Republik*, Berlin: Akademie Verlag.
Beck, H. and U. Walter (2004), *Die frühen römischen Historiker 2: Von Coelius Antipater bis Pomponius Atticus. Herausgegeben, übersetzt und kommentiert*, Darmstadt: Wissenschaftliche Buchgesellschaft.

Beck, H. and H.-U. Wiemer, (eds.) (2010a), *Feiern und Erinnern: Geschichtsbilder im Spiegel antiker Feste*, Berlin: Verlag Antike.

Beck, H. and H.-U. Wiemer (2010b), "Feiern und Erinnern—Eine Einleitung," in H. Beck and H.-U. Wiemer (eds.), *Feiern und Erinnern. Geschichtsbilder im Spiegel antiker Feste* [Studien zur Alten Geschichte 12], 9–54, Berlin: Verlag Antike.

Bedu-Addo, J. T. (1991), "Sense-experience and the Argument for Recollection in Plato's *Phaedo*," *Phronesis* 36, 27–60.

Beekes, R. (2010), *Etymological Dictionary of Greek*. 2 vols., Leiden and Boston: Brill.

Beltrametti, A. (2011), *La storia sulla scena. Quello che gli storici antichi non hanno raccontato*, Rome: Feltrinelli.

Bendlin, A. (2013), "The Urban Sacred Landscape," in P. Erdkamp (ed.), *The Cambridge Companion to Ancient Rome*, 461–77, Cambridge: Cambridge University Press.

Bendlin, A. (2015), "Rezension zu: Nicola Cusumano, Valentino Gasparini, Attilio Mastrocinque Und Jörg Rüpke (eds.), Memory and Experience in the Greco-Roman World," *Bonner Jahrbücher*, 215: 537–41.

Benoist, S. (2001), "Le prince en sa ville: conditor, pater patriae et divi filius," in N. Belayche (ed.), *Rome, les Césars et la Ville aux deux premiers siècles de notre ère*, 23–49, Rennes: Presses universitaires de Rennes.

Benoist, S. (2005), *Rome, le prince et la Cité. Pouvoir impérial et cérémonies publiques (I$^{er}$ siècle av. – début du IV$^{e}$ siècle ap. J.-C.)*, Paris: Presses universitaires de France.

Benoist, S. (2008), "Les processions dans la cité: de la mise en scène de l'espace urbain," in Ph. Fleury and O. Desbordes (eds.), *Roma Illustrata. Représentations de la Ville*, 49–62, Caen: Presses universitaires de Caen.

Benoist, S. (2011), "Les *Kaisereia* de Gytheion," in A. Hermary and B. Jaeger (eds.), *Thesaurus Cultus et Rituum Antiquorum (ThesCRA)*, VII, *Festivals and Contests*, III, 271–2, Los Angeles: J. Paul Getty Museum.

Benoist, S. (2016), "*Coloni* et *incolae*, vingt ans après: mobilité et identité sociales et juridiques dans le monde romain occidental," in E. Lo Cascio and L.E. Tacoma (eds.), *The Impact of Mobility and Migration in the Roman Empire* (Twelfth Workshop of the International Network Impact of Empire, 17–19 June 2015), 205–21, Leiden and Boston: Brill.

Benoist, S. and A. Daguet-Gagey (eds.) (2007), *Mémoire et histoire. Les procédures de condamnation dans l'Antiquité romaine*, Metz: CRUHL.

Benoist, S. and A. Daguet-Gagey (eds.) (2008), *Un discours en images de la condamnation de mémoire*, Metz: CRUHL.

Benoist, S., A. Daguet-Gagey, C. Höet-van Cauwenberghe, and S. Lefebvre (eds.) (2009), *Mémoires partagées, mémoires disputées. Écriture et réécriture de l'histoire*, Metz: Centre de Recherche Universitaire d'Histoire Lorrain–Metz.

Bergemann, J. (1990), *Römische Reiterstatuen. Ehrendenkmäler im öffentlichen Bereich*, Mainz: Ph. Von Zabern.

Berger, S., H. Feldner, and K. Passmore (eds.) (2020), *Writing History: Theory and Practice*, London: Bloomsbury Publishing.

Bernabé, A. and A.I. Jiménez San Cristóbal (2008), *Instructions for the Netherworld: The Orphic Gold Tablets*, Leiden and Boston: Brill.

Bershadsky, N. (2012), "The Border of War and Peace. Myth and Ritual in Argive-Spartan Dispute over Thyreatis," in J. Wilker (ed.), *Maintaining Peace and Interstate Stability in Archaic and Classical Greece*, 49–77, Mainz: Verlag Antike.

Betegh, G. (2004), *The Derveni Papyrus. Cosmology, Theology and Interpretation*, Cambridge: Cambridge University Press.

Bleicken, J. (1995), *Die athenische Demokratie*. 4th and completely revised and extended edn, Paderborn: UTB.

Bloch, D. (2007), *Aristotle on Memory and Recollection*. Leiden and Boston: Brill.

Blösel, W. (2000), "Die Geschichte des Begriffes mos maiorum von den Anfängen bis zu Cicero," in B. Linke and M. Stemmler (eds.) *Mos maiorum: Untersuchungen zu den Formen der Identitätsstiftung und Stabilisierung in der römischen Republik*, 25–97, Stuttgart: Steiner.

Bodnar, J.E. (1992), *Remaking America: Public Memory, Commemoration, and Patriotism in the Twentieth Century*, Princeton: Princeton University Press.

Bolter, J.D. and Grusin, R. (eds.) (1999), *Remediation: Understanding New Media*, Cambridge: MIT Press.

Bommas, M. (ed.) (2011), *Cultural Memory and Identity in Ancient Societies*, London and New York: Bloomsbury Academic.

Bommas, M., J. Harrisson, and Ph. Roy (eds.) (2012), *Memory and Urban Religion in the Ancient World*, London and New York: Bloomsbury Academic.

Bonamente, G. (2017), "Il silenzio di Augusto sul culto imperiale," in A. Galimberti, R. Cristofoli, and F. Rohr Vio (eds.), *Costruire la memoria: uso e abuso della storia fra tarda repubblica e primo principato*, 139–64, Rome: L'Erma di Bretschneider.

Bonanno, D. (2013), "Memory Lost, Memory Regained. Considerations of the Recovery of Sacred Texts in Messenia and in Biblical Israel: A Comparison," in N. Cusumano et al. (eds.), *Memory and Religious Experience in the Graeco-Roman World*, 63–80, Stuttgart: Steiner.

Borg, B. (ed.) (2004), Paideia: *The World of the Second Sophistic*, Berlin and New York: De Gruyter.

Borgeaud, Ph. (1988), "Pour une approche anthropologique de la mémoire religieuse," in Ph. Borgeaud (ed.), *La mémoire des religions*, 7–20, Geneva: Labor et Fides.

Bostock, D. (1986), *Plato's* Phaedo, Oxford: Oxford University Press.

Bostock, D. (1988), *Plato's* Theaetetus, Oxford: Clarendon Press.

Bosworth, A.B. (1988), *Conquest and Empire: The Reign of Alexander the Great*, Cambridge; New York: Cambridge University Press.

Bosworth, A.B. (2002), *The Legacy of Alexander: Politics, Warfare, and Propaganda under the Successors*, Oxford and New York: Oxford University Press.

Bourdieu, P. (2010), *Distinction: A Social Critique of the Judgement of Taste*, trans. R. Nice, 2nd edn, London: Routledge (*La distinction. Critique sociale du jugement*, Paris, 1979).

Bourriot, F. (1995), Kalos kagathos—kalokagathia: *d'un terme de propagande de sophistes à une notion sociale et philosophique*, 2 vol, Hildesheim: G. Olms.

Bowie, E.L. (1970), "Greeks and their Past in the Second Sophistic," *PP* 46, 3–41.

Bowra, C.M. (1961), *Greek Lyric Poetry: From Alcman to Simonides*, 2nd edn, Oxford: Clarendon Press.

Bradley, G. (2015), "Investigating Aristocracy in Archaic Rome and Central Italy: Social Mobility, Ideology and Cultural Influences," in N. Fisher and H. van Wees (eds.), *'Aristocracy' in Antiquity. Redefining Greek and Roman Elites*, 85–124, Swansea: Classical Press of Wales.

Briant, P. (2010), *Alexander the Great and his Empire: A Short Introduction*, trans. A. Kuhrt, Princeton and Oxford: Princeton University Press.

Brind'Amour, P. (1983), *Le Calendrier romain. Recherches chronologiques*, Ottawa: Éditions de l'Université d'Ottawa.

Briquel, D. (2008), "Rome comme ville étrusque," in Ph. Fleury and O. Desbordes (eds.), *Roma Illustrata. Représentations de la Ville*, 63–84, Caen: Presses universitaires de Caen.

Brown, P. (1981), *The Cult of the Saints. Its Rise and Function in Latin Christianity*, Chicago: The University of Chicago Press.

Burkert, W. (1983; German original 1972), *Homo Necans. The Anthropology of Ancient Greek Sacrificial Ritual and Myth*, tr. by P. Bing, Berkeley: University of California Press.

Burnyeat, M.F. (1977), "Socratic Midwifery, Platonic Inspiration," *Bulletin of the Institute of Classical Studies* 24, 7–16.

Burnyeat, M.F. (1987), "Wittgenstein and Augustine *De magistro*," *Proceedings of the Aristotelian Society*, s.v. 61, 1–24.

Burnyeat, M.F. (1990), *The* Theaetetus *of Plato*, translation by M.J. Levett, Indianapolis and Cambridge, Mass.: Hackett.

Busine, A. (2012), "The Discovery of Inscriptions and the Legitimation of New Cults," in B. Dignas and R.R.R. Smith (eds.), *Historical and Religious Memory in the Ancient World*, 241–56, Oxford: Oxford University Press.

Buxton, B. and R. Hannah (2005), "OGIS 458, the Augustan calendar, and the succession," in C. Deroux (ed.), *Studies in Latin Literature and Roman History*, XII (Collection Latomus 287), 290–306, Brussels: Éditions Latomus.

Buxton, R., ed. (1999), *From Myth to Reason? Studies in the Development of Greek Thought*, Oxford: Oxford University Press.

Calame, C. (2009), *Poetic and Performative Memory in Ancient Greece*, Washington: Trustees for Harvard University.

Camia, F., and D. Marchiandi (2011), "L'Arco di Adriano," in E. Greco (ed.), *Topografia di Atene: sviluppo urbano e monumenti dalle origini al III secolo d. C. Tomo 2, Colline sud-occidentali, Valle dell'Ilisso*, 449–51, Athens and Paestum: Pandemos.

Candau, J. (2005), *Anthropologie de la mémoire*, Paris: Armand Colin.

Canevaro, M. (2017a), "La memoria, gli oratori e il pubblico nell'Atene del IV secolo a.C.," in E. Franchi and G. Proietti (eds.), *Communities in Conflict. Forward-looking Memories in Classical Athens*, 171–212, Trento: Università degli Studi di Trento.

Canevaro, M. (2017b), "The Popular Culture of the Athenian Institutions: 'Authorized' Popular Culture and 'Unauthorized' Elite Culture in Classical Athens," in L. Grig (ed.), *Popular Culture in the Ancient World*, Cambridge: Cambridge University Press.

Capra, A. (2014), *Plato's Four Muses: The* Phaedrus *and the Poetics of Philosophy*, Cambridge, Mass. and Washington: Center for Hellenic Studies.

Carandini, A. (1997), *La nascita di Roma. Dèi, Lari, eroi e uomini all'alba di una civiltà*, Torino: Giulio Einaudi.

Carandini, A. and R. Cappelli (eds.) (2000), *Roma. Romolo, Remo e la fondazione della città*, catalogue of an exhibition in Rome (Museo Nazionale Romano, Terme di Diocleziano, 28 June–29 October 2000), Rome and Milan: Electa.

Carrié, J.-M. (2001), "Antiquité tardive et 'démocratisation de la culture': un paradigme à géométrie variable," *An Tard* 9, 27–46.

Cartledge, P. and A. Spawforth (2002), *Hellenistic and Roman Sparta: A Tale of Two Cities*, London and New York: Routledge.

Castagnoli, L. (2006), "Liberal Arts and Recollection in Augustine's *Confessions*," *Philosophie Antique* 6, 107–35.

Castagnoli, L. (2019), "Is Memory of the Past? Aristotle on the Objects of Memory," in L. Castagnoli and P. Ceccarelli (eds.), *Greek Memories: Theories and Practices*, 236–55, Cambridge: Cambridge University Press.

Castagnoli, L. and P. Ceccarelli (eds.) (2019), *Greek Memories: Theories and Practices*, Cambridge: Cambridge University Press.

Castelli, E. (2004), *Martyrdom and Memory: Early Christian Culture Making*, New York: Columbia University Press.

Chaniotis, A. (1988), *Historie und Historiker in den griechischen Inschriften. Epigraphische Beiträge zur griechischen Historiographie*, Stuttgart: Steiner.

Chaniotis, A. (1991), "Gedenktage der Griechen: Ihre Bedeutung für das Geschichtsbewusstsein griechischer Poleis," in J. Assmann (ed.), *Das Fest und das Heilige. Religiöse Kontrapunkte zur Alltagswelt*, 123–45, Gütersloh: G. Mohn.

Chaniotis, A. (2005), "Akzeptanz von Herrschaft durch ritualisierte Dankbarkeit und Erinnerung," in C. Ambos et al. (eds.), *Die Welt der Rituale. Von der Antike bis heute*, 188–204, Darmstadt: Wissenschaftliche Buchgesellschaft.

Chaniotis, A. (2007), "La divinité mortelle d'Antiochos III à Téos," *Kernos* 20, 153–71.

Chaniotis, A. (2013), "Mnemopoetik: die epigraphische Konstruktion von Erinnerung in den griechischen Poleis," in O. Dahly et al. (eds.), *Medien der Geschichte. Antikes Griechenland und Rom*, 132–69, Berlin and Boston: DeGruyter.

Chaniotis, A. (2016), "Memory, Commemoration and Identity in an Ancient City: The Case of Aphrodisias," *Daedalus* 145:2, 88–100.

Chantraine, P. (1968–80), *Dictionnaire étymologique de la langue grecque. Histoire des mots*, Paris: Klincksieck.

Chartier, R. (1982), "Intellectual History or Socio-Cultural History?" in Dominick LaCapra and Steven L. Kaplan (eds.), *Modern European Intellectual History: Reappraisals and New Perspectives*, 30, Ithaca, NY: Cornell University Press.

Chartier, R. (1998), "Introduction," in Roger Chartier (ed.), *Cultural History. Between Practice and Representations*, 4, Cambridge: Cambridge University Press.

Chen, X. (2015), "Reflection: Memory and Forgetfulness in Daoism," in D. Nikulin (ed.), *Memory: A History*, 176–83, Oxford: Oxford University Press.

Chiai, F.G. (2013), "The Origins and Deeds of our Gods: Inscriptions and Local Historical-Religious Memories in the Hellenistic and Roman World," in N. Cusumano, V. Gasparini, A. Mastrocinque, and J. Rüpke (eds.), *Memory and Religious Experience in the Graeco-Roman World*, 81–114, Stuttgart: Steiner.

Chiaradonna, R. (2019), "Plotinus on Memory, Recollection and Discursive Thought," in L. Castagnoli and P. Ceccarelli (eds.), *Greek Memories: Theories and Practices*, 310–24, Cambridge: Cambridge University Press.

Chrubasik, B. (2016), *Kings and Usurpers in the Seleukid Empire: The Men Who Would Be King*, Oxford Classical Monographs, Oxford: Oxford University Press.

Chrubasik, B. forthcoming, "Succession Seleukid Style," in S. Dieffenbach, U. Gotter, and W. Havener (eds.), *The Arts of Succession: Creating Dynasties in the Ancient World and Beyond*, Stuttgart: Steiner.

Clark, A. and D. Chalmers (1998), "The Extended Mind," *Analysis* 58:1, 7–19.

Clark, S.R.L. (2019), "Plotinus: Remembering and Forgetting," in L. Castagnoli and P. Ceccarelli (eds.), *Greek Memories: Theories and Practices*, 325–39, Cambridge: Cambridge University Press.

Clarke, J. R. (2003), *Art in the Lives of Ordinary Romans: Visual and Non-Elite Viewers in Roman Italy*, 100 BC–AD 315, Berkeley and Los Angeles: University of California Press.

Clay, D. (2004), *Archilochos Heros. The Cult of Poets in the Greek Polis*, Cambridge, Mass: Harvard University Press.

Coarelli, F. (1990), "Roma, i Volsci e il Lazio antico," in *Crise et transformation des sociétés archaïques de l'Italie antique au V$^e$ siècle av. J.-C.*, 135–54, Rome: École française de Rome.

Cole, T. (1983), "Archaic Truth," *Quaderni Urbinati di Cultura Classica* 13, 7–28.

Coleman, J. (1992), *Ancient and Medieval Memories: Studies in the Reconstruction of the Past*, Cambridge: Cambridge University Press.

Collins, D. (1999), "Hesiod and the Divine Voice of the Muses," *Arethusa* 32, 241–61.
Connerton, P. (1989), *How Societies Remember*, Cambridge: Cambridge University Press.
Corbier, M. (2006), *Donner à voir, donner à lire. Mémoire et communication dans la Rome ancienne*, Paris: CNRS éd.
Cordovana, O. and M. Galli (eds.) (2007), *Arte e memoria culturale nell'età della Seconda Sofistica*, Catania: Edizioni del Prisma.
Cornell, T.J. (1995), *The Beginnings of Rome. Italy and Rome from the Bronze Age to the Punic War (c. 1000–264 BC)*, London and New York: Routledge.
Couldry, N. (2012), *Media, Society, World. Social Theory and Digital Media Practice*, Cambridge and Malden: Polity.
Courrier, C. (2014), *La plèbe de Rome et sa culture (fin du IIe s. av. J.-C.-fin du Ier s. ap. J.-C.)*, Rome: EFR.
Crawford, M.H. (1974), *Roman Republican Coinage*, Cambridge: Cambridge University Press.
Cubitt, G. (2007), *History and Memory*, Manchester and New York: Manchester University Press.
Cullhed, M. (1994), Conservator Urbis Suae, *Studies in the Politics and Propaganda of the Emperor Maxentius*, Stockholm: Åström.
Curran, J. (2000), *Pagan City and Christian Capital. Rome in the Fourth Century*, Oxford Classical Monographs, Oxford: Oxford University Press.
Currie, B. (2005), *Pindar and the Cult of Heroes*, Oxford: Oxford University Press.
Cusumano, N., V. Gasparini, A. Mastrocinque, and J. Rüpke (eds.) (2013), *Memory and Religious Experience in the Graeco-Roman World*, Stuttgart: Steiner.
Dally, O., T. Hölscher, S. Muth, and R.M. Schneider (eds.) (2014), *Medien der Geschichte— Antikes Griechenland und Rom*, Berlin: De Gruyter.
Dancy, R. (2004), *Plato's Introduction of Forms*, Cambridge: Cambridge University Press.
Darbo-Peschanski, C. (2019), "Place and Nature of Memory in Greek Historiography," in L. Castagnoli and P. Cecarelli (eds.), *Greek Memories. Theories and Practices*, 158–78, Cambridge: Cambridge University Press.
Dasen, V. (2010), "Wax and Plaster Memories: Children in Elite and Non-elite Strategies," in V. Dasen and Th. Späth (eds.), *Children, Memory, and Family Identity in Roman Culture*, 109–45, Oxford and New York: Oxford University Press.
Daux, G. (1936), *Pausanias à Delphes*, Paris: Picard.
Daverio Rocchi, G. (2013), "Ethnic Identity, Cults and Territorial Settlement: East and West Lokrians," in P. Funke and M. Haake (eds.), *Greek Federal States and their Sanctuaries. Identity and Integration*, 139–61, Stuttgart: Steiner.
Daverio Rocchi, G. (2015), "The Lokrians and their Federal Leagues," in H. Beck and P. Funke (eds.), *Federalism in Greek Antiquity*, 179–98, Cambridge: Cambridge University Press.
David, J.-M. (1996), *The Roman Conquest of Italy*, Oxford: Blackwell.
Davies, J. (1999), *Death, Burial and Rebirth in the Religions of Antiquity*, London: Routledge.
Davies, J.K. (1971), *Athenian Propertied Families, 600–300 B.C.*, Oxford: Oxford University Press.
Davies, Ph. (2013), "*Kalos kagathos* and Scholarly Perceptions of Spartan Society," *Historia* 62, 259–79.
Day, J. (ed.) (1994), *Plato's* Meno *in Focus*, London and New York: Routledge.
De Angelis, F., J.-A. Dickmann, F. Pirson, and R. von den Hoff (eds.) (2012), "Kunst von unten? Stil und Gesellschaft in der antiken Welt von der 'arte plebea' bis heute," Internationales Kolloquium anlässlich des 70. Geburtstages von Paul Zanker, Roma Villa Massimo, 8. bis 9. Juni 2007, Wiesbaden: Dr. Ludwig Reichert Verlag.

Dean-Jones, L. (2003), "Literacy and the Charlatan in Ancient Greek Medicine," in H. Yunis (ed.), *Written Texts and the Rise of Literate Culture in Ancient Greece*, 97–121, Cambridge: Cambridge University Press.

DeGloma, T. (2015), "The Strategies of Mnemonic Battle: On the Alignment of Autobiographical and Collective Memories in Conflicts over the Past," *American Journal of Cultural Sociology* 3:1, 156–90.

Derderian, K. (2001), *Leaving Words to Remember: Greek Mourning and the Advent of Literacy*. Leiden and Boston: Brill.

Derrida, J. (1972), *Dissemination*, Chicago: University of Chicago Press.

Deshours, N. (2006), *Les mystères d'Andania: étude d'épigraphie et d'histoire religieuse*, Bordeaux: De Boccard.

Dignas, B. (2002a), *Economy of the Sacred in Hellenistic and Roman Asia Minor*, Oxford: Oxford University Press.

Dignas, B. (2002b), "*Inventories* or *Offering Lists*? Assessing the Wealth of Apollo Didymeus," *ZPE* 138, 235–42.

Dignas, B. (2007), "A Day in the Life of a Greek Sanctuary," in D. Ogden (ed.), *A Companion to Greek Religion*, 163–77, Malden, Mass. and Oxford: Blackwell.

Dignas, B. (2012), "Rituals and the Construction of Identity in Attalid Pergamon," in B. Dignas and R.R.R. Smith (eds.), *Historical and Religious Memory in the Ancient* World, 119–43, Oxford: Oxford University Press.

Dignas, B. (2013), "Greek Priests in the First Three Centuries AD: Traditional, Diverse, Wholly New?" in B. Dignas, R. Parker, and G. Stroumsa (eds.), *Priests and Prophets among Pagans, Jews and Christians*, 80–112, Louvain: Peeters.

Dignas, B. and K. Trampedach (eds.) (2008), *Practitioners of the Divine. Greek Priests and Religious Officials from Homer to Heliodorus*, Cambridge, Mass.: Harvard University Press.

Dignas, B. and R.R.R. Smith (eds.) (2012), *Historical and Religious Memory in the Ancient World*, Oxford and New York: Oxford University Press.

Dillery, J. (2005), "Greek Sacred History," *AJPh* 126:4, 505–26.

Dimas, P. (2003), "Recollecting Forms in the *Phaedo*," *Phronesis* 48, 175–214.

Domínguez-Monedero, A.J. (2008), "Ethnos, Koinon and Polis among the Locrians," in M. Lombardo and F. Frisone (eds.), *Forme sovrapoleiche e interpoleiche di organizzazione nel mondo antico*, 321–34, Galatina: Congedo.

Domínguez-Monedero, A.J. (2010), "La organización simbólica del espacio en el mundo griego: el caso Locrio," in J. Carruesco García (ed.), *Topos-Chôra: l'espai a Grècia I: perspectives interdisciplinàries*, 75–83, Tarragona: ICAC.

Doody, A. (2009), "Pliny's 'Natural History: Enkyklios Paideia' and the Ancient Encyclopedia," *Journal of the History of Ideas* 70:1, 1–21.

Dorandi, T. (1991), "Den Autoren über die Schulter geschaut. Arbeitsweise und Autographie bei den antiken Schriftstellern," *ZPE* 87, 11–33.

Dowden, K. (2012), "Memory Shift: Reinventing the Mythology, 100 BC–AD 100," in M. Bommas, J. Harrisson, and Ph. Roy (eds.), *Memory and Urban Religion in the Ancient World*, 129–47, London and New York: Bloomsbury Academic.

Dumézil, G. (1970), *Archaic Roman Religion with an Appendix on the Religion of the Etruscans*, Chicago: University of Chicago Press.

Dunbabin, K. (2004), *The Roman Banquet: Images of Conviviality*, Cambridge: Cambridge University Press.

Eder, W. (2005), "Augustus and the Power of Tradition," in G.K. Galinsky (ed.), *The Age of Augustus*, 13–32, Cambridge: Cambridge University Press.

Edmonds, R.G. III (ed.) (2011), *The "Orphic" Gold Tablets and Greek Religion: Further Along the Path*, Cambridge: Cambridge University Press.

Edmondson, J. (2016), "Monuments of Empire in Roman Spain and Beyond: Augusta Emerita (Mérida), the *Spanish Rome*," in J.M.D. Pohl and C.L. Lyons (eds.), *Altera Roma: Art and Empire from Mérida to México*, 69–107, UCLA Cotsen Institute of Archaeology Press Monographs 83, Los Angeles: Cotsen Institute of Archaeology Press.

Edmondson, J., S. Mason, and J. Rives (eds.) (2005), *Flavius Josephus and Flavian Rome*, Oxford: Oxford University Press.

Edwards, C. (1996), *Writing Rome. Textual Approaches to the City*, Cambridge: Cambridge University Press.

Edwards, E. (2020), "Photography and technological memory in Britain during the Age of Empire," in *A Cultural History of Memory*, vol. 5, London: Bloomsbury.

Ehling, K. (2008), *Untersuchungen zur Geschichte der späten Seleukiden. Vom Tode des Antiochos IV. bis zur Einrichtung der Provinz Syria unter Pompeius*, Stuttgart: Steiner.

Eidinow, E., J. Kindt, and R. Osborne (eds.) (2016), *Theologies of Ancient Greek Religion*, Cambridge: Cambridge University Press.

Ekroth, G. (2007), "Heroes and Hero-Cults," in D. Ogden (ed.), *A Companion to Greek Religion*, 100–14, Oxford and Malden, Mass.: Blackwell.

Elsner J. and I. Rutherford (eds.) (2005), *Pilgrimage in Graeco-Roman and Early Christian Antiquity*, Oxford: Oxford University Press.

Elsner, J. (2000), "From the Culture of Spolia to the Cult of Relics: The Arch of Constantine and the Genesis of Late Antique Forms," *Papers of the British School at Rome* 68, 149–84.

Elsner, J. and M. Squire (2016), "Sight and Memory. The Visual Art of Roman Mnemonics," in M. Squire (ed.), *Sight and the Ancient Senses*, 180–204, New York and Abingdon: Routledge.

Erll, A. (ed.) (2008), *Cultural Memory Studies: An International and Interdisciplinary Handbook*, Berlin: de Gruyter.

Erll, A. (2011$^2$), *Kollektives Gedächtnis und Erinnerungskulturen. Eine Einführung*, Stuttgart: Metzler.

Erll A. and A. Nünning (eds.) (2010), *A Companion to Cultural Memory Studies*, Berlin and New York: DeGruyter.

Erll, A. and A. Rigney (eds.) (2009a), *Mediation, Remediation, and the Dynamics of Cultural Memory*, Berlin and New York: De Gruyter.

Erll, A. and A. Rigney (2009b), "Introduction: Cultural Memory and its Dynamics," in *Mediation, Remediation, and the Dynamics of Cultural Memory*, 1–14, Berlin and New York: De Gruyter.

Erskine, A. (2001), *Troy Between Greece and Rome. Local Tradition and Imperial Power*, Oxford: Oxford University Press.

Estienne, S. (2015), "La construction du divin au prisme des processions à Rome," in N. Belayche and V. Pirenne-Delforge (eds.), *Fabriquer du divin*, 105–25, Liège: Presses universitaires de Liège.

Farney, G.D. (2007), *Ethnic Identity and Aristocratic Competition in Republican Rome*, Cambridge: Cambridge University Press.

Farrell, J. and D. Nelis (eds.) (2013), *Augustan Poetry and the Roman Republic*, Oxford: Oxford University Press.

Favro, D. (1996), *The Urban Image of Augustan Rome*, Cambridge: Cambridge University Press.

Favro, D. (2014), "Moving Events: Curating the Memory of the Roman Triumph," in K. Galinksy (ed.), *Memoria Romana: Memory in Rome and Rome in Memory*, 85–101, Ann Arbor: The University of Michigan Press.

Feeney, D. (2007), *Caesar's Calendar. Ancient Time and the Beginnings of History* (Sather Classical Lectures 65), Berkeley and Los Angeles: University of California Press.

Felton, D. (2007), "The Dead," in D. Ogden (ed.), *A Companion to Greek Religion*, 86–99, Oxford and Malden, Mass.: Blackwell.

Ferrari, J. (1987), *Listening to the Cicadas: A Study of Plato's* Phaedrus. Cambridge: Cambridge University Press.

Fine, G. (2014), *The Possibility of Inquiry: Meno's Paradox from Socrates to Sextus*, Oxford: Oxford University Press.

Fine, G. forthcoming, "Recollection and Innatism in the *Phaedo*."

Fischer, T. (1970), *Untersuchungen zum Partherkrieg Antiochos VII.*, Tübingen: Eigenverlag.

Flaig, E. (1992), *Den Kaiser Herausfordern: Die Usurpation im römischen Reich* [Historische Studien 7], Frankfurt and New York: Campus Verlag.

Flaig, E. (1995), "Die Pompa Funebris. Adlige Konkurrenz und annalistische Erinnerung in der römischen Republik," in O.G. Oexle (ed.), *Memoria als Kultur*, 115–48, Göttingen: Vandenhoeck & Ruprecht.

Fleischer, R. (1996), "Hellenistic Royal Iconography on Coins," in P. Bilde, T. Engberg-Pedersen, and J. Zahle (eds.), *Aspects of Hellenistic Kingship* [Studies in Hellenistic Civilization 7], 28–40, Oakville, CT: Aarhus University Press.

Fless, Fr. (2004), "Processions, Rom./Prozessionen, Röm./Processioni, Rom.," in *Thesaurus Cultus et Rituum Antiquorum* I, 33–58, Los Angeles: The J. Paul Getty Museum.

Fleury, P. (2011), "Vitruve et le métier d'ingénieur," *Cahiers des études anciennes* 48, 7–34.

Flower, H. (1995), "Fabulae praetextae in Context: When were Plays on Contemporary Subjects Performed in Republican Rome?" *CQ* 45:1, 170–90.

Flower, H. (1996), *Ancestor Masks and Aristocratic Power in Roman Culture*, Oxford: Clarendon Press.

Flower, H. (2000), "The Tradition of the Spolia Opima: M. Claudius Marcellus and Augustus," *ClAnt* 19:1, 34–64.

Flower, H. (2006), *The Art of Forgetting. Disgrace and Oblivion in Roman Political Culture*. Chapel Hill, NC: The University of North Carolina Press.

Forsdyke, S. (2012), *Slaves Tell Tales: And Other Episodes in the Politics of Popular Culture in Ancient Greece*, Princeton and Oxford: Princeton University Press.

Foster, E. And D. Lateiner, D. (eds.) (2012), *Thucydides and Herodotus*, Oxford: Oxford University Press.

Foucault, M. (1975), "Film and Popular Memory," *Radical Philosophy* 11, 24–9.

Foxhall, L., H.-J. Gehrke, and N. Luraghi (eds.) (2010), *Intentional History: Spinning Time in Ancient Greece*, Stuttgart: Steiner.

Franchi, E. (2009), "Spartani dalle lunghe chiome e Argivi rasati: interpretazioni iniziatiche moderne e costruzioni di senso antiche," *IncidAnt* 7, 61–88.

Franchi, E. (2015a), "*Memory Studies* e *Classics*," in E. Franchi and G. Proietti (eds.), *Guerra e memoria nel mondo antico*, 39–126, Trento: Università degli Studi di Trento.

Franchi, E. (2015b), "The Phocian Desperation and the Third Sacred War," *Hormos* 7, 49–71.

Franchi, E. (2016), *Die Konflikte zwischen Thessalern und Phokern. Krieg und Identität in der griechischen Erinnerungskultur des 4. Jahrhunderts*, Munich: Utz.

Franchi, E. (2017), "La pace di Filocrate e l'enigma della clausola focidese," in E. Franchi and G. Proietti (eds.), *Communities in Conflict. Forward-looking Memories in Classical Athens*, 255–88, Trento: Università degli Studi di Trento.

Franchi, E. (2018), "Continuity and Change in Phocian Spatial Politics: Commemorating Old and New Victories in 4th Century Delphi," in S. Montel and A. Pollini (eds.), *Les questions de l'espace au IVe siècle av. J.-C.: continuités, ruptures, reprises*, 35–69, Besançon: PUF.

Franchi, E. and G. Proietti (eds.) (2012), *Forme della memoria e dinamiche identitarie nell'antichità greco-romana*, Trento: Università degli Studi di Trento.

Franchi, E. and G. Proietti (eds.) (2015), *Guerra e memoria nel mondo antico*, Trento: Università degli Studi di Trento.

Franchi, E. and G. Proietti (eds.) (2017), *Communities in Conflict. Forward-looking Memories in Classical Athens*, Trento: Università degli Studi di Trento.

Frede, M. (1990), "An Empiricist View of Knowledge: Memorism," in S. Everson (ed.), *Companions to Ancient Thought 1: Epistemology*, 225–50, Cambridge: Cambridge University Press.

Fredouille, J.-C. (2012), *Tertullien et la conversion de la culture antique*, Turnhout: Brepols (1st ed. 1972).

Fromentin, V. (2001), "Denys d'Halicarnasse: historien grec de Rome," J. Leclant and Fr. Chamoux (eds.), *Histoire et historiographie dans l'Antiquité*, 123–42, Paris: De Boccard.

Gabba, E. (1999), Review of A. Carandini (1997), *Athenaeum* 87, 324–6.

Gabba, E. (2000), *Roma arcaica. Storia e storiografia*, Rome: Edizioni di Storia e Letteratura.

Galimberti, A. (2017), "Claudio, Tacito e la memoria dei Balbi," in A. Galimberti, R. Cristofoli, and F. Rohr Vio (eds.), *Costruire la memoria: uso e abuso della storia fra tarda repubblica e primo principato*, 195–203, Rome: L'Erma di Bretschneider.

Galimberti, A., R. Cristofoli. and F. Rohr Vio (eds.) (2017), *Costruire la memoria: uso e abuso della storia fra tarda repubblica e primo principato*, Rome: L'Erma di Bretschneider.

Galinsky, K. (1996), *Augustan Culture. An Interpretive Introduction*, Princeton: Princeton University Press.

Galinsky, K. (ed.) (2005), *The Cambridge Companion to the Age of Augustus*, Cambridge: Cambridge University Press.

Galinsky, K. (2007), "Continuity and Change: Religion in the Augustan Semi-century," in J. Rüpke (ed.), *A Companion to Roman Religion*, 71–82, Oxford: Blackwell.

Galinsky, K. (ed.) (2014), *Memoria Romana: Memory in Rome and Rome in Memory*, Ann Arbor: The University of Michigan Press.

Galinsky, K. (2015), "Introduction," in K. Galinsky and K. Lapatin (eds.), *Cultural Memories in the Roman Empire*, 1–22, Los Angeles: J. Paul Getty Museum.

Galinsky, K. (ed.) (2016a), *Memory in Ancient Rome and Early Christianity*, Oxford and New York: Oxford University Press.

Galinsky, K. (2016b), "Introduction," in K. Galinsky (ed.), *Memory in Ancient Rome and Early Christianity*, 1–39. Oxford and New York: Oxford University Press.

Galinsky, K. and K. Lapatin (eds.) (2015), *Cultural Memories in the Roman Empire*, Los Angeles: Paul Getty Museum.

Galli, M. (2005), "Pilgrimage as Elite *Habitus*: Educated Pilgrims in Sacred Landscape during the Second Sophistic," in J. Elsner and I. Rutherford (eds.), *Pilgrimage in Graeco-Roman and Early Christian Antiquity*, 253–90, Oxford: Oxford University Press.

Gallia, A.B. (2012), *Remembering the Roman Republic: Culture, Politics and History under the Principate*, Cambridge and New York: Cambridge University Press.

Gallop, D. (1975), *Plato. Phaedo*, Oxford: Clarendon Press.

Gangloff, A. (2006), *Dion Chrysostome et les mythes. Hellénisme, communication et philosophie politique*, Grenoble: Millon.

Gangloff, A. (2012), "L'adaptation du langage et la diffusion de normes chez Dion de Pruse," in F. Brizay (ed.), *Les formes de l'échange. Communiquer, diffuser, informer de l'Antiquité au XVIIIe siècle*, 11937, Rennes: PUR.

Gangloff, A., ed. (2013), *Lieux de mémoire en Orient grec à l'époque impériale*, Bern: P. Lang.

Garbarino, G. (1973), *Roma e la filosofia greca dalle origini alla fine del II sec. a.C.*, Torino: Paravia.

Garde-Hansen, J. (2011), *Media and Memory*, Edinburgh: Edinburgh University Press.

Garde-Hansen, J., L. McEwen, and O. Jones (2016), "Towards a Memo-Techno-Ecology: Mediating Memories of Extreme Flooding in Resilient Communities," in A. Hajek, Ch. Lohmeier, and Ch. Pentzold (eds.), *Memory in a Mediated World: Remembrance and Reconstruction*, 55–73, Basingstoke: Palgrave Macmillan.

Garland, R. (1992), *Introducing New Gods. The Politics of Athenian Religion*, Ithaca: Cornell University Press.

Gawlinski, L. (2011), *The Sacred Law of Andania: A New Text with Commentary*, Berlin and Boston: DeGruyter.

Gehrke, H.-J. (2001), "Myth, History and Collective Identity: Uses of the Past in Ancient Greece and Beyond," in N. Luraghi (ed.), *The Historian's Craft in the Age of Herodotus*, 286–313, Oxford: Oxford University Press.

Gehrke, H.-J. (2004), "Was heißt und zu welchem Ende studiert man intentionale Geschichte? Marathon und Troja als fundierende Mythen," in G. Melville and K.-S. Rehberg (eds.), *Gründungsmythen, Genealogien, Memorialzeichen. Beiträge zur institutionellen Konstruktion von Kontinuität*, 21–36, Cologne, Weimar and Vienna: Böhlau.

Gehrke, H.-J. (2010), "Greek Representations of the Past," in L. Foxhall, H.-J. Gehrke, and N. Luraghi (eds.), *Intentional History. Spinning Time in Ancient Greece*, 15–33, Stuttgart: Steiner.

Gehrke, H.-J. (2014), Geschichte als Element antiker Kultur, Berlin: De Gruyter.

Gehrke, H.-J. and A. Möller (eds.) (1996), *Vergangenheit und Lebenswelt: Soziale Kommunikation, Traditionsbildung und historisches Bewusstsein*, Tübingen: Narr.

Gell, A. (1998), *Art and Agency: An Anthropological Theory*, Oxford: Oxford University Press.

Giangiulio, M. (2005), *Erodoto e il "modello erodoteo". Formazione e trasmissione delle tradizioni storiche in Grecia*, Trento: Università degli Studi di Trento.

Giangiulio, M. (ed.) (2010a), *Memorie coloniali*, Rome: L'Erma di Bretschneider.

Giangiulio, M. (2010b), "Collective Identities, Imagined Past, and Delphi," in Foxhall, L., H.-J. Gehrke, and N. Luraghi (eds.), *Intentional History: Spinning Time in Ancient Greece*, 121–35, Stuttgart: Steiner.

Giangiulio, M. (2010c), "Memoria e tradizione orale," in M. Giangiulio (ed.), *Memorie coloniali*, 13–27, Rome: L'Erma di Bretschneider.

Giangiulio, M. (2016), "Aristocrazie in discussione. Verso un nuovo modello per la società greca arcaica?" *IncidAnt* 14:2, 305–16.

Giangiulio, M. (2019), "Do Societies Remember? The Notion of 'Collective Memory': Paradigms and Problems (from Maurice Halbwachs on)," in M. Giangiulio, E. Franchi, and G. Proietti (eds.), *Commemorating War and War Dead. Ancient and Modern*, 19–33, Stuttgart: Steiner.

Giangiulio, M., E. Franchi, and G. Proietti (eds.) (2019), *Commemorating War and War Dead. Ancient and Modern*, Stuttgart: Steiner.

Goetz, G. and F. Schöll (1910), *De lingua Latina quae supersunt*, Leipzig: Teubner.

Goldmann, L. (1967), *The Hidden God. A Study of Tragic Vision in the Pensées of Pascal and the Tragedies of Racine*, 17, London: Routledge.

González, J. (1986), "The Lex Irnitana: A New Copy of the Flavian Municipal Law," *JRS* 76, 147–243.

Goodman, M. (2012), "Memory and Its Uses in Judaism and Christianity in the Early Roman Empire: The Portrayal of Abraham," in B. Dignas and R.R.R. Smith (eds.), *Historical and Religious Memory in the Ancient World*, 69–82, Oxford: Oxford University Press.

Goody, J. (1978), *The Domestication of the Savage Mind*, Cambridge: Cambridge University Press.

Gordon, R. (2012), "Memory and Authority in the Magical Papyri," in B. Dignas and R.R.R. Smith (eds.), *Historical and Religious Memory in the Ancient World*, 145–80, Oxford: Oxford University Press.

Gotter, U. (1996), *Der Diktator ist tot! Politik in Rom zwischen den Iden des März und der Begründung des zweiten Triumvirats*, Historia Einzelschriften 110, Stuttgart: Steiner.

Gotter, U. (2015), "Penelope's Web, or: How to Become a Bad Emperor *Post Mortem*," in H. Börm (ed.), *Antimonarchic Discourses in Antiquity* [Studies in Ancient Monarchies 2], 215–33, Stuttgart: Steiner.

Gould, J. (1999), "Myth, Memory and the Chorus: 'Tragic Rationality'," in R. Buxton (ed.), *From Myth to Reason? Studies in the Development of Greek Thought*, 107–16, Oxford: Oxford University Press.

Gould, J. (ed.) (2001a), *Myth, Ritual, Memory, and Exchange. Essays in Greek Literature and Culture*, Oxford: Oxford University Press.

Gould, J. (2001b), "Epimetrum: On the Nature of Collective Memory," in J. Gould (ed.), *Myth, Ritual, Memory, and Exchange. Essays in Greek Literature and Culture*, 415–18, Oxford: Oxford University Press.

Gowing, A.M. (2005), *Empire and Memory: The Representation of the Roman Republic in Imperial Culture, Roman Literature and Its Contexts*, Cambridge and New York: Cambridge University Press.

Graf, F. (2009), "Serious Singing: The Orphic Hymns as Religious Texts," *Kernos* 22, 169–82.

Graf, F. (2011), "Myth and Hellenic Identities," in K. Dowden and N. Livingstone (eds.), *A Companion to Greek Mythology*, 211–26, Malden, Mass. and London: Wiley-Blackwell.

Graf, F. and Johnston, S.I. (2007), *Ritual Texts for the Afterlife. Orpheus and the Bacchic Gold Tablets*, London and New York: Routledge.

Grethlein, J. (2008), "Memory and Material Objects in the *Iliad* and the *Odyssey*," *JHS* 128, 27–51.

Grethlein, J. (2010), *The Greeks and Their Past: Poetry, Oratory and History in the Fifth Century BCE*, Cambridge: Cambridge University Press.

Grethlein, J. (2013), *Experience and Teleology in Ancient Historiography. "Futures Past" from Herodotus to Augustine*, Cambridge: Cambridge University Press.

Grethlein, J. (2014), "Future Past. Time and Teleology in (Ancient) Historiography," *History and Theory* 53:3, 309–30.

Grig, L. (ed.) (2017a), *Popular Culture in the Ancient World*, Cambridge: Cambridge University Press.

Grig, L. (2017b), "Introduction: Approaching Popular Culture in the Ancient World," in L. Grig (ed.), *Popular Culture in the Ancient World*, 1–36, Cambridge: Cambridge University Press.

Griswold C.L. (1986), *Self-knowledge in Plato's Phaedrus*, New Haven: Yale University Press.

Gros, P. (1976), Aurea Templa. *Recherches sur l'architecture religieuse de Rome à l'époque d'Auguste* (Bibliothèque des Écoles françaises d'Athènes et de Rome 231), Rome: École française de Rome.

Grunaeur-von Hoerschelmann, S. (1978), *Die Münzprägung der Lakedaimonier*, Berlin: De Gruyter.

Guettel-Cole, S. (2008), "Professionals, Volunteers, and Amateurs in the Cult of Demeter: Serving the Gods *kata ta patria*," in B. Dignas and K. Trampedach (eds.), *Practitioners of the Divine. Greek Priests and Religious Officials from Homer to Heliodorus*, 55–72, Cambridge, Mass.: Harvard University Press.

Haake, M. and M. Jung (eds.) (2011), *Griechische Heiligtümer als Erinnerungsorte. Von der Archaik bis in den Hellenismus*, Stuttgart: Steiner.
Hackforth, R. (1955), *Plato's Phaedo*. Cambridge: Cambridge University Press.
Hägg, R. (ed.) (1999), *Ancient Greek Hero Cult. Proceedings of the Fifth International Seminar on Ancient Greek Cult, organized by the Department of Classical Archaeolgy and Ancient History, Göteborg University, 21–23 April 1995*, Stockholm: Coronet Books.
Hajek, A., Ch. Lohmeier, and Ch. Pentzold (eds.) (2016), *Memory in a Mediated World: Remembrance and Reconstruction*, Basingstoke: Palgrave Macmillan.
Halbwachs, M. (1925, 2nd edn 1952), *Les cadres sociaux de la mémoire*, Paris: Librairie Félix Alcan.
Halbwachs, M. (1950; 2nd edn 1967), *La mémoire collective*. Paris: Les presses universitaires de France (Engl. tr. 1980, New York).
Halliwell, S. (2007), "The Life-and-Death Journey of the Soul: Interpreting the Myth of Er," in G.R.F. Ferrari (ed.), *The Cambridge Companion to Plato's Republic*, 445–73, Cambridge: Cambridge University Press.
Hannah, R. (2005), *Greek and Roman Calendars. Constructions of Time in the Classical World*, London: Duckworth.
Hansen, S. (1996), "Weihegaben zwischen System und Lebenswelt," in H.-J. Gehrke and A. Möller (eds.), *Vergangenheit und Lebenswelt: Soziale Kommunikation, Traditionsbildung und historisches Bewusstsein*, 257–76, Tübingen: Narr.
Harris, W.V. (1989), *Ancient Literacy*, Cambridge, Mass. and London: Harvard University Press.
Hartmann, A. (2010), *Zwischen Relikt und Reliquie. Objektbezogene Erinnerungspraktiken in antiken Gesellschaften*, Berlin: Verlag Antike.
Hartmann, A. (2012), "Vergessen, bewahren, erfinden. Vergleichende Perspektiven auf den Umgang mit Überresten der Vergangenheit in Griechenland und Rom," in G.F. Chiai, B.M. Gauly, A. Hartmann, G. Zimmer, and B.M. Zapff (eds.), *Athen, Rom, Jerusalem. Normentransfers in der antiken Welt*, 257–311, Regensburg: Verlag Friedrich Pustet.
Haselberger, L. (2007), *Urbem adornare: Die Stadt Rom und ihre Gestaltumwandlung unter Augustus / Rome's Urban Metamorphosis under Augustus* [Journal of Roman Archaeology Suppl. 64], Portsmouth, RI: Journal of Roman Archaeology.
Havelock, E. (1986), *The Muse Learns to Write. Reflections on Orality and Literacy from Antiquity to the Present*, New Haven and London: Yale University Press.
Havelock, E.A. (1963), *Preface to Plato*. Cambridge, Mass.: Harvard University Press.
Havelock, E.A. (1982), *The Literate Revolution in Greece and its Cultural Consequences*, Princeton: Princeton University Press.
Havener, W. (2016), *Imperator Augustus: Die diskursive Konstituierung der militärischen Persona des ersten römischen Princeps* [Studies in Ancient Monarchies 4], Stuttgart: Steiner.
Hawes, G. (2014), *Rationalizing Myth in Antiquity*, Oxford: Oxford University Press.
Hawes, G. (ed.) (2017), *Myths on the Map: The Storied Landscapes of Ancient Greece*, Oxford: Oxford University Press.
Hekster, O. (2002), *Commodus. An Emperor at the Crossroads*, Amsterdam: J.C. Gieben.
Helmig, C. (2012), *Forms and Concepts: Concept Formation in the Platonic Tradition*, Berlin and Boston: De Gruyter.
Herbert-Brown, G. (1994), *Ovid and the* Fasti. *A Historical Study*, Oxford: Oxford University Press.
Hermary, A. and B. Jaeger (eds.) (2011), *Thesaurus Cultus et Rituum Antiquorum (ThesCRA)*, VII, *Festivals and Contests*, III. "Fêtes et jeux dans le monde romain," 195–272, Los Angeles: J. Paul Getty Museum.

Heusch, Ch. (2011), *Die Macht der Memoria: Die "Noctes Atticae" des Aulus Gellius im Licht der Erinnerungskultur des 2. Jahrhunderts n. Chr.*, Berlin and New York: De Gruyter.

Hickson Hahn, F. (2007), "Performing the Sacred: Prayers and Hymns," in J. Rüpke (ed.), *A Companion to Roman Religion*, 235–48, Oxford: Blackwell.

Higbie, C. (2003), *The Lindian Chronicle and the Greek Creation of their Past*, Oxford: Oxford University Press.

Higbie, C. (2014), "Greeks and the Forging of Homeric Pasts," in B. Alroth and Ch. Scheffer (eds.), *Attitudes Towards the Past in Antiquity. Creating Identities, Proceedings of an International Conference Held at Stockholm University, 15–17 May 2009* [Stockholm Studies in Classical Archaeology 14], 9–20, Stockholm: Stockholm University.

Higgins, D. (1966), *Intermedia*, New York: Fluxus and Something Else Press.

Hobsbawm, E. J. (1983), "Introduction: Inventing Traditions," in E.J. Hobsbawm and T.O. Ranger (eds.), *The Invention of Tradition*, 1–14, Canto, Cambridge and New York: Cambridge University Press.

Hochschild, P.E. (2012), *Memory in Augustine's Theological Anthropology*, Oxford: Oxford University Press.

Hölbl, G. (2001), *A History of the Ptolemaic Empire*, London: Routledge.

Hölkeskamp, K.J. (1996), "Exempla und mos maiorum: Überlegungen zum kollektiven Gedächtnis der Nobilität," in H.-J. Gehrke and A. Möller (eds.), *Vergangenheit und Lebenswelt: Soziale Kommunikation, Traditionsbildung und historisches Bewusstsein*, 301–33, Tübingen: Narr.

Hölkeskamp, K.J. (2016), "In the Web of (Hi-)stories. Memoria, Monuments and their Myth-historical Interconnectedness," in K. Galinsky (ed.), *Memory in Ancient Rome and Early Christianity*, 169–213, Oxford and New York: Oxford University Press.

Hölscher, T. (1998), "Images and Political Identity," in D. Boedecker and K.A. Raaflaub (eds.), *Democracy, Empire, and the Arts in Fifth-Century Athens*, 153–83, Cambridge, Mass.: Harvard University Press.

Hölscher, T. (2001), "Die Alten vor Augen. Politische Denkmäler und öffentliches Gedächtnis im republikanischen Rom," in G. Melville (ed.), *Institutionalität und Symbolisierung. Kulturelle Ordnungsmuster in Vergangenheit und Gegenwart*, 183–211, Cologne, Weimar and Vienna: Böhlau.

Hoover, O.D. (2011), *Handbook of Coins of the Peloponnesos: Achaia, Phleiasia, Sikyonia, Elis, Triphylia, Messenia, Laconia, Argolis, and Arkadia: Sixth to First Centuries BC*, Lancaster, PA: Classical Numismatic Group.

Hornblower, S. (2002), "Herodotus and his Sources of Information," in E.J. Bakker, I.J.F. de Jong, and H. van Wees (eds.), *Brill's Companion to Herodotus*, 373–86, Leiden: Brill.

Hornblower, S. (2004), *Thucydides and Pindar. Historical Narrative and the World of Epinikian Poetry*, Oxford: Oxford University Press.

Hornblower, S. (2008), *A Commentary on Thucydides: Volume III: Books 5.25–8.109*, Oxford and New York: Oxford University Press.

Horsfall, N. (2003), *The Culture of the Roman Plebs*, London: Duckworth.

Hubbard, Th.K. (2008), "Getting the Last Word: Publication of Political Oratory as an Instrument of Historical Revisionism," in E.A. Mackay (ed.), *Orality, Literacy, Memory in the Ancient Greek and Roman World*, 183–200, Leiden and Boston: Brill.

Humphreys, S.C. (1981), "Death and Time," in S. Humphreys and H. King (eds.), *Mortality and Immortality: The Anthropology and Archaeology of Death*, 261–83, London: Academic Press.

Humphreys, S.C. (2004), *The Strangeness of Gods. Historical Perspectives on the Interpretations of Athenian Religion*, Oxford: Oxford University Press.

Humphreys, S.C. (2018), *Kinship in Ancient Athens: An Anthropological Analysis*, Oxford: Oxford University Press.

Hunt, L. (1989), "Introduction: History, Culture, Text," in L. Hunt (ed.), *The New Cultural History*, 19, Berkeley: University of California Press.

Hurst, A. (1982), "Un critique grec dans la Rome d'Auguste. Denys d'Halicarnasse'" *ANRW*, II-30:1, 39–865.

Hutton, P.H. (2020), "Memory Issue in the Democratization of Print Culture," *A Cultural History of Memory*, vol. 4, London: Bloomsbury.

Ierodiakonou, K. (2007), "The Stoics and the Skeptics on memory," in M.M. Sassi (ed.), *Tracce nella mente: teorie della memoria da Platone ai moderni*, 47–65, Pisa: Edizioni della Normale.

Inglebert, H. (2005), *Histoire de la civilisation romaine*, Paris: Presses universitaires de France.

Jacoby, F. (1949), *Atthis. The Local Chronicles of Ancient Athens*, Oxford: Clarendon Press.

Jacquemin, A. (1999), *Offrandes monumentales à Delphes*, Athens and Paris: DeBoccard.

Jacquemin, A. (2011), "Le sanctuaire de Delphes come *lieu de mémoire*," in M. Haake and M. Jung (eds.), *Griechische Heiligtümer als Erinnerungsorte. Von der Archaik bis in den Hellenismus*, 19–27, Stuttgart: Steiner.

Jaeger, M. (1997), *Livy's Written Rome*, Ann Arbor: The University of Michigan Press.

Jaeger, W. (1957), "Aristotle's Use of Medicine as Model of Method in His Ethics," *JHS* 77:1, 54–61.

Jaeger, W. (1978; 1944), *Paideia: the Ideals of Greek Culture*, vol. III. *The Conflict of Cultural Ideals in the Age of Plato* (Engl. tr. G. Highet), New York: Oxford University Press.

Johne, R. (1991), "Zur Entstehung einer 'Buchkultur' in der zweiten Hälfte des 5. Jahrhunderts v. u. Z.," *Philologus* 135, 45–54.

Jones, C.P. (1991), "Dinner-theater," in W.J. Slater (ed.), *Dining in a Classical Context*, 185–98, Ann Arbor: University of Michigan Press.

Jouanna J. (1999), *Hippocrates* (tr. M.B. DeBevoise), Baltimore: Johns Hopkins University Press.

Julião, R. (2018), "Galen on Memory, Forgetting and Memory Loss," in C. Thumiger and P.N. Singer (eds.), *Mental Illness in Ancient Medicine. From Celsus to Caelius Aurelianus*, 222–45, Berlin: De Gruyter.

Julião, R., R. Lo Presti, D. Perler, and P. van der Eijk (2016), "Mapping Memory: Theories in Ancient, Medieval and Early Modern Philosophy and Medicine," *eTopoi* 6, 678–702.

Jung, M. (2006), *"Marathon and Plataiai". Zwei Perserschlachten als "lieux de mémoire" im antiken Griechenland* [Hypomnemata 164], Göttingen: Vandenhoeck&Ruprecht.

Jung, M. (2011), "Methodisches: Heiligtümer und *lieux de mémoire*," in M. Haake and M. Jung (eds.), *Griechische Heiligtümer als Erinnerungsorte. Von der Archaik bis in den Hellenismus*, 9–19, Stuttgart: Steiner.

Kahn, C. (2006), "Plato on Recollection," in H.H. Benson (ed.), *A Companion to Plato*, 119–32, Oxford: Oxford University Press.

Kahn, C.H. (2003), "Writing Philosophy: Prose and Poetry from Thales to Plato," in H. Yunis (ed.), *Written Texts and the Rise of Literate Culture in Ancient Greece*, 139–61, Cambridge: Cambridge University Press.

Kalifa, D. (2010), "Culture savante/Culture Populaire," in Chr. Delacroix, Fr. Dosse, and P. Garcia (eds.), *Historiographies: Concepts et débats*, II, 994–9, Paris: Gallimard.

Kallet, L. (2003), "*Dēmos Tyrannos*: Wealth, Power, and Economic Patronage," in K. Morgan (ed.), *Popular Tyranny: Sovereignty and its Discontents in Ancient Greece*, 117–53, Austin: University of Texas Press.

Karim, K.H. (2003), "Mapping Diasporic Mediascapes," in K.H. Karim (ed.), *The Media of Diaspora*, 1–18, London: Routledge.

Kaun, A. and F. Stiernstedt (2016), "Media, Memory Practices and Community of Remembrance: Youth Radio DT64," in A. Hajek, Ch. Lohmeier, and Ch. Pentzold (eds.), *Memory in a Mediated World: Remembrance and Reconstruction*, 195–209, Basingstoke: Palgrave Macmillan.

Keightley, E. and M. Pickering (2016), "Memory, Media and Methodological Footings," in A. Hajek, Ch. Lohmeier, and Ch. Pentzold (eds.), *Memory in a Mediated World: Remembrance and Reconstruction*, 36–52, Basingstoke: Palgrave Macmillan.

Kellum, B.A. (1990), "The City Adorned: Programmatic Display at the Aedes Concordiae Augustae," in K. Raaflaub and M. Toher (eds.), *Between Republic and Empire: Interpretations of Augustus and his Principate*, 276–307, Berkeley: University of California Press.

Kelly, G. (2008), *Ammianus Marcellinus. The Allusive Historian*, Cambridge: Cambridge University Press.

Keramopoullos, E. (1907), "Φωκικὸν ἀνάθημα ἐν Δελφοῖς," *EphArch*, 91–104.

Kidron, C.A. (2016), "Memory," http://oxfordbibliographiesonline.com. [accessed 26 August 2017].

Kierdorf, W. (1980), *Laudatio Funebris. Interpretationen und Untersuchungen zur Entwicklung der römischen Leichenrede*, Meisenheim: Hain.

King, C. (2010), "Macedonian Kingship and Other Political Institutions," in J. Roisman and I. Worthington (eds.), *A Companion to Ancient Macedonia*, 373–91, Oxford: Wiley-Blackwell.

King, R.A.H. (2009), *Aristotle and Plotinus on Memory*, Berlin and New York: De Gruyter.

King, R.A.H. (2019), "Memory and Recollection in Plato's *Philebus*: Use and Definitions," in L. Castagnoli and P. Ceccarelli (eds.), *Greek Memories: Theories and Practices*, 216–35, Cambridge: Cambridge University Press.

König, J. and G. Woolf (eds.) (2017), *Authority and Expertise in Ancient Scientific Culture*, Cambridge and New York: Cambridge University Press.

Kõresaar, E., Võsu, E. and K. Kuutma (2008), "Mediation of Memory: Towards Transdisciplinary Perspectives in Current Memory Studies," *TRAMES* 12 (62/57): 3, 243–63.

Koselleck, R. (2004), *Futures Past: On the Semantics of Historical Time*, New York: Columbia University Press.

Kosmin, P. (2014), *The Land of the Elephant Kings: Space, Territory, and Ideology in the Seleucid Empire*, Cambridge, Mass.: Harvard University Press.

Kosmin, P. (2018), *Time and its Adversaries in the Seleucid Empire*, Cambridge, Mass.: Harvard University Press.

Kousser, R. (2015), "Monument and Memory in Ancient Greece and Rome: A Comparative Perspective," in K. Galinsky and K. Lapatin (eds.), *Cultural Memories in the Roman Empire*, 33–48, Los Angeles: J. Paul Getty Museum.

Krämer, S. (ed.) (1998a), *Medien-Computer-Realität. Wirklichkeitsvorstellungen und neue Medien*, Frankfurt: Suhrkamp.

Krämer, S. (1998b), "Was haben die Medien, der Computer und die Realität miteinander zu tun?" in S. Krämer (ed.), *Medien-Computer-Realität. Wirklichkeitsvorstellungen und neue Medien*, 9–26, Frankfurt: Suhrkamp.

Krauter, S. (2004), *Bürgerrecht und Kultteilnahme. Politische und kultische Rechte und Pflichten in griechischen Poleis, Rom und antikem Judentum* [Beihefte zur Zeitschrift für die neutestamentliche Wissenschaft und die Kunde der älteren Kirche 127], Berlin and New York: De Gruyter.

Kuntze, C. (1985), *Zur Darstellung des Kaisers Tiberius und seiner Zeit bei Velleius Paterculus*, Frankfurt: Lang.

Kurke, L. (2011), *Aesopic Conversations: Popular Tradition, Cultural Dialogue, and the Invention of Greek Prose*, Princeton and Oxford: Princeton University Press.

Kurlansky, K. (2016), *Paper. Paging through History*. New York: W.W. Norton & Co.
Kyriakou, P. (2011), *The Past in Aeschylus and Sophocles*, Berlin and Boston: De Gruyter.
La Rocca, E. (1995), "Il programma figurativo del foro di Augusto," in E. La Rocca, L. Ungaro, and R. Meneghini (eds.), *I luoghi del consenso imperiale: Il foro di Augusto, il foro di Traiano: Introduzione Storico-Topografica*, 74–87, Rome: Progetti musealli editore.
Laehn, T.R. (2013), *Pliny's Defence of Empire*, New York and London: Routledge.
Laffi, U. (1967), "Le iscrizioni relative all'introduzione nel 9 a.C. del nuovo calendario della Provincia d'Asia," *Studi Classici e Orientali* 16, 5–98.
Lahusen, G. (1983), *Untersuchungen zur Ehrenstatue in Rom: literarische und epigraphische Zeugnisse*, Rome: L'Erma di Bretschneider.
Landrea, C. (2014), "Traditions, mémoire nobiliaire et savoirs d'Etat à la fin de la République romaine," in J. Dubouloz, S. Pittia, and G. Sabatini (eds.), *L'imperium Romanum' en perspective: les savoirs d'empire dans la République romaine et leur héritage dans l'Europe médiévale et moderne*, 117–30, Besançon: Presses universitaires de France.
Lane Fox, R. (2018), "Travelling Myths, Travelling Heroes," in L. Audley-Miller and B. Dignas (eds.), *Wandering Myths. Transcultural Uses of Myth in the Ancient World*, XXXIII–LIV, Berlin: De Gruyter.
Latham, J.A. (2016), *Performance, Memory, and Processions in Ancient Rome: the Pompa Circensis from the Late Republic to Late Antiquity*, New York: Cambridge University Press.
Laurence, R. (1993), "Emperors, Nature and the City: Rome's Ritual Landscape," *The Accordia Research Papers* 4, 79–87.
Laurence, R. and C. Smith (1995–6), "Ritual, Time and Power in Ancient Rome," *The Accordia Research Papers* 6, 133–51.
Le Goff, J. (1977), *Storia e memoria*, Turin: Einaudi.
Le Roux, P. (2015) "Le doit latin *(ius Latii)*: une relecture," in G. Cresci Marrone (ed.), Trans Padum. . .usque ad Alpes. *Roma tra il Po e le Alpi: dalla romanizzazione alla romanità*, 179–95, Rome: Quasar.
Lefkowitz, M.R. (1981), *The Lives of the Greek Poets*. London: Duckworth.
Leonhard, N. (2002), "Politikbewusstsein und Vergangenheitsbezug in der dritten Generation. Ein Forschungsprojekt zum Wandel der Erinnerung an Nationalsozialismus und Holocaust," in J.-F. Pyper (ed.), *Uns hat keiner gefragt. Positionen der dritten Generation zur Bedeutung des Holocaust*, 67–100, Berlin and Vienna: Philo.
Leroi, A.M. (2014), *The Lagoon. How Aristotle Invented Science*, London: Bloomsbury.
Létoublon, F. (2011), "Homer's Use of Myth," in K. Dowden and N. Livingstone (eds.), *A Companion to Greek Mythology*. Malden, Mass. and Oxford: Blackwell.
Levene, D. (2012), "'You Shall Blot out the Memory of Amalek': Roman Historians on Remembering to Forget," in B. Dignas and R.R.R. Smith (eds.), *Historical and Religious Memory in the Ancient World*, 217–39, Oxford: Oxford University Press.
Levy, D. and N. Sznaider (2006), *The Holocaust and Memory in the Global Age*, Philadelphia: Temple University Press.
Lindsay, H. (1998), "Eating with the Dead: The Roman Funerary Banquet," in I. Nielsen and N. Sigismund Nilsen (eds.), *Meals in a Social Context: Aspects of the Communal Meal in the Hellenistic and Roman World*, 66–80, Aarhus: Aarhus University Press.
Liou-Gille, B. (2005), "La fondation de Rome: lectures de la tradition," *Histoire urbaine* 13, 67–83.
Lloyd, G.E.R. (1970), *Early Greek Science: Thales to Aristotle*, London: Chatto & Windus.
Loraux, N. (2002), *The Divided City: On Memory and Forgetting in Ancient Athens*, tr. C. Pache with J. Fort, New York: Zone Books.

Lord, A.B. (1960), *The Singer of Tales*, Cambridge: Harvard University Press.
Lowenthal, D. (1975), "Past Time, Present Place: Landscape and Memory," *Geographical Review* 65, 1–36.
Luce, T. J. (1990), "Livy, Augustus, and the Forum Augustum," in K.A. Raaflaub and M. Toher (eds.), *Between Republic and Empire: Interpretations of Augustus and his Principate*, 123–38, Berkeley: University of California Press.
Luckmann, T. (1967), *The Invisible Religion. The Problem of Religion in Modern Society*, New York: Macmillan.
Luraghi, N. (ed.) (2001), *The Historian's Craft in the Age of Herodotus*, Oxford: Oxford University Press.
Luraghi, N. (2008), *The Ancient Messenians: Constructions of Ethnicity and Memory*, Cambridge: Cambridge University Press.
Ma, J. (2002), *Antiochos III and the Cities of Western Asia Minor*, Oxford: Oxford University Press.
Ma, J. (2007), "Hellenistic Honorific Statues and their Inscriptions," in Z. Newby and R. Leader-Newby (eds.), *Art and Inscriptions in the Ancient World*, 203–20, Cambridge: Cambridge University Press.
Ma, J. (2009), "City as Memory," in G. Boys-Stones, B. Graziosi, and P. Vasunia (eds.), *The Oxford Handbook of Hellenic Studies*, 248–59, Oxford: Oxford University Press.
Ma, J. (2013), *Statues and Cities: Honorific Portraits and Civic Identity in the Hellenistic World*, Oxford: Oxford University Press.
MacDowell, D. M. (2007), "Hereditary 'Sitesis' in Fourth-Century Athens," *ZPE* 162, 111–13.
Mackay, E.A. (ed.) (2008), *Orality, Literacy, Memory in the Ancient Greek and Roman World*, Leiden and Boston: Brill.
Malkin, I. (1998), *The Returns of Odysseus. Colonization and Ethnicity*, Berkeley: University of California Press.
Malkin, I. (2003), "'Tradition' in Herodotus: The Foundation of Cyrene," in P. Derow and R. Parker (eds.), *Herodotus and his World. Essays from a Conference in Honour of George Forrest*, 153–70, Oxford: Oxford University Press.
Marincola, J., ed. (2011), *A Companion to Greek and Roman Historiography*, Oxford and New York: Wiley-Blackwell.
Marincola, J., L. Llewellyn-Jones, and C.A. Maciver (eds.) (2012), *Greek Notions of the Past in the Archaic and Classical Eras: History without Historians*, Edinburgh: Edinburgh University Press.
Martin, P.M. (ed.) (1993), *II<sup>e</sup> table ronde internationale sur Denys d'Halicarnasse, historien des origines de Rome, Pallas* 39, 3–214.
Martínková, I. (2010), "Three Interpretations of kalokagathia," in P. von Mauritsch (ed.), *Körper im Kopf: Antike Diskurse zum Körper*, 17–28, Graz: Grazer Universitätsverlag.
Matthews, J. (1989), *The Roman Empire of Ammianus*, London: Duckworth.
McAuley, A. (2018). "The Tradition and Ideology of Naming Seleucid Queens," *Historia* 67: 472–94.
McClay, M.F. (2018), "Memory and Performance: Strategies of Identity in the Orphic-Bacchic Lamellae," PhD diss., University of California, Berkeley.
Meadows, A.R. (2001), "Money, Freedom, and Empire in the Hellenistic World," in A.R. Meadows and K. Shipton (eds.), *Money and its Uses in the Ancient Greek World*, 53–63, Oxford: Oxford University Press.
Mehl, A. (1986), *Seleukos Nikator und sein Reich* [Studia Hellenistica 28], Leuven: Leuven University Press.

Meier, C. (2017), *Res publica amissa. Eine Studie zur Verfassung und Geschichte der späten römischen Republik*, Stuttgart: Steiner.

Merrill, M. (1976), "Interview with E.P. Thompson," in H. Abelove, et al. (eds.), *Visions of History*, 20f, Manchester: Manchester University Press.

Meuli, K. (1946), "Griechische Opferbräuche," in O. Gigon (ed.), *Phyllobolia. Für Peter van der Mühll zum 60. Geburtstag am 1. August 1945*, 185–288, Basel: Benno Schwabe & Co.

Miano, D. (2012), "Moneta. Sacred Memory in Mid-Republican Rome," in M. Bommas, J. Harrisson, and P. Roy (eds.), *Memory and Urban Religion in the Ancient World*, 89–109, London: Bloomsbury.

Michels, A.K. (1967), *The Calendar of the Roman Republic*, Princeton: Princeton University Press.

Migliario, E. (2015), "Commemorare conflitti e generali a Roma fra il I secolo a.C. e il I secolo d.C.," *Commemorating War and War Dead. Ancient and Modern* (Trento, 4–5th June 2015): https://www.youtube.com/watch?v=k1PXLr56ijc&t=2553s.

Migliario, E. (forthcoming), "La narrazione della morte di Cicerone," *Interférences*.

Mikalson, J.D. (1998), *Religion in Hellenistic Athens*, Berkeley and London: University of California Press.

Mikalson, J.D. (2010$^2$; 2005), *Ancient Greek Religion*, Chichester: Wiley-Blackwell.

Miles, G. (1995), *Livy: Reconstructing Ancient Rome*, Ithaca and London: Cornell University Press.

Millar, F. (1987), "Polybius between Greece and Rome," in J.A.T. Koumoulides (ed.), *Greek Connections: Essays on Culture and Diplomacy*, 1–18, Bloomington: Indiana University Press [= H.M. Cotton and G.M. Rogers (eds.) (2006), *Rome, the Greek World, and the East*, III: *The Greek World, the Jews, and the East*, 91–105, Chapel Hill and London: The University of North Carolina Press].

Millar, F. (1993), "Ovid and the *Domus Augusta*: Rome seen from Tomoi," *JRS* 83, 1–17 [= H.M. Cotton and G.M. Rogers (eds.) (2002), *Rome, the Greek World, and the East*, I. *The Roman Republic and the Augustan Revolution*, 321–49, Chapel Hill and London: The University of North Carolina Press.]

Millar, F. (2006), *A Greek Roman Empire: Power and Belief under Theodosius II (408–450)* (Sather Classical Lectures 64), Berkeley and Los Angeles: University of California Press.

Minchin, E. (2001), *Homer and the Resources of Memory: Some Applications of Cognitive Theory to the* Iliad *and the* Odyssey, Oxford: Oxford University Press.

Minchin, E. (2006), "Can one Ever Forget? Homer on the Persistence of Painful Memories," *Scholia* 15, 2–16.

Minchin, E. (2012a), "Commemoration and Pilgrimage in the Ancient World. Troy and the Stratigraphy of Memory," *Greece & Rome* 59:1, 76–89.

Minchin, E. (2012b), "Memory and Memories: Personal, Social, and Cultural Memory in the Poems of Homer," in F. Montanari, A. Rengakos, and C. Tsagalis (eds.), *Homeric Contexts: Neoanalysis and the Interpretation of Oral Poetry*, 83–99, Berlin: De Gruyter.

Minchin, E. (2017), "Mapping the Hellespont with Leander and Hero: The Swimming Lover and the Nightly Bride," in G. Hawes (ed.), *Myths on the Map: The Storied Landscapes of Ancient Greece*, 65–82, Oxford: Oxford University Press.

Mineo, B. (2015), *A Companion to Livy*, Chichester: Wiley-Blackwell.

Minon, S., ed. (2012), *Dion de Pruse. Ilion n'a pas été prise: Discours troyen 11*, Paris: Les Belles Lettres.

Misztal, B.A. (2003), *Theories of Social Remembering*, Maidenhead: Open University Press.

Mittag, P.F. (2006). *Antiochos IV. Epiphanes. Eine politische Biographie*, Berlin: Akademie Verlag.

Moatti, C. (2003), "Experts, mémoire et pouvoir à Rome, à la fin de la république," *Revue Historique* 626, 303–25.

Momigliano, A. (1942), "Camillus and Concord," *CQ* 36, 111–20.

Morgan, C. (2014), "Archaeology of Memory or Tradition in Practice?" in B. Alroth and Ch. Scheffer (eds.), *Attitudes towards the Past in Antiquity. Creating Identities, Proceedings of an International Conference Held at Stockholm University, 15–17 May 2009* [Stockholm Studies in Classical Archaeology 14], 173–81, Stokholm: Stockholm University.

Morgan, K.A. (2000), *Myth and Philosophy from the Presocratics to Plato*. Cambridge: Cambridge University Press.

Mørkholm, O. (1991), *Early Hellenistic Coinage from the Accession of Alexander to the Peace of Apamea (336–186 B.C.)*, Cambridge: Cambridge University Press.

Morstein-Marx, R. (2004), *Mass Oratory and Political Power in the Late Roman Republic*, Cambridge and New York: Cambridge University Press.

Munson, R. (ed.) (2013), *Herodotus: vol. 1, Herodotus and the Narrative of the Past*, Oxford and New York: Oxford University Press.

Münzer, Fr. (1930), s.v. Marcius (90) Rex, in *RE* 14:2, 1582–3.

Murphy, T.M. (2004), *Pliny the Elder's Natural History: The Empire in the Encyclopedia*, Oxford: Oxford University Press.

Nadali, D. (ed.) (2016), *Envisioning the Past Through Memory: How Memory Shaped Ancient Near Eastern Societies*, London: Bloomsbury Academic.

Neigers, M., O. Meyers, and E. Zandberg (eds.) (2011), *On Media Memory: Collective Memory in a New Media Age*, Basingstoke and New York: Palgrave Macmillan.

Neisser, U. (1989), "Domains of Memory," in P.R. Solomon, G.R. Goethals, C.M. Kelley, and B.R. Stephens (eds.), *Memory: Interdisciplinary Approaches*, 67–83, New York: Springer-Verlag.

Newby, Z. (2005), *Greek Athletics in the Roman World: Victory and Virtue*, Oxford: Oxford University Press.

Newby, Z. (2006) "Reading the Archelaos Relief," in Z. Newby and R. Leader-Newby (eds.), *Art and Inscriptions in the Ancient World*, 156–78, Cambridge: Cambridge University Press.

Newby, Z. and R. Leader-Newby (eds.) (2006), *Art and Inscriptions in the Ancient World*, Cambridge: Cambridge University Press.

Ng, D. (2016), "Monuments, Memory, and Status Recognition in Roman Asia Minor," in K. Galinsky (ed.), *Memory in Ancient Rome and Early Christianity*, 235–60, Oxford and New York: Oxford University Press.

Nicolai, R. (1992), *La storiografia nell'educazione antica*, Pisa: Giardini.

Nielsen, J. (2012), "Marduk's Return: Assyrian Imperial Propaganda, Babylonian Cultural Memory, and the *Akītu* Festival of 667 BC," in M. Bommas, J. Harrisson, and Ph. Roy (eds.), *Memory and Urban Religion in the Ancient World*, 3–32; London and New York: Bloomsbury Academic.

Nielsen, Th.H. (2000), "Epiknemidian, Hypoknemidian, and Opountian Locrians. Reflections on the Political Organisation of East Lokris in the Classical Period," in P. Flensted-Jensen (ed.), *Further Studies in the Ancient Greek Polis*, 91–120, Stuttgart: Steiner.

Nora, P. (1984–92), *Les lieux de mémoire*, 7 vols., Paris: Gallimard.

Nora, P. (1989), "Between Memory and History: Les lieux de mémoire," *Representations* 26, 7–24.

Nöth, W. (1997), *Semiotics of the Media: State of the Art, Projects, and Perspectives*, Berlin: De Gruyter.

Notopoulos, J.A. (1938), "Mnemosyne in Oral Literature," *Transaction and Proceedings of the American Philological Association* 69, 465–93.

Nuffelen, P. van (2004), "Le culte royal de L'empire des Séleucides: une reinterpretation," *Historia* 53:3, 278–301.
Nutton, V. (2013), *"Avoiding Distress,"* [English translation of Galen's Περὶ ἀλυπίας] in P.N. Singer (ed.), *Galen. Psychological Writings*, 45–99, Cambridge: Cambridge University Press.
O'Neill, Sh. (2008), *Interactive Media: The Semiotics of Embodied Interaction*, Stuttgart: Springer.
Ogden, D. (ed.) (2007), *A Companion to Greek Religion*, London: Blackwell.
Ogden, D. (2017), *The Legend of Seleucus*, Cambridge: Cambridge University Press.
Olick, J.K. and J. Robbins (1998), "Social Memory Studies: from 'Collective Memory' to the Historical Sociology of Mnemonic Practices," *Annual Review of Sociology* 24, 105–40.
Olick, J. K., V. Vinitzky-Seroussi, and D. Levy (eds.) (2011), *The Collective Memory Reader*, Oxford: Oxford University Press.
Ong, Walter J. (1982), *Orality and Literacy. The Technologizing of the Word*, London: Methuen.
Ooteghem, J. van (1961), *Lucius Marcius Philippus et sa famille*, Brussels: Palais des Académies.
Orlin, E. (2016), "Augustan Reconstruction and Roman Memory," in K. Galinsky (ed.), *Memory in Ancient Rome and Early Christianity*, 115–44, Oxford and New York: Oxford University Press.
Osborne, J.F. (2017), "Counter-monumentality and the Vulnerability of Memory," *JSA* 17:2, 163–87.
Osborne, M. J. (1981), "Entertainment in the Prytaneion at Athens," *ZPE* 41, 153–70.
Osborne, P. (2002), *Conceptual Art*, London: Tate Publications.
Osborne, R. (2011), "Local Environment, Memory, and the Formation of the Citizen in Classical Attica," in S.D. Lambert (ed.), *Sociable Man: Essays on Ancient Greek Social Behaviour in Honour of Nick Fisher*, 25–43, Swansea: Classical Press of Wales.
Ostwald, M. (1969), *Nomos and the Beginnings of the Athenian Democracy*, Oxford: Clarendon Press.
Ostwald, M. (1988), "The Reform of the Athenian State by Cleisthenes," *CAH*² 4, 303–46.
Pagkalos, M. (2015), "The Coinage of King Areus I revisited: Uses of the Past in Spartan Coins," *GLB* 20:2, 145–59.
Paivio, A. (1983), "The Mind's Eye in Arts and Science," *Poetics* 12, 1–18.
Paivio, A. (1986), *Mental Representations: A Dual Coding Approach*, New York: Oxford University Press.
Palagia, O. (1986), "Imitation of Herakles in Ruler Portraiture: A Survey, from Alexander to Maximinus Daza," *Boreas* 9, 137–51.
Palagia, O. (2006), "Art and Royalty in Sparta of the 3rd Century B.C.," *Hesperia* 75, 205–17.
Papini, M. (2004), *Antichi volti della repubblica. La ritrattistica in Italia Centrale tra IV e II secolo a.C.*, Rome: L'Erma di Bretschneider.
Parker, H. N. (2011), "Toward a Definition of Popular Culture," *History and Theory* 50:2, 147–70.
Parker, R.C.T. (2011), *On Greek Religion*, Ithaca: Cornell University Press.
Parry, M. (1950; 1932), "Studies in the Epic Technique of Oral Verse-Making. II: The Homeric Language as the Language of an Oral Poetry," *Harvard Studies in Classical Philology* 43, 1–50.
Pébarthe, Chr. (2006), *Cité, démocratie et ecriture. Histoire de l'alphabétisation d'Athènes à l'époque classique*, Paris: De Boccard.
Pelling, Chr. (1997), *Greek Tragedy and the Historian*, Oxford: Clarendon Press.
Pernot, L. (2005), "Athènes, lieu de mémoire," in Y. Lehmann, G. Freyburger, and J. Hirstein (eds.), *Antiquité tardive et humanisme: de Tertullien à Beatus Rhenanus. Mélanges offerts à François Heim à l'occasion de son 70ᵉ anniversaire*, 101–20, Turnhout: Brepols.

Perrett, R. W. (1999) "History, Time, and Knowledge in India," *History and Theory* 38, 307–21.
Petersen, L. H. (2006), *The Freedman in Roman Art and Art History*, Cambridge and New York: Cambridge University Press.
Picard, G.C. (1957), *Les trophées romains. Contribution à l'histoire de la religion et de l'art triomphal de Rome*, Paris: De Boccard.
Pietri, Ch. (1997), Christiana respublica. *Éléments d'une enquête sur le christianisme antique* (Collection de l'École française de Rome 234, 3 vols), Rome: École française de Rome.
Piovan, D. (2011), *Memoria e oblio della guerra civile: strategie giudiziarie e racconto del passato in Lisia*, Pisa: ETS.
Pirenne-Delforge, V. (2004), "Mythe et histoire dans la Périégèse de Pausanias (fin IIe s. ap. J.-C.): une question de vocabulaire?" in M.E. Henneau et al. (eds.), *Temps, culture, religions: autour de Jean-Pierre Massaut*, 48–62, Louvain-la-Neuve and Brussels: Collège Érasme.
Pirenne-Delforge, V. (2008), *Retour à la source: Pausanias et la religion grecque*, Liège: Presses universitaires Liège.
Pirenne-Delforge, V. and E. Suárez de la Torre (eds.) (2000), *Héros et héroïnes dans les mythes et les cultes grecs* [Kernos Suppl. 10], Liège: Presses universitaires Liège.
Pleket, H. W. (1972), "Isonomia and Cleisthenes: A Note," *Talanta* 4, 63–81.
Podlecki, A.J. (1966), "The Political Significance of the Athenian 'Tyrannicide'-Cult," *Historia* 15:2, 129–41.
Pomtow, H. (1915), "202B, 203A," in W. Dittenberger, *Sylloge Inscriptionum Graecarum* 1, 3rd edn, Leipzig: Hirzel.
Poole, R. (2008), "Memory, History and the Claims of the Past," *Memory Studies* 1, 149–66.
Prescendi, F. (2010), "Children and the Transmission of Religious Knowledge," in V. Dasen and Th. Späth (eds.), *Children, Memory, and Family Identity in Roman Culture*, 73–93, Oxford: Oxford University Press.
Price, S.R.F. (2012), "Memory and Ancient Greece," in B. Dignas and R.R.R. Smith (eds.), *Historical and Religious Memory in the Ancient World*, 15–36, Oxford: Oxford University Press.
Price, S.R.F. and P. Thonemann (2010), *The Birth of Classical Europe. A History from Troy to Augustine*, London: Penguin.
Prim, J. (2016), "L'Aventin et la plèbe: représentations politiques d'un espace urbain dans les sources littéraires des IIe et Ier siècles av. n. è.," in S. Benoist, A. Daguet-Gagey, and Chr. Hoët-van Cauwenberghe (eds.), *Une mémoire en actes: espaces, figures et discours dans le monde romain*, 89–117, Villeneuve d'Ascq: Presses universitaires du Septentrion.
Pritchard, D.H. (2010), "Cognitive Ability and the Extended Cognition Thesis," *Synthese* 175, 133–151.
Raaflaub, K. (2002), "Philosophy, Science, Politics: Herodotus and the Intellectual Trends of his Time," in E.J. Bakker, I.J.F. de Jong, and H. van Wees (eds.), *Brill's Companion to Herodotus*, 149–86, Leiden: Brill.
Raaflaub, K. (2005), "The Conflict of the Orders in Archaic Rome: A Comprehensive and Comparative Approach," in K.A. Raaflaub (ed.), *Social Struggles in Archaic Rome. New Perspectives on the Conflict of the Orders*, 2nd edn, 1–46, Malden, Mass., Oxford and Victoria: Blackwell.
Raaflaub, K. (2003), "Stick and Glue: The Function of Tyranny in Fifth-Century Athenian Democracy," in K. Morgan (ed.), *Popular Tyranny: Sovereignty and Its Discontents in Ancient Greece*, 59–93, Austin: University of Texas Press.
Rausch, M. (1999), *Isonomia in Athen: Veränderungen des öffentlichen Lebens vom Sturz der Tyrannis bis zur zweiten Perserabwehr*, Frankfurt am Main and New York: Peter Lang.

Rawson, G. (2006), "Platonic Recollection and Mental Pregnancy," *Journal of the History of Philosophy* 44, 137–55.
Reddé, M. (ed.) (2003), *La naissance de la ville dans l'Antiquité*, Paris: De Boccard.
Reeve, C.D.C. (2012), *Blindness and Reorientation: Problems in Plato's Republic*, Oxford: Oxford University Press.
Rehak, P. and J.G. Younger (2006), *Imperium and Cosmos: Augustus and the Northern Campus Martius*, Madison: The University of Wisconsin Press.
Rhodes, P.J. (1992), "The Athenian Revolution," *CAH*² 5, 62–95.
Rhodes, P.J. (1993), *A Commentary on the Aristotelian "Athenaion Politeia"* [Clarendon Paperbacks], Oxford: Clarendon Press.
Rhodes, P.J. (1998), "Isonomia," *DNP* 5, 1143.
Richardson, J. (2008), *The Language of Empire. Rome and the Idea of Empire from the Third Century BC to the Second Century AD*, Cambridge: Cambridge University Press.
Ricoeur, P. (1984), *Temps et récits* 2, Paris: Le Seuil.
Ricoeur, P. (2000), *La memorie l'histoire l'oubli*, Paris: Le Seuil.
Ricoeur, P. (2004), *Memory, History and Forgetting* (Engl. tr. K. Blamey and D. Pellauer), Chicago: The University of Chicago Press.
Rigsby, K.J. (1996), *Asylia: Territorial Inviolability in the Hellenistic World*, Berkeley: University of California Press.
Robert, J. and L. Robert (1983), *Fouilles d'Amyzon en Carie*, Paris: De Boccard.
Roberto, U. (2015), *Rome face aux Barbares. Une histoire des sacs de la Ville*, Paris: Le Seuil.
Robinson, M. (2011), *A Commentary on Ovid's* Fasti, *Book 2*, Oxford: Oxford University Press.
Robson, J. (2017), "Humouring the Masses: The Theatre Audience and the Highs and Lows of Aristophanic Comedy," in L. Grig (ed.), *Popular Culture in the Ancient World*, 66–87, Cambridge: Cambridge University Press.
Rohr Vio, F. (2017), "Protagoniste della memoria, interpreti del passato, artefici del futuro: 'matronae doctae' nella tarda repubblica," in A. Galimberti, R. Cristofoli, and F. Rohr Vio (eds.), *Costruire la memoria: uso e abuso della storia fra tarda repubblica e primo principato*, 95–112, Rome: L'Erma di Bretschneider.
Romano, A. (2012), "Tragic Pasts and Euripidean Explainers," in J. Marincola, L. Llewellyn-Jones, and C.A. Maciver (eds.), *Greek Notions of the Past in the Archaic and Classical Eras: History without Historians*, 127–43, Edinburgh: Edinburgh University Press.
Rösler, W. (2002), "The *Histories* and Writing," in E.J. Bakker, I.J.F. de Jong, and H. van Wees (eds.), *Brill's Companion to Herodotus*, 79–94, Leiden: Brill.
Rössler-Köhler, U. and T. Tawfik (eds.) (2009), *Die ihr vorbeigehen werdet . . . Wenn Gräber, Tempel und Statuen sprechen*, Berlin and New York: De Gruyter.
Rubin, D. (1995), *Memory in Oral Traditions: The Cognitive Psychology of Epic, Ballads, and Counting-out Rhymes*, New York and Oxford: Oxford University Press.
Rudhardt, J. (1988), "Mnémosyne et les Muses," in Ph. Borgeaud (ed.), *La mémoire des religions*, 37–62, Geneva: Labor et Fides.
Rupert, R.D. (2004), "Challenges to the Hypothesis of Extended Cognition," *The Journal of Philosophy* 101:8, 389–428.
Rüpke, J. (1995), *Kalender und Öffentlichkeit. Die Geschichte der Repräsentation und religiösen Qualifikation von Zeit in Rom*, Berlin: De Gruyter.
Rüpke, J. (2000), "Räume literarischer Kommunikation in der Formierungsphase römischer Literatur," in B. Braun and F.H. Mutscher (eds.), *Moribus antiquis res stat Romana: Römische Werte und römische Literatur im dritten und zweiten Jahrhundert v. Chr.*, 31–52, Munich and Leipzig: Saur.

Rüpke, J. (2007a), *The Religions of the Romans*, London: Wiley.
Rüpke, J. (ed.) (2007b), *A Companion to Roman Religion*, Malden, Mass. and London: Blackwell.
Rüpke, J. (2011), *The Roman Calendar from Numa to Constantine: Time, History, and the Fasti*, London: Wiley-Blackwell.
Rüpke, J. (2012), *Religiöse Erinnerungskulturen. Formen der Geschichtsschreibung in der römischen Antike*, Darmstadt: Wissenschaftliche Buchgesellschaft.
Rüpke, J. (2016), "Knowledge of Religion in Valerius Maximus' Exempla: Roman Historiography and Tiberian Memory Culture," in K. Galinsky (ed.), *Cultural Memory in Ancient Rome and Early Christianity*, 89–111, Oxford: Oxford University Press.
Rutledge, S.H. (2015), "Conflict, Culture, and Concord: Some Observations on Alternative Memory in Ancient Rome," in K. Galinsky and K. Lapatin (eds.), *Cultural Memories in the Roman Empire*, 225–37, Los Angeles: J. Paul Getty Museum.
Sablayrolles, R. (1981), "Espace urbain et propagande politique: l'organisation du centre de Rome par Auguste (*Res Gestae*, 19 à 21)," *Pallas* 28: *L'espace dans l'Antiquité Classique*, 59–77.
Salzman, M. (1999), "The Christianization of sacred time and sacred space," in W.V. Harris (ed.), *The Transformations of Vrbs Roma in Late Antiquity*, 123–34, Portsmouth: Journal of Roman Archaeology.
Samuel, A. E. (1972), *Greek and Roman Chronology. Calendars and Years in Classical Antiquity* [Handbuch Der Altertumswissenschaft 7:1], Munich: C.H. Beck.
Santaniello, E. (2011), "L'*Olympieion*," in E. Greco (ed.), *Topografia di Atene: sviluppo urbano e monumenti dalle origini al III secolo d. C. 2, Colline sud-occidentali, Valle dell'Ilisso*, 458–63, Athens and Paestum: Pandemos.
Sassi, M. M. (2019), "The Greek Philosophers on How to Memorise—And Learn," in L. Castagnoli and P. Ceccarelli (eds.), *Greek Memories: Theories and Practices*, 343–61, Cambridge: Cambridge University Press.
Schacter, D. (2001), *The Seven Sins of Memory: How the Mind Forgets and Remembers*, Boston and New York: Houghton Mifflin.
Scheer, T.S. (1993), *Mythische Vorväter. Zur Bedeutung griechischer Heroenmythen im Selbstverständnis kleinasiatischer Städte* [Münchener Arbeiten zur Alten Geschichte 7], Munich: Maris.
Scheer, T.S. (1996), "Ein Museum griechischer 'Frühgeschichte' im Apollontempel von Sikyon," *Klio* 78:2, 353–73.
Scheer, T.S. (2018), "Myth, Memory and the Past. Wandering Heroes between Arcadia and Cyprus," in L. Audley-Miller and B. Dignas (eds.), *Wandering Myths. Transcultural Uses of Myth in the Ancient World*, 71–91, Berlin: De Gruyter.
Scheid, J. (1987), "Les sanctuaires de confins dans la Rome antique. Réalité et permanence d'une représentation idéale de l'espace romain," in *L'Urbs. Espace urbain et histoire (I$^{er}$ siècle avant J.-C.–III$^e$ siècle après J.-C.)*, 583–95, Rome: École française de Rome.
Scheid, J. (2003), *An Introduction to Roman Religion [La Religion des Romains, Paris 1998]*, Engl. tr. Janet Lloyd, Edinburgh: Edinburgh University Press.
Scheid, J. (2007), "Sacrifices for Gods and Ancestors," in J. Rüpke (ed.), *A Companion to Roman Religion*, 263–71, Malden, Mass. and London: Blackwell.
Scheid, J. (2012), "Le *suburbium* de Rome. Recherches sur l'organisation religieuse du territoire de Rome," in: *Annuaire du Collège de France 2010–2011*, 461–68, Paris: Collège de France.
Scheid, J. (2015), *The Gods, the State, and the Individual. Reflections on Civic Religion in Rome*, translated and with a foreword by C. Ando, Philadelphia: University of Pennsylvania Press.

Schmid, W. (1887), *Der Atticismus in seinen Hauptvertretern, von Dionysius von Halikarnass bis auf den zweiten Philostratus*, I, Stuttgart: Kohlhammer.

Schmuhl, Y. (2008), *Römische Siegesmonumente republikanischer Zeit: Untersuchungen zu Ursprüngen, Erscheinungsformen und Denkmalpolitik*, Hamburg: Kovac.

Schudson, M. (1995), "Dynamics of Distortion in Collective Memory," in D. Schacter (ed.), *Memory Distortion: How Minds, Brains and Societies Reconstruct the Past*, 346–64, Cambridge, Mass.: Harvard University Press.

Scodel, R. (2008), "Social Memory in Aeschylus' Oresteia," in E.A. Mackay (ed.), *Orality, Literacy, Memory in the Ancient Greek and Roman World*, 115–41, Leiden and Boston: Brill.

Scodel, R. (2012), "Debating the Past in Euripides' Troades and Orestes and in Sophocles' Electra," in J. Marincola, L. Llewellyn-Jones, and C.A. Maciver (eds.), *Greek Notions of the Past in the Archaic and Classical Eras: History without Historians*, 113–26, Edinburgh: Edinburgh University Press.

Scodel, R. (ed.) (2014), *Between Orality and Literacy: Communication and Adaptation in Antiquity*, Leiden and Boston: Brill.

Scolnicov, S. (1988), *Plato's Metaphysics of Education*, London: Routledge.

Scott, D. (1987), "Platonic Anamnesis Revisited," *CQ* n.s. 37, 346–66.

Scott, D. (1995), *Recollection and Experience: Plato's Theory of Learning and Its Successors*, Cambridge: Cambridge University Press.

Scott, D. (2006), *Plato's Meno*, Cambridge: Cambridge University Press.

Scullard, H.H. (1981), *Festivals and Ceremonies of the Roman Republic*, Ithaca: Cornell University Press.

Sedley, D.N. (1998), *Lucretius and the Transformation of Greek Wisdom*, Cambridge: Cambridge University Press.

Sedley, D.N. (2004), *The Midwife of Platonism: Text and Subtext in Plato's* Theaetetus, Oxford: Oxford University Press.

Seebacher, C. (forthcoming), *Zwischen Augustus und Antinoos. Tradition und Innovation in der Imago Kaiser Hadrians* [Studies in Ancient Monarchies 5], Stuttgart: Steiner.

Seel, M. (1998), "Medien der Realität und Realität der Medien," in S. Krämer (ed.), *Medien-Computer-Realität. Wirklichkeitsvorstellungen und neue Medien*, 244–68, Frankfurt: Suhrkamp.

Sehlmeyer, M. (1999), *Stadtrömische Ehrenstatuen der republikanischen Zeit. Historizität und Kontext von Symbolen nobilitären Standesbewußtseins*, Stuttgart: Steiner.

Seider, A.M. (2013), *Memory in Vergil's Aeneid: Creating the Past*, Cambridge and London: Cambridge University Press.

Sérida, R. (2018), "Myth, Memory, and Mimesis. The Inaros Cycle as Literature of Resistance," in L. Audley-Miller and B. Dignas (eds.), *Wandering Myths. Transcultural Uses of Myth in the Ancient World*, 281–307, Berlin: De Gruyter.

Sharma, A. (1983), "The Role of Memory in Hindu Epistemology and its Religious Implications," *Indian Philosophical Quarterly* 10, 485–91.

Shaya, J. (2005), "The Greek Temple as Museum: the Case of the Legendary Treasure of Athena from Lindos," *AJA* 109, 423–42.

Shaya, J. (2013), "The Public Life of Monuments: The Summi Viri of the Forum of Augustus," *AJA* 117:1, 83–110.

Sheffield, F. (2001), "Psychic Pregnancy and Platonic Epistemology," *Oxford Studies in Ancient Philosophy* 20, 1–33.

Shumka, L.J. (2000), "Designing Women: Studies in the Representation of Femininity in Roman Society," PhD Diss., Victoria: University of Victoria.

Simondon, M. (1982), *La mémoire et l'oubli dans la pensée grecque jusqu'à la fin de V$^e$ siècle av. J-C. Psychologie archaïque, mythes et doctrines*, Paris: Les Belles Lettres.

Sion-Jenkis, K. (2000), *Von der Republik zum Prinzipat. Ursachen für den Verfassungswechsel in Rom im historischen Denken der Antike*, Stuttgart: Steiner.

Skydsgaard, J.E. (1968), *Varro the Scholar. Studies in the First Book of Varro's* De re rustica [Analecta Romana Instituti Danici IV Suppl.], Copenhagen: Munksgaard.

Small, J.P. (1997), *Wax Tablets of the Mind. Cognitive Studies of Memory and Literacy in Classical Antiquity*, London and New York: Routledge.

Small, J.P. (2012), "Memory and the Roman Orator," in W. Dominik and J. Hall (eds.), *A Companion to Roman Rhetoric*, 195–206, Oxford: Blackwell.

Smith, Ch. (2019), "Revisiting the Roman Clan," in M. Di Fazio and S. Paltineri (eds.), *La società gentilizia nell'Italia antica fra realtà e mito storiografico*, 25–45, Bari: Edipuglia.

Smith, R.R.R. (2012), "Defacing the Gods at Aphrodisias," in B. Dignas and R.R.R. Smith (eds.), *Historical and Religious Memory in the Ancient World*, 283–323, Oxford: Oxford University Press.

Sommerstein, A. (ed.) (1993), *Tragedy, Comedy and the Polis*, Bari: Levante editori.

Sorabji, R. (1972), *Aristotle On Memory*. London: Duckworth.

Sorabji, R. (2006a), *Aristotle On Memory*. 2nd edn, Chicago: University of Chicago Press. [cf. BMCR 2006.08.08].

Sorabji, R. (2006b), *Self: Ancient and Modern Insights about Individuality, Life, and Death*, Chicago: University of Chicago Press.

Sourvinou-Inwood, Ch. (1995), *"Reading" Greek Death to the End of the Classical Period*, Oxford: Oxford University Press.

Sourvinou-Inwood, Ch. (2000), "What is *Polis* Religion?" and "Further Aspects of *Polis* Religion," in R. Buxton (ed.), *Oxford Readings in Greek Religion*, 13–37 and 38–55, Oxford: Oxford University Press.

Spannagel, M. (1999), *Exemplaria principis: Untersuchungen zur Entstehung und Ausstattung des Augustusforums*, Heidelberg: Verlag Archäologie und Geschichte.

Späth, Th. (2016), "Au lieu des lieux, les actes de mémoire. Figurations du passé et pratiques sociales," in S. Benoist, A. Daguet-Gagey, and Chr. Hoët-van Cauwenberghe (eds.), *Une mémoire en actes: espaces, figures et discours dans le monde romain*, 23–46, Villeneuve d'Ascq: Presses universitaires du Septentrion.

Spinelli, E. (2019), "*Physiologia medicans*: The Epicurean Road to Happiness," in L. Castagnoli and P. Ceccarelli (eds.), *Greek Memories: Theories and Practices*, 278–91, Cambridge: Cambridge University Press.

Stafford, E. (2012), *Herakles*, London and New York: Routledge.

Stahl, H. (2010), "Mediascape and Soundscape. Two Landscapes of Modernity in Cold War Berlin," in P. Broadbent and S. Hake (eds.), *Berlin. Divided City, 1945–1989*, 56–65, Oxford and New York: Berghahn Books.

Starzmann, M.T. (2016), "Engaging Memory: an Introduction," in M.T. Starzmann and J.R. Roby (eds.), *Excavating Memory: Sites of Remembering and Forgetting*, 1–22, Gainesville: University Press of Florida.

Stedman Jones, G. (1983), *Languages of Class: Studies in English Working-Class History 1832–1986*, 22, Cambridge: Cambridge University Press.

Steinbock, B. (2013), *Social Memory in Athenian Public Discourse. Uses and Meanings of the Past*, Ann Arbor: University of Michigan Press.

Stein-Hölkeskamp, E. (2016), "Marius, Sulla, and the War over Monumental Memory and Public Space," in K. Galinsky (ed.), *Memory in Ancient Rome and Early Christianity*, 214–34, Oxford and New York: Oxford University Press.

Stern, S. (2012), *Calendars in Antiquity: Empires, States, and Societies*, Oxford: Oxford University Press.

Stevens, K. (2014), "The Antiochus Cylinder, Babylonian Scholarship and Seleucid Imperial Ideology," *JHS* 134, 66–88.

Stock, K.-A., H. Gajsar, and O. Güntürkün (2016), "The Neuroscience of Memory," in K. Galinsky (ed.), *Memory in Ancient Rome and Early Christianity*, 369–92, Oxford and New York: Oxford University Press.

Strauss Clay, J. (2011), *Homer's Trojan Theater: Space, Vision, and Memory in the Iliad*, Cambridge and New York: Cambridge University Press.

Strothmann, M. (2000), *Augustus—Vater der res publica. Zur Funktion der drei Begriffe restitutio—saeculum—pater patriae im augusteischen Prinzipat*, Stuttgart: Steiner.

Tarrant, H. (2005), *Recollecting Plato's* Meno, London: Routledge.

Taub, L. (2017), *Science Writing in Greco-Roman Antiquity*, Cambridge: Cambridge University Press.

Teegarden, D.A. (2014a), "Acting like Harmodius and Aristogeiton: Tyrannicide in Ancient Greek Political Culture," in C. Dietze and C. Verhoeven (eds.), *The Oxford Handbook of the History of Terrorism*, oxfordshandbooks.com DOI: 10.1093/oxfordhb/9780199858569.013.001 [accessed 26 August 2017].

Teegarden, D.A. (2014b), *Death to Tyrants! Ancient Greek Democracy and the Struggle against Tyranny*, Princeton and Oxford: Princeton University Press.

Ternes, Ch.M. (ed.) (1992), *Condere Urbem*, Luxembourg: Publications du Centre Universitaire de Luxembourg.

Teske, R. (2001), "Augustine's Philosophy of Memory," in E. Stump and N. Kretzmann (ed.), *The Cambridge Companion to Augustine*, 148–58, Cambridge: Cambridge University Press.

Thomas, R. (1989), *Oral Tradition and Written Record in Classical Athens*, Cambridge: Cambridge University Press.

Thomas, R. (1992), *Literacy and Orality in Ancient Greece*, Cambridge: Cambridge University Press.

Thomas, R. (2019), *Polis Histories, Collective Memories and the Greek World*, Cambridge: Cambridge University Press.

Thompson, E. (2013), "Self, No-Self? Memory and Reflexive Awareness," in M. Siderits, E. Thompson, and D. Zahavi (eds.), *Self, No-Self? Perspectives from Analytical, Phenomenological and Indian Traditions*, 157–75, Oxford: Oxford University Press.

Thonemann, P. (2012), "Abercius of Hierapolis. Christianization and Social Memory in Late Antique Asia Minor," in B. Dignas and R.R.R. Smith (eds.), *Historical and Religious Memory in the Ancient World*, 257–82, Oxford: Oxford University Press.

Thonemann, P. (2015), "The Calendar of the Roman Province of Asia," *ZPE* 196, 123–41.

Thornton, J. (2017), "Motivi tradizionali del dibattito sugli imperi nella memoria dei primi decenni della provincia d'Asia," in A. Galimberti, R. Cristofoli, and F. Rohr Vio (eds.), *Costruire la memoria: uso e abuso della storia fra tarda repubblica e primo principato*, 35–58, Rome: L'Erma di Bretschneider.

Timpe, D. (2011), "Memoria and Historiography in Rome," in J. Marincola (ed.), *A Companion to Greek and Roman Historiography*, 150–74, Oxford and New York: Wiley-Blackwell.

Toews, J. E. (1987), "Intellectual History after the Linguistic Turn: The Autonomy of Meaning and the Irreducibility of Experience." *American Historical Review* 92, 4 (Oct.): 879–907.

Tölle-Kastenbein, R. (1994), *Das Olympieion in Athen*, Cologne: Böhlau.

Toner, J. (2009), *Popular Culture in Ancient Rome*, Cambridge and Malden, Mass: Polity.

Tracy, S.V. (2016), *Athenian Lettering of the Fifth Century B.C.: The Rise of the Professional Letter Cutter*, Berlin: De Gruyter.

Traill, J.S. (1975), *The Political Organization of Attica: a Study of the Demes, Trittyes, and Phylai, and their Representation in the Athenian Council* [Hesperia Supplement 14], Princeton: American School of Classical Studies at Athens.

Trampedach, K. (2011), "Götterzeichen im Heiligtum: das Beispiel Delphi," in M. Haake and M. Jung (eds.), *Griechische Heiligtümer als Erinnerungsorte. Von der Archaik bin in den Hellenismus*, 29–44, Stuttgart: Steiner.

Trillmich, W. (2009), "Colonia Augusta Emerita, Capital of Lusitania," in J. Edmondson (ed.), *Augustus* [Edinburgh Readings on the Ancient World Series], 427–67, Edinburgh: Edinburgh University Press.

Tsouratsoglou, I. (2002), "Νομισματική και Αρχαιολογία," in Grammatikopoulou, E. (ed.), Η ιστορική διαδρομή της νομισματικής μονάδας στην Ελλάδα, Εθνικό Ίδρυμα Ερευνών, 11–23, Athens: Εθνικό Ίδρυμα Ερευνών.

Ungern-Sternberg, J., "The Tradition on Early Rome and Oral History," in J. Marincola (ed.), *A Companion to Greek and Roman Historiography*, 119–49, Oxford and New York: Wiley-Blackwell.

Vansina, J. (1985), *Oral Tradition as History*, London: James Currey; Nairobi: Heinemann Kenya.

Vernant, J.-P. (1983), *Myth and Thought among the Greeks* (Engl. tr. of Vernant (1965), *Mythe et pensée chez les Grecs. Études de psychologie historique*, Paris: Maspero), London: Routledge.

Veyne, P. (2005²), *L'Empire gréco-romain*, Paris: Le Seuil.

Vincent, A. (2017), "The Music of Power and the Power of Music: Studying Popular Auditory Culture in Ancient Rome," in L. Grig (ed.), *Popular Culture in the Ancient World*, 149–64, Cambridge: Cambridge University Press.

Vittinghoff, Fr. (1936), *Der Staatsfeind in der römischen Kaiserzeit. Untersuchungen zur "damnatio memoria,"* Berlin: Junker und Dünnhaupt.

Vlastos, G. (1994), "Anamnesis in the *Meno*", in J. Day (ed.), *Plato's* Meno *in Focus*, 88–111, London and New York: Routledge.

Von Staden, H. (1996), "'In a Pure and Holy Way': Personal and Professional Conduct in the Hippocratic Oath?" *Journal of the History of Medicine and Allied Sciences* 51, 404–37.

Wagner-Pacifici, R. and B. Schwartz (1991), "The Vietnam Veterans Memorial: Commemorating a Difficult Past," *The American Journal of Sociology* 97:2, 376–420.

Walbank, F.W. (1957), *A Historical Commentary on Polybius*, vol. 1, Oxford: Clarendon Press.

Walker, S. (1985), *Memorials to the Roman Dead*, London: British Museum Publications.

Walter, U. (2004), *Memoria und res publica. Zur Geschichtskultur im republikanischen Rom*, Frankfurt am Main: Verlag Antike.

Walter, U. (2007), "Wer in die Schuhe der Eltern steigt, bekommt keine größeren Füße," *Frankfurter Allgemeine Zeitung* 29.06.2007, 41 (review of M. Jung, *Marathon and Plataiai*, Göttingen 2006).

Warren, J. (2001), "Lucretian *Palingenesis* Recycled," *CQ* 51, 499–508.

Wecowski, M. (2016), "Herodotus in Thucydides: A Hypothesis," in J. Priestley and V. Zali (eds.), *Brill's Companion to the Reception of Herodotus in Antiquity and Beyond*, 17–32, Leiden and Boston: Brill.

Wees, H. van (2002), "Herodotus and the Past," in E.J. Bakker, I.J.F. de Jong, and H. van Wees (eds.), *Brill's Companion to Herodotus*, 321–49, Leiden: Brill.

Welzer, H., S. Moller, and K. Tschuggnall (2002³), *Opa war kein Nazi: Nationalsozialismus und Holocaust im Familiengedächtnis. Die Zeit des Nationalsozialismus*, Frankfurt am Main: Fischer.

Werner, D.S. (2012), *Myth and Philosophy in Plato's* Phaedrus, Cambridge: Cambridge University Press.
West, M.L. (1983), *The Orphic Poems*, Oxford: Oxford University Press.
Whitehead, A.N. (1929), *Process and Reality: An Essay in Cosmology,* New York and Cambridge.
Whitmarsh, T. (2015), "The Mnemology of Empire and Resistance: Memory, Oblivion, and Periegesis in Imperial Greek Culture," in K. Galinsky and K. Lapatin (eds.), *Cultural Memories in the Roman Empire*, 49–64, Los Angeles: J. Paul Getty Museum.
Wienand, J. (2012), *Der Kaiser als Sieger. Metamorphosen triumphaler Herrschaft unter Constantin I*, Klio. Beiträge zur alten Geschichte. New Series 19, Berlin: De Gruyter.
Wilhelm, A. (1911), "Die lokrische Mädcheninschrift," *ÖAW* 14, 163–256.
Wilhite, D.E. (2007), *Tertullian the African. An Anthropological Reading of Tertullian's Context and Identities*, Berlin and New York: De Gruyter.
Willers, D. (1990), *Hadrians panhellenisches Programm: Archäologische Beiträge zur Neugestaltung Athens durch Hadrian*, Basel: Vereinigung der Freunde Antiker Kunst.
Williamson, G. (2005), "Mucianus and a Touch of the Miraculous: Pilgrimage and Tourism in Roman Asia Minor," in J. Elsner and I. Rutherford (eds.), *Pilgrimage in Graeco-Roman and Early Christian Antiquity*, 219–52, Oxford: Oxford University Press.
Winograd E. and V.E. Church (1988), "Role of Spatial Location in Learning Face-Name Associations," *Memory and Cognition* 16, 1–7.
Winter, J. and E. Sivan (1999), *War and Remembrance in the Twentieth Century*, Cambridge: Cambridge University Press.
Winterling, A. (2003³), *Caligula: Eine Biographie*, Munich: C.H. Beck.
Winterling, A. (2005), "Dyarchie in der römischen Kaiserzeit. Vorschlag zur Wiederaufnahme der Diskussion," in W. Nippel and B. Seidensticker (eds.), *Theodor Mommsens langer Schatten. Das römische Staatsrecht als bleibende Herausforderung für die Forschung*, 177–98, Hildesheim: Georg Olms.
Winterling, A. (2011), *Caligula: A Biography* (Engl. tr. of Winterling 2003), Berkeley: University of California Press.
Wiseman, T.P. (1994), "Roman Legend and Oral Tradition," in T.P. Wiseman (ed.), *Historiography and Imagination*, 23–36, Liverpool: Liverpool University Press.
Wiseman, T.P. (1995), *Remus. A Roman Myth*, Cambridge: Cambridge University Press.
Wiseman, T.P. (2008), *Unwritten Rome*, Exeter: University of Exeter Press.
Wiseman, T.P. (2009), *Remembering the Roman People: Essays on Late-Republican Politics and Literature*, Oxford: Oxford University Press.
Wiseman, T.P. (2014), "Popular Memory," in K. Galinsky (ed.), *Memoria Romana, Memory in Rome and Rome in Memory*, 43–62, Ann Arbor: The University of Michigan Press for the American Academy in Rome.
Wolpert, A. (2002), *Remembering Defeat: Civil War and Civic Memory in Ancient Athens*, Baltimore: Johns Hopkins University Press.
Woolf, G. (1997), "Polis-Religion and its Alternatives in the Roman Provinces," in H. Cancik, and J. Rüpke (eds.), *Römische Reichsreligion und Provinzialreligion*, 72–81, Tübingen: Mohr.
Woolf, G. (1998), *Becoming Roman. The Origins of Provincial Civilization in Gaul*, Cambridge: Cambridge University Press.
Wright, J.C. (2004), "The Mycenean Feast,' *Hesperia* 73:2, 121–32.
Wygoda, Y. (2019), "Socratic Forgetfulness and Platonic Irony," in L. Castagnoli and P. Ceccarelli (eds.), *Greek Memories: Theories and Practices*, 195–215, Cambridge: Cambridge University Press.
Yamagata, N. (2005), "Plato, Memory and Performance," *Oral Tradition* 20, 111–29.

Yates F.A. (1966; 2001), *The Art of Memory*, London: Routledge and Kegan Paul.
Yunis, H. (ed.) (2003), *Written Text and the Rise of Literate Culture in Ancient Greece*, Cambridge: Cambridge University Press.
Zanker, P. (1987; 2003), *Augustus und die Macht der Bilder*, Munich: C.H. Beck.
Zanker, P. (1988), *The Power of Images in the Age of Augustus*, Ann Arbor: The University of Michigan Press.
Zecchini, G. (2017), "Conclusioni," in A. Galimberti, R. Cristofoli, and F. Rohr Vio (eds.), *Costruire la memoria: uso e abuso della storia fra tarda repubblica e primo principato*, 245–8, Rome: L'Erma di Bretschneider.
Zeitlin, F. (2001), "Visions and Revisions of Homer," in S. Goldhill (ed.), *Being Greek under Rome: Cultural Identity, the Second Sophistic and the Development of Empire*, 195–266, Cambridge: Cambridge University Press.
Ziótkowski, A. (2009), "Frontier sanctuaries of the ager Romanus antiquus: did they exist?" *Palamedes* 4, 91–130.

# CONTRIBUTORS

**Han Baltussen** is the Walter W. Hughes Professor of Classics at the University of Adelaide and a Fellow of the Australian Academy of Humanities. His research interest in intellectual history has led to articles, edited volumes, and monographs on sense perception, grief and consolations, ancient commentators, and self-censorship. He is currently working on a book about consolation strategies in antiquity, a commentary on Theophrastus' doxographical fragments, and a new Loeb translation of Eunapius' *Lives of Philosophers and Sophists*.

**Stéphane Benoist** is Professor of Roman History at the University of Lille and is the Chair of the research team HALMA (UMR 8164, CNRS, U Lille, MC). He has published widely on imperial power, political discourses and memory, festivals and ceremonies in the city of Rome.

**Ilaria Bultrighini** received her PhD in Ancient History and Archaeology from G. d'Annunzio University of Chieti-Pescara in 2012 and is currently Post-doctoral Research Fellow at the Institute of Classical Studies, University of London. She has previously worked as a researcher for the ERC project *Calendars in Antiquity and the Middle Ages*, based in the UCL Department of Hebrew and Jewish Studies. Her research interests also include Greek and Roman measurement and perceptions of time, ancient astrology, and the religions of the Roman Empire.

**Luca Castagnoli** is Associate Professor of Ancient Greek Philosophy at the University of Oxford, and Stavros Niarchos Foundation Clarendon Fellow at Oriel College. He is the Author of *Ancient Self-Refutation: The Logic and History of the Self-Refutation Argument from Democritus to Augustine* (CUP, 2010), the co-editor of *Greek Memories: Theories and Practices* (CUP, 2019), and the editor of *The Cambridge Companion to Ancient Logic*. He has published on a number of topics in ancient philosophy, with special focus on dialectic, logic, epistemology and philosophical method, from the Presocratics to Augustine.

**Boris Chrubasik** is Associate Professor of Ancient History at the University of Toronto. His research focuses on the political and cultural history of the Eastern Mediterranean from Achaemenid to early Roman eras. He has published a monograph on *Kings and Usurpers in the Seleukid Empire* (OUP, 2016), a co-edited volume with Daniel King on *Hellenism and the Local Communities of the Eastern Mediterranean* (OUP, 2017) and several articles and chapters. He teaches Greek History, broadly conceived, at the University's Mississauga Campus and the School of Graduate Studies.

**Beate Dignas** is Associate Professor at the University of Oxford and the Barbara Craig Fellow and Tutor of Ancient History at Somerville College. Her research focuses on Greek Religion and the History of Asia Minor. She is the author of *Economy of the Sacred* in *Hellenistic and Roman Asia Minor* (OUP, 2002) and co-authored *Rome and Persia in Late Antiquity* (CUP, 2007). Together with R.R.R. Smith, she edited *Historical and Religious Memory in the Ancient World* (OUP, 2012).

**Elena Franchi** is Assistant Professor of Ancient Greek History the University of Trento and Assistant Manager of the Laboratorio di Scienze dell'antichità (LabSA) of the Center for Advanced Studies in the Humanities there. In 2016 she published *Die Konflikte zwischen Thessalern und Phokern. Krieg und Identität in der griechischen Erinnerungskultur des 4. Jahrhunderts* (Munich: UTZ). Her research focuses on interstate relations, frontier wars, ethnogenesis, and memory studies. She has also published on Greek historiography and oratory, the periegetic genre (esp. Pausanias), and Plutarch.

**Anne Gangloff** is Senior Lecturer of Ancient History at the University of Rennes, member of the LAHM-CReAAH, UMR 6566, and of the Institut universitaire de France. Her research focuses on imperial Hellenism and Roman political thought and communication.

**Elizabeth Minchin** is Emeritus Professor of Classics at the Australian National University in Canberra. She is the author of *Homer and the Resources of Memory* (OUP, 2001) and *Homeric Voices* (OUP, 2007), and several articles and book chapters that address different aspects of memory and remembering, memory in the landscape, and memory over time.

# INDEX

*ab Urbe condita* (Livy) 41
*Acharnians* (play) 19
Achilles 134–35, 137, 142
Acropolis at the Erechtheum 143
*Aeneid* (Virgil) 9
Afghanistan 21
Agiadai 63
*agoge* 54
Agrippa 79
Ajax 59, 111, 134, 137, 142, 168n.42
Alexander the Great 21–22, 129
Alexandria 1
Alkibiades 30
Alkmaionidai 27–29, 31
Ammianus Marcellinus 46–47
Amphictyony of Delphi 59
*anabasis* 23
ancestor masks 120
*Ancient Medicine* 71–72, 159n.15
Ancus Marcius, King 63–64
Anderson, Greg 28
Anna Perenna 105, 162n.5
*Anthesteria* 127
Antigonos 33
Antiocheia 22
Antiochos I 21–22
Antiochos III 22–23, 27, 33, 129–30, 151n.18, 165nn.33/35
Antiochus IV 40
Antiochos V 32
antiquarianism 123, 132, 149n.36
*Antiquitates rerum humanarum et divinarum* (Varro) 77, 159n.21
Antoninus Pius 42
Apollo 21–22, 57
Apotheosis of Homer relief *see* Archelaos of Priene
Archelaos of Priene 1–2, 5, 8–10, 147nn.2–5,16
*arete* 86
Areus, King 63
Argives 53–55
Argolas, Battle of 57
Aristogeiton 17–20, 28
Aristophanes 27–30, 33, 107

Aristotle,
 and the ease of forgetting 144
 the first scientist 75–76, 159n.18
 literacy and orality 66
 pioneer of biology 67
 and Plato's imagery on wax 98, 161n.30
 and rote memorization 86
 and students needing memory skills 80–81
Artemisium, the 71
Artemis Leukophryene (festival) 129
Asclepius 131
Assmann, Aleida 124–27
Assmann, Jan,
 and bicultural ancient Egypt 6
 communicative memories 28
 cultural memories 3–4, 20, 34, 152n.44
 impact of writing 7–8
 interplay between oral and written media 51, 54
 and memory distinctions 103, 130, 137–38, 165n.2
 and religion 117–18
 and reversal of media significance 130, 165nn.36-7
 and sacred texts 131, 165n.37
Athena 6–8, 20, 143
Athena at Ilion (Troy) 59
*Athenaion Politeia* 17, 28–30
Athenaios of Naukratis 19, 150n.3
Athena Lindia 10, 121, 123
Athens,
 and the 403 BCE amnesty 143
 and the altar to Forgetfulness 143
 an oral culture 133
 aristocratic genealogies of 104
 classical 138–39
 commemoration of death and funerals 125–27, 164nn.29–30
 conveying memories of the past 53
 and cultural memory of the tyrannicides 34
 and democracy 19–20, 150nn.6–7
 *demos* of 26–30, 32
 end of the tyranny 28
 and the *ephebeia* 105

    funeral orations in 139, 166–67nn.19–20
    granting dining rights 17
    re-establishment of democracy in 144
    and social memory 142–43
    symbol of tyranny in 40
Augustine 100
Augustus Caesar,
    celebration of the *dies natales* 34
    and the *cognomen* Romulus 41
    creation of cultural memories 24–27, 31–32
    and C. Sosius 33
    received name from the Senate 58, 157n.30
    renaming of *sextilis* month 39
    restoration programme of 43, 154n.25
    and the Secular Games 42
    true defender of Rome 47

Babylonia 11, 118, 149n.38
Bacchylides 52
Baltussen, Han 105
Baroin, Catherine 107
Baths of the Seven Sages, Ostia 108
Battle of Argolas 57
Battle of the Champions 53–54
Battle of Marathon 29
Beard, M. 61
biology 67, 75–76
*bissextilis* days 38
Boeotians 57–58
Bonanno, Daniela 131
Book of Law 131
Borgeaud, Philippe 104
*bouleuterion* 22–23
Bourdieu, Pierre 101

Caius Marius 61–63
Calame, C. 52
Calliope 89
Calvisius Sabinus 110–11
Camillus 45
Campus Martius 24–26, 34, 45–47
'Capture of Miletus' (Phrynichus) 142
Caracalla 42
Carrié, Jean-Michel 112
caryatids 106
case studies 53, 138–40, 142–44, 155–56nn7–9
Cassandra 59
Cassius Dio 47
Castagnoli, L. 131
Cato 25, 46
Ceccarelli, P. 131
Celsus 77

C. Gracchus 58
Chalmers, D. 66
Champions, Battle of the 53–54
Chaniotis, Angelos 7, 127
children 53–54, 103, 110, 113–15, 128
Chremonidean War 63
Christianity,
    and approaches to social memory 131, 165n.38
    belief in the afterlife 127
    and change and continuity 129
    and memory formation 132
    a new approach 48, 155n.34
    and pagan symbols 49
    and pilgrimages 123
    rise of 15, 118
    role of women in spread of 107
*Chronos* (time) 2
Chrubasik, Boris 125
Cicero 25, 112
*circulators* 114
civic identity 118
Clark, A. 66
Clarke, John R. 108
Claudius 42, 104
C. Marcus Censorinus 63–64
coins 63–64
Colosseum 115
Commodus 41
*Confessions* (St. Augustine) 15, 100
Connerton, Paul 59, 104
Constantinople 46–47
Constantius II 47
*contio* (meeting) 54
Courrier, Cyril 103, 109
Cresconius 107
C. Sosius 33–34, 152n.43
culture,
    definition 102
    elite 110
    high 101
    local 112
    popular 101, 109, 112

*damnatio memoriae* 49, 155n.35
Darbo-Peschanski, Catherine 5
Dasen, Véronique 114
*das kulturelle Gedächtnis* (Assmann) 20
*De architectura* (Vitruvius) 105
*De articulis* 74
Decimus Cossutius 40
de Gaulle, Charles 29

Delphi 56, 129
Delphic Amphictyonic League 57
*deltoi* (tablets) 94
Demodocus 135
*De origine linguae Latinae* (Varro) 77
*De rerum natura* (Lucretius) 76
Diderot, Denis 78
Didyma 22, 151n.16
*dies natalis* 43–44
Dignas, Beate 53
Dillery, John 121–22, 163n.15, 164n.20
Dion of Prusa 114
Dionysius of Halicarnassus 41
*diuus* (god) 46
Domitian 42
Drusus 24

Egypt,
  described as bicultural 6
  function of cultic language in 131
  priestly authority in 11, 149n.38
  religious practices in 118
  and Socrates 95–96
  and Tlepolemos, son of Artapates 33
*elenchus* Socrates 86
*Elogium* of Marius 61–63
Emerita Augusta, Lusitania 35
Empedocles 66, 97, 158n.3
*Encyclopaedia Britannica* 77
Epicurus 76–77
*Epidemics* 72
Erechtheum, Athens 143
Erll, A. 4, 148n.12
Er (myth) 90–91
Eurypontidai 63
*Exempla* (Valerius Maximus) 56

*fabulae praetextae* (Roman tragedies) 54
*Fasti* (Ovid) 11, 37
Flavius Josephus 47
Forsdyke, S. 107, 109
Forum of Augustus 24, 26, 35, 61, 106
Forum Romanum 24, 47
Foucault, Michel 29
Fundania (wife of Varro) 112
*funus publicum* 125

Galen 67, 80
Galinsky, K. 5, 148n.14
Gangloff, Anne 11
Gehrke, Hans-Joachim 122
*Genesia* (state festival) 127, 165n.32

Giangiulio, Maurizio 53
Goody, Jack 68
Gordon, Richard 11
Gorgias 86
Gowing, A. M. 63
Greece,
  conveying memories of the past 53
  cultural memory took precedence 104
  hero cult centered on tombs 124–25
  and the Muses 84
  no collective memory of a Dark Age 123
  orality, literacy, archiving 107
  oral stories in 53–54
  overlapping legal subdivisions in 103
  and 'polis' religion 132
  and Rome's cultural identity 46, 76
  tradition of learning poems by heart 86
Grethlein, Jonas 5
Grig, Lucy 109

Hadrian,
  celebrated for his philhellenism 47
  innovative ways to be successful 32
  and Romaia 41–42
  and Temple of Olympian Zeus 40
*Hadrianis phyle* (tribe) 40
Halbwachs, Maurice 4, 51, 117, 162n.1
Harmodios 17–20, 28
Havelock, Eric 51, 66
Havener, Wolfgang 24
Hector 135
Heracles 57, 63, 121
Heraclitus 71
hero cults 120, 123–25, 164n.26
Herodotus,
  and ancient historiography 55, 57–58, 157n.21
  and Athenian general Miltiades 19
  and *Histories* 53
  master-narratives of 10
  and memories 133–34, 142, 144–45, 148n.15
  and tyranny 27–30
  and writing 140, 142, 167nn.28–33
Hesiod 52, 83–84
Hipparchos 17, 20, 27–28
Hippias 17, 40
Hippocrates 71–72, 75, 159n.13
Hippocratic Corpus 71–75, 81
Hippocratic Oath 72

Hispania 42
*Histories* (Herodotus) 5, 19, 53
historiography 10, 55–56, 149n.35
Hobsbawm, Eric 30, 32
Hölkeskamp, Karl-Joachim 63
Hölscher, Tonio 20
Homer,
    and the Archelaos relief 1–2
    birthplace of 9
    and death and funerals 125, 139
    and the *Iliad* 84
    and the *Odyssey* 136–37, 166nn.11–12
    and oral tradition 67
    relationship with myth 8, 148–49n.23
    and remembering 52, 142
    and selective culture 110
    and suffering of individuals 142
    testimonies of 10
*Homeristai* (actors) 111
Honorius 48
Horace 112
Horsfall, N. 106, 112
Humphreys, Sally 125, 127, 164–65nn.30–31
*hypomnemata* (inscriptions) 119

*Iliad* (Homer) 84, 110, 133–34, 137, 142, 144
*Inquiry into Nature* (Pliny the Elder) 67
inscriptions 120
intertextuality 55, 157n.20
Isocrates 81
*isonomia* 19–20, 28

Jesus 15, 123, 130
    *see also* Christianity
Judaism 48, 118, 127
Jugurtha, King of Numidia 61–62
Julian calendar 39
Julião, Ricardo 80
Julius Caesar 112
Jupiter Stator 26

Kadmos 121
*kaloi kagathoi* 110
Kedon 28
Kleisthenes 27–30
Kleomenes, King 27
*kleos* 134
Kurlansky, Mark 65–66

*La distinction* (Bourdieu) 101
Laehn, T. R. 77–79
Lakedaimonians 27–30

*lamellae* 89, 131
*La mémoire et l'oubli dans la pensée grecque* (Simondon) 107
Laodike III 22
*La plèbe de Rome et sa culture* (Courrier) 103
Lebenswelt 119, 163n.7
*Liber Memorialis* (Lucius Ampelius) 122
*lieux de mémoire* 5, 14–15, 20-21, 119, 129, 148n.11, 150n.12, 155n.8, 164n.24
*Lindian Chronicle* 10–11, 121–22, 164n.19
Lindos 121–22
Linear B 68, 158n.8
literacy 67, 70–71
Livius Andronicus 63
Livy 41, 44
L. Marcius Philippus 64
Locrian territories 59
L. Opimius 58
Loraux, N. 143
Lord, Albert 68
Lucius Ampelius 122
Lucretius 76–77
*Lucretius and the Transformation of Greek Wisdom* (Sedley) 77
Lysias (orator) 111
*Lysistrata* (Aristophanes) 28–29, 33

McClay, Mark 131
Macedonia 21, 57–58
Magnesia on the Maeander 121–22, 129
Marathon, Battle of 29
Marcellus (consul) 64
Marcii, the 63
Marcus Antonius 24–25, 32–33
*Marmor Parium* 20
martyrs 130
Maxentius 41
Mazzarino, Santo 107
media memory 51–54, 155nn.3–4
medicine 76
*Meno* 86–91, 93, 95, 160n.15, 161n.24
metempsychosis 91
meter (music) 68
Miletus 142
mimesis II 51, 155n.2
Minos 121
M. Livius Drusus 55–56
*Mnemosyne* (goddess) 1, 70, 83–84, 90, 101, 147n.3
Moatti, Claudia 111

monumental landscapes 56–59
Muses, the 84
Mycenae 123

*Naturalis Historia* (Pliny the Elder) 76–77, 159n.22
Naupactus 59
Niceratus 110
Nicias 110
Nora, Pierre 20–21
Numa Pompilius, king 63–64
Nünning, A. 4, 148n.12

Octavian *see* Augustus Caesar
*Odyssey* (Homer) 110, 133–34, 137, 142
*oikistes* 124
*Oikumene* (inhabited world) 2
Olbia 7
Olympieion *see* Temple of Olympian Zeus, Athens
*On Agriculture* (Varro) 112
*On Ancient Medicine* 73
Ong, Walter 66
*On How to Recognize the Best Doctor* (Galen) 80
*On the Latin Language* (Varro) 38
*On Medicine* (Celsus) 77
*On Memory and Recollection* (Aristotle) 76, 98
Opountian Locris 59
Opous 59
*optimus princeps* 32
oral stories 53–54, 142, 156n.13, 168n.34
Orlin, Eric 58
Orpheus 89
Orphic-Bacchic gold leaves 131
Orphic mysteries 131
Orphism 89–90
Osborne, Robin 128
Ovid 37

*Paeans* (Pindar) 84
paganism 118
*paideia* 84, 86, 91, 103
Palatine 26
Pales (goddess) 42
*Panathenaea* (festival) 138, 166n.16
*Parentalia* 54
Parilia 41
Parry, Milman 68
*Parva naturalia* (Aristotle) 80
Paulus Fabius Maximus 39

Pausanias 123
pedagogues 105
Peisistratids 40
Peloponnesian War 143
*pepaideumenoi* (cultured people) 103, 114
*Periegesis* (Pausanias) 123
Perikles 30
Persia and the sack of Athens 19, 29
Persian Wars 139
Pertinax 47
Petersen, Lauren H. 108
Petronius 110–11
*Phaedo* 88–92, 160n.18
*Phaedrus* 88–91, 95–97
*Philebus* (Plato) 92–94, 97
Philhellenes 40
Philip the Arab 42
Phocians 56–59
Phrynichus 142
Physcus 59
*physis* 97
Pieres 57
pilgrimage 122–23, 128, 164nn.21–4
Pindar 84, 87
Piraeus 144
'Plain of Oblivion' 90
Plato,
 called writing 'artificial memory' 66
 footnotes to 97–100, 99n.32
 and memory 91–97, 160nn.21, 24–26
 and the 'Meno paradox' 85–86, 88
 and pre-school learning 113
 recollection and human existence 89–90, 160n.21
 students and good memory 80–81
 the threshold of writing use 71, 158n.12
*plebs* 103, 105, 108–9, 161n.2
Pliny the Elder 34, 37, 76–79, 81, 159n.24
Plotinus 100
Plutarch 24, 84
Polybius 5, 46, 112
polytheism 119
*pomœrium* (sacred boundary) 46
pompae funebres (funeral processions) 54
Pompey 79
Porticus Octaviae 25–26
Poseidon 143
*Precepts 1* 72
Price, Simon 4, 52–53, 59
*Prometheus Bound* 94
Proust, Marcel 56
*prytaneion* 20

Ptolemy Philadelphus 63
Pyrrhonists 99
Pythian Apollo 123

Q. Haterius Tychicus (freedman) 115
Q. Marcius Rex 64
*Quaestiones naturales* (Seneca) 76

religious festivals 127–28
Remus 41
*Republic* (Plato) 90–91
Rhamnous (coastal community) 128
Rhodes 121
Rhodes, P.J. 28
Ricoeur, Paul 51
Romaia 41–42
Rome,
    and ancient pilgrimages 123
    calender of 38, 153n.9
    and civic religion 44–45
    civil war of 32
    communication memory specialists in 104
    control of sacred memory in 130
    cultural memory of 24
    culture of remembering 34
    defining a city as Roman 43
    extraordinary memories in 111–12, 162n.14
    foundation of city 40–42, 153n.17, 154n.24
    introspective view of 79
    lack of book reading in 139, 166n.17
    memory sanctions in 144, 168n.43
    monuments an important medium in 58
    and the *nomenclatores* 105
    oral stories in 53–54, 156n.17
    overlapping legal subdivisions in 103, 161n.2
    and private/public remembrance of dead 125–27
    public funerals 112, 114
    and the rise of Christianity 118
    and the Second Sophistic 8
    and *terminus* 37–40, 153n.10
    transition from Greece 76
    and writing 54
Romulus 40–43
rote memorization 86, 160n.7
Rubin, David 137
Rüpke, Jörg 56

sacred texts 130–31
sacred tourism *see* ancient pilgrimages

St. Aberkios of Hierapolis 131
St. Augustine 15, 107
sanctuaries 122
Sarapis cult 129
*Satyricon* 108
Schacter, Daniel 134
Schudson, Michael 134, 140
Schwartz, Barry 27
Second Sophistic 15, 103, 123
Sedley, David 77
Seleukid era 21–23, 26–27, 30–35, 150n.15–16, 151n.17, 152nn38–9
Seneca 76, 110–11
Septimius Severus 42, 47
Shaya, Josephine 35
Sicyon 122
Simondon, Michèle 107
Simonides of Keos 68, 70, 81, 158n.10
Sinn-Zirkulation 51, 81
skeptics 99
*skolia* 19
slavic bards 68
Socrates 86–88, 92–96, 160n.9
Solon 125
*Sophistical Refutations* 86
Sorabji, R. 76
Soranus 80
souls 89
Sparta,
    and 30 Years' Peace with Argives 55
    and the amnesty of 403 BC 134, 143–44, 168n.40
    and the end of tyranny 28
    hairstyles in 53–54
    and relations with the Ptolemies 63, 158n.33
    role of in Athenian democracy 29–30, 33, 151n.30
statues 7, 19–20, 24, 56–57, 105–6, 119–20, 128–30
Stilicho 47–48
Stoics, the 98
*Suda* 70
Suetonius 104
*summi viri* 26
*Symposium* (Plato) 91

Tacitus 104
Telchines, the 121
Temple of Apollo, Delphi 56, 157n.24
Temple of Apollo, Sicyon 122
Temple of Apollo Sosianus 26, 33

Temple of Bellona 26
Temple of Castor 64
Temple of Concordia Augusta 58–59
Temple of Olympian Zeus, Athens 40
Teos 22
Terminalia festival 37–38
Terminus 37–39, 153nn.6,13
Tertullian 47
Thamus 96
*Theaetetus* (Plato) 91, 93–95, 97
*Theogony* (Hesiod) 83–84, 101
theory of recollection (Plato) 85, 100, 160n.6
Theseus 40
Thessalians 57–58
Theuth (Egyptian god) 71, 95–96
Third Sacred War 57–58
*tholos* tombs 139
Thomas, Rosalind 29, 103–4
Thonemann, P. 131
Thorikos, Attic deme 128
Thrasybulus 143–44
Thucydides 5, 27–30, 55, 142, 168n.35
Thyreatis, Cynouria 53
Tiberius 32, 54, 56
Timarchos 32
Titus 47
Titus Livius 107
Tlepolemos, son of Artapates 33–34
tourism 123
Trajan 103
Trampedach, Kai 11
Tremulus 64
Trimalchio 108, 110–11

Trojan War 9, 135, 142
Trophonios, oracle of 131
Troy 8-10, 59, 88, 135
Turkey 21

Valentinian III 48
Valerius Maximus 56
Varro 37–38, 77, 112
Velleius Paterculus 54–55
Vespasian 47
Vestal Virgins 104
Vietnam 30
Virgil 9, 107
Vitruvius 105–7, 114
Vlastos 85
Volsci, the 44–45

Warburg, Aby 103
wax block model 93–95
Whitehead, Alfred North 97
Whitmarsh, Tim 40
Winterling, Aloys 34
Wiseman, T. P. 107
Wolpert, A. 144, 168n.40
women 107, 128
writing 65–67, 72, 77, 94, 158n.4
*Written Texts and the Rise of Literate Culture in Ancient Greece* (Yunis) 66

Xanthos 33
Xenophon 5, 143–44

Zanker, Paul 106
Zeus 1, 101